GUARDIANS
OF
THE GAA

GUARDIANS
OF
THE GAA

Noel Hynes & Brian Willoughby

Published by
Noel Hynes & Brian Willoughby
© 2018

*All rights reserved. No part of this publication may be reproduced in any form
or by any means, electronic or mechanical including photocopying or recording,
or by any information storage or retrieval systems, without permission in writing
from the publisher.*

*The photographs and text remain the property of the photographers,
individual owners and contributors, and the author respectively,
where attributed.*

Printed by
Naas Printing Ltd.

2018

Authors' Dedications

I would like to dedicate this book to my late father-in-law, Noel Oates,
a proud member of An Garda Síochána, an exceptional GAA man – who
won a Roscommon senior club championship medal with Elphin in 1951
– and one of the greatest people I have ever had the pleasure of knowing,
and also to my late parents Con and Joan Willoughby
for all their love and support.
Brian Willoughby

To my late wife, Eimer, whose love and support encouraged me to
complete this daunting task and in memory of her father, Chief
Superintendent Sean Gantly, who captained the Garda intermediate
hurling team to victory in 1928.
Noel Hynes

Contents

Réamhrá

This fascinating book by Noel Hynes and Brian Willoughby is a great demonstration of the strong ties between two of the country's most community-focused organisations – An Garda Síochána and the GAA.

Spanning from 1922 to 2016, it profiles over 1,500 Garda members – male and female – who have made great contributions to their communities, both on and on off the pitch.

From internal Garda competitions, to the Garda College's participation in the college competitions, to members who have won All-Ireland medals and All Star Awards, this book shows the commitment of Garda members to their clubs, colleges and counties over the decades since the service's foundation.

Illustrated by some wonderful photographs, this book contains a treasure trove of interesting information and insights into the impact that An Garda Síochána has had on the GAA and vice versa.

I want to congratulate Noel and Brian on completing what was an incredible task and in writing a book that is a real tribute to two organisations which have made lasting marks on the development of this country.

Nóirín O'Sullivan
Former Garda Commissioner

Réamhrá

Bhí agus tá páirt nach beag ag an gCumann Lúthchleas Gael agus ag An nGarda Síochána i bhforbairt pobail ó cheann ceann na tíre.

Tá ceangal láidir le muintir na hÉireann ag an dá eagraíocht a bhfuil rannpháirtíocht pobail mar éiteas lárnach acu araon.

Taispeánann an leabhar seo an chaoi a d'eascair na ceangail láidir idir an dá eagraíocht ó bhunú an Stáit.

Taispeánann sé freisin an ról tábhachtach a bhí ag comhaltaí An Gharda Síochána i ndul chun cinn an Chumann Lúthchleas Gael anuas tríd na blianta. Ar ndóigh, tá a mhalairt fíor freisin – an tionchar dearfach a bhí ag an gCumann Lúthchleas Gael ar shaol go leor de chomhaltaí An Gharda Síochána.

Comhghairdeas ó chroí leis na húdair, Noel Hynes agus Brian Willoughby. Tugann an leabhar síos bóithrín na smaointe muid maidir le héachtaí fir agus mná An Gharda Síochána a bhí, sa chéad dul síos, ag déanamh ionadaíocht thar a gceann féin ach freisin thar ceann An Gharda Síochána ag an leibhéal is airde spóirt in Éirinn.

Dónall Ó Cualáin
Acting Garda Commissioner

ix

Message from Uachtarán, Cumann Lúthchleas Gael

A chairde,

Is cúis mhór áthais dom a deis seo a bheith agam na focail seo a leanas a scríobh don foilseacháin seo agus é ag ceiliúradh na dlúthbhainte idir An Garda Síochána agus Cumann Lúthchleas Gael.

It gives me great pleasure to pen these words to highlight the strong bonds between two of the country's most important entities – An Garda Síochána and the GAA.

The area of overlap between the organisations is considerable and taking a rounded view we're entitled to ask – 'how could it be any other way?' given our respective roles in Irish society since the foundation of the State.

The close ties between and An Garda and the GAA are of course highly visible throughout the year wherever and whenever our games our played.

The role played by members of the force in helping us to stage our fixtures, not least at Croke Park on the biggest days in the Irish sporting calendar, are apparent to anyone who attends our games and the relationship is a valued one.

However, the ties run deeper and further than that.

So many of our members and indeed players have served An Garda with distinction and of course legions of teams down throught the decades have competed with each other in internal competitons, and against other units in colleges competitons and in the case of Dublin, in the Dublin leagues and championships.

Many have won the highest honours in our games.

That this has all been captured in a body work that stretches back to the 1920s underlines the feat overseen by Brian Willoughby and Noel Hynes.

The profiling of over 1,600 members gives you an idea of the breadth of the work and the strength of the relationship and of course many of our shared values.

I wish everyone involved with the project every success and I sincerely hope this work gets the audience it deserves.

Rath Dé ar an obair!

Seán Ó hÓráin
Uachtarán, Chumann Lúthchleas Gael
Feabhra, 2018

Sponsor's note

As a former member of An Garda Síochána - second generation - and an avid supporter of the GAA, it is an absolute honour to be involved in the release of ' *"Guardians of the GAA"* . It also gives me great pleasure to host the launch of the book in Copper Face Jacks and to see the two worlds of The GAA and An Garda Síochána come together.

I would firstly like to congratulate Brian and Noel on their fantastic achievement and the work they have put into capturing this interwoven relationship. No doubt it was an enjoyable and richly fulfilling experience researching all the history and stories that contributed to making the book such a pleasant read. It is a huge credit to them and their families.

When Copper Face Jacks opened its doors in February 1996, Sam Maguire was residing in the Capital, whilst Liam McCarthy had found its way to the Banner County after a 71-year absence. Since the foundation of the state, many different counties have tasted All-Ireland success, nearly all featuring a multitude of representatives from An Garda Síochána. On a personal level, there has been a long-standing relationship between The GAA, An Garda Síochána and Coppers. Some say it is a 'rite of passage', that if you are in one organisation or the other, at some point, you will have to serve your time in Coppers! We are incredibly grateful for the loyal and reciprocal support that the GAA and An Garda Síochána members have shown us over the years. Long may it continue.

I would like to wish Brian, Noel and everyone involved with *"Guardians of the GAA"* a massive success in the release of this new book and we look forward to seeing you all on the launch night.

Cathal Jackson- Copper Face Jacks

Disclaimer

We are aware of the possibility that inter-county GAA players who were members of An Garda Síochána are entitled to inclusion in this publication, and may have been omitted. If that has happened, after the most painstaking research, we beg forgiveness and suggest that the omissions, if any have occurred, should be forwarded for inclusion in a future revised edition of the book – a planned Volume 2. We also acknowledge the huge amount of members who have starred at underage levels for their counties and for their clubs over the years, but we regret we had to confine the criteria to senior level; space was the final arbiter in this case. In addition, there have been thousands of members over the years who have given tremendous service to the GAA at underage coaching level and in administrative positions. We also acknowledge the countless members of the Force who fit the criteria of being fanatical supporters of their counties down through the years. Unfortunately, we were unable to include these categories. There were members who were contacted and, modestly, expressed little interest in having a profile in the book, but these profiles are included as they meet the criteria of being senior inter-county players. We have also referenced a number of names of individuals who, research indicated, did play at inter-county level, but we were unable to ascertain the identity of the counties they played for, or the code in which they participated.

While every effort has been made to ensure that the contents of this book are accurate, neither the publisher, editor or contributors can accept responsibility for loss, distress or damage, occasioned to any person resulting from any errors or omissions.

Chapter 1

Introduction

When the Gaelic Athletic Association (GAA) was founded in Hayes Hotel, Thurles, Co. Tipperary on 1 November 1884, Royal Irish Constabulary (RIC) Inspector Thomas St McCarthy – a Tipperary native who was stationed in Templemore – attended that very first meeting and is credited with being a founder member. This first connection began the unique relationship between the Gaelic Athletic Association and An Garda Síochána which has since flourished, and continues to this day.

18 November 2009, Uachtarán CLG Gael Criostóir Ó Cuana with, from left,
Gerry O'Callaghan, Chief Superintendent of the PSNI, Fachtna Murphy, Garda Commissioner,
Gerry Murray, Superintendent of the PSNI, and James Brannigan, Detective Constable, PSNI,
at the Unveiling of the Headstone to Thomas St. George McCarthy, Deansgrange Cemetery, Dublin.

Leabharlanna Poiblí Chathair Baile Átha Cliath
Dublin City Public Libraries

Chapter 2

The GAA
and the Garda connection

When General Eoin O'Duffy was appointed Garda Commissioner on September 18, 1922, he immediately recognised the real value of sport, both for creating true comradeship between the members of the new force, and for breaking the long established barrier of animosity that existed between the Irish people and "policemen". Sport, he said, would bring the the people and the new "Guardians of the Peace" into contact under most favourable conditions, and thereafter the influence of true and steadfast men would establish a lasting bond of trust and friendship.

The Garda GAA Club was formed in Dublin in 1923 by Commissioner O'Duffy. Right from the beginning the club attracted some of the greatest hurlers and footballers in the country. The club made an immediate impact in the Dublin hurling and football championships, with the hurlers crowned county champions from 1925-29 and in 1931, and the footballers victorious in 1927 and 1929, before winning three-in-a-row from 1933 to 1935.

Yet for all the footballers' achievements, it was the greatness of the hurlers which shone most luminously during this period. The team reached its Everest peak of greatness in 1927, when it provided nine members of the Dublin team which won the All-Ireland title that year.

The side which contained Mick Gill, Pat 'Fowler' McInerney, Garrett Howard, Matty Power and Ned Tobin from Garda is still considered one of the finest McCarthy Cup-winning sides. The footballers of that era included such players as the legendary Larry Stanley (Kildare), Dick Creagh (Mayo), and Paddy Colleran (Sligo).

Inevitably the Garda Club became a victim of its success, and it was disbanded because its sides were considered too strong, and members were transferred to various parts of the country. However, the club reformed in 1947, and as was the case in the 1920s, it made an immediate impact by winning the 1948 Dublin senior football championship with a memorable victory over St Vincent's. That set the stage for a series of magnificent matches which culminated in 1952 with a then record 25,000 spectators attending that year's county final. That Garda team included Paddy Kennedy, Bill Carlos, Brendan Lynch, Liam Gilmartin and Tom Langan. While the footballers never reached such heights for the rest of the 1950s and 1960s, the force continued to produce extraordinary talent.

In the ten years comprising 1953 to 1963, a total of 3,893 recruits were trained in the Garda Depot, Phoenix Park. A record was taken of the sporting activities of the recruits before they joined the force and it showed that 2,040 played Gaelic football and 1,300 played hurling.

In 1966, the Garda Recreation Club donated a cup for an inter-divisional competition, which has since become the premier competition. Cork East were the first winners, while Garda hurlers and footballers have always played an integral part in the representative series in the Combined Universities and the Defence Forces.

After being briefly disbanded, Michael O'Connor and Jim Murphy were the driving forces behind the reformation of the Garda club in 1969. Since winning the intermediate championship in 1986, the team has proven to be a major power in the Dublin championship, with the 1993 side containing such players as Dermot Deasy, Jack Sheedy (Dublin), John Newton (Roscommon) and Davy Byrne (Monaghan).

Marcus de Búrca, referring to the years 1922-34 in his 2010 book *The GAA: a history*, has stated: "The appearance in Dublin of Army and Garda teams provided a welcome new element in metropolitan competitions; elsewhere throughout the country Garda support provided a badly needed stimulus in areas where native games had previously not gained wide local acceptance."

The last fifty years has been something of a golden era for the Gardaí nationwide, with the force producing some of the greatest players in the history of Gaelic games. Matt Connor, John Egan, Páidí Ó Sé, John McCarthy, Tom Prendergast, Seamus Bonner, Anthony Davis, Brian Murray and the late John Morley of Mayo embellished the reputation of the force in the football arena, and more recently John Crowley, Declan O'Keeffe, Kevin Walsh, Cathal Daly, Aidan O'Mahony, Colm Boyle and David Clarke add lustre in their county colours. Meanwhile, Joachim Kelly, Ken Hogan, Frank Cummins, Mossie Walsh, Ollie Baker, Jerry O'Connor and Eddie Brennan all hit the top in the hurling area.

Another Garda, Brian Murphy of Cork, was amongst the most honoured dual players in the history of Gaelic games.

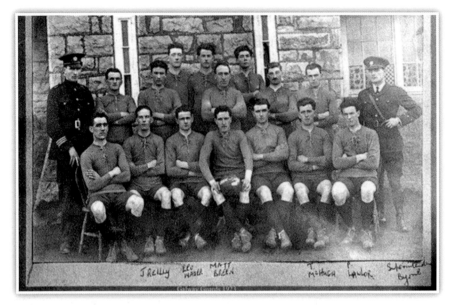

The Galway Garda Gaelic football team, 1923

A Garda hurling team from the 1920s.
ront, right with uniform cap: Mattie Power of Kilkenny.
Back, right: Mick Gill of Galway.

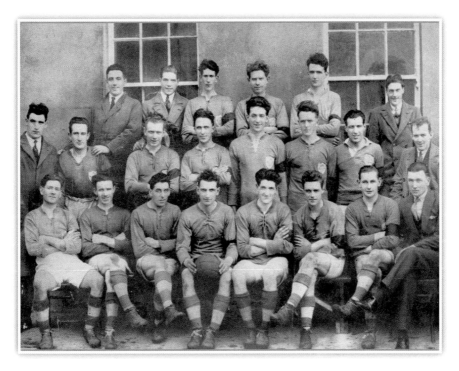

Garda Síochana Footballers

Standing (from left):
Garda Frank Wedick (69A), Wicklow, Hon. Sec.; John Forde (Depot);
John Mullen (134E), Laois; Frank Benson, Cavan; Thomas Teeling (203C), Dublin;
Patrick Kevlin (Depot).
Second row (standing, from left):
Gdas Con O'Connell, Joe O'Toole (144C), Dublin; John Lynam (104E), Kildare;
Martin McCoy, Sligo; Joe Reilly (76B), Kildare; John Kirwan, Galway;
Jim Healy (Depot), Hon. Secretary, IABA.
Sitting, from left:
Gdas John Sherlock, Dublin; Patrick Flynn, Sligo; George Magan, Kildare;
Inspector Patrick Colleran, Sligo; Capt. Jim Smyth, Cavan; John J. Scanlon, Clare;
Jim Kirwan, Wexford; Jim Kielt (trainer).

Other well-known Garda footballers:
St J. Murphy, Kerry); Gda P. Russell, Kerry; D/O P. Kirwan, Cavan;
Supt R. Creagh, Mayo; Supt P. Kilroy, Monaghan; Gda M. Keating, Wicklow;
Gda M. Langton, Wicklow; T. Kelly, Mayo; R. Hearts, Mayo; K. Kenny, Sligo;
T. Carthy, Wicklow; J. Farrell, Monaghan; J McGetterick, Sligo; G. Comerford, Clare;
St J. Moran, Mayo.

Winners of the Co. Dublin Senior League, 1926.
Co. Dublin Senior Championship, 1927 and 1929.
Winners of the President's Cup, Aonach an Garda, Garda vs Army 1926-27, 1929.

Garda Síochana Hurlers

Standing (at back, from left):
Gdas William Phelan, Laois; Patrick Cusack, Offaly; Mattie Power, Kilkenny;
Jim Began, Cork.
Second row (standing, from left):
Gdas Patrick McInerney, Clare; Edward Tobin, Laois (Hon. Sec.); William O'Brien, Kilkenny;
Jim Doherty, Tipperary; Jim Smyth, Cavan (Hon. Treasurer); Tom Burnell, Clare;
Patrick Browne, Tipperary; John Ryan, Cork; Tommy Maloney, Dublin (trainer).
Sitting (on bench, left to right):
Gdas Edward Fahy, Clare; Jeremiah Burke, Cork; Mick Gill, Galway (capt.);
Comdt McCarthy (chairman); Garrett Howard, Limerick; John Kirwan, Galway;
Mick Finn, Galway. Sitting (front): Gdas Joe Cahill, Limerick and William Dunphy, Kilkenny.

*Winners of the Co. Dublin Senior Leagues 1924, 1926–30,
and the Co. Dublin Senior Championship 1924, 1926–29 and 1931.
Winners of the President's Cup, Aonach an Garda, Garda vs Army (1926, 1927 and 1929).
The Garda selection won the Leinster and All-Ireland Championships in 1927.*

*Other well-known Garda hurlers:
Gdas James McInerney, T. Burke, D. McHugh, J. Browne, T. Quinlan, M. Flynn,
Tony Flanagan and Tommy O'Rourke, Clare.*

18

Michael Collins addressing Mattie Power (second from left).

Playing their way "into the hearts of the people": The central role of An Garda Síochána in revitalising the GAA in the 1920s

Michael Lang[1]

Cavan dominated the Ulster Senior Football Championship from the 1910s to the 1950s, during which period Monaghan was the only county which could occasionally manage to wrestle the provincial title from the grasp of the Breffni men. The Gaels of these two neighbouring counties have always enjoyed a keen rivalry on the field of play and a close friendship off it. This article tells the tale of two such men, John McGahern of Cavan and Eoin O'Duffy of Monaghan, and how their paths in life were interwined between the years 1918 to 1933 through their mutual involvement in the GAA and An Garda Síochána. The story begins in Ulster, and ends in Mayo.

1   Michael Lang is a lecturer in the School of Business and Economics at NUI Galway and is also the secretary of Tourmakeady GAA Club, Co. Mayo. He and his father, Sergeant Thomas Lang, and uncle, Detective Garda Michael Lang, all played inter-county football with Sligo.

The GAA and the Irish Volunteers in Ulster

Eoin O'Duffy was a member of the Clones Harps GAA Club in Monaghan and became secretary of the Ulster GAA Council in 1912. In April of that same year, the British Prime Minister, H. H. Asquith, introduced a Home Rule Bill which promised to confer powers of self-government upon an Irish parliament. Ulster Unionists vehemently opposed this and formed the Ulster Volunteers as a local defence force. In turn, nationalists raised their own force, the Irish Volunteers (Óglaigh na hÉireann).

The formation of the Irish Volunteers greatly impacted the activities of the GAA in the years that followed. Most of the recruits to the Volunteers were fit young men, many of whom were also involved in the GAA. Although according to its own rules the GAA was technically a non-political organisation, it was no secret that many of the key individuals within the association were at least sympathetic to the republican movement. Daniel McCarthy, a leading GAA official and Sinn Féin member, had openly declared that "we want our men to be physically strong [so that] when the time comes, the hurlers will cast aside the camán for the steel that will drive the Saxon from our land". In January 1914, the president of the GAA recommended that members should join the Volunteers "to learn to shoot straight".

Following the execution of the leaders of the 1916 Rising, public opinion in Ireland was transformed. In a 50th anniversary article re-printed in the Mayo GAA 1970 Yearbook, war veteran Paddy Mullaney wrote that:
"if there was no general uprising and no general sympathy with the Rebellion, the executions changed all that. There was no prisoner-of-war treatment for the Irish rebels but the Germans who, we were told, were guilty of every outrage against civilisation, were treated according to the Geneva international code… [The executions] resulted in an eruption of national feeling unbelievable in such a short time. From then on to 1921 were the years when the GAA showed their mettle. The Association was the great reservoir from which the IRA was drawn. Captains of teams became captains of companies. County Board officers met to plan military operations". And this indeed was how it was. In Mayo, for example, the Chairman of the GAA County Board, Dick Walsh, was a leading figure in the IRA. In Monaghan, Eoin O'Duffy joined the Irish Volunteers and rose to the rank of Chief of Staff of the IRA. There was such a level of cross-membership between the GAA and the IRA that the Director of British Military Intelligence considered the GAA to be practically under the full control of the IRA.

In 1918, John McGahern from Gowna was in his début season with the Cavan senior football team. The Ulster final was scheduled to take place in

Cootehill, but had to be called off because there was a prohibition against Gaelic games, and Crown forces occupied the venue. In the aftermath, Eoin O'Duffy and several other members of the Ulster Council were pursued by a posse of RIC men on bicycles. O'Duffy knew that he was being followed, so he deliberately took a circuitous route, to the great discomfort of the heavily uniformed policemen who pedalled after him in the sweltering heat.

The Bureau of Military History witness statements tell of similar stories from elsewhere in the country, such as in Ballyvarry, Co. Mayo, where the captain of the local GAA team, Patrick Lyons, recalled that "the RIC always followed us so I often marched the team back home across the country, which made the things difficult for the police over hedges and ditches" (BMH WS1645). At that time, members of the RIC were banned from joining the GAA, but the reverse was also the case; RIC men or Irish soldiers in the British Army who dared to play Gaelic football were heavily censured by their commanding officers. This was the fate of Constable Paddy McGuinness from Carnaross, Co. Meath, who was dismissed from the RIC for participating in a GAA game while off-duty (BMH WS1648).

The 1918 Ulster final was eventually played on 15 September, and John McGahern won his first senior provincial medal with Cavan. Eoin O'Duffy was arrested that same weekend for the charge of organising an illegal GAA match. He was released in November 1918 shortly before the general election. Some time about this period, McGahern also joined the Irish Volunteers. It is likely, given that he was a prominent member of the Cavan team that jousted for Ulster senior honours with the so-called team of "O'Duffy's men" from neighbouring Monaghan, that McGahern became personally acquainted with O'Duffy at this time.

John McGahern in the colours of his native county Cavan about 1918

McGahern won his second Ulster senior medal in August 1920, when Cavan beat Armagh in the final. The Ulster championships of 1921 and 1922 were disrupted by the War of Independence and the Civil War, and the fixtures backlog was not cleared up until 1923, in which year Monaghan played in three separate Ulster finals in a most unusual sequence. On 22 April 1923, they drew with Cavan in the 1922 decider and won the replay on 20 May; they then lost to Cavan in the 1923 decider on 2 September 1923, before bizarrely regaining bragging rights by winning the delayed 1921 decider against Derry on 28 October 1923.

By this stage, Eoin O'Duffy had become the Commissioner of An Garda Síochána and John McGahern was a trainee in the Garda Depot. Given his own personal experiences with the RIC, O'Duffy was anxious that the Garda Síochána would be accepted by the people of Ireland and not regarded as a continuation of the old colonial style police force with just a change of uniform. In a circular issued to all stations in 1923, O'Duffy encouraged the guards to join local football, hurling and athletics clubs. He urged his men to be "Irish in thought and in action" and to "play their way into the hearts of the people" by actively promoting Irish sport, music, language and dancing. In Dublin, the Garda Síochána football and hurling clubs were to the fore in county competitions and O'Duffy was a strong supporter of these activities.

The Garda Síochána Club
in the Dublin Senior Football Championship

From 1922 to 1935, the Dublin Senior Football Championship was dominated by O'Toole's and the Garda Síochána Club, who between them won all but two of the titles during that period. The Dublin county team which won three All-Ireland senior championships in a row from 1921 to 1923 was backboned by O'Toole's players.

On 23 January 1924, Commissioner O'Duffy was in attendance at Croke Park to watch An Garda Síochána play O'Toole's in the Dublin County Championship final of 1923. Eight of the O'Toole's players were on the Dublin team which won the delayed 1922 All-Ireland Championship final, which was played three months previously at the same venue. The Garda team also had several inter-county players within their line-up. Among them was John McGahern, the holder of two Ulster senior medals with Cavan, who was selected at left-half forward. Ahead of him in the full-forward line were Paddy Colleran of Sligo and Paddy Kilroy of Galway. There is an interesting cameo here, because it was Paddy Kilroy's Galway team which contested the All-Ireland final against Dublin the previous October, but Sligo – and in particular Paddy Colleran – had every reason to feel badly aggrieved about this. Paddy Colleran had actually played on the Mayo team reached the 1921 All-Ireland final against Dublin but he transferred back to his native Sligo for the 1922 championship. He was set to achieve the remarkable feat of playing with two different counties in consecutive All-Ireland finals after Sligo beat Galway in the Connacht

The Garda football team about 1923.
John McGahern is standing at the right of the picture, other players unidentified.

final, and subsequently beat favourites Tipperary in the semi-final to qualify for the All-Ireland final for the first and only time in the county's history. Alas, it was not to be. Galway raised an objection and Sligo's place in the final was denied.

O'Toole's won that Dublin final of 1923 on a scoreline of 1-4 to 0-4, but McGahern, Kilroy and Colleran were to the fore for the Garda attack and they were unfortunate not to win the match. Also in the Garda forward line on that day was Michael Smyth, who came from the footballing stronghold of Kilbride GAA Club in Co. Roscommon. Smyth, who was described as an "ardent follower of the GAA" all his life, signed up to join the new police force the same week as John McGahern, just days after the IRA Executive ordered an end to the Civil War in May 1923. They became very good friends, and were dispatched to serve together in Partry, Co. Mayo. The arrival in the village of two excellent Garda footballers led to a revival in the fortunes of the local team.

Partry Garda Station about 1925.
Standing:
Michael Smyth, John McGahern, Martin Reynolds.
Seated:
Sergeant Michael Mullane, Michael Dwyer.

The revival of the GAA in South Mayo in the 1920s

In 1923, the *Western People* remarked that "there are few counties in which the fine old game [of Gaelic football] suffered such a setback as a result of the disturbed conditions of the last few years as in Mayo". At last, a sense of normality finally returned and one of the first visible signs of independence was the arrival of the new police force, An Garda Síochána, the "guardians of the peace". Following renovation work to repair extensive damage inflicted during the War of

Independence, the former RIC barracks in Partry, Co. Mayo re-opened as a Garda station in November 1924. The first sergeant in charge was Michael Mullane, a native of Mallow, who a few years later was awarded a Scott Medal for bravery for his part in an incident in Drumshanbo. Along with Sergeant Mullane, three guards commenced service at Partry in that month. Their names were Martin Reynolds, John McGahern and Michael Smyth. All three came from rural communities where there was an established tradition of Gaelic games.

Given their strong GAA backgrounds, it was little wonder that within a short time of their arrival in Partry, these three Gardaí played a central role in revitalising Gaelic football in the area.

The men probably needed little encouragement to lace up their football boots, but actually were under instructions from Commissioner Eoin O'Duffy to do so. At the time that Partry barracks opened, football had not been played on an organised basis in the area for a few years. The three Gardaí, with the help of some locals from Partry and Ballintubber, sought to rectify this. In the spring of 1926 the newly formed Partry football team ventured to play in the South Mayo League competition hosted by Ballinrobe GAA Club. A number of teams entered, including Ballinrobe, The Farm, Shrule, Kilmaine, Loughmask, Cloonacastle and Partry. Partry had an easy win over Cloonacastle at Ballinrobe on Sunday, 7 February 1926 and the same two teams met again in the semi-final on Sunday, 14 March, which Partry again won. The scene was then set for the league final between Shrule and Partry to be played on Sunday, 21 March in Ballinrobe, with attractive medals as the prize. Partry came out on top by 0-4 to 0-1.

Connacht Senior Football League winners' medal, 1926

Photographs of local Gaelic football teams from the 1920s are rare, but at that time there happened to be an American photographer living in Ballinrobe, who was on hand to capture the occasion for posterity. The Partry team were smartly dressed, and proudly displayed their winners' medals on their lapels. A number of them also wore what appears to be shamrock, it being the first Sunday after St Patrick's Day. Garda John McGahern is standing at the very centre of the photograph. In front of him (seated) is his colleague, Garda Michael Smyth, on whose shoulders he rests his hands in a very clear gesture of friendship. To McGahern's left is Garda Martin Reynolds, who in addition to playing football, was also involved briefly with the club hurling scene in Mayo. The three guards occupy central positions in the photograph and the image conveys a sense that they galvanised the group together. Several of the men in this photograph fought in the War of Independence and were amongst the local brigade of Volunteers who were captured in 1921 and imprisoned in Galway.

John McGahern's career with Mayo and Connacht

John McGahern stood 5'9" in height and was of strong physique. Contemporary newspaper reports told of his ability to kick neat scores from tight angles, and he was also very quick to react to any goalscoring opportunity. Within a few months of his arrival in Partry, he was selected to play for the Mayo junior team, and was dominant at midfield against Sligo in the Connacht championship in July 1925. 1926 was a very successful year for him, commencing in March, when he won the South Mayo League with Partry. Two months later, he played a starring role for the Mayo seniors against Galway in the opening round of the Connacht Senior Football League. The previous October, Galway defeated Mayo in the delayed 1925 Connacht senior final, and in so doing, deprived Mayo not just of a provincial title, but also an All-Ireland title because of the bizarre circumstances of that year's championship. So it was with much glee that 3,000 Mayo supporters witnessed their team give Galway a good beating on 3 May 1926 in Balla. The Western People reported that "McGahern was playing a wonderful game", and despite their best endeavours, the Galway backs simply had no answer to his "brilliant play". Time and again, he cut through for score after score and set up numerous moves. One wonders if he had been playing for the Mayo seniors the previous season, they might have won their first senior All-Ireland title. As it turned out, he so very nearly delivered an All-Ireland title for Mayo with his outstanding performance in the junior All-Ireland final of 1925, which was played in Croke Park on 21 June 1926. Again, he was Mayo's chief scorer that day, but his efforts came up narrowly short, as the team lost by just one point to Louth. Further disappointment came three weeks later, when he was on the Mayo senior team which lost the Connacht Senior Championship final to rivals Galway. In November 1926, he was selected on the Connacht team, and scored the winning point in an inter-provincial semi-final against Leinster.

Word of John McGahern's talent reached the ears of the Castlebar Mitchels captain, John Egan. Speaking in the 1980s, he remembered that:

> "There was a fellow called John McGahern, a guard in Partry ... He was a lovely footballer. I cycled to Partry and asked him to play for

> *us. He came down and won two or three medals with us and without him we would not have been as good."*

In 1927, he was a substitute on the Connacht team in the Railway Cup final in Croke Park, and he also played on the Mayo senior team which lost to Galway in the Connacht championship semi-final. In the spring of the following year, he played in the National Football League play-offs against Kildare and Kerry, but he either fell out of favour or out of form for the rest of the 1928 season because he was dropped from the Mayo panel. Finally, in 1929, he won a Connacht Senior Football Championship medal to add to his two Ulster medals. Several members of the Mayo team, including Chief Superintendent Dick Creagh, were members of An Garda Síochána, and Commissioner O'Duffy allowed them to take a week off work to prepare for the game. An expectant Mayo crowd travelled en masse to support their team in the All-Ireland semi-final, but they lost badly to Kerry, who subsequently went on to win the 1929 championship as their first of four-in-a-row. That 1929 All-Ireland semi-final was McGahern's last appearance in the green and red of Mayo. At club level, he helped Castlebar Mitchels win the 1930 Mayo Senior Championship – their first county title in 27 years, breaking the dominance of Ballina Stephenites.

In 1931, he married Nora Horan from Tourmakeady, whose father Thomas was an innocent victim of an atrocious Black and Tans act of reprisal ten years previously. They settled in Westport, where he spent the remainder of his life until his death from illness in 1956. It was unusual that John McGahern should have been permitted to be stationed in Westport, given that his wife's homeplace was just twelve miles away and Garda regulations at the time was they a member could not serve within 50 miles of his wife's native place. Perhaps this concession was granted because his wife's family had suffered a tragic loss, or maybe it was a case of Eoin O'Duffy again pulling strings for the man he first came to know several years previously. If so, the irony was that when O'Duffy attended a Blueshirt demonstration in Westport in 1933, having been dismissed as Commissioner by the new Taoiseach Éamon de Valera, it was Garda John McGahern who was sent to the square with orders to take his former superior officer into custody. He did so reluctantly, with tears in his eyes.

Thus came full circle a relationship which began many years beforehand, through their mutual involvement in Ulster GAA.

P.S.: please note that the John McGahern mentioned above was not related to the author John McGahern (1934-2006), son of Sgt Francis McGahern who occupied the barracks in Cootehall, Co. Roscommon, and author of the novel 'The Barracks' (1963), for which he was awarded the McCauley Fellowship in 1964.

Chapter 3

Coiste Siamsa

A brief history of Coiste Siamsa

Coiste Siamsa evolved from a need in the infant force for sporting and cultural activities to occupy 500 energetic new recruits, who crowded the temporary depot in Kildare during the formative months of the Civic Guard in 1922.

Formal organisation of the body developed over the ensuing years. The history of the sport itself in An Garda Síochána began in Kildare, when the first tournaments were held on 24 September 1922. In its early constitution, Coiste Siamsa fostered an esprit de corps in An Garda Síochána.

In 1923, the official organ of the force, *Iris an Gharda*, identified sport as a "bond of unity in every organisation … to cement the ties of comradeship and co-operation as characteristics of our force". It was stated at that time that the aim of Coiste Siamsa was "… not the production of champion athletes, but to ensure that the Garda as a body should contain a high proportion of men who can hold their own with the average athlete in every form of sport – from such participation will in due course spring champion athletes".

New beginnings

As the years advanced, the stalwarts of the early decades faded from the headlines. Many of the clubs survived as hobbies for their members, but organised sport was in decline.

In 1962, An Garda Síochána again became a young organisation, as the first generation retired in increasing numbers. It was at this time that Coiste Siamsa experienced a re-birth. Thursday, 21 June 1962 saw the opening meeting of the Ard Comhairle of the Coiste Siamsa at the Depot Library in Garda Headquarters.

Then Minister for Justice, Charles J. Haughey, addressed the meeting, which was also attended by then Garda Commissioner, Mr Daniel Costigan, senior Garda officers, and others with an interest in sport within An Garda Síochána. The existence of Coiste Siamsa was put on a solid footing, and has gone from strength to strength since that day.

The last 50 years have seen some major sporting achievements by Garda Members at local, national and international level. Many of those sporting heroes have been honoured by their induction into the An Garda Síochána Coiste Siamsa Sportstar Awards in November of each year.

The present

In its present form, Coiste Siamsa is the governing body of sporting clubs at national level in the organisation. At local level, each Chief Superintendent is asked to assume chairmanship of his/her divisional Coiste Roinne.

The efficient operation of the sporting body is facilitated by a network of Sports Representatives and Provincial and Divisional Secretaries.

Coiste Siamsa logo

The Coiste Siamsa logo was designed by the late Moira Willoughby-O'Shea of "Aisling", Ballyrafter, Lismore, Co. Waterford. Moira was a graphic artist by profession.

Her design depicts half a shamrock to represent Ireland, a silhouette to represent a member of An Garda Síochána, male or female, who as the picture shows is in the process of warming up for a sporting event. The colours are green and gold to represent Ireland, and navy blue to represent An Garda Síochána. The shamrock and the figure symbolise the unity which the Gardaí have with Ireland.

Moira was presented with her prize with her prize by Commissioner Patrick Culligan on 13 February 1992 in the Garda Recreational Club in Harrington Street, Dublin.

Moira died tragically from a brain haemorrhage on 13 September 2004, leaving behind her husband Aidan, and her four children, Abbie, Leah, Alex and Louise. She was a sister of this book's co-author, Brian Willoughby.

Chapter 4

Divisional/Regional Competition (Gaelic Football)

The DMA Recreation Club Cup

Every year, an internal Gaelic football competition is run between all the participating Garda divisions in the country. Over the years, this competition has featured all the inter-county Garda players. The competition is extremely competitive and each Division strives to get their names on the cup.

Many members mentioned in this book, plus the other members who took part in the internal competitions, are proud holders of All-Ireland Garda Gaelic football and hurling medals. It was not possible to list this fact. For a long number of years, J. Forde, Sean O'Mahony, Michael O'Connor (Mayo) and Eamonn Barry (Meath) ran the competition successfully, with Brian Willoughby (Waterford) taking over the position in 2013. In 2009, to celebrate the 125th year of the GAA's existence, the annual Gaelic football and hurling finals were held in Croke Park. In the football final, the DMA South defeated Mayo/Sligo/Leitrim, and in the hurling final, Leinster defeated Limerick.

The roll of honour is as follows:

1966:	Cork East	1972:	DMA South
1967:	DMA South	1973:	DMA South
1968:	Roscommon/Galway	1974:	Cork East
1969:	Roscommon/Galway	1975:	DMA North Central
1970:	Roscommon/Galway	1976:	Cavan/Monaghan
1971:	DMA South	1977:	Cavan/Monaghan

1978: Laois/Offaly

1979: Cavan/Monaghan

1980: DMA North Central

1981: Cork East

1982: Laois/Offaly

1983: Wexford/Wicklow

1984: Galway West

1985: Kerry

1986: DMA South Central

1987: DMA South Central

1988: Laois/Offaly

1989: Cavan/Monaghan

1990: DMA North Central

1991: DMA North Central

1992: DMA North Central

1993: Donegal

1994: Garda College

1995: Cavan/Monaghan

1996: DMA North Central

1997: Cork East

1998: Limerick/Clare/Galway

1999: DMA North Central

2000: DMA South Central

2001: No competition because of 'foot and mouth' disease outbreak

2002: Carlow/Kildare

2003: Mayo/Sligo/Leitrim

2004: DMA South

2005: Louth/Meath

2006: Longford/Westmeath

2007: Cork

2008: DMA South

2009: DMA South Central

2010: Laois/Offaly

2011: Galway

2012: Galway

2013: Galway

2014: DMA West

2015: DMA South

2016: Garda College

Donegal, Inter–Divisional Football Champions 1993.

Back row, from left:
Hugh Gilvarry, Paul McHugh, Gerry Newton, Sean Paul Barrett,
Dessie Sheridan, Martin Conroy, Bosco Gallagher, Joe Doherty, Tony Moran,
Padraic Scanlon, Padraig Farragher.
Front row, from left:
Seamus Marley, Hugh McGurn, Michael Galvin, Tom Connolly, Brendan Martin,
Denis Swift, Adrian Flynn, David Gaffney, Declan McFarland (captain).

*Cavan/Monaghan, All-Ireland Garda Inter–Divisional Football Champions
1995.*

Back row, from left:
Sean Boyle, Micheál O'Donoghue, Des Brannock, Michael Lee, Kevin Swan,
Martin McGowan, Shane Heslin, Joe O'Connor, Pat Donohoe, Brian Doyle, Hugh Gilsenan.
Front row, from left:
Shaun Gallagher, Padraig Shanagher, John Farrelly, Damian Helferty, Jimmy Stenson,
Brian Leamy, Garry O'Callaghan, T. P. McLoughlin, Gerry Butler, Dave Hanrahan,
John O'Gara.

Carlow/Kildare All-Ireland Inter-Divisional Football Champions 2002,
who defeated Roscommon/Galway 0-10 to 0-8 at Westmanstown on 20 August 1992.
Back row, from left:
Michael Keevans, Dermot Cagney, Diarmuid Daly, Leonard Donlan, Brendan Costello,
Enda Coleman, Niall Brambrick, Alan Murphy, Paul O'Reilly, Mark Doran, Dessie Brannock,
P.J. O'Brien.
Front row, from left:
Jim Kelly, Pauric Kenny, Mark Carley, Eamon Whelan, Brian Monaghan (captain),
Pat McGirl, Jason Hughes, Brian Kearney, Brian Murphy, Paul Harris, Kevin Byrne,
Bernard Graham, Sean Galvin.

Longford/Westmeath, All-Ireland divisional football winners 2006.
Back row, left to right:
Martin McGowan, Brian Willoughby, Paddy Moran, Cian Finan, Padraig Fahey,
Declan Tanner, Roghan Headen, Derek McDonnell, Aidan Lyons, Derek Duggan,
Adrian O'Reilly, Donal Carroll, Mark Carty, Ronan Loftus, Denis Shields, Brian Monaghan,
Tom Judge, Tommy Farrell.
Front row, left to right:
Ray Tubman, Ian Bradley, Alan Hogan, Ken Duggan, Danny Maguire, Padraic Jones,
Conor Egan, Fergal Reynolds, Ray Greenan, Joe Kenny, Dave Mead, Damien Dorr,
Enda Daly.

DMA South Central,
All-Ireland Inter-Divisional Football Champions, 2009

Rear Left to Right
Shane Cooke, Declan McDermott, Barry O'Donnell, Graham Dunne, Niall Cahalan,
Declan Conlon, Martin Cahill, Bat Moriarity, Liam McGraynor, Mark Crompton,
Dennis Carrigan, Padraig Boyce, Martin Clavin, Damien Broughall, Brian O'Connor,
Derek Thomson, Gerry Russell.
Front Left to Right,
John Carney, Shane McNamara, Ronan Mulligan, Peter O'Brien, Dave Marshall,
Andy Dermody, Paul Cornish, Shane McGrath, Colin Coleman, Brian O'Connor, Sean O'Neill,
Noel Galvin, Enda Kenny, John Keane

Galway, All-Ireland Inter-Divisional Football Champions, 2011.

Back row, left to right:
Conor Barrett, Michael Gallagher, Mark Walkin, Brian Meaney, Shane Waldron,
Mark Caffrey, Don Connellan, Pat Kelly, Shane Fitzmaurice, Shaun Durkin, Shane Nallen,
Shane Igoe, Emmet Rocke, Alan Keane,
Shane Prendergast, Padraig O'Connor, Jason Kelly, Darragh Bolton.
Front row, left to right:
Paul McBride, Nicholas Delaney, Declan Fawl, Niall Lennon, Colm Boyle, Neil Lydon
(captain), Cian Flanagan (mascot), Padraig Kelly, Cormac Bane, Pat Casey,
Seamus McDonnell (manager).
Absent from photo:
Sean McHugh, Charlie Cawley, Anthony Pender and Ronan Steede.

Galway, All-Ireland Inter-Divisional Football Champions, 2012.

Back row, left to right:
John Gallagher, Mark Walkin, Rob Molloy, Pat Kelly, Don Connellan, Shane Nallen,
Shane Fitzmaurice, Alan Keane, Padraig O'Connor, Emmet Rocke, Paul Mc Bride, Pat Casey.

Front row, left to right:
Seamus McDonnell (manager), Mark Caffrey, Niall Lennon, Padraig Kelly, Anthony Pender,
Cormac Bane (captain), Brian Meaney, Jason Kelly, Aonghus Tierney, Padraig Moran,
Brendan Ryan.

Absent from photo:
Colm Boyle, Shaun Durkin, Neil Lydon, Eugene Boyce, Declan Fawl, Shane Igoe
and Dermot O'Brien.

Galway, All-Ireland Inter-Divisional Football Champions, 2013.

Back row, left to right:
Seamus McDonnell (manager), John Gallagher, Mark Walkin, Padraig O'Connor,
Shaun Durkin, Emmet Rocke, Shane Fitzmaurice, Rob Molloy, Shane Nallen, Niall O'Brien,
Conor Barrett, Mark Caffrey, Marvin Lee, Pat Kelly, Pat Casey.

Front row, left to right:
Alan Keane, Paul McBride, James Kavanagh, Cormac Bane, Brian Meaney, Michael Farragher,
Padraig Kelly (captain), Anthony Pender, Don Connellan, Declan Fawl, Nicholas Delaney.

Absent from photo:
Ger Brady, Darren Griffin, Neil Lydon and Brendan Ryan.

DMA West, All-Ireland Inter-Divisional Football Champions 2014.

Back row, left to right:
Brian Concannon, Dave Howard, Joe Green, Graham Dillon, Sean Breheny, Colm Hanley,
Gary Brennan, Barry Hehir, Ronan O'Reilly, Mark Ferris, Andy McGuill, John Mulcahy.
Front row, left to right:
Damien Reilly, Eoin Pelly, Mark Brennan, Eamonn Callaghan, Joe Kavanagh, Dave Fahy,
Paul Govern.

Inter Divisional Championship Winners, DMA South, 2015

Back Row (Left to right)
Danny Kelly (Manager), Mark Twomey, Darren Rooney, Dan Redmond, Conor Flannery,
Mick Cunningham, Niall Gaynor,Mick Divilly, PJ Foley, Paddy Browne, Damien Quirke,
Paul Flood (Selector)
Front Row (Left to right)
Alan Marshall, Dave O'Neill, Barry John Molloy, Paraic Syron, Mick Degan, Barry Curtin,
James Lambe, Ian Ward, Dave Costigan and Wayne Gilgunn

Garda College, All-Ireland Inter-Divisional Football Champions, 2016.
Panel:
Damien O'Sullivan, Joe Blake, Fergal Battrim, Cathal O'Reilly, Rory O'Connor,
Ronan Gallagher, Paul Varley, Leon Fox, Andy McDonnell, Shane Cunnigham, Gary Rogers,
Johnny Ryan, Shane Ryan, Ciaran Russell, Joe Hayes, James Cush, Alan Gaughan, Eoin Duffy,
Dara O'Shea, Mike Alyward, Gene Casey, Steven Dwyer, Sean Kane, Tom Currid,
Mark Heffernan, Dean Hyland.
Management:
Andrew Lacey, Peter Fahy, Joe Hayes, Dan Barry, James Cush, Lee Hunt.

Chapter 5

Divisional/Regional Competition (Hurling)

For many years, Dan Devitt, Finbarr Kelly, Phil Verdon and John O'Shea (Tipperary) ran the competition. In 2006, Mick Morrissey (Kilkenny) took over. Trophies competed for: the Edmond Garvey Memorial Cup; the DMG Recreation Cup.

The roll of honour is as follows:

1967: Wexford
1968: Cork East
1969: Cork West
1970: DMA South
1971: DMA South
1972: DMA South
1973: DMA South
1974: DMA South
1975: Cork
1976: Galway West
1977: Galway West
1978: Garda College
1979: Limerick
1980: DMA
1981: Waterford/Kilkenny
1982: Galway West
1983: Galway West
1984: Waterford/Kilkenny
1985: Galway West
1986: Waterford/Kilkenny

1987: Waterford/Kilkenny
1988: DMA
1989: DMA
1990: Garda College
1991: DMA South
1992: DMA South
1993: DMA South
1994: Garda College
1995: Garda College
1996: Garda College
1997: Waterford/Kilkenny
1998: Garda College
1999: Garda College
2000: Waterford/Carlow/Kildare
2001: Garda College
2002: Garda College
2003: Garda College
2004: Tipperary/Limerick
2005: Leinster
2006: Leinster

2007: Cork	2012: Cork
2008: Cork	2013: Limerick
2009: Leinster	2014: Eastern Region
2010: Cork	2015: Cork/Kerry
2011: South Eastern Region	2016: Garda College

CORK GARDA DIVISION HURLING TEAM
Cork Garda Division Hurling Team who beat the DMA selection in the All-Ireland Garda Hurling Final, played in Croke Park, 1975:
Front Row (l-r): Tadgh O'Mahoney, Ned Kirby, Jim Seymour, Jim Cremins, Pat O'Brien, Seán Doyle, Eugene O'Connor, Gerry McNamara, Justin Byrne, Frank Fallon, and Teddy Holland
Back Row (l-r): Tom McCarthy, Batt Kirby (RIP), Matt Kirwan, Pat Sheehan, Pat Galvin, Pat Doyle, Dan Brislane, John O'Brien (RIP), Frank Cummins, and Tom Kirby (RIP)

Photo courtesy of Gerry McNamara, Limerick City Branch.

Waterford/Kilkenny Garda Hurling Team
Winners of Garda Munster and All-Ireland Title 1981.

Back row, left to right:
Gordan Ryan, Pat Starr, Colman Loughnane, Mossy Walsh, Johnny Cleary, Tony Flynn, Donal Loughnane, Cormac Quinn, Gerry Mulligan, Tom O'Grady.
Front row, left to right:
John J. Duggan, Pat O'Hanlon, Terry Butler, Mick McCormack, Dinny Connolly, John Killeen, Jimmy Wafer, Johnny Grace, John Direen, Brian Murphy (inset)

*Waterford/Kilkenny Garda Hurling Team
Winners of Garda Munster and All–Ireland Title 1984.*

Back row, left to right:
C. Quinn, D. Loughnane, C. Loughnane, C. Ryan, G. Ryan, D. Foely, P. Starr,
J. Curran, T. Butler.
Front row, left to right:
G. Mulligan, J. Killeen, J. McDonald, M. Walsh (Capt), P. O'Hanlon, J.J. Duggan,
F. Sweeney, D. Sheehan, J. Wafer, B. Murphy.

*Waterford/Kilkenny Garda Hurling Team
Winners of Garda Munster and All–Ireland Title 1986.*

Back row, left to right:
M. Galway, J.J.Duggan, P. Starr, L. Maher, G. Mulligan (Capt.), B. Murphy, D. Sheehan,
F. Sweeney, D. Loughnane, J. Curtin, J. Wafer
Front row, left to Rigth:
T. Butler, D. Foley, G. Ryan, M. Walsh, C. Loughnane, J. McDonald, L. Kelly, C. Quinn,
J. Cleary, J. Direen

Waterford/Kilkenny Garda Hurling Team
Winners of Garda Munster and All-Ireland Title 1987.

Back row, left to right:
C. Quinn, M. Galway, J. McDonald, J. Direen, G. Ryan, C. Loughnane, D. Foely,
M. Walsh, T. Butler, J. Cleary, E. Carley, L. Farrell
Front Row left to Right:
J. Wafer, D. Sheehan, G. Mulligan, P. Starr (Capt), L. Maher, J.J. Duggan,
B. Murphy, L. Kelly.

Garda College, All-Ireland Inter-Divisional Hurling Champions, 1994.

Back row, left to right:
Eoin Ó Gríofa (Corcaigh), Alan Waters (Áth Cliath), Joachim Kelly (Uibh Fháilí), Ken Hogan
(Tiobraid Árann), Niall Guinan (Loch Gorman), Mick Cuffe (Áth Cliath), Mark Dowling
(Cill Chainnigh), Gerry Kennedy (Tiobraid Árann), Vinny Byrne (Cill Chainnigh).
Front row, left to right:
Peter Queally (Port Láirge), Pat O'Connell (Ciarraí), Tom McGlinchey (Corcaigh),
Padraig Tobin (Luimneach), James Aherne (Corcaigh), Sean Collum (Tiobraid Árann).

41

Waterford/Carlow/Kildare
Winners of Garda All–Ireland Title 2000

Leinster
Winners of Garda All–Ireland Title 2009

South east region All Ireland Garda Hurling Champions 2011

Panel

Cormac Quinn, Larry Smith, John Bugler, Emmett Dunphy, James Woodlock, Conor Cleere,
Ronan O'Donoghue, Anthony Owens, Brian Morris, Paul Hayes, Darren Colfer,
Brian Dignam, Paul *Kinsella, Jimmy Bourke, Darren Kelly, Mark Carley, Liam O'Reilly*
Stephen Hogan, Darin Sane, Pat Walsh, John O'Flynn, Graham Gohery, Pat Kelly, Ronan
O'Callaghan, Pater Kennedy, Conor Gleeson, Donal Keogh

Chapter 6

The history of Garda GAA Club, Dublin, Cork and Limerick

Garda GAA Club, Dublin
by Eugene O'Sullivan

Senior football champions: 1927, 1933, 1934, 1935 and 1948
Senior hurling champions: 1925, 1927, 1928, 1929 and 1931

The Garda GAA Club has been involved in Dublin GAA affairs with varying degrees of success since the foundation of the state and the transfer of policing responsibility from the RIC to the new unarmed force the Civic Guard which subsequently became An Garda Síochána. In the early 1920s after the War of Independence and a very bitter civil war, the GAA was seen as a great healing influence in communities and indeed families divided by strife. People who took different sides in the civil war came together on the playing fields and having members of the GAA join the new police service helped it to gain acceptance. It was the start of a long and enduring relationship between the GAA and An Garda Síochána, and it is rare to find a club which does not have a member of the Garda as a player or administrator.

The inaugural meeting for the formation of the new police force was held in the Gresham Hotel on 9 February 1922, and Michael Staines was selected as the first Commissioner. On 9 September 1922, Michael Staines resigned, and was succeeded by Eoin O'Duffy. For the next ten years, O'Duffy actively encouraged the recruitment of young footballers, hurlers and handballers to the Civic Guard, which was renamed An Garda Síochána in 1923 on the proposal of Cathal O'Shannon.

Officially, the Civic Guard GAA Club came into existence in the spring of 1922 when the affiliation was accepted by the Dublin County Board. But because of the circumstances of the time, it would be another year before football and hurling teams participated in Dublin competitions.

The club has been a constant presence on Dublin GAA fields for nearly a century, with the odd lapse which usually coincided with a fall-off in recruiting. What Eoin O'Duffy started as an all-police, all-male club with no ground to call their own has now evolved into Garda Westmanstown Gaels, playing football, hurling, camogie, and ladies' football from nursery through to adult level, and enjoys the facilities of the Westmanstown Sports Complex.

The 1920s proved to be a very fruitful period for the newly formed Civic Guard GAA Club, with the policy of recruiting some of the best hurlers and footballers in the country paying rich dividends.

The hurlers won five senior championships in a row from 1925 to 1929, a feat only recently equalled by Ballyboden St Endas, who won from 2007 to 2011. They also won the Dublin Senior League on four occasions: 1924, 1925, 1928 and 1929.

Some of the star hurlers of that era such as Pat 'Fowler' McInerney of Clare, Garrett Howard of Limerick and Mick Gill lined out with the Garda club.

Withinztwelve months of affiliation, the football side of the club was also making an impression, reaching the county final in 1923 and losing to O'Tooles, who were a dominant force in Dublin at the time. The first championship success came in 1927, followed by a second win in 1929. Again, several stars of the time lined out in the blue of the Garda club, such as Paul Russell of Kerry, Larry Stanley of Kildare and Jim Smith of Cavan.

After the initial success of the 1920s, the hurlers' fortunes declined somewhat in the 1930s with an aging team and a lack of recruitment – a situation which has repeated itself throughout the decades. One more title was won in 1931 to make it six wins in nine years, but after that there was little success, with the club withdrawing from competition in 1939 and players transferring to other clubs in the city.

The 1930s was a most successful period for the club's footballers, winning three senior championships and three senior leagues – all in consecutive years. They replaced O'Tooles as the powerhouse of Dublin club football, and this led to mutterings of the Garda Club being a semi-professional team, in that nearly all members were stationed in Garda HQ and trained every day as part of their duties. One of the most prominent players of that era was Tim O'Donnell of Kerry, who was a brother of John 'Kerry' O'Donnell of Gaelic Park fame in New York.

Just like the hurlers, an aging squad and no recruiting led to the withdrawal of the club from Dublin competition in the late 1930s, and it was only resurrected again in the 1940s with the arrival of a new generation of young Gardaí. During the Emergency and World War II, spasmodic efforts were made to field Garda teams, but an absence of youth and demands on manpower made it impossible.

At the end of the Emergency, a new recruiting drive saw many young men who were already inter-county players join the force. This gave rise to the formation of a committee with the sole intention of putting the Garda GAA Club back in business on Dublin GAA fields. The club was re-established in late 1947, with many of the stars of the time who were serving Gardaí in Dublin opting to play football with their colleagues. Players like Brendan Lynch and Bill Carlos of Roscommon, Paddy Kennedy and Teddy O'Sullivan of Kerry, and the great Tom Langan of Mayo became the backbone of the team in that period.

Success followed very quickly with a senior championship win in 1948, beating a very strong St Vincents in the final in Croke Park. This was the start of a decade of rivalry with the Donnycarney giants, with both clubs vying for the top spot in Dublin football. They met again in the 1952 final in Croke Park before a crowd of 30,000. This game ended in a draw, with Tom Langan in outstanding form for the Guards; unfortunately, Vincents prevailed in the replay. winning in extra time. The same clubs met yet again in the 1955 final – which was played in March 1956 – with victory going once more to St Vincents.

In 1956, three members of the Garda Club played in the All-Ireland final. Paddy Harrington from Bere Island – father of golfer Padraig – and Eric Ryan lined out with Cork, and Frank Evers played with Galway.

The fortunes of the Garda Club again went into decline as the 1950s drew to a close, with the familiar pattern of an aeing team and an absence of recruiting.

At the start of the 1960s, life in Ireland was changing with an improving economy and improvements in transport and mobility. This in turn created problems for GAA clubs in the capital, with players opting to play for their home clubs down the country. While the club continued to participate in Dublin competition in the early 1960s, it was in serious decline. After a league tie in 1964 against Rialto Gaels, the Garda team was described as a "slow and cumbersome fifteen". By 1965, the team had dropped into Division 2, suffered successive defeats and eventually had to concede a number of walkovers. The inevitable was near and on May 24, the county board received a letter from the Garda Club withdrawing from Dublin competition because of inability to field a team. The letter was accepted with regret, and a glorious era had ended for the Garda Club. But yet again, the phoenix would rise from the ashes.

After three years in the wilderness, the club once more reappeared on the playing fields of Dublin when a group in Pearse Street Station – under the chairmanship of Michael O'Connor and with Jim Murphy as secretary – affilliated a new club of Gardai to be called St Andrews, adopting the name of the Westland Row parish. Initally it was to be confined to members of Pearse Street and Store Street Districts, but having been accepted back into competition by the Dublin County Board, it was open to any serving member in the then DMA to join.

For a few years there was considerable success, with the club winning Divisions 3 and 2 of the Dublin Leagues and getting to two county semi-finals in 1972 and 1974, losing on both occasions to old rivals St Vincents. At that time, some prominent inter-county players wore the blue of the Garda Club, such as Willie McGee (Mayo), John McCarthy (Dublin), Seamus Bonner (Donegal, RIP) and Eugene Sheelin (Louth).

Towards the end of the 1970s, a junior team was formed for the first time, and with an influx of young recruits, an U21 team played in the Dublin championship of 1978. In the late 1970s and early 1980s, while playing numbers were strong, success on the field was scarce, and in 1984 the club was relegated to intermediate status for the first time.

Yet again, a recruiting drive in the mid 1980s saw the arrival of an exceptional group of players, leading to a resurrection and a decade of great success. The winning of the intermediate championship in 1986 – under the management of Phil Kelly and the captaincy of Ken Brennan – led to a return to senior status. In the following years, all four divisions of the senior league were won, and with a little luck, a senior championship would have surely followed. John Newton (Roscommon), Davy Byrne (Monaghan), Dermot Deasy (Dublin), Jack Sheedy (Dublin), Willie Hughes (Dublin) and Ashley O'Sullivan (Wicklow) were some of the prominent inter-county stars who played for the club at that time.

At present, the club operates in Division 3 of the Dublin Leagues and in the intermediate championship. There have been many changes over the years, with membership now open to civilians, the formation of a ladies' team in 1997 and the juvenile section Westmanstown Gaels in 2004.

The changing of Rule 21 of the GAA led to the formation of clubs in the PSNI and London Metropolitan Police, and this has opened up a new line of activity for the Garda Club, with regular games against our colleagues in those services. In 2002, history was made when the PSNI GAA Club took to the field in Westmanstown for the first time for the MacCarthy Cup, in honour of Thomas St George MacCarthy, who was an RIC Inspector and a founding member of the GAA. This has become an annual event, and led to the Tom Langan Tournament every two years – a competition between Garda, PSNI, London Met and NYPD GAA Clubs.

The Civic guard Football team in 1923
Back(left to right)
Guard McNamee, Guard Dalton, Guard Langton, Sergeant Colleran, Guard McCormack,
Guard Smith,
Front (left to right)
Sergeant Cunnffe, Guard Flynn, Guard Haves, Sergeant Moron (Capt), Guard Redmond,
Guard McGahern, GuardMahon.
Sitting (left to right)
Guard Williams, Guard Kirwan.

A hurling team from1923
Back (left to right)
Gd. O'Brien. Gal. Driscoll, Sgt. McMahon, Gd. Healy, Gal. McInerney, Gd. Holmes,
Gd. Cahill, Gd. Bennett.
Middle (left to right)
Gd. Foster 9 (trainer), Gd. M. Noonan, Cadet T. Noonan, (secretary), Gd. Hayes,
Sgt. Barry (Captain), Inspector Feore (treasurer), Gd. O'Sullivan, Gd. Conroy
Front (left to right)
Gd. Burke, Sgt. Ryan, Gd. Howard, Gd. Tobin.

County Champions
The team and subs who won the Dublin hurling title in 1925.
Back (left to right)
J. Doherty, J. Grace, P. McInerney, J. Burke, T. Conway, M. Dunphy,
J. Cahill, J. Conroy, T. Burnell, J. Ryan.
Front (left to right)
J. Kelly, W. O'Brien, N. Tobin, J. Smith, M. Gill (Capt), J. Burke, G. Howard, M. Power,
W Phelan.

Garda Team c.1930

Once More
Many of the Hurlers were entering the twilight of their careers when they won back the county title in 1931.
Here they are pictured four years earlier before their annual game against the Army selection.

Garda Team c.1930

Title Regained

Players pictured at Croke Park befor the Dublin Final in June 1948
Back left to Right:
Paddy Kennedy, Johnny McEvoy, Ned Kennedy Ned Carroll, Murt O'Shea, Gerry McArdle,
Pat McGrath, Tom Prendergast, Bill Carlos
Front left to Righ:
Tony Burke, Jim Healy, Brendan Lynch (Captain), John F. Sullivan, Liam Queally
Tom Lanagan, Teddy O'Sullivan, Sid Harkin

Garda Team Winners of Dublin Senior Championship Football 1948. They beat St. Vincents by 2-8 to 2-3.
Front: T. Burke, J. Healy, R.I.P., B. Lynch (Capt.), J. F. O'Sullivan, L. Quigley, R.I.P., T. Langan, R.I.P., T. Sullivan, S. Harkins, R.I.P.
Back: P. Kennedy, R.I.P., J. McEvoy, E. Keneally, R.I.P., E. Carroll, M. O'Shea, G. McArdle, J. Hurley, P. McGrath, T. Prendergast, R.I.P., B. Carlos, R.I.P.,
Mentors: P. McTiernan, R.I.P., T. McNamara, R.I.P., M. Murray, C. O'Sullivan, R.I.P., J. Brannigan, R.I.P., L.Stanley, R.I.P., P. O'Shea, D. Hearns (Trainer) R.I.P.,
Photo courtesy of Peg McNamara and Tony Burke

- **GARDA SENIOR FOOTBALL TEAM (1972)**

In May 1972, the Garda team reached the semi-final of the Dublin Senior Football championship and were drawn against St Vincent's who had their sights set on 'three in a row'.

Played at Parnell Park match ended in a draw, with the replay resulting in success for St Vincent's who went on beat UCD in the county final. The Garda players acknowledge the huge efforts made by their manager Mick O' Connor and trainer Niall McGready (RIP).

Pictured are members who played on the Garda team:

Front Row (l-r): Sean Galway (RIP); Michael Mulryan; Seamus Hughes; Martin Donnellan; Kevin Connell (RIP); John Healy and Tom Harty.

Back Row (l-r): Ollie Hanley; Vinny O'Donnell (RIP); Ned Ryan; Tom Flanagan; Willie Magee; Ray Prenderville (RIP); Noel McDermott and Mick Quinn.

Photo courtesy of Michael Mulryan, Galway.

The Garda Guinness Tournament
The Garda Side which took part in the first Garda/Guinness Tournament in 1977
Back Left to Right:
Paul Curran, Eugene Murphy, Ray Doyle, P.J. Gallagher, Noel McDermott, Pat Gavin,
Aidan McNulty, Pat Rrehony, Owen Greene
Front Left to Right:
Gerry McManus, Martin Donnellon, Andy Gillick, Hugh White, Pat Driscoll, Noel Bourke,
Brian McGrodan, Gus Keating.

The Garda Club first travelled overseas in 1980, visiting New York, Boston, Toronto and Chicago. This was the first of ten foreign trips which have taken the club to places such as Washington, Las Vegas, San Francisco, Hawaii, Barcelona and London. It is doubtful that Eoin O'Duffy would have envisaged a Garda team playing Clan na Gael of Hawaii, but that fixture took place in Kapiolani Park in Honolulu in October 1992.

Perhaps the most significant development in recent times was the construction of the Westmanstown Sports Centre, where the Garda GAA Club owns its pitches and all-weather facilities. It was felt by many members that the club should share these facilities with the local community, and in 2004 – under the chairmanship of George Kyne – the juvenile section Westmanstown Gaels was formed. Over a decade later, this has grown to twenty teams of boys and girls playing football, hurling and camogie at all ages from nursery to minor, as well as the adult Garda men's and ladies' teams.

The future looks bright for the Garda Club, and as well as being the club of choice for members serving in the DMR, it will also continue to serve the local people in the Westmanstown area.

Garda GAA Club, Limerick
by Brian Kelly

Senior football champions: 1924 and 1958

Limerick Garda Club won the Limerick senior football championship on two occasions – 1924, when they defeated Rathkeale, and 1958 when they defeated Pallasgreen. They got to the final on one other occasion: in 1926, when they were defeated by Glin. The club won the 1924 county senior football crown, travelling to Rathkeale on 22 February 1925 to beat the local lads 1-2 to 0-3. It was a very satisfying game and produced some first class football. The referee on the day was Albie Quillinan.

Limerick Garda Club was the first Garda team to win a county GAA championship anywhere. The team was as follows: Sgt Keyes (captain), Charlie McArdle, Gardas Fulham, Lawlor, Walsh (John Street Station), Sgts Sean Rabbitt, Baker, Ruane, Reilly, (William Street Station), Gardas Mick Keating, Pat Sheeran, McQuillan, Reynolds, Rogers (William Street Station), Sgt Flynn (Edward Street Station), Sgt Marron (Abbeyfeale Station), Garda O'Sullivan (Caherconlish Station) and Garda Fenlon (Bruff Station). Garda were again in the final two years later, but by the time the decider was arranged, many of their players had been transferred elsewhere, and they conceded a walkover to Glin.

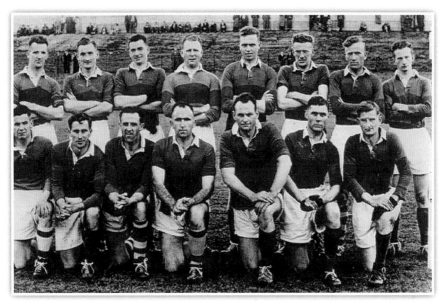

Limerick Garda Club, Limerick Senior Football Champions 1958.

Back row, from left:
L Duffy (Roscommon), T Roche (Kerry), L Egan (Mayo), T Coleman (Mayo),
P. J. McDonagh (Sligo), P Donnellan (Galway), J Whelan (Galway), J O'Brien (Wexford).

Front row, from left:
A Scannell (Cork), J. J. Masterson (Mayo), P Silke (Galway, captain), L Brady (Cavan),
M Jones (Kerry), M Freeman (Sligo), F Lyons (Mayo).

Limerick Garda also won in 1958, when they defeated Pallasgreen 0-7 to 1-1. The date was 21 September 1958, and the gate was then a record. Gerry Fitzgerald, Rathkeale, was the referee. Team: P. J. McDonagh, Pat Courtney, Paddy Donnellan, J F Lyons, E McDonagh, Gerry O'Sullivan, J Whelan, Pat Silke, Andy Scannell, Leo Duffy, Maurice Jones, Con O'Brien, Tom Coleman, J Finnerty, P Brady.

Cork Garda GAA Club
by Tim Bowe

Senior football champions: 1950

Gaelic games and Gaelic football in particular were in a healthy state in Cork as 1950 dawned. The Cork hurling team had lost to Tipperary in both the Munster final and the National League finals in 1949, but hopes were high that those results would be reversed in 1950.

The Cork senior football team won the Munster football championship in 1949, before losing narrowly to Cavan in the All-Ireland semi-final. The Rebels' football community was hopeful that elusive All-Ireland title could be captured in 1950.

The county teams' hopes were underpinned by a strong and vibrant club scene. The senior county football championship was particularly strong in the late 1940s and early 1950s. No less than nineteen teams entered the 1950 Cork county senior football championship, and this compares well to the 13 teams which had entered the hurling championship.

Part of the reason for the strength and subsequent public interest in the county football championship at that time was that the Army and Gardaí both entered teams in the championship. Some of the best footballers in Ireland were available to the Army and Garda teams, which added huge interest and often spice to games that featured the protectors of the state and guardians of the peace.

The army under the name 'Collins' had played in the Cork championship since the 1920s. They won the County Cork championship in 1929, but did not feature strongly in the 1930s. It was not until the Defence Forces

Cork Garda GAA club, the team that won the championship
Back row, from left:
Insp Cotter, Pat Spillane, Eugene Monahan, Mick Reddy, Jas Murphy, Sgt Buckley,
John Courtney, Con Kearney, Jack Behan-O'Brien, Jim Clifford, Richard O'Connor,
Jim Downing, Phil 'Gunner' Brady, Con McGrath, Alfie O'Rourke, Frank Scanlon,
Paddy McMahon, Dominic Murray and Paddy O'Driscoll

was expanded during the Emergency of 1939 to 1945 that the Army club re-emerged as a strong championship contender. They won the 1949 Cork County football championship when they hammered Macroom in a replayed final. That was also the first year the Gardaí entered the Cork senior football championship.

The first round of the 1950 championship produced some spicy games. Garda were paired against the tough divisional side Beara, while St Nicholas were pitted against 1949 runners-up Macroom. The big upset and talking point of the round, however, was the defeat of Clonakilty by Castlemagner. There was a sequel to this defeat, and Clonakilty were re-instated in the championship after an objection was lodged against the Castlemagner side.

The quarter-finals generated a lot of talk too. The biggest games were the clashes of perennial rivals Clonakilty and Fermoy and the championship heavyweights St Nicks and 'Collins' (Army). Clonakilty defeated Fermoy with an injury time point. The St Nicks versus Collins game was even closer. It is estimated that 5,000 spectators went to the Mardyke Sports Grounds to witness a bruising encounter which ended level. The *Cork Examiner* described it as "the most exciting game seen in Cork for years". The referee, Cork and Garda star Con McGrath, strongly disagreed with this account.

He wrote in his referee's report: "I have nothing good to say about the game except it ended. It was a rough and tumble affair where the ball seemed to be only of secondary consideration." According to the *Cork Examiner*, the replay was even more exciting. St Nicks won with a late Dave Creedon goal.

The semi-finals were also bruising affairs. St Nicks got the better of Millstreet in Macroom, where top scorers were Jack Lynch, Dave Creedon and Christy Ring. In the other semi-final game, Garda edged past Clonakilty by 1-4 to 0-4, a disputed penalty goal the difference between the sides.

These results set the stage for a unique final on 8 October 1950. St Nicks were laden with star hurlers and footballers. Two weeks earlier, many of their team county senior hurling medals with Glen Rovers. They had injury problems, which meant they had to line out without team captain Joe Hartnett, Jack Lynch and Donie Twomey, while their corner back Paddy Martin had to box in an Irish trial in Dublin the night before, and travel back overnight to Cork for the game.

The Garda team was put on a special course free of all normal duties for three weeks prior to the game. There star men were Cork players Paddy Driscoll, Con McGrath, former St Nicks player James 'Jas' Murphy (later captained Kerry to All-Ireland victory in 1953), and Phil 'Gunner' Brady, an All-Ireland medallist with Cavan. On the down side, the Garda panel was small and they could not afford any injuries. In fact 'Gunner' Brady had been transferred away from Union Quay Station in Cork during the year, and travelled to Cork from Monaghan for the final. Garda missed the services of John Guiry in goal and T Walsh in the forwards.

There was a lot of talk in football circles that the game would be a blood and murder affair. The reality was that while it was an extremely tough match, it was also a game of high quality football.

The *Cork Examiner* reported: "In the many finals that have taken place (since 1890) it is doubtful if there was ever a harder, more keenly contested game than yesterday's final which was witnessed by a large crowd". Despite playing into a strong breeze, the Garda club made the better start. Nicks did not score until the tenth minute, when Dave Creedon intercepted a Garda clearance and fired home a goal.

Con McGrath scored a point for Garda. Nicks used the wind well and points by Creedon, Gerald Lenihan, and John Lyons gave them a five point lead as half time approached. Then Garda goaled following a melee in the St Nicks goal, but in the five minutes of injury time, Mick Murphy and Dave Creedon pointed to put Nicks ahead by 2-4 to 1-1 half time.

The second half was even tougher. A slick move between James Murphy, 'Gunner' Brady and Dominic Murray resulted in a Garda goal, and they moved a point ahead with fifteen minutes remaining. The next nine minutes were described as "some of the hardest and toughest ever witnessed in a county final". There were no scores during that period.

The clinching score came when 'Gunner' Brady picked up a loose ball in the middle of the field. There was no apparent danger to St Nicks, but in the twinkling of an eye, he had side-stepped two tackles and fired an unstoppable rocket to the roof of the St Nicks net. Nicks rallied with a Creedon point, but two late scores by Con McGrath secured a famous victory for Garda.

The Garda were the nineteenth team to add their name to the roll of honour of senior county football championship winners in Cork. It was to be their only county senior title. They fell to St Nicks in the 1951 county championship ,and even though they competed every year until 1965, they were never the same power as they were in the first three years of their existence.

Garda team: Insp Cotter, Pat Spillane, Eugene Monahan, Mick Reddy, Jas Murphy, Sgt Buckley. John Courtney, Con Kearney, Jack Behan O'Brien, Jim Clifford, Richard O'Connor, Jim Downing, Phil 'Gunner' Brady, Con McGrath, Alfie O'Rourke, Frank Scanlon, Paddy McMahon, Dominic Murray, Paddy O'Driscoll.

Final Score: Garda 3-7, St Nicholas 2-5.

Garda line-up:

1. C Kearney, 2. J Murphy, 3. J Courtney, 4. J Downing,
5. R O'Connor, 6. P O'Driscoll, 7. A O'Rourke, 8. C McGrath (capt.),
9. P 'Gunner' Brady, 10. P McMahon, 11. M Reddy, 12. P Spillane
13. D Murray, 14. F Scanlon, 15. E Monahan. **Sub:** T Lawlor.

By J. D. HICKEY

CO. CORK based Gardai have formed a football club which will compete in next year's senior and junior Rebel County competitions, including the championships.

At a meeting on Thursday night, Clonakilty stationed Pat Griffin who led Kerry in this year's all-Ireland senior final against Down was appointed captain. The Kerry centre-forward told me yesterday that his decision to play with the Cork side will not alter his allegiance to the "Kingdom."

Also on call by the law-men will be the Cork midfielder Mick O'Loughlin and Clare's Josie Tubridy. Cork inter-county player Johnny Crowley has not, it is understood, yet decided if he will assist the Garda club which went out of existence two years after having won the 1951 Cork senior title.

SELECTOR, TRAINER

Seamus Garvey, the well-known referee who is also one of the selectors has been appointed trainer of the senior team.

Other officers are: President—Chief Supt. P. McLoughlin. Chairman—Eric Ryan, the former Munster and Cork player; vice-Chairman—Jas. Murphy, who captained Kerry when they won the 1953 all-Ireland senior crown; hon. sec.—Paul Downey (Waterford); hon. Treas.—Jerry Moran (Limerick).

The return of Garda should add considerably to the interest in Cork football.

Cork Examiner, 21 December 1968

Chapter 7

The Garda College's Participation in:
The Fitzgibbon Cup, Sigerson Cup, Trench Cup, Ryan Cup, Purcell Cup, Lynch Cup, Lynch Shield and Ashbourne Shield

Fitzgibbon Cup

The Fitzgibbon Cup, the trophy for the Higher Education Hurling Championship, is named after Dr Edwin Fitzgibbon, a Capuchin priest who was Professor of Philosophy in University College, Cork from 1911 to 1936. In 1912, Dr Fitzgibbon donated most of his annual salary to present the trophy that bears his name for the hurling championship between the constituent colleges of the National University of Ireland (NUI).

The Garda College reached the final of the Fitzgibbon Cup on one occasion, in 1996/97, managed by Ken Hogan.

Quotes below are adapted from 'The Cups That Cheered' by Donal McAnallen, regarding the Garda College involvement in the Fitzgibbon Cup (with kind permission of Donal McAnallen).

1995/96

Garda College made as dramatic an entrance to the Fitzgibbon Cup series as in the Sigerson competition. The trainee policemen devoured the light servings of Trinity and UUJ for hors d'oeuvres. For their main course, in the quarter-final in Templemore, they polished off Waterford RTC's pretensions at retaining the Cup, a storming centre back showing from Peter Queally (Waterford),and a late goal from Denis Byrne (Kilkenny) sufficing to produce a 1-9 to 0-9 upset. In the semi-final, Damien Cleere (Kilkenny) struck 1-5 in the process of putting the Garda College in a promising position. But three late points saw Limerick steal through by 1-9 to 1-8.

1996/97

The Garda College visited Belfield to apprehend UCD's efforts to return to glory by 0-16 to 2-8 and moved on to close the case on Maynooth with eight points in their quarter-final in Templemore. The College played Waterford RTC in the semi-final, a goal from Niall Moloney (Kilkenny), buttressed Garda's seven point lead at half time. With Conor Gleeson (Tipperary) at centre back and Ollie Baker (Clare) i lár na páirce, the physically formidable Garda side would not concede scores easily to anyone. Garda just managed to keep control and advanced by 1-8 to 1-7.

Fitzgibbon Cup Panel 1996

Back row, from left:
Pat O'Connell, Conor Gleeson, Gerry Kennedy, Lorcan Looby, Darren Sane, Ken Hogan,
David Gleeson, Paudge Tobin, Aidan Flanagan, John Finnegan, Mark Dowling, Tom Kennedy,
Tom McGlinchey.
Front row, from left:
Damien Cleere, Hud Kelly, Anthony Teefey, Peter Queally, Kevin Long, Sean Collum,
Denis Byrne, Francis Corey.

UCC threatened a runaway success the next day at Páirc Uí Rinn on 2 March 1997, but Garda strode into a three point lead, largely due to Damien Cleere's accurate free taking. John Enright starred for UCC, and although Denis Byrne's goal for the College reinvigorated the contest, UCC stayed safely on terra firma and won by 0-14 to 1-8.

The Garda team on the day was: Cathal Jordan (Galway), Niall O'Donnell (Cork), Seamus McIntyre (Kerry, captain), John Finnegan (Dublin), Kevin Long (Cork), Conor Gleeson (Tipperary), Stephen Hogan (Tipperary), Ollie Baker (Clare), Tommy Kennedy (Tipperary), Damien Cleere (Kilkenny), Brian O'Dwyer (Tipperary), Tom Kavanagh (Galway), Niall Moloney (Kilkenny), Dennis Byrne (Kilkenny), Aidan Flanagan (Tipperary). Subs: Jimmy Smiddy (Cork), for Flanagan, Seamus Maher (Tipperary) for O'Dwyer and Nigel Carey (Limerick) for Kennedy.

1997/98

In the second round in Templemore, Damien Cleere's eleven points steered the College past UCG, 0-16 to 0-11. In the quarter-final, the boys in blue raided Plassey where Ollie Baker did yeoman service, scoring two early

Fitzgibbon Cup Panel 1997/98

Back row, from left:
Nigel Carey, Michael O'Mahony, Tom Kennedy, Niall Moloney, Brian O'Donnell,
Cathal Jordan, Tom Kavanagh, Pat Treacy, John Finnegan, Brian O'Dwyer, Jimmy Smiddy.
Middle row, from left:
Hud Kelly, Conor Gleeson, Seamus Maher, Francis Corey, Darren Sane, Brendan B. Murphy,
Kevin Long, Michael O'Rourke.
Front row, from left:
Damien Cleere, Ollie Baker, Aidan Flanagan, Stephen Hogan, Niall O'Donnell, Greg Baker,
Seamus McIntyre (captain), Denis Byrne, Barry Smythe, Colm O'Flaherty.

points from sideline cuts and clearing a last minute UL penalty from the line, while substitute Niall Moloney snapped up the all important goal in a 1-9 to 0-9 away triumph. In the semi-final at Claughhaun, Limerick, Damien Cleere (1-6) and Henry Shefflin (0-9) tied the battle of the marksmen and WIT mustered a slim majority of scores from play. The Déise Institute ground down the Garda by 1-11 to 1-9.

1998/1999

The Garda College qualified by navigating its way past NUIG at Dangan. A hat-trick from John Flanagan (Galway) sealed the deal for the Gardaí on a score of 5-9 to 3-9. In the semi-final, goals from John Flanagan and Niall Moloney kept Garda in touch with WIT for much of the game, but they lost on a scoreline of 1-17 to 2-4.

1999/2000

DCU knocked out the Garda College at Templemore by 1-12 to 1-9.

2000/2001

NUIG beat the Garda College by 3-14 to 2-7, despite two goals from Brian Begley (Limerick).

2001/2002

In the first round, the Garda College quashed Queen's by 5-14 to 1-1 at Malone. The men in blue amassed a 22-point first half lead owing mostly to Owen Behan (Kilkenny) who scored 4-6 in total. The referee blew the whistle early when Garda had charge 5-14 to 1-1. In the quarter-final, a feisty clash between the College and UL, UL took the honours by 1-9 to 0-9.

2002/2003

Did not participate.

2003/2004

Did not participate.

2004/2005

In the first round, GMIT beat the Garda College by 3-11 to 1-13 at Shannon, despite ten points from Tony Carmody (Clare).

2005/2006

DIT beat the Garda College by 1-17 to 1-16 after extra time in the quarter-final despite Vincent Hurley's prolific scoring.

2006/2007

UCC defeated the Garda College in the first round in Templemore by 1-12 to 0-10.

2007/2008

A new structure changed the dynamic of the championship. There were a dozen teams with four groups of three teams were drawn in a round robin format, with the top two in each going through to the quarter-finals. The Garda College failed to progress.

2009/2010

Drumcondra/Mater Dei beat the Garda College by 1-18 to 1-8 in Templemore in the first round. The Garda College has not played in the Fitzgibbon Cup since 2010.

Sigerson Cup

The Sigerson Cup, the trophy for the Higher Education Gaelic football championship, was presented by Strabane man, Dr George Sigerson – a professor in UCD – in 1911, and has been played for ever since. The Garda College has reached the final on three occasions – 1995/96, 1998/99 and 2007/08 – but has never won the competition.

Quotes below are adapted from 'The Cups That Cheered' by Donal McAnallen, regarding the Garda College involvement in the Fitzgibbon Cup (with kind permission of Donal McAnallen).

1994/95

A new type of student team joined in, with the entry of the Garda Training College in 1995. Typically Garda teams were older than most sides, with many of their players having studied elsewhere beforehand; and they were also perceived as being physically stronger, albeit a somewhat exaggerated factor. Garda hit the ground running with ten points from Derek Duggan (Roscommon) to overcome St Mary's by 0-22 to 3-11 after extra time in an epic first round tie in Santry. In the quarter-final, Garda's maiden voyage continued with a one point win over Maynooth at Westmanstown, its home ground. In the semi-final, UCG arrested Garda's progress on the score of 2-12 to 1-6.

1995/96

In the quarter-final, DCU deferred to the force of the law in a four-point

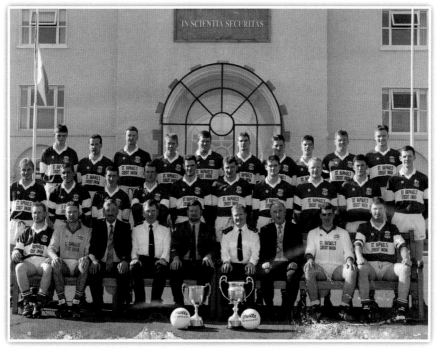

Sigerson Cup Panel 1994/95

Back row, from left:
Martin Power (Waterford), Michael Galvin (Sligo), Padraig Boyce (Galway),
Ollie Rua O'Sullivan (Cork), Liam Kearns (Kerry) (Manager), Marin Doran (Dublin),
Patrick Murphy (Cork), Declan Farrell (Offaly), Ken Duggan (Roscommon),
Derek Duggan (Roscommon).

Middle row, from left:
Sean Collum (Tipperary), Peter Queally (Waterford), Niall Lennon (Roscommon),
Chris Coleman (Roscommon), Pat Hegarty (Cork), Fergal O'Donnell (Roscommon),
Joe Hughes (Offaly), Aidan Bracken (Offaly), Brian O'Donovan (Cork),
Seamus Murphy (Laois).

Front row, from left:
Karl Kearns (Sligo), Chris Grogan (Roscommon), P. J. Ruddy, Tony Finnerty, Eoin Liston,
Liam Harris, John Cooper (Wexford), Brendan Rouine (Clare).

defeat at the Garda Training Centre, Templemore. In the semi-final, a relatively unknown Garda side discharged an illustrious UUJ line-up by 1-7 to 0-5 courtesy of four points from Fergal O'Donnell (Roscommon) and a fortieth minute goal from Martin Power (Waterford). In the final played on 12 March 1995 at Plassey, UL, Limerick, UCD scored two goals in the first ten minutes, but Garda's hopes were kept alive by a goal from Brian O'Donovan (Cork) after a weaving run. The tempo was raised in the last twenty minutes when James O'Shea (Kerry) and Jim O'Donoghue pierced the Dublin edifice to maximum effect. Suddenly the side were level but UCD scored two points to secure victory on a scoreline of 2-11 to 3-5. The Garda team was: Kevin O'Dwyer (Cork), Jason Lynch (Cork), Brian McCarthy (Kerry), Fergal Reynolds (Leitrim), Ollie O'Sullivan (Cork), Kevin McGettigan (Donegal), Colm O'Flaherty (Tipperary), Padraig Boyce (Galway), Adrian Phelan (Laois), James O'Donoghue (Cork), Brian O'Donovan (Cork), Enda Freaney (Kildare), James O'Shea (Kerry), Fergal O'Donnell (Roscommon), John Barrett (Cork). Subs: James Kingston (Cork) for Lynch and Colin Coleman (Roscommon) for Barrett.

1996/97

In the quarter-final, UL beat the Garda College after extra time.

1997/98

In the second round, UUJ nicked victory from the Garda side for whom a penalty from Cathal Sheridan (Meath) was cancelled out by the issuing of marching orders to two of the future law enforcers.

1998/99

In the second round, Garda College narrowly got the better of Jordanstown at Athy. In the quarter-final, the Garda College ghosted past St Mary's by three points and into the semi-final.

Queen's University, Belfast's semi-final against Garda started like a dream. In good weather and before a partisan home crowd the Belfast students went eight points ahead, 1-8 to 0-3 but inexplicably it turned into the stuff of nightmares for them when standing on the edge of the square, Declan Lynch (Kerry) was allowed to fist a high ball unchallenged to the net. Then a defensive mix-up allowed a 45-metre kick from Cathal Sheridan to sail straight under the crossbar. In a surreal atmosphere of stunned silence, Garda piled on further points to emerge with a true "smash and grab" victory by 2-9 to 1-10. Centre back Cathal Daly (Offaly), Don Connellan (Roscommon) at midfield and Aaron Hoey (Louth) led the raid. Garda had achieved the unique feat of beating all three Belfast teams on the way to the final.

In the final against IIT on 7 March 1999 at Malone DUB, Queen's University, Belfast, the Garda College side – fielding players from fourteen counties, and either through fatigue or being the lesser team on the day – could not light the comeback spark which they did the previous day and lost 1-8 to 0-7.

The Garda team was: John McCallion (Mayo), Anton McNulty (Dublin), Michael O'Donoghue (Kerry), Robbie Doyle (Galway), Colin White (Sligo), Cathal Daly (Offaly), Michael Ryan (Roscommon), John

Whelan (Kildare), Don Connellan (Roscommon), Aaron Hoey (Louth), Colin Crowley (Cork), David Earley (Kildare), Declan Lynch (Kerry), Tom Bowe (Laois), Cathal Sheridan (Meath). Subs: Mark Moynihan (Kerry) for Hoey, Rory McGrath (Kerry) for Bowe and Sean McDaid (Donegal) for Earley.

Sigerson Cup Panel 1998/99

Back row, from left:
Michael Ryan (Roscommon), Colin White (Sligo), Robert Doyle (Galway), John Whelan (Kildare), Declan Lynch (Kerry), John McCallion (Mayo), Anto McNulty (Dublin), Cathal Daly (Offaly), Michael O'Donoghue (Kerry).
Front row, from left:
Don Connellan (Roscommon), David Earley (Kildare), Aaron Hoey (Louth), Colin Crowley (Cork), Tom Bowe (Laois) Cathal Sheridan (Meath).

1999/2000
CIT beat the Garda College by six points in the first round in Ballincollig.

2000/2001
UL beat the Garda College by 1-8 to 1-7 in the first round.

2001/2002
UUJ beat the Garda College by 2-7 to 1-3 in the first round.

2002/2003
Did not participate.

2003/2004

In the first round, goals from Darren Rooney and John Madden advanced the Garda College against Trinity at Templemore, but in their next match they were felled by UCD, who won 0-9 to 0-3.

2004/2005

The Garda College, who had outflanked UUC and Maynooth, stood in UCC's way in a last eight clash at the Mardyke. Although aCork player, James Masters, led the Garda offensive, the home team dominated throughout and emerged winners on a scoreline of 0-14 to 0-7.

2005/2006

In the first round, the Garda College had seven points to spare over UCD in Templemore. The College almost derailed DCU at the same venue on quarter-final day, and although they held a slim lead in the second half, they were beaten by 1-6 to 0-8.

2006/2007

The Garda College were beaten in the first round by ITS, thanks to a goal from a player called Colm Boyle (Mayo), who went on to join the force.

Sigerson Cup Panel 2005/6

Back row, left to right:
Joe Hayes (Clare), Cormac Bane (Galway), Batt Moriarty (Kerry), Pat Kelly (Mayo), Mike O'Shea (Clare), Padraig Mullarkey (Kildare), David Hickey (Waterford), James Lambe (Kildare).
Front row, from left:
Vincent Hurley (Cork), Marvin Lee (Galway), Arthur O'Connor (Longford), David Marshall (Dublin), Brian Coen (Tipperary), Tommy Brosnan (Kerry), James Masters (Cork). In total, there were twelve inter-county players on the 2005/06 Garda College team.

The 2008 Garda Sigerson Cup team.

Back Row left to right
Brian Kelly (Carlow), Mick Riordan (Tipperary), Niall Cahalane (Tipperary),
Keith King (Clare), Mark Twomey (Dublin), Denis Glennon (Westmeath),
Ambrose O'Donovan (Kerry), Kieran McGrath (Galway), Darren Mullaly (Galway),
John O'Brien (Dublin), Eamon O'Callaghan (Kildare), Rory Guinan (Offaly),
Brian McCormack (Galway), Denis Carrigan (Dublin)
Front Row Left to Right:
Shane McGrath (Clare), Paudi O'Connnor (Mayo), Seanie Buckley (Limerick),
Mark Harrington (Cork), Anthony Pender (Galway), Aidan O'Mahony (Kerry),
Graham Dillon (Dublin), Andrew Dermody (Kildare), Joe Malone (Mayo), Not Identified

2007/2008

This year saw problems with the eligibility of several Garda College players. In the first round against IT Carlow in Carlow, a fiftieth minute goal from Denis Glennon (Westmeath) did the trick for the Garda College, who won by 1-11 to 0-12. The Carlow club lodged an objection which was upheld by the CA executive, and the Garda College was thrown out of the competition. However, upon appeal, the CAC overturned the decision. The Garda College went on to beat CIT by two points in the quarter-final in Bishopstown. CIT then lodged a fresh objection, which in turn convinced IT Carlow to lodge a claim for arbitration to the GAA's Disputes Resolution Authority (DRA). The DRA delivered its verdict in favour of the Garda College. The semi-final took place in Athlone on 15 April, when a whopping 1-6 from John O'Brien (Dublin) did the trick for Garda after extra time.

In the final on 22 April at Carlow IT, UUJ galloped into a three-point lead in a high-tempo match and then scored a goal. But a John O'Brien goal direct from a thirteen-metre free kick, a rash of points from Rory Guinan (Offaly) and an equaliser from substitute James Martin (Longford) propelled the game into injury time. In a fractious supplementary instalment, one Garda and two UUJ players were sent off. In the end, UUJ emerged victorious by 1-16 to 1-14.

The Garda team was: Páidí O'Connor (Mayo), Cormac McGill (Meath), Ciaran McGrath (Galway), Anthony Pender (Galway), Graham Dillon (Westmeath), Darren Mullahy (Galway), Eamonn Callaghan (Kildare), Aidan O'Mahony (Kerry), Ambrose O'Donovan (Kerry), Seanie Buckley (Limerick), Rory Guinan (Offaly), Denis Glennon (Westmeath), John O'Brien (Dublin), Mark Harrington (Cork), J. Keane (Mayo). Subs: Barry Brennan (Laois) for Keane and James Martin (Longford) for O'Donovan.

2008/2009

The Garda College were beaten in the quarter-finals by UCD on a scoreline of 0-15 to 0-12.

Garda College, Sigerson League winners 2009.

Back row, from left:
James Kavanagh (Kildare), Enda Devenney (Mayo), Emlyn Mulligan (Leitrim), Mick Cussen (Cork), Darren Mullahy (Galway), Anthony Pender (Galway), Eamonn Callaghan (Kildare).
Front row, from left:
Sean Breheny (Dublin), Shane Mulligan (Longford), Mick Milner (Cork), Ronan O'Connor (Kerry), Mark Harrington (Cork), John Miskella (Cork), Ger Brady (Mayo).
Missing from photo: Nigel Shevlin (Louth) and Brendan McMahon (Clare).
Management.
Mick Riordan and Pat McCabe.
The team boasted twelve inter-county players.

2015/2016

Because of the recruitment ban, the Garda College did not compete again in the Sigerson Cup until January 2016, and although they defeated Cork IT by 1-13 to 0-8 in the first round, they were beaten by Ulster University, Jordanstown on a score of 2-14 to 0-11 in the second round.

Garda College, winners of the Sigerson Junior League, 2016

Panel:

Niall McGraynor, Damien Cronin, Paddy Brown, Colm O Cuiv, Connor Guckian,
Jeoff Scally, Matthew Galvin, Peter Sheerin, Shane Thornton, Alan Jones, Eamon McAndrew,
Niall Murphy, Kevin Larkin, Don McCarthy, Dara Melia, Tom McCarrick,
Niall Carolan (Capt), Emmett Lyney, Fintan Coffee, Teddy Doyle, Conor Langan.

Trench Cup

The Trench Cup is the second division Gaelic football championship trophy for third level education colleges, Institutes of Technology and Universities of Ireland and England. The Trench Cup championship is administered by Comhairle Ard Oideachais, the GAA Higher Education Council, which oversees the third level GAA championship.

In 1975, moves were made by non-university colleges to set up their own knockout Gaelic football championship tournament as a consequence of being shut out of the Sigerson Cup championship. The initiative came from St Joseph's Training College, Belfast. The concept of the Trench Cup was proposed by Pat Blake, Comhairle Ard Oideachais Chairman (1978-83) and Peter McGinnity (later a Fermanagh all star) as a knock out competition for all higher education institutions not in the Sigerson Cup tournament. Pat Blake purchased a trophy costing £80 (sterling) at Tommy Lennon's Jewellers, Smithfield Market, Belfast. The trophy was named the Trench Cup after Trench House, St Joseph's Training College, Belfast.

The competition first came into existence in the 1975/76 season. The inaugural final was played between St Joseph Training College, Belfast and National College of Physical Education, Limerick at Croke Park. NCPE became the inaugural champions. In the 1980s, the Sigerson Cup championship was opened up to allow an increasing number of universities, Regional Technical Colleges and institutes of higher education to participate on the basis of their league success. Subsequently, the Trench Cup became the second-tier competition for the third level institutions which were not in the Sigerson Cup championship.

The Garda College has won the Trench Cup on three occasions: 1993, 1994 and 2015.

21 March 1993, Thurles
Garda College 1-13, Dundalk RTC 1-5
Garda panel: Ian Breen (Cork), Mark McElkenney (Cork), Pat Hegarty (Cork), Derek Duggan (Roscommon), Pat Walsh (Galway), Phil O'Dea (Dublin), Fergal Dardis (Dublin), Brendan Rouine (Clare), Dean Kerins

Garda College, Trench Cup Winners, 1993.
Back row, from left:
Ian Breen (Cork), Mark McElkenney (Cork), Pat Hegarty (Cork),
Derek Duggan (Roscommon), Pat Walsh (Galway), Phil O'Dea (Dublin),
Fergal Dardis (Dublin), Brendan Rouine (Clare).
Front row, from left:
Dean Kerins (Meath), Karl Kearns (Sligo), John Cooper (Wexford),
David O'Connor (Roscommon), Martin Coyle (Mayo), Greg McGovern (Dublin/Fermanagh),
Don Davis (Cork).

(Meath), Karl Kearns (Sligo), John Cooper (Wexford), David O'Connor (Roscommon), Martin Coyle (Mayo), Greg McGovern (Dublin), Don Davis (Cork), Peter Oates (Dublin).

27 February 1994, VEC Grounds, Terenure
Garda College 1-10, Dublin Institute of Technology 1-7
Garda panel: Derek Duggan (Roscommon), Fergal O'Donnell (Roscommon), Pat Murphy (Cork), Pat Hegarty (Cork), Tom McGlinchey (Cork), Ken Duggan (Roscommon), Joe Hughes (Offaly), Seamus Murphy (Laois), Brendan Rouine (Clare), Mick Galvin (Sligo), Karl Kearns (Sligo), Sean Collum (Tipperary), Martin Coyle (Mayo, captain), John Cooper (Wexford), Peter Queally (Waterford).

Garda College, Trench Cup Winners 1994.
Back row, from left:
Derek Duggan (Roscommon), Fergal O'Donnell (Roscommon), Pat Murphy (Cork),
Pat Hegarty (Cork), Tom McGlinchey (Cork), Kenneth Duggan (Roscommon),
Joe Hughes (Offaly), Seamus Murphy (Laois), Brendan Rouine (Clare).
Front row, from left:
Mick Galvin (Sligo), Karl Kearns (Sligo), Sean Collum (Tipperary),
Martin Coyle (Mayo, captain), John Cooper (Wexford), Peter Queally (Waterford).

21 February 2015
Garda College 1-13, St Patrick's College, Drumcondra 0-10
Garda panel: Shane O'Gara (Donegal), Gary Farren (Donegal), Joe Kearney (Galway), Paul Smith (Cavan), Barry John Molloy, (Carlow), Fintan Coffey (Kerry), Ivor Whyte, (Clare), Peter McGee (Donegal), Colm Ó Cuív (Galway), Emmet Lynskey (Sligo), Conor Boyle (Laois), Seamus Corcoran (Donegal), Johnny Burke (Galway), Colin Compton, (Roscommon), Johnny Kerrigan (Galway), Niall Carolan (Meath), Matthew Galvin (Kerry), Geoff Scally (Offaly), Padraig Scott (Roscommon), Alan Jones (Longford), Damien Cronin (Cork), Sean Blanchfield (Dublin), Seamus Mac Gearailt (Kerry), Dara Melia (Galway), Thomas McCarrick (Dublin), Peter Sheeran (Kerry), Shane Thornton (Kerry), Kevin Larkin (Tipperary), Peter Naughton (Galway), Joe Bell (Dublin), Cillian Fitzmaurice (Kerry), Eoin O'Malley (Galway), Killian O'Gorman (Wexford), Lonan McKenna (Cavan), Patrick Browne (Wicklow).

Garda College, Trench Cup Winners, 2015.

Lynch Cup

The Garda College won the Lynch Cup (ladies' football) on one occasion, in 1999.

Lynch Shield

The Garda College won the Lynch Shield (ladies' football) on one occasion, 2006.

Fr Meachair Shield

Garda College won this camogie competition in 2000, by beating NUI Maynooth in the final. The Garda College hosted the competition and it was played in a seven-a-side format.

Garda College, Fr Meachair Shield winners in 2000

Purcell Cup

The Purcell Cup is Division 2 of the Third Level Colleges camogie competition. It is in existence since 1977. The cup was donated by Úna Uí Phuirséil, President of the Camogie Association, 1976-1978 and her husband, Pádraig Puirséil.

Purcell Cup panel 2004:
Suzanne Ford, Patricia O'Riordan, Ruth O'Sullivan, Triona Gallagher, Sandra Johnson, Therese Keoghan, Ann Roche, Niam O'Connor, Laura

Burns, Ethel D'ilínn, Julie May Keane, Geraldine McCarthy, Brid Troy, Cora Dowling, Aine O'Connell, Jacinta Gordon, Liz Bulger, Aoife Walsh, Valerie O'Keefe, Jenny Martin, Denise Fitzgerald, Ann Cahill, Aoife Cullen, Ciara Moran. Mentors: Sandra Gillick, Ailish Myles.

The Garda College has won the competition on one occasion, in 2005. The managers were Ailish Myles and Sandra Gillick, with coach Ken Hogan.

2005 results:

Round one: Garda College 4-11, Carlow IT 1-3
Round two: Garda College 0-17, Dublin City University 1-3
Quarter-final: Garda College beat Athlone IT
Semi-final: Garda College 6-10, Tralee IT 3-5
Final: Garda College beat Queen's University, Belfast

Five Garda College players were named on the 2005 Purcell Cup All Star team: Aoife Cullen, Liz Glennon (Roscommon), Sheena Howard (Tipperary), Niamh O'Connor (Wexford) and Louise Young (Tipperary). Paula Kenny was named on the Purcell All Star team of 2010

Garda College, Purcell Cup winners 2005

Purcell Cup 2007 Garda College panel

Valerie O'Keeffe, Elizabeth Glennon, Marie O'Connor, Michelle Shortt, Jane Ryan, Louise Young, Edel Fitzgerald, Emer Phelan, Faith Noonan, Fiona O'Connell, Michelle Casey, Liz Power, Mary Dorgan, Josie Dwyer, Lisa Prendergast, Vanessa O'Donnell, Georgina Kelly, Aoife Hayes, Fiona O'Keeffe, Collette Farragher, Emer Griffin.

Ashbourne Cup

Garda College, Ashbourne Cup finalists 2006.

The Garda College reached the final of the Ashbourne Cup in 2006. The results were as follows:

Semi-final: Garda College 3-10, Mary Immaculate College, Limerick 1-6
Scorers; Marie O'Connor (2-4), Louise Young (0-6), Aoife Cullen (1-0).
Final: CIT 0-9, Garda College 0-8
Scorers: Marie O'Connor (0-5), Louise Young (0-3).

Garda College panel:
Therese Keoghan, Emer Phelan, Fiona Connell, Triona Gallagher, Jane Ryan, Niamh O'Connor, Michelle Shortt, Liz Glennon, Sheena Howard, Noelle Bergin, Aoife Cullen (captain), Louise Young, Julie May Keane, Marie O'Connor, Jacinta Gordon, Aoife Walsh, Liz Bugler, Denise Fitzgerald, Edel Fitzgerald, Ann Roche, Grace O'Sullivan, Geraldine O'Connor, Paula Malcolmson, Catherine McCarthy, Gemma Browne, Helen Tierney, Stephanie Power, Ethel O'Flynn.

Ashbourne Shield

The Garda College won the Ashbourne Shield in February 2007. Managers: Ailish Myles and Sandra Gillick. Coach: Seamus Delaney. The results were as follows:

Semi-final: Garda College 2-6, NUI Galway 1-5
Final: Garda College 3-9, Ulster University, Jordanstown 0-6
Among the panel of players were Sheena Howard (captain, Tipperary),

Marie O'Connor (Kilkenny, who scored 3-3 in the final), Josie Dwyer (Wexford), Liz Power (Tipperary), Louise Young (Tipperary), Michelle Shortt (Tipperary), Liz Glennon (Roscommon), Michelle Casey (Limerick), Emer Phelan, Mary Dorgan, Jane Ryan, Vanessa O'Donnell and Georgina Kelly. Michelle Shortt was named on the All Star Ashbourne Shield team in 2007.

Garda College, Ashbourne Shield winners 2007.
Back row, from left:
Seamus Delaney (coach), Ciara Moran, Mary Dorgan, Vanessa O'Donnell, Emer Phelan,
Liz Power, Niamh Keogh, Edel Fitzgerald, Michelle Casey, Fiona Connell, Collette Farragher,
Georgina Kelly, Jane Ryan, Louise Young, Ailish Myles (manager), Valerie O'Keeffe.
Front row, from left:
Sandra Gillick (manager), Josie Dwyer, Emer Griffin, Stephanie Power, Marie O'Connor,
Lizzie Glennon, Michelle Stones, Sheena Howard (captain), Lisa Prendergast, Aoife Hayes,
Niamh Keogh, Carina Daly.

Garda College, Ashbourne Shield winners 2007.

The inaugural camogie match between An Garda Síochána and the Police Service of Northern Ireland

17 November 2012 will go down in the history books as a momentous occasion, when the first representative camogie match between An Garda Síochána and the Police Service of Northern Ireland (PSNI) took place.

Superintendent Gerald Murray extended an invitation to the Gardaí via the Assistant Commissioner, Fintan Fanning, to a camogie match against the PSNI. Sergeant Marie Daly from the Garda College, Templemore was the liaison person co-ordinating the event.

The match was hosted by the PSNI in the Police Club, Newforge Lane, Belfast. An Garda Síochána camogie team was captained by Garda Elizabeth Power, with Garda Maureen Finnerty as vice-captain. They were managed by Ms Sandra Gillick from the Garda College, Templemore. The team was met by Superintendent Murray (PSNI), who extended a warm welcome and reception before the match.

Deputy Chief Constable Judith Gillespie OBE also welcomed the team and addressed both sides on the significance of the occasion. This was followed by a minute's silence in memory of Garda Jane Heaney (RIP) and Northern Ireland prison office David Black (RIP).

The match commenced at 2pm and after one minute, Garda Liz Power had put herself into the history books having got the first score between these two police forces, with a fine goal into the top corner of the net – the start of a personal tally of 4-2.

Goals followed from Gdas Aoife Walsh, Maureen Finnerty and Rosie Kenneally, and points from Gda Noelle O'Riordan (2) and Sgt Michelle Gillick. The final score was 7-5 to 1-0 in favour of Garda College.

The teams came together for refreshments after the game. You could sense from the occasion that this was the start of something new, and that Gaelic games was once again becoming the catalyst for the development of strong relationships between the two forces.

An Garda Síochána panel: Ms Sandra Gillick (manager), Caroline Griffin, Rosie Kenneally, Vanessa O'Donnell, Lisa Power, Aoife Walsh, Michelle Gillick, Noelle O'Riordan, Sinead Daffy, Liz Power, Faith Noonan, Sharon Kehoe, Rachel Rogers-Kiernan, Maureen Finnerty.

Police Service of Northern Ireland panel: Jayne Perry, Christine Drain, Rayenne Denvir, Seaneen Hughes, Briege McFadden, Joanne McGuigan, Marie McArdle, Danielle McVarnock and Deirdre Mahony.

13 February 2008, Ashbourne Cup Qualifier,
Garda College teammates celebrate at the final whistle

Ryan Cup

The Ryan Cup is the Division 2 hurling championship for third level colleges. The Ryan Cup is administered by Comhairle Ard Oideachais Cumann Lúthchleas Gael (CLG), the GAA's Higher Educational Council. In the late 1980s or early 1990s, the Ryan Cup, the trophy for the Divisional Gaelic Football League, was presented to the winners of what was then the Division 2 Championship (non-university). The Higher Education First Division Football League Trophy is also known as the Ryan Cup. The Garda College captained by John Cooper (Wexford) and managed by Ken Hogan (Tipperary) won the Ryan Cup in 1995.

Result
25 March 1995, Limerick Gaelic Grounds: Garda College 2-15, Galway Regional Technical College 2-7.

Garda College, Ryan Cup Hurling Winners 1995.
Back row, from left:
Hud Kelly (Waterford), Tom McGlinchey (Cork), Paddy Lenihan (Dublin),
Alan Waters (Dublin), Peter Queally (Waterford), James Aherne (Cork),
Mark Dowling (Kilkenny), Mick Cuffe (Dublin), Gerry Kennedy (Tipperary),
Padraig Tobin (Limerick), Austin Cleere (Kilkenny), Niall McKeigue (Galway),
Eoin Ó Gríofa (Cork), Niall Bambrick (Carlow), Sean O'Regan (Cork).
Front row, from left:
John Scanlan (Limerick) (Mentor), David Bourke (Limerick), Anthony Teefey (Limerick),
Pat O'Connell (Kerry), John Finnegan (Dublin), Seamus McIntyre (Kerry),
John Cooper (Wexford), Mick Brophy (Kilkenny), Seamus Delaney (Tipperary),
Sean Collum (Tipperary), Ciaran Whelan (Tipperary), Ken Hogan (Tipperary, manager).

Garda College won Ryan Cup Football on one occasion
2 December 2008, Kildorrery, Cork: Garda College 0-12, Cork IT 1-6
Garda College panel: D O'Brien (Clare), S Breheny (Dublin), R O'Connor (Kerry), D Mullahy (Galway), S Mulligan (Longford), E Callaghan (Kildare), A Pender (Galway), M Cussen (Cork), M Milner (Cork), E Devenney (Mayo), J Kavanagh (Kildare), J Miskella (Cork), M Harrington (Cork), G Brady (Mayo), E Mulligan (Leitrim). Subs: J Martin (Longford) for Kavanagh, N Shevlin (Louth) for E Mulligan. Scorers: M Harrington 0-4 (1f), E Callaghan 0-3, J Kavanagh, J Miskella and D. J. Martin (0-1 each).

Garda College, Ryan Cup Hurling Winners 2017.

The Garda College won the Ryan Cup hurling competition on a second occasion in 2017. Results were as follows:
Thurles, 24 January 2017: Garda College 6-23, Athlone Institute of Technology 0-7
Belfast, 7 February 2017: Garda College 3-15 Queen's University of Belfast 1-17
Semi-final, 24 February 2017: Garda College 5-18, Cork Education and Training Board 1-9
Final, 25 February 2017: Garda College 5-24, Institute of Technology, Sligo 1-9.
Ryan Cup football
The Garda College, including twelve inter-county players, won the Ryan Cup football trophy on one occasion.

Chapter 8

Garda Vs Defence Forces and Combined Universities Matches

Combined Universities

Combined Universities GAA was a Gaelic football and hurling team which consisted of players from the major universities of Ireland. The players were taken from St Patrick's College Maynooth, Queen's University Belfast, Trinity College Dublin, University College Cork, University College Dublin, University of Ulster at Jordanstown and University College Galway.

In the 1980s, Combined Advanced Colleges GAA (Combined Colleges) joined in to make the annual contests between Combined Universities, Army (Defence Forces), and Garda a quadrangular tournament. The Gardaí have won the competition on three occasions in Gaelic football, and twice in hurling.

Gaelic football

In the beginning, the Garda vs Army Cup in Gaelic football was known as the Minister for Defence Cup, then the Fitzgerald Kenny Cup. Finally, it became the John Morley Memorial Cup. As has once been written in the Irish Independent: "These games rank as second in importance to the All-Ireland finals and often the displays even equal the latter."

Croke Park, 25 June 1927: Garda 2-4, Army 0-3
Garda panel: O'Reilly, Creagh, Sherlock, Toole, Russell, Mullens, John Kirwan, Forde, Colleran, Kilroy, Smith, Larry Stanley, Carthy, Jim Kirwan, Scanlon.

Croke Park, 1 July 1928: Garda 2-1, Army 1-1

Clondalkin, 25 February 1929: Garda 1-7, Army 1-4
Team included Russell, Teeling, McCann, Kirwan and Kelly.

24 March 1963: Army 1-10, Garda 1-6
Garda panel: S McGuinness (Mayo), P Harrington (Cork), H McDonnell (Laois), P. J. Kennedy (Clare), J Hughes (Laois), M Carolan (Kildare), S Keevans (Wexford), T Browne (Laois), S Ferriter (Donegal), G Reilly (Roscommon), F Kennedy (Clare), J. J. Reilly (Cavan), T Mongey (Meath), F Gilton (Dublin), P Roberts (Carlow). Sub: G Starkin for Harrington. Scorers: T Browne (1-0), G Reilly (0-2), P Roberts (0-2), J. J. Reilly and F Gilton (0-1 each).

Croke Park, 25 June 1964: Garda 0-11, Army 0-8
Garda panel: J McGuinness (Mayo), F Kennedy (Clare), M McDonnell (Laois), T Morris (Cavan), T Sands (Galway), S Keevans (Wexford), J Hughes (Louth), M Carolan (Kildare), C Cawley (Sligo), T Browne

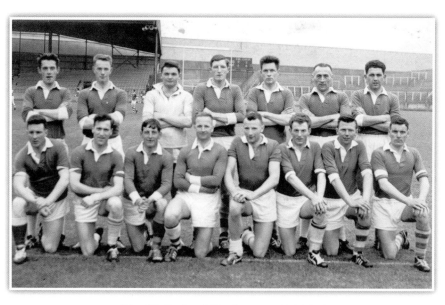

The All-Ireland Garda team 1964/65,
which beat the Army 0-11 to 0-8 in Croke Park.

Back row, from left:
Donie Mulligan (Dublin), John Morley (Mayo), John McGuinness (Mayo),
Cathal Cawley (Sligo), J. J. O'Reilly (Cavan), Frank Kennedy (Clare), Paddy Dolan (Mayo).
Front row, from left:
Mick McDonnell (Laois), Jim Hughes (Laois), Tom Browne (Meath),
Seamus Keevans (Wexford), Mick Carolan (Kildare), Tom Sands (Galway),
Tony Morris (Cavan), George Rankin (Laois).

(Meath), J. J. Reilly (Cavan), J Morley (Mayo), D Mulligan (Dublin), P Dolan (Mayo), G Rankin (Laois). Subs: S Gibbons for Reilly, P Roberts for Cawley.

Scorers: J Morley (0-6), T Browne (0-2), P Dolan (0-1), D Mulligan (0-1), M Carolan (0-1)

Croke Park, 19 June 1966; Army 0-13, Garda 1-7

Garda panel: P Casey (Cork), B O'Connor (Roscommon), F Kennedy (Clare), B Gilmore (Longford), P Roberts (Carlow), T Harrington (Cork), J Hughes (Laois), M Murphy (Westmeath), A Feeley (Roscommon), M O'Loughlin (Cork), P Hanlon (Dublin), O Shanley (Meath), P King (Carlow), T Mee (Clare). Subs: J Moran (Westmeath) for Hanlon, P Griffin (Kerry) for Harrington, K Donnelly (Kerry) for Mee.

Scorers: J Moran (0-3), P King (0-1).

Brothers Pat King played for Garda and Sean for the Army.

O'Toole Park, Kimmage, 31 May 1967: Garda 3-13, Army 2-7

Garda panel: J McGuinness, A Morris (Leinster), M McDonnell (Munster), B Gilmore (Leinster), J Cassidy (Connaught/Ulster), C Cawley (Connaught/Ulster), M Murphy (Leinster), M Carolan (DMA), S Ferriter (Connaught/Ulster), M O'Loughlin (Munster), P Hallinan (DMA), T Browne (Leinster), T Mee (Munster), J. J. O'Reilly (DMA, captain), O Shanley (Leinster), J Hughes (Munster), C Grogan (Leinster), T Sheehan (Munster), D Thomas (Connaught/Ulster), F Reynolds (Connaught/Ulster), P Lambe (Leinster), F McArdle (DMA), S Keevans (Munster), P Griffin (Munster).

Scorers: J. J. O'Reilly (2-1), O Shanley (1-2), C Cawley (0-4), P Griffin (0-2), M O'Loughlin, P Hallinan, T Browne and S Ferriter (0-1 each).

Croke Park, 30 May 1968: Garda 3-9, Army 1-9

Garda panel: C Grogan (Leinster), J Carey (Connaught/Ulster), O'Moynihan (Munster), N Colleran (DMA), P Lambe (Leinster), J Morley (Connaught/Ulster), M Murphy (Leinster), C Cawley (Connaught/Ulster), T Brennan (Munster), DJ Crowley (Munster), K Brennan (DMA), G Clifford (Leinster), O Shanley (Leinster).

Scorers: J Morley (1-5), DJ Crowley (1-3), O Shanley (1-0), C Cawley (0-1).

Croke Park, 30 May 1969: Army 3-8, Garda 1-9

Scorers: D. J. Crowley (0-5), M O'Loughlin (1-0), W Molloy (0-2), W Murphy and P Roberts (0-1 each).

Army Grounds, Phoenix Park, 28 May 1971: Garda 2-14, Army 2-6
Garda panel: E O'Hara (Leitrim), J N Galvin (Westmeath), P Somers (Kerry), J Reynolds (Leinster), M Behan (Dublin), N Colleran (Galway), K Brennan (Laois), B Murphy (Sligo), S O'Grady (Mayo), W Molloy (Offaly), F Murphy (Cork), C Dolan (Mayo), D Fenton (Cork), W McGee (Mayo). Sub: M Noonan for Fenton.
Scorers: W Molloy (1-3), E Kirby (1-1), F Murphy (0-3), C Dolan (0-2), M Noonan (0-2), J N Galvin (0-1).

The Mardyke, Cork, 19 April 1976: Combined Universities 0-10, Combined Services 0-7
Panel: M Carolan, J. J. Martin, S Cloonan, M McGrath, K Brennan, B Murphy, J Kearns, S Bonner, J Courtney, E Sheelin, S Coughlan, T Holland, G Aherne, V O'Donnell, D Aherne. Subs: B Murphy for Cloonan, T Doyle for Coughlan, N Farragher for G Aherne.
Scorers: S Bonner (0-3), E Sheelin, J Courtney and V O'Donnell (0-1 each).

Croke Park, 6 March 1977: Advanced Colleges 2-10, Combined Services 1-11
Panel: M Carolan, G Barnes, S Cloonan, B Murphy, P O'Shea, B Murphy, M O'Connor, C Moore, D Earley, J Courtney, E Murphy, E Kirby, J Kearns, S Coghlan, D Aherne. Subs: S McBridge for E Murphy
Scorers: J Courtney (0-4), S McBride (1-0), D Early and E Kirby (0-2 each), C Moore, D Aherne and E Murphy (0-1 each).

Páirc Chiarán, Athlone, 26 February 1978: Advanced Colleges 2-14, Combined Services 2-9
Panel: M Carolan (Galway), J. J. Martin (Cavan), P Fingleton (Laois), D Brennan (Laois), P O'Shea (Kerry), C Moore (Kildare), P Begley (Clare), D Earley (Roscommon), S Bonner (Donegal), P Mulhern (Kildare), S Coughlan (Cork), B Dooley (Wicklow), M McGrath (Longford), J Keane (Westmeath), J McCarthy (Dublin).
Scorers: J Keane (1-2), M McGrath (1-0), S Coughlan (0-3), S Bonner (0-2), D Earley (0-2).

Croke Park, 4 March 1979: Garda 3-10, Advanced Colleges 1-11
Garda panel: E McHale (Mayo), D Hobbs (Dublin), S Mulvanney (Cavan), J Evans (Kerry), P O'Shea (Kerry), C Browne (Laois), J Marshall (Wexford), G O'Driscoll (Kerry), P Lee (Galway), P O'Mahony (Kerry), S Bonner (Donegal), T Prendergast (Laois), J Egan (Kerry), E Sheelin (Louth), J McCarthy (Dublin). Subs: W McGee for E Sheelin.

Scorers: S Bonner (2-1), T Prendergast (1-0), G O'Driscoll (0-3), P O'Mahony (0-2), P Lee (0-2), J Egan (0-1), E Sheelin (0-1).

Devlin Park, 29 April 1979: Combined Universities 2-11, Garda 1-11
Garda panel: P Forristal, J Mulvaney, S Kinneavy, D Brennan, P O'Shea, C Browne, J Marshall, D Brogan, V O'Connor, W O'Connor, E Sheelin, T Prendergast, J Evans, W McGee, J McCarthy. Subs: P O'Mahony for Brogan, P Begley for Evans.
Scorers: E Sheelin (0-8) W McGee (1-1), W O'Connor (0-1) J Evans (0-1).

Croke Park, 16 April 1980: Garda 0-11, Combined Universities 1-7
Garda panel: P Forristal, J Martin, B Murphy, D Brennan, W O'Connor, C Browne, J Keane, G O'Driscoll, P Lee, T Prendergast, M O'Connor, V O'Donnell, J Kearns, W McGee, S Bonner. Sub: G Ryan for G O'Driscoll.
Scorers: M O'Connor (0-5), S Bonner (0-2), W McGee (0-2), P Lee and T Prendergast (0-1 each).

The All-Ireland Garda team
Back Row Left to Right
Mick O'Connor (Manager), Mick Prendergast, Mattie Coleman, Matt Connor, Seamus Bonner, Tom O'Connell, Paidi Forresstal, Des McGrath, Ben Tansey, Seamus Burke, Mick Enright (Selectcor)
Front Row Left to Right
Eamon Barry, ? O'Mahony, Liam Shanahan, John Keane, John Clarke, James Kearns, Des Brennan, Jimmy McManus, Peter Lee, Mick Lillis

Croke Park, 30 April 1980: Garda 5-8, Army 0-22

Garda panel: P Forristal, J Kane, B Murphy, D Brennan, M Coleman, C Browne, J Marshall, P Lee, S Bonner, T Prendergast, M O'Connor, W O'Connor, P O'Mahony, M Connor, J O'Connell. Subs: J Egan for O'Connell, G O'Driscoll for W O'Connor.

Scorers: P O'Mahony (2-2), M Connor (1-4), T Prendergast (1-0), M O'Connor (og), J Egan and S Bonner (0-1 each).

Croke Park, semi-final, 1982: Garda 2-13 Combined Universities 2-9

Garda panel: P Forristal, J Keane, J Clarke, D Brennan, T McManus, C Browne, J Marshall, P Lee, D McGrath, L Shanahan, S Bonner, J Kearns, M Gallagher, M Connor, E McHale. Subs: E Barry for Gallagher, B Tansey for Barry.

Scorers: M Connor (1-6), B Tansey (1-1), P Lee (0-2), E McHale (0-2), C Browne (0-1), J Kearns (0-1).

Croke Park, final, 28 April 1982: Army 3-8, Garda 0-5

Garda panel: P Forristal, J Keane, J Clarke, D Brennan, J McManus, B Tansey, M Coleman, P Lee, D McGrath, T O'Connell, M Connor, L Shanahan, J Kearns, S Bonner, P O'Mahony. Subs: M Prendergast for O'Connell, E Barry for Shanahan, S Burke for E Barry.

Scorers: M Connor (0-2), S Bonner, P O'Mahony anD. J. Kearns (0-1 each).

Croke Park, 6 April 1983: Advanced Colleges 2-8, Garda 2-6

Garda panel: P Forristal, D Brennan, B Murphy, M Coleman, J Marshall, C Browne, J Keane, P Lee, S Bonner, E McGrath, W Hughes, J Kearns, E McHale, M Connor, D McGrath. Sub: M Lowry for McGrath.

Scorers: E McHale (1-2), J Kearns (1-0), P Lee (0-2), M Connor (0-1), D McGrath (0-1).

Croke Park, 4 April 1984: Combined Universities 1-10, Garda 1-7

Garda panel: V Murphy (Wexford), B Murphy (Cork), S Kinneavy (Galway), D Brennan (Laois), J McManus (Roscommon), C Browne (Laois), M Coleman (Galway), P Lee (Galway), D Deasy (Dublin), E O'Mahony (Cork), E McManus (Roscommon), P Spollen (Offaly), M Connor (Offaly), S Bonner (Donegal). Subs: E Barry for Spollen, F McGrath (Dublin) for Murphy.

Scorers: M Connor (0-4), E O'Mahony (1-0), J Egan (0-2), F McGrath (0-1).

Santry, 17 April 1985: Advanced Colleges 1-17, Garda 0-9
Scorers: T O'Beirne (0-4), A O'Sullivan (0-2), T Prendergast (0-2), K O'Rourke (0-1).

1986
Both the Garda hurling and football teams pulled out of the representative matches because of their "inability to field teams".

1987
Croke Park, 1 April 1987: Combined Universities 4-12, Garda 1-17
Scorers: W Hughes (0-4), K O'Rourke (1-2), E McManus (0-3), D Deasy (0-4), D Byrne (0-2), J Sheedy (0-2).
Semi-final: Garda 2-8, Combined Sigerson 0-7
Scorers: B Murray (2-1), J McGrath (0-3), R Culhane (0-3), L Conlon (0-1).
Final, St Vincents, 15 April 1989: Garda 1-15, Combined Colleges 1-11
Scorers: J Sheedy (1-2), B Redmond (0-4), R Culhane (0-2), J McGrath (0-3), B Murray (0-2), J Newton (0-1), T Flanagan (0-1).

1991
Semi-final, Santry, 27 March 1991: Garda 2-9, Combined Colleges 0-7
Scorers: J Mullen, B Murray (1-0) each, E McManus, J Sheedy (0-3 each), G Mahon (0-1).
Final, Parnell Park, 3 April 1991: Garda 2-11, Combined Sigerson 1-9
Scorers: B Murray (1-2), P Costello (1-1), L Conlon (0-4), J Sheedy (0-2), E McManus, D Deasy (0-1 each).

Belfield, 25 March 1992: Combined Universities 1-15, Garda 1-12
Garda panel: D Smyth, E Leonard, P Moran, P McConnon, C Murphy, D Deasy, T Davis, J Newton, K Kelliher, D Davis, J Sheedy, D Byrne, L Conlon, B Murphy, E McManus Jnr. Sub: D O'Connor for Kelliher.
Scorers: E McManus (0-4), C Murphy (1-0), J Sheedy (0-3), L Conlon, D Davis (0-2 each), B Murray, J Newton, D Byrne and D O'Connor (0-1 each).

Belfield, 1 April 1992: Defence Forces 1-13 Garda 1-10 (aet)
Garda panel: N O'Donnell, E Leonard, P Moran, P McConnon, C Murphy, D Deasy, D O'Connor, J Newton, K Walsh, D Davis, B Murray, G McGovern, L Conlon, J Mullen, E McManus. Subs: P Costello for McManus, P Ivess for Deasy, P Donoghue for Conlon, W Hughes for McGovern.
Scorers: B Murray (0-8), K Walsh, C Murphy (0-1 each).

Belfield, 20 April 1994: Combined Sigerson 2-14, Garda 2-5
Garda panel: C Grogan, F Dardis, P Moran, M McElhinney, C Murphy, T McLoughlin, P McConnon, J Newton, B Murray, J. P. McManus, G Ware, E Sweeney, M Doran, S Murphy, L Conlon. Subs: D Kearns for Moran, P O'Dea for Dardis.
Scorers: M Doran (1-1), E Sweeney (1-0), J. P. McManus (0-2), P McConnon (0-1), C Murphy (0-1).

Westmanstown, 27 April 1995: Combined Sigerson 1-18, Garda 0-8
Garda panel: C Grogan, G Sheridan, P Moran, F Dardis, S Boyle, B Rouine, P McConnon, J Sheedy, J Newton, B O'Donovan, J Mullen, G McGovern, L Conlon, M Doran, A McGauran. Subs: R Culhane for Newton, E Sweeney for McConnon, P Caffery for Sheridan.
Scorers: A McGauran (0-2), B O'Connor, M Doran, G McGovern, S Boyle, R Culhane, J Mullen (0-1 each).

Westmanstown, 3 April 1996: Combined Colleges 1-15, Garda 2-10
The Garda line-up included Brian Murray, Derek Duggan, Eamonn McManus, Connie Murphy and Jack Sheedy.

After a gap of many years, Brian Willoughby and Mick Morrissey resurrected the Garda versus Army matches.

Cusack Park, Mullingar, 14 October 2014: Garda 2-15, Defence Forces 0-9.
Back row, from left:
Brian Monaghan (Offaly, selector), Padraic Jones (Longford, selector),
Martin McGowan (Leitrim, selector), Anthony Pender (Galway), David Hickey (Waterford),
David Clarke (Mayo), Rob Molloy (Galway), James Masters (Cork), Páidí O'Connor (Mayo),
Darren Mullahy (Galway), Kevin Mulryan (Tipperary), Timmy Stokes (Wicklow),
Dave Scahill (Roscommon), Brian Willoughby (Waterford, manager).
Front row, from left:
Aidan O'Mahony (Kerry), Eamonn Callaghan (Kildare), Paul Deeley (Offaly),
Mike O'Shea (Clare), Colm Boyle (Mayo), Andy Dermody (Kildare), Sean Buckley (Limerick),
Emlyn Mulligan (Leitrim), Shane Mulligan (Longford).

Army Grounds, Phoenix Park: Garda 3-14, Defence Forces 0-11.
Garda panel:

Niall Cahalane (Tipperary), Dave Scahill (Roscommon), Fintan Coffey (Kerry), Peter McGee (Donegal), Denis Glennon (Westmeath), Denis Carrigan (Dublin), Darren Mullahy (Galway), Michael Cussen (Cork), Paul Deeley (Offaly), Shane Mulligan (Longford), Páidí O'Connor (Mayo), Hugh Coghlan (Tipperary), Paul Smith (Cavan), Ciaran McGrath (Galway), Andrew Tormey (Meath), Johnny Burke (Galway), Shane O'Malley (Roscommon), Colin Compton (Roscommon), Seanie Buckley (Limerick), Conor Boyle (Laois), Eamonn McKenna (Mayo). Manager: Brian Willoughby (Waterford). Selector: Brian Monaghan (Offaly).

The All-Ireland Garda football team (2017), who defeated the All-Ireland Defence Forces team 6-15 to 2-14 in Templemore on 8 November 2017.
Back row, from left:
Brian Willoughby (Waterford, manager), Páidí O'Connor (Mayo), Páidí O'Leary (Cork),
David Clarke (Mayo), Mick Cussen (Cork), Denis Glennon (Westmeath),
David Shannon (Cork), Tom Featherstone (Roscommon), Caoileann Fitzmaurice (Roscommon),
Graham Pettit (Roscommon), Darren Gallagher (Longford), Martin McGowan (Leitrim),
Joe Hayes (Clare), Enda Coughlan (Clare).
Front row, from left:
Killian Brady (Cavan), Eamonn Callaghan (Kildare), Barry John Molloy (Carlow),
Killian Daly (Westmeath), Tommy McDaniel (Westmeath), Colin Compton (Roscommon),
Gary Farren (Donegal), Niall Murphy (Meath), Ciaran Kendrick (Tipperary).

Hurling

The Garda College won the President's Cup in 1923 and 1924.

Croke Park, 18 July 1926: Garda 3-4, Army 3-4
D McHugh, P McInerney, J Gleeson, Phelan, Meagher, Tobin, Finn, Gill, J McGann, O'Rourke, Howard, Quinlan, Conroy, Fahy, Power.
Replay, Croke Park: Garda 4-2 Army 2-5
M Gill (captain), J Burke, J McGann, P McInerney, W Phelan, W Meagher, E Tobin, M Finn, J Gleeson, P Browne, G Howard, T Burnell, T O'Rourke, E Fahy, J Smith.

The Garda team featured eight players who had helped Dublin beat Cork in the All-Ireland final.

Croke Park, 1 July 1928: Garda 8-3, Army 3-3
The hurling team fielded five Clare, six Dublin, one Laois and one Cork inter-county players.

Dundalk, 12 September 1932: Army 3-5, Garda 4-1
Scorers: Brown, Phelan, Burnell and O'Neill (1-0) each, Gill (0-1).

The 1964 Garda panel which lined out against the Army.
Back row, from left:
Mick Regan (Cork), John Kennedy (Cork), Ned Coogan (Kilkenny), Peter McGovern (Carlow),
Brian Cooney (Dublin), Sean Nealon (Tipperary), Jim Prendergast (Kilkenny).
Front row, from left:
Willie Walsh (Carlow), Mick Hayes (Limerick), Seamus Quaid (Limerick),
Eamonn Carey (Limerick), Jimmy Conroy (Galway), Mick Regan (Galway),
Nicky Power (Kilkenny), Phil Verdon (Tipperary).

Croke Park, 25 June 1964: Garda 4-11, Army 2-7

Garda panel: P Verdon (Tipperary), S Nealon (Tipperary), J Prendergast (Kilkenny), E Coogan (Kilkenny), W Walsh (Carlow), J Kennedy (Wexford), J Conroy (Galway), B Cooney (Dublin), N Power (Kilkenny), E Carey (Limerick), P McGovern (Carlow), S Quaid (Limerick), M Regan (Galway), M Regan (Cork), M Hayes (Limerick). Subs: B Kenny for Coogan, Coogan for Conroy, J Lane for Hayes.
Scorers: M Regan (Galway) (2-1), M Regan (Cork) (0-3), M Hayes (1-1), P McGovern (0-3), S Conway (1-0), S Quaid (0-2), N Power (0-1).

Croke Park, 27 June 1965: Garda 5-18, Army 3-8

Garda panel: C Doocey, T Carberry, B Kenny, J Nealon, S English, J O'Donnell, E Coogan, G Lohan, N Power, J Conroy, E Carey, J Lane, M Regan, N Lane, L Doyle.
Scorers: E Carey (2-5), L Doyle (1-0), J Conroy (1-3), J Lane (1-0), N Power (0-2), M Regan (0-2).

Croke Park, 19 June 1966: Garda 6-14, Army 2-4

Garda panel: T Ahern (Cork), W Walsh (Waterford), B Kenny (Tipperary), J Kinsella (Wexford), V Duff (Tipperary). J Hearne (Tipperary), J Conroy (Galway), S Quaid (Limerick), G Lohan (Galway), E Sullivan (Kerry), P McGovern (Waterford), P Daly (Limerick), M Regan (Galway), M O'Brien (Limerick), M Hayes (Limerick). Subs: J Kennedy (Wexford) for Sullivan, Sullivan for Regan.
Scorers: P McGovern (0-5), M Hayes (0-3), P Daly (4-0), E Sullivan (0-3), V Duff (0-1), M O'Brien (2-2).

Croke Park, 30 May 1967: Garda 3-10 Army 1-5

Garda panel: T Aherne (Enniscorthy), E Coogan (Kevin Street), B Kenny (Wexford), J. J. Kinsella (Killane), J O'Donnell (Blackrock), J Hearne (Dublin Castle), S English (Nenagh), N Power (Dublin Castle), G Lohan (Newmarket-on-Fergus), V Duff (Kevin Street), P McGovern (Adelphi Quay, captain), S Quaid (Wexford), F Cummins (Templemore), J Kennedy (Wexford), M Hayes (Dalkey), J Doran (Blackrock), P Verdon (Pearse Street), E Carey (Dublin Castle), B Cooney (Store Street), P Daly (Donnybrook), W Walsh (Wexford), M Regan (Store Street), C Doocey (Callan), B Johnson (Training Centre), N Smith (Training Centre), B Maher (Training Centre).
Scorers; J. Kennedy (2-1), P McGovern (0-5), E Carey (0-2), N Power (1-0), M Hayes (0-1), F Cummins (0-1).

Croke Park, 30 May 1968: Garda 6-10, Army 3-11

Garda panel: M Hyland (Cork East), J Conroy (Tipperary), W Maloney (Kerry), J Lordan (Clare), T Kirby (Cork East), N Power (Kerry), J Doyle (Cork East), G Lohan (Clare), F Cummins (Cork East), E Doyle (Cork East), P McGovern (Waterford), P Freaney (Cork East), E O'Sullivan (Kerry), J Cullinane (Tipperary), M Keane (Cork East). Subs: M O'Loughlin for Keane, K Mannion for Cullinane.
Scorers: E O'Sullivan (2-2), P McGovern (1-4), F Cummins (1-1), P Freaney (1-2), E Doyle (1-0), G Lohan (0-1).

Phoenix Park, 30 May 1969: Garda 5-8, Army 3-11

Scorers: M Regan (1-2), E Carey (1-2), B Cooney (1-1), T O'Donoghue and T Purcell (1-0) each, W Power (0-3).

An All-Ireland Garda team that played the Tipperary senior team to celebrate the opening of the GAA football pitch in Templemore, circa 1970.
Back row, from left:
Johnny Carey, Dan Fenton, Seán O'Grady, Noel Colleran, Seán Galway (RIP),
Eugene Rooney, Willie McGee, John Morley (RIP), Mick Quinn, Michael Reynolds (RIP),
Evans Byrne (manager).
Front row, from left:
Jimmy Donegan, Gerry Gallagher, Ned Kirby, unknown, Charlie O'Reilly, Frank McGowan,
Willie Gallagher, Brian Colleran, P.J. Moolick.
Two members of the team lost their lives in the line of duty – John Morley and Michael Reynolds.

Army Grounds, Phoenix Park, 5 June 1970: Army 2-10 Garda 1-9; Garda 2-14 Army 2-6

Garda panel: D Quigley (Kilkenny), J Moran (Westmeath), M Hearne (Waterford), F Byrne (Laois), J Brennan (Wexford), J Hearne (Waterford), E Hogan (Tipperary), M Walsh (Kilkenny), T Coughlan (Waterford), J

Norton (Tipperary), D Corcoran (Tipperary), M Kelliher (Tipperary), P Enright (Limerick), T Bowe (Kilkenny), A Kiely (Tipperary). Subs: D Fenton (Cork) for Coughlan, T Donoghue (Clare) for Enright.
Scorers: D Corcoran (0-3), D Norton (1-0), M Kelliher (0-2), J Hearne, T Donoghue, D Fenton, A Kiely (0-1 each).

Army Grounds, Phoenix Park, 28 May 1971: Garda 5-13, Army 5-6
Garda panel: P Byrne, M Behan, B Cooney, J McGuane, M Collins, J O'Donnell, T Mahoney, N Power, J Aherne, T Purcell, B Maher, T Donoghue, E Carey, K Brennan, L Kennedy. Sub: N Kirby for Brennan.
Scorers: E Kirby (2-0), N Power (1-4), E Carey (1-3), T Purcell (1-1), B Maher (0-3), L Kennedy (0-2).

Semi-final, Mardyke, Cork, 19 April 1976: Combined Universities 3-13, Combined Services 4-8
Panel: F Larkin (Garda, Galway), J O'Donnell (Garda, Limerick), O Hanley (Garda, Roscommon), B Murphy (Garda, Cork), P Hayes, F Cummins (Garda, Kilkenny), J Cooper, P Butler, D McCormack N Casey (Garda, Clare), W O'Brien, P Butler (Garda, Kilkenny), D Prendergast, G Mahony. Subs: G Grehan for Brennan, P Mulcahy (Garda, Kilkenny) for Prendergast, G Lohan (Garda, Clare) for Mahony.
Scorers: P Mulcahy (0-3), G Lohan (1-0), P Butler (1-1), F Cummins (2-0), W O'Brien (0-2), N Casey and D Prendergast (0-1) each.

Semi-final, Croke Park, 3 April 1977: Combined Universities 2-11, Combined Services 1-9
Panel: F Larkin (Garda), P. J. Keane, I O'Donnell (Garda), J Cooper, S Cloonan (Garda), G Lohan (Garda), B Murphy (Garda), F Cummins (Garda), P Mulcahy (Garda), P Grace (Garda), D Prendergast, F Houlihan, W O'Brien, G Burke (Garda), F Grehan. Subs: O'Hanley (Garda), S Farrell for Burke.
Scorers: G Lohan (1-0), P Grace (0-4), D Prendergast (0-2), F Cummins (0-2), F Houlihan (0-1).

1979
Semi-final, Phoenix Park, 29 March 1979: Garda 6-10, Army 2-2
Final, Croke Park, 22 April 1979: Combined Universities 2-7, Garda 0-9
Garda panel: F Larkin, G Finch, B Brady, C Quinn, L Craven, D McCormack, D Collins, G Ryan, P Grace, J Kelly, M Walsh, M O'Shea, K Donoghue, M Murphy, P Mulcahy. Subs: M O'Riordan for Mulcahy, B Johnston for Murphy, D Loughnan for Donoghue.
Scorers: G Ryan (0-4), M Walsh (0-3), J Kelly, M O'Riordan (0-1 each).

Final, Croke Park, 23 April 1980: Combined Universities 1-11, Garda 2-6

Garda panel: F Larkin, J O'Donnell, C Quinn, O Hanley, L Craven, B Murphy, G Ryan, J Kelly, D McCormack, M Murphy, N Smith, M O'Shea, M Cashen, G Lohan, W Browne. Subs: P Mulcahy for Smith, K Kennedy for Browne.

Scorers: G Lohan (2-0), N Smith (0-2), G Ryan, W Browne, M Murphy andD. J. Kelly (0-1 each).

The All-Ireland Garda Hurling team, 1980.
Back row, from left:
John O'Shea (Tipperary), Kevin Kennedy (Clare), Liam Craven (Galway),
Ollie Hanley (Roscommon), Dinnie McCormack (Kilkenny), Joachim Kelly (Offaly),
Frank Larkin (Galway), Cormac Quinn (Wexford), Jim O'Donnell (Limerick),
Gordon Ryan (Kilkenny), Martin O'Shea (Kilkenny).
Front row, from left:
Tony Donoghue, P. J. Stokes (Cork), Willie Browne (Dublin), Dan Walsh (Galway), Noel Lane
(Tipperary), Gus Lohan (Galway), Brian Murphy (Cork), Martin Cashen (Offaly), Noel
Smyth (Offaly), Mick Murphy (Wexford), Gerry Curtin (Galway).

Semi-final, Santry, 21 April 1983: Advanced Colleges 1-18, Garda 1-12

Garda panel: J O'Shea, J Hayes, J O'Donnell, L Galvin, C Crinn, D McCormack, G Keating, M Cleere, F Larkin, D Keating, K Kennedy, L Meagher, W Hughes, D Brogan, P Cleary. Sub: G Curtin for Keating.

Scorers: D Brogan (1-2), L Meagher (0-3), M Cleere (0-2), G Curtin (0-2), P Cleary (0-1), D Keating (0-1), W Hughes (0-1).

Semi-final, Croke Park, 11 April 1984: Garda 3-11, Army 3-9
Garda panel: F Larkin (Galway), K Hogan (Tipperary), J O'Donnell (Limerick), P Finnerty (Galway), L Craven (Galway), G Ryan (Kilkenny), J Twomey (Dublin), L Maher (Tipperary), J Kelly (Offaly), M O'Shea (Kilkenny), M Walsh (Waterford), J Lynch (Kilkenny), G Curtain (Galway), B Tansey (Meath), J McDonald (Wexford). Subs: M Nash for Curtin, V McCormack for Craven.
Scorers: M O'Shea (0-6), B Tansey (2-0), G Curtain (1-2), J McDonald (0-2), M Walsh (0-1).

Final, Galway, 23 April 1984: Advanced Colleges beat Garda

Semi-final, Santry, 18 April 1985: Garda 2-13, Advanced Colleges 1-12

Final, Croke Park, 25 April 1985: Garda 1-17 Combined Universities 0-16

Semi-final, Croke Park, 1 April 1987: Combined Universities 2-17, Garda 2-12
Scorers: P Cleary (2-3), L Maher (0-3), M O'Shea (0-2), E Breen (0-2), J McDonald (0-1), D Keating (0-1).

Semi-final, Phoenix Park, 30 April 1988: Garda 0-17, Combined Colleges 0-10

Final, Drumcondra, 30 April 1988: Combined Fitzgibbon 3-13, Garda 1-9
Scorers: M Nash (0-3), J O'Shea (1-1), L Maher (0-2), J Hayes, M Hayes, M Cleere, M O'Riordan (0-1) each.

Semi-final, Belfield, 29 April 1989: Combined Fitzgibbon 4-10, Garda 2-12
Scorers: J Twomey (0-5), G Hogarty (1-2), M O'Sullivan, (1-0), L Maher (0-2), W Hughes, L Byrne and S O'Doherty (0-1) each.

Semi-final, 27 March 1991: Combined Colleges 1-12, Garda 1-9
Scorers: P Cleary (1-1), P Martin, P Kelly (0-2) each, L Byrne, C Bonner, D Flanagan, A O'Connor (0-1) each.

Semi-final, Belfield, 25 March 1992: Combined Fitzgibbon 0-16, Garda 0-4
Garda panel: P Hession, C Ó Giollain, B Carey, J Shortall, C O'Leary,

J Lyng, P Kelly, M Morrissey, J Twomey, M Nash, J Hayes, W Hughes, J McDonald, J Rigney, G Hogarty. Subs: B Leamy for Nash, D Flanagan for McDonald, T Dwyer for Ó Giollain.
Scorers: J Rigney (0-2), G Hogarty, J Lyng (0-1) each.

1996
Semi-final, Westmanstown, 3 April 1996: Garda beat Combined Fitzgibbon
Final, Westmanstown, 3 April 1996: Garda 2-12, Army 0-10

The All-Ireland Garda hurling team, 1996.
Back row, from left:
John O'Shea (Tipperary, manager), Aidan Flanagan (Tipperary), John Twomey (Dublin),
Seamus Delaney (Tipperary), Tom Kennedy (Tipperary), Gerry Kennedy (Tipperary),
Brendan Carey (Tipperary), Padraig Hession (Galway), Austin Cleere (Kilkenny),
Michael Cuffe (Dublin), Paudge Tobin (Limerick), Tony Donoghue (manager),
Chris Bonar (Tipperary).
Front row, from left:
Ken Hogan (coach), Tom O'Dwyer (Tipperary), John Shortall (Laois), Denis Byrne (Kilkenny),
Peter Queally (Waterford), John Finnegan (Dublin), Kevin Long (Cork),
Mike Nash (Limerick), Mick Morrissey (Kilkenny).
Mascot: Padraig Morrissey.

Cusack Park, Mullingar, 14 October 2014: Garda 2-14, Defence Forces 5-17.
Panel of Garda players:
Paul Delaney (Cork), John Bugler (Clare), Niall O'Connor (Clare), Donal Kehoe (Tipperary),
Conor O'Brien (Tipperary), Kevin Dilleen (Clare), Alan Kelly (Tipperary),
James Woodlock (Tipperary), Damien Ring (Cork), Brian Coen (Tipperary),
Ronan O'Meara (Tipperary), Conor Egan (Offaly), Ger Flynn (Limerick),
David Hickey (Waterford), Mick Fitzgerald (Limerick), Dave Boland (Limerick),
James Young (Laois), Peter Kennedy (Tipperary), Pat Kelly (Waterford),
Owen McGrath (Kilkenny), Ian Delaney (Tipperary), Paddy Nolan (Wexford),
Darren Sane (Wexford).
Management: Mick Morrissey (Kilkenny), John Rigney (Offaly), Jim Doyle (Kilkenny).

The All-Ireland Garda hurling team, 2016.
Panel:
Tom Delaney (Kilkenny), Ciaran Finn (Mayo), Darren Rooney (Laois),
Shane O'Neill (Wexford), Declan Mulqueen (Clare), Mark Harrington (Cork),
Vincent Hurley (Cork), Seamus O'Carroll (Limerick), Richie Ryan (Limerick),
Peter O'Boyle (Dublin), Alan Kelly (Tipperary), Paddy Mulcahy (Tipperary),
Ian Mulcahy (Clare), Conor Dooley (Dublin), M. J. Farrell (Tipperary),
Keith Horgan (Dublin), James Phelan (Offaly), Barry Moran (Tipperary).
Manager: Mick Morrissey (Kilkenny). **Selector:** John Rigney (Offaly).

2017

The 2017 Garda hurling panel.

The All-Ireland Garda hurling team were defeated by the All-Ireland Defence Forces side on a scoreline of 2-21 to 3-12 in Templemore on 8 November 2017. Garda panel: Jimmy Smiddy, Conor Walsh, Enda Naughton, Declan Mulqueen, Enda Barrett, Padraic Maher, Ray Ryan, Damien Fenlon, Conor O'Brien, Eamonn Cahill, Ger Flynn, Mike Fitzgerald, Declan Byrne, Colin O'Loughlin, Eddie Brennan. Management Mick Morrissey and Jim Doyle.

The Garda camogie team which faced off against the Army in 2012.

The All-Ireland Garda hurling team on a trip to New York to play an exhibition match in 2013.

Hurlers led all the way

Garda, 4-11; Army, 2.7

A STAR-STUDDED Garda team was far superior in the hurling game and after leading 2-7 to 1-2 at half-time had little difficulty in increasing their lead as the game progressed.

All round, the Garda were more polished while their main strength lay in the forward line where Peter McGovern of Carlow, Seamus Quaid of Limerick and the two Mick Regans from Galway and Cork were in devastating form.

Garda goalkeeper, Phil Vernon, settled down to play an outstanding game after a rather shaky start. Right full-back Sean Nealon, brother of the Tipperary star, combined with Jim Prendergast in a solid full-back line; John Kennedy was an extremely confident centre-half, and Nick Power was the better of the two mid-fielders.

For the Army, John Dillon, Tony Wall and Albie Sullivan were the best in defence; P. J. Keane and John Armstrong did well at midfield, and Rory Campion, Paddy Cobbe and Christy Leaney starred up front.

Mick Bohane, of Dublin, who is due to play in the Leinster semifinal against Carlow on Sunday, did not line out with the Army due to an injury received on Tuesday night. He hopes to be fit by the week-end.

Scorers for Garda were: M. Regan (Galway) (2-1), M. Regan (Cork) (0-3), M. Hayes (1-1), P. McGovern (0-3), S. Conway (1-0), S. Quaid (0-2) and N. Power (0-1); and for Army, C. Leaney (1-0), J. Armstrong (1-2), R. Campion (0-2), P. J. Keane (0-1), T. Kiely (0-1) and J. Duff (0-1).

Garda—P. Vernon (Tipperary), S. Nealon (Tipperary), J. Prendergast (Kilkenny), E. Coogan (Kilkenny), W. Walsh (Carlow), J. Kennedy (Wexford), J. Conroy (Galway), B. Cooney (Dublin), N. Power (Kilkenny), E. Carey (Limerick), P. McGovern (Carlow), S. Quaid (Limerick), M. Regan (Galway), M. Regan (Cork), M. Hayes (Limerick). Subs.: B. Kenny for Coogan, Coogan for Conroy, J. Lane for Hayes.

Army—J. Noonan (Limerick), J. Dillon (Tipperary), A. Cross (Tipperary), C. McNamara (Clare), T. O'Meara (Tipperary), T. Wall (Tipperary), A. Sullivan (Cork), P. J. Keane (Limerick), J. Armstrong (Dublin), T. Brennan (Tipperary), R. Campion (Laois), P. Cobbe (Limerick), T. Kiely (Cork), C. Leaney (Dublin), M. Cregan (Limerick). Subs.: J. Duff for Cregan, M. Quinn for Wall.

Chapter 9

Garda Internal All Star Awards

An Garda Síochána's top Gaelic footballers and hurlers are honoured at a gala Coiste Siamsa Sportstar awards ceremony held in different locations around the country on a yearly basis. The following is a list of the winners and the venues:

Westmanstown 1994
Football: Dermot Deasy (Dublin)
Hurling: Mike Nash (Limerick)

Templemore 1995
Football: Brian Murray (Donegal)
Hurling: no name
Hall of Fame: Matt Connor (Gaelic football)

Westmanstown 1996
Football: Garvan Ware (Carlow)
Hurling: Padraig Tobin (Limerick)
Hall of Fame: Brian Murphy (Gaelic football and hurling)

Malahide 1997
Football: Declan O'Keeffe (Kerry)
Hurling: Ollie Baker (Clare)
Hall of Fame: Tim O'Donnell (Gaelic football)

Limerick 1998
Football: Gerry Burke (Galway)
Hurling: Peter Queally (Waterford)
Hall of Fame: John Egan (Gaelic football)

Wexford 1999

Football: Martina O'Ryan (Waterford)
Hurling: Ollie Baker (Clare)
Hall of Fame: Michael Carolan (Gaelic football)

Malahide 2000

Football: Declan O'Keeffe (Kerry)
Hurling: Eddie Brennan (Kilkenny)

Westport 2001

Football: Kevin Walsh (Galway)
Hurling: David Kennedy (Tipperary)
Hall of Fame: Mick Higgins (Gaelic football)

Cork 2002

Football: Sean Collum
Hurling: Eddie Brennan (Kilkenny)
Hall of Fame: John McCarthy (Gaelic football)

Monaghan 2003

Football: Darren Rooney (Laois)
Hurling: Eddie Brennan (Kilkenny)

Waterford 2004

Football: John Crowley (Kerry)
Hurling: Jerry O'Connor (Cork)
Hall of Fame: Brendan Lynch (Gaelic football)

Salthill 2005

Football: Kieran Fitzgerald (Galway)
Hurling: Jerry O'Connor (Cork)
Hall of Fame: Sean Ferriter (Gaelic football)

Templemore 2006

Football: Tom O'Sullivan (Kerry)
Hurling: Eddie Brennan (Kilkenny)
Hall of Fame: Joachim Kelly (Hurling)

Mullingar 2007

Football: Aidan O'Mahony (Kerry)
Hurling: Eddie Brennan (Kilkenny)
Hall of Fame: James Murphy (Gaelic football)

Sligo 2008

Football: Darren Mullally (Galway)
Hurling: Eddie Brennan (Kilkenny)

Kilkenny 2009

Football: Tom O'Sullivan (Kerry)
Hurling: Eddie Brennan (Kilkenny)
Hall of Fame: Frank Cummins (Kilkenny, hurling)

Trim 2010

Football: James Kavanagh (Kildare)
Camogie: Josie Dwyer (Wexford)

Limerick 2011

Football: Aaron Hoey (Louth)
Hurling: Eddie Brennan (Kilkenny)

Westmanstown 2012

Football: David Clarke (Mayo)
Camogie: Josie Dwyer (Wexford)

Westport 2013

Football: Colm Boyle (Mayo) and Joanne Moore (Louth)

Killarney 2014

Football: Aidan O'Mahony (Kerry)
Hurling and camogie: James Woodlock (Tipperary) and Michelle Casey
(Limerick)
Hall of Fame: Willie McGee (Mayo, Gaelic football)

Killiney 2015

Football: Colm Boyle (Mayo)
Hurling: Conor O'Brien (Tipperary)

Ballincollig 2016

Football: David Clarke and Colm Boyle (Mayo)
Hurling: Pádraic Maher (Tipperary)

Portlaoise 2017

Football: David Clarke, Colm Boyle and Martha Carter (all Mayo)
Team of the year: Garda College Hurling Club

Chapter 10

Members who have received All Star Awards

Football All Stars

2017

Colm Boyle (Mayo) – Right Wing Back
David Clarke (Mayo) – Goalkeeper

2016

Colm Boyle (Mayo) – Centre Back
David Clarke (Mayo) – Goalkeeper

2014

Colm Boyle (Mayo) – Left Half Back

2013

Colm Boyle (Mayo) – Left Half Back

2009

Tom O'Sullivan (Kerry) – Left Full Back
John Miskella (Cork) – Left Half Back

2007

Aidan O'Mahony (Kerry) – Centre Half Back

2006

Aidan O'Mahony (Kerry) – Left Half Back

2004

Tom O'Sullivan (Kerry) – Right Full Back

2003

Kevin Walsh (Galway) – Midfield

2001

Kieran Fitzgerald (Galway) – Right Full Back
Kevin Walsh (Galway) – Midfield
Johnny Crowley (Kerry) – Left Corner Forward

2000

Declan O'Keeffe (Kerry) – Goalkeeper
Martina O'Ryan (Waterford) – Centre Back

1999

Kevin O'Dwyer (Cork) – Goalkeeper

1998

Kevin Walsh (Galway) – Midfield

1997

Cathal Daly (Offaly) – Left Full Back

1994

Jack Sheedy (Dublin) – Midfield
Martina O'Ryan (Waterford) – Full Back

1993

Dermot Deasy (Dublin) – Full Back

1992

Martina O'Ryan (Waterford) – Full Back

1991

Martina O'Ryan (Waterford) – Full Back
Julie Kavanagh (Dublin) – Midfield

1990

John Kerins (Cork) – Goalkeeper

1989

Connie Murphy (Kerry) – Right Half Back

1987
John Kerins (Cork) – Goalkeeper

1986
Colm Browne (Laois) – Left Half Back

1983
Stephen Kinneavy (Galway) – Full Back
Matt Connor (Offaly) – Centre Half Forward

1982
John Egan (Kerry) – Right Corner Forward
Matt Connor (Offaly) – Left Half Forward

1980
John Egan (Kerry) – Left Corner Forward
Matt Connor (Offaly) – Right Corner Forward

1978
John Egan (Kerry) – Right Corner Forward

1977
John Egan (Kerry) – Right Corner Forward

1976
Brian Murphy (Cork) – Left Full Back

1975
John Egan (Kerry) – Right Corner Forward

1973
Brian Murphy (Cork) – Left Full Back

1971
Johnny Carey (Mayo) – Right Full Back
Jack Cosgrove (Galway) –Full Back

1966
Mick Carolan (Kildare) – Centre Half Back (Cú Chulainn Award)

Hurling All Stars

2017
Pádraic Maher (Tipperary) – Right Half Back

2016
Pádraic Maher (Tipperary) – Left Half Back

2014
Pádraic Maher (Tipperary) – Centre Half Back

2011
Pádraic Maher (Tipperary) – Left Half Back

2010
Pádraic Maher (Tipperary) – Full Back

2008
Eddie Brennan (Kilkenny) – Right Corner Forward

2007
Eddie Brennan (Kilkenny) – Left Corner Forward

2006
Jerry O'Connor (Cork) – Midfield
Eddie Brennan (Kilkenny) – Left Half Forward

2005
Jerry O'Connor (Cork) – Midfield

2004
Jerry O'Connor (Cork) – Midfield

2003
Eddie Brennan (Kilkenny) – Left Half Forward

2000
Denis Byrne (Kilkenny) – Right Half Forward

1998
Ollie Baker (Clare) – Midfield

1995
Ollie Baker (Clare) – Midfield

1987
Ken Hogan (Tipperary) – Goalkeeper

1985
Pat Cleary (Offaly) – Right Corner Forward

1984
Joachim Kelly (Offaly) – Midfield

1981
Brian Murphy (Cork) – Right Full Back

1980
Mossie Walsh (Waterford) – Midfield
Joachim Kelly (Offaly) – Midfield

1979
Brian Murphy (Cork) – Right Full Back

Ex-members:
Frank Cummins (Kilkenny, hurling) – 1983, 1982, 1972 and 1971
Pete Finnerty (Galway, hurling) – 1990, 1988, 1987, 1986, and 1985

Chapter 11

Members who have Won All-Ireland Medals

Football

1923
Paddy Kirwan, John Sherlock, Larry Stanley, Dublin

1924
Jack Murphy, Paul Russell, Kerry

1925
Frank Benson, Galway

1926
Paul Russell, Kerry

1927
Tom Keogh, Paddy Martin, Kildare

1928
Tom Keogh, Paddy Martin, Kildare

1929
Paul Russell, Tim O'Donnell, Kerry

1930
Paul Russell, Tim O'Donnell, Kerry

1931
Paul Russell, Tim O'Donnell, Kerry

1932
Paul Russell, Tim O'Donnell, Kerry

1933
Jim Smith, Cavan

1934
Martin Kelly, Galway

1935
Jim Smith, Cavan

1936
Peter Laffey, George Ormsby, Mayo

1937
Tim O'Donnell, Charlie O'Sullivan, Kerry

1938
Martin Kelly, Frank Cunniffe, Galway

1939
Paddy Kennedy, Charlie O'Sullivan, Kerry

1940
Paddy Kennedy, Charlie O'Sullivan, Kerry

1941
Paddy Kennedy, Charlie O'Sullivan, Kerry

1942
Joe Fitzgerald, Dublin

1943
Brendan Lynch, Bill Carlos, Liam Gilmartin, Roscommon

1943
Brendan Lynch, Bill Carlos, Liam Gilmartin, Roscommon

1946
Paddy Kennedy, Teddy O'Sullivan, Kerry

1947
Phil Brady, Mark Higgins, Cavan

1948
Phil Brady, Mark Higgins, Cavan

1950
Paddy Prendergast, Tom Langan, Chris Hegarty, Mayo

1951
Paddy Prendergast, Tom Langan, Paddy Irwin, Mayo

1952
Mick Higgins, Phil Brady, Liam Maguire, Cavan

1953
James Murphy, Kerry

1954
Paddy Carrie, Meath

1956
Gerry Daly, Frank Evers and Joe Lowney, Galway

1957
Dan O'Neill, Seamus O'Donnell, Aidan McGennis, Louth

1964
Tom Sands, Galway

1965
Tom Sands, Galway

1966
Tom Sands, Tommy Brennan, Galway

1967
Oliver Stanley, Meath

1969
D. J. Crowley, Pat Griffin, Kerry

1970
D. J. Crowley, Pat Griffin, Kerry

1973
Brian Murphy, Ned Kirby, Cork

1974
John McCarthy, Dublin

1975
Páidí Ó Sé, John Egan, Ger O'Driscoll, Kerry

1976
John McCarthy, Dublin

1977
John McCarthy, Dublin

1978
John Egan, Páidí Ó Sé, Pat O'Mahony, Kerry

1979
John Egan, Páidí Ó Sé, Kerry

1980
John Egan, Páidí Ó Sé Kerry

1981
John Egan, Páidí Ó Sé, Kerry

1982

Matt Connor, Liam Mahony, Offaly

1983

Willie Hughes, Frank McGrath, Dublin

1984

John Egan, Páidí Ó Sé, Kerry

1985

John Egan, Páidí Ó Sé, Kerry

1986

John Egan, Páidí Ó Sé, Kerry

1987

Donal Smyth, Meath

1988

Donal Smyth, Meath

1989

Anthony Davis, John Kerins, Cork

1990

Anthony Davis, John Kerins, Cork

1992

Brian Murray, Donegal

1995

Dermot Deasy, Sean Cahill, Dublin

1996

Cathal Sheridan, Meath

1997

Declan O'Keeffe, John Crowley, Tom O'Sullivan, Kerry

2000

Declan O'Keeffe, John Crowley, Tom O'Sullivan, Kerry

2001
Kieran Fitzgerald, Kevin Walsh, Galway

2004
Aidan O'Mahony, Tom O'Sullivan, John Crowley, Kerry
Annette Clarke, Mayo

2006
Aidan O'Mahony, Tom O'Sullivan, Kerry

2007
Aidan O'Mahony, Tom O'Sullivan, Kerry

2009
Aidan O'Mahony, Tom O'Sullivan, Kerry.

2010
John Miskella, Cork. John Gleeson

2012
Peter McGee, Donegal

2014
Aidan O'Mahony, Kerry.

Hurling

1922
Mattie Power, Kilkenny

1923
Mick Gill, Galway

1924
Mick Gill, Garrett Howard, Dublin

1925
Jim O'Regan, Cork

1927
Mick Gill, Mattie Power, Pat 'Fowler' McInerney, Garrett Howard, Ned Tobin, Bill Phelan, Tom O'Rourke, Ned Fahy, John Gleeson, Willie Meagher, Bob McGann, Mick Finn, Tom Burnell and Paddy Browne – all Dublin, but none a Dublin native

1928
Jim O'Regan, Cork

1929
Jim O'Regan, Cork

1931
Jim O'Regan, Cork

1932
Mattie Power and Jim Grace, Kilkenny

1933
Mattie Power and Jim Grace, Kilkenny

1934
Garrett Howard, Limerick

1938
Mick Gill, Mick Flynn, Dublin

1954
Terry Kelly, Cork

1955
Tom Ryan, Wexford

1956
Tom Ryan, Wexford

1960

Seamus Quaid, Sean English, John Kennedy, John Mitchell, Wexford

1969

Frank Cummins, Kilkenny

1971

Noel Lane, Tipperary

1972

Frank Cummins, Kilkenny

1973

Jim O'Donnell, Limerick

1974

Frank Cummins, Kilkenny

1975

Frank Cummins, Kilkenny

1976

Brian Murphy, Cork

1977

Brian Murphy, Cork

1978

Brian Murphy, Cork

1979

Frank Cummins, Kilkenny

1980

Gerry Curtin, Galway

1981

Joachim Kelly, Martin Cashen, Offaly

1982

Frank Cummins, Denis McCormack, Kilkenny

1983

Frank Cummins, Kilkenny

1985

Joachim Kelly, Pat Cleary, Martin Cashen, Offaly

1987

Peter Finnerty, Galway

1988

Peter Finnerty, Galway

1989

Ken Hogan, Joe Hayes, John Leamy, Tipperary

1991

Ken Hogan, Joe Hayes, Tipperary

1992

Mick Morrissey, Kilkenny

1995

Ollie Baker, Clare

1997

Ollie Baker, Clare

2000

Eddie Brennan, Denis Byrne, Kilkenny

2001

Conor Gleeson, David Kennedy, Tipperary

2002

Eddie Brennan, Kilkenny

2003
Eddie Brennan, Kilkenny

2004
Jerry O'Connor, Cork

2005
Jerry O'Connor, Cork

2006
Eddie Brennan, Kilkenny

2007
Eddie Brennan, Kilkenny

2008
Eddie Brennan, Kilkenny

2009
Eddie Brennan, Kilkenny

2010
Conor O'Brien, Pádraic Maher, Tipperary

2011
Eddie Brennan, Kilkenny

2016
Conor O'Brien, Pádraic Maher, Tipperary

All-Time Hurling All Star Winners (1980-1994)

1982
Garrett Howard

1983
Pat 'Fowler' McInerney

Camogie

1999
Ciara Gaynor, Tipperary

2000
Ciara Gaynor, Tipperary

2001
Ciara Gaynor, Sheena Howard, Tipperary

2003
Ciara Gaynor, Michelle Shortt, Tipperary

2004
Ciara Gaynor, Tipperary

2010
Josie Dwyer, Wexford

2011
Josie Dwyer, Wexford

2012
Josie Dwyer, Wexford

Chapter 12

Members who have Won All-Ireland Club Championship Medals

Football/Ladies' Football

1989, 1990, 1991, 1992, 1993, 1994, 1995, 1997 and 1998
Martina O'Ryan, Ballymacarbry, Waterford

1973, 1979, 1982 and 1984
Brian Murphy, Nemo Rangers, Cork

1976
Mick Behan, St Vincents, Dublin

1981
Teddy Holland, St Finbarrs, Cork

1983
Colm Browne, Mick Lillis and Tom Prendergast Portlaoise, Laois

1987
John Kerins, St Finbarr's, Cork

1989
Eoin O'Mahony, Nemo Rangers, Cork
1990
Brian Fitzpatrick (captain), Baltinglass, Wicklow

1992

Connie Murphy, Dr Crokes, Kerry

1993

Tony Davis, Pat Davis, Don Davis, Brian O'Donovan, Kevin O'Dwyer,
O'Donovan Rossa, Cork

1998

Gerry Burke, Corofin, Galway

2001

Linda O'Connell, Donoughamore, Cork

2005

Ger Brady and David Clarke, Ballina Stephenites, Mayo

2015

Kieran Fitzgerald and Kieran McGrath, Corofin, Galway

2018

Kieran Fitzgerald and Kieran McGrath, Corofin, Galway

Hurling/Camogie

1972

Frank Cummins, Blackrock, Cork

1974

Frank Cummins, Blackrock, Cork

1976

Dinnie McCormack, James Stephens, Kilkenny

1979

Frank Cummins, Blackrock, Cork

1982

Dinnie McCormack, James Stephens, Kilkenny

1998
Ollie Baker, St Josephs Doora Barefield, Clare

2003
Jerry O'Connor, Newtownshandrum, Cork

2004
Marie O'Connor, St Lachtains, Kilkenny

2005
Marie O'Connor, St Lachtains, Kilkenny

2006
Marie O'Connor, St Lachtains, Kilkenny

2010
Ciara Gaynor, Burgess Duharra, Tipperary

Chapter 13

World Police and Fire Games
Belfast, 2013

WPFG Chair and PSNI Deputy Police Constable Judith Gillespie,
and Uachtarán Chumann Lúthchleas Gael Liam Ó Néill
at Croke Park in 2013.
WPFG organisers were at GAA headquarters to meet officers representing
the Garda, Irish Fire Services, Prison, Customs and Coastguard Services to profile
opportunities for competitors and spectators at this year's World Police and Fire Games.
The Games, a biennial event for serving and retired police, fire, prison and border security officers
will take place in Northern Ireland from 1–10 August.

Senior County Footballers, from left, Eamonn O'Callaghan, Kildare, Emlyn Mulligan, Leitrim, Denis Glennon, Westmeath, and David Clarke, Mayo, at the same event in Croke Park in 2013.

In August 2013, Belfast welcomed 7,000 competitors from sixty-seven countries for the World Police and Fire Games (WPFG), the third largest international multi-sport event in the world, and the largest sporting event to ever take place in Northern Ireland.

About The Games

The WPFG is a biennial event for serving and retired police, fire prison and border security officers comprising a wide range of individual and team sports. It was established by an organisation called the World Police and Fire Games Federation, based in San Diego, California.

It was a massive coup for Northern Ireland to win the right to stage the Games, as it involved a very competitive process, with numerous other cities bidding against Belfast. Indeed, the 2013 event was the first time that they were hosted in the British Isles, and only the third time in their twenty-eight year history that they were hosted in Europe.

A company (2013, World Police and Fire Games Ltd)

was set up to deliver the event. It was overseen by a board of directors, chaired by Deputy Chief Constable Judith Gillespie, including representatives from partner organisations including DCAL, PSNI, NIPS, NIFRS, Belfast City Council, NITB, and Sport NI, plus three independent nominees.

The games were also privileged to have Dame Mary Peters acting as patron. Dame Mary's tireless support and enthusiasm helped raised the profile of the games and gave it credibility locally with people who had never heard of WPFG.

Unprecedented Public Support

The games captured the imagination of the Northern Irish public and proved to be a massive success. Almost every event was open to the public and free of charge. This was widely promoted, and as a result there were unprecedented numbers of spectators attending the events. The ice hockey competition alone, which took place in the Odyssey Arena and Dundonald Ice Bowl, brought over 50,000 spectators through the turnstiles.

The support of the local population, helped enormously by the fantastic enthusiasm of the WPFG volunteer team, generated an electric atmosphere at WPFG venues.

The Garda GAA contingent at the World Police and Fire Games in 2013.
Back row, from left:
Eamonn Barry, Martin McGowan, Denis Glennon (captain), Páidí O'Connor,
Denis Carrigan, Shane McGrath, John O'Brien, Paddy Mulvihill, Brian Willoughby,
Padraic Jones.
Front row, from left:
James Masters, Emlyn Mulligan, Shane Mulligan, John Miskella, Hugh Coghlan,
Cormac Bane, Matthew Willoughby, Brian Monaghan.

The Garda GAA (Ireland) team clinched the gold medal in Gaelic football at the games. The Irish team was managed by Mullingar-based Detective Sergeant Brian Willoughby, assisted by mentors Martin McGowan, Brian Monaghan and Padraic Jones. Winning the gold medal was a tremendous achievement by all concerned, as this was the third largest sporting event in the world, with police and firemen from all over the globe competing in fifty-six different sports.

Because of the diversity of players, the Garda team had only one get-together before the games, when they played a very strong Mullingar Shamrocks side – a match sportingly organised by Pearse Corroon of Mullingar Shamrocks. The Shamrocks side – who were, at that time, the reigning Westmeath senior football champions – certainly tested the panel, and this was very important in the lead up to the games.

Despite being minus a few inter-county players due to injuries and unavailability, the squad that travelled to Belfast still consisted of many current and ex-county players.

The Gaelic matches were played between seven-a-side teams on Wednesday and Thursday, 7/8 August, on the beautiful playing fields of Queen's University, in Upper Malone Road, Belfast, where the pitches were incredibly good – almost like billiards tables.

The Garda team played their first match in brilliant sunshine, and proved too strong for their opponents, Western GAA. In their next two games, also played on the first day, the Garda team defeated the PSNI 'B' team and Cavan/Monaghan to qualify for the semi-final the next day.

In the semis, Garda defeated the PSNI 'A' team and progressed to the final to play the holders of the gold medal, the Northern Ireland Fire and Rescue Services.

The final was played before a very large and enthusiastic attendance, and before the match the team were introduced to Páraic Duffy, Árd-Stiúrthóir (director general) of the GAA. The final began at a brisk pace, with the NIFC team being cheered on by a strong local support, and the teams went in at half time with the Garda team leading by just a solitary point, 1-10 to 1-9. However, the Garda team came out in the second half and put in a scintillating performance to run out winners by 4-21 to 2-11.

Results

Wednesday, 7 August 2013
1st round: Garda 10-10, Western GAA 0-7
2nd round: Garda 13-6, PSNI 'B' 0-1
3rd Round; Garda 4-14, Cavan/Monaghan Garda 0-6

Thursday, 8 August 2013
Semi-final: Garda 10-16, PSNI 'A' 2-5
Final: Garda 4-21, NIFRS 2-11

Garda panel: Denis Glennon (Westmeath, captain), John Miskella (Cork), Emlyn Mulligan (Leitrim), Páidí O'Connor (Mayo), Denis Carrigan (Dublin), Shane McGrath (Clare), James Masters (Cork), John O'Brien (Dublin), Shane Mulligan (Longford), Hugh Coghlan (Tipperary), Cormac Bane (Galway), Paddy Mulvihill (Westmeath). Management team: Brian Willoughby (Waterford), Martin McGowan (Leitrim), Brian Monaghan (Offaly), Padraic Jones (Longford), Eamonn Barry (mentor, Meath). Maor uisce: Matthew Willoughby (Westmeath).

Garda Stars Sparkle

(A report by Jonathan Bradley of the *Belfast Telegraph*, 9 August 2013)

Cracking contest:
Winners Garda and runners-up NIFRS after the final at the Dub

Director-General of the GAA Paraic Duffy enjoyed a chuckle after he presented the Gaelic football winners medals to An Garda Siochána, conquerors of the Northern Ireland Fire and Rescue Service at the Queen's Dub complex.

"It was the first time I heard at a GAA match someone shouting 'Come on Northern Ireland'!" said Duffy.

Boosted by stellar inter-county talent such as Leitrim's Emlyn Mulligan, Westmeath's Denis Glennon and Cork's All-Ireland winner John Miskella, An Garda Siochána ran out winners on a 4-21 to 2-10 scoreline, but the Northern Ireland firemen made life difficult.

Peter Turley was a human battering ram and goalkeeper Tim Harney pulled off many memorable saves, and they drew level with 10 minutes to go until the superior conditioning of so many county players told.

It was a fitting end to a competition played in brilliant spirit and the skills in the senior final were an impressive showcase for the many athletes gathered in the social quarters right beside the location for Gaelic games.

The PSNI had two teams taking part, and there's a chance that some spectators might have been attending their first Gaelic football contest as a result of that.

In the bar, it was all "Oh my gosh!" and "You guys" and that kind of chat. Americans. Of course, they were there for the softball, naturally.

Elsewhere Aussies, Italians and Kiwis knocked back glasses that looked cold and frothy as they occasionally gave a glance at this curious spectacle outside.

A man and woman who appeared to have dropped straight out of 'Eurotrash' central casting, wearing Doc Martens and T-shirts emblazoned with 'Antwerp Fire Brigade' appeared bemused by it all, while on the sidelines a character with 'Deputy Sheriff' on his baseball cap took dozens of photos.

A strange, wonderful and peculiar day for sport in this corner of the world. Good to see. Great to see, in fact.

There was the poignant sight of Peader Heffron on the sidelines.

Three and a half years ago, the Irish-speaker and keen Gaelic footballer was caught in a booby-trap bomb and his life, and body, was altered forever. To see him encouraging the PSNI team here was to witness a triumph of the human spirit.

The shield final featured the Western Fire and Rescue Service who were comfortable winners against the PSNI, while Cavan and Monaghan Gardai beat another PSNI selection in the Bronze Medal Match.

The senior final was a marked improvement in standard with some fine score-taking and plenty of big men thumping into each other in the sunshine, before the Garda side eventually pulled away at the end.

Paraic Duffy added: "It was a very competitive final, a very enjoyable game and fair play to the Fire Service team for their performance against a star-studded Garda team. It was played in a great spirit.

"You could also see the enjoyment all teams got out of representing their organisations.

"It was very well run and the whole mood and spirit of the day was extremely positive.

"It was great to see so many people from different countries watching it, people who would never have been exposed to Gaelic games before.
"I think they will have enjoyed what they have seen."

Cavan/Monaghan Garda: Senior Bronze Medalists

Panel: Padraig Murtagh (Longford), Conor Gurn (Donegal), John Callinan (Meath), Damien Walsh (Louth), Kevin Jones (Longford), David Pettit (Longford), Patrick Flanagan (Fermanagh), Colm McDonagh (Mayo), Stephen McLoughlin (Louth).

Ladies' Garda, Gaelic Football Gold Medallists

The ladies' matches were played in the salubrious surroundings of the Mary Peters Centre at Queen's University, Belfast. Unfortunately there were only three participating teams – an All-Ireland Garda team, a Donegal team and

The All-Ireland Garda Ladies' Football Panel ('Brucie's Banners'):
Caroline Griffin, Edel Hanley, (Tipperary), Paula Harkin, Martha Carter (Mayo),
Johanna Connolly (Galway), Laura King, Grainne Shaughnessy, Jenny Weldon,
Roisin O'Dea, Liz Bugler, Annette Clarke (Galway), Denise Fitzgerald.

a team from the Irish Prison Service. The All-Ireland team featured three former All Stars, Annette Clarke (Galway), Edel Hanley (Tipperary) and Martha Carter (Mayo), and current Galway goalkeeper, Johanna Connolly.

The All-Ireland team beat the Donegal ladies and the Irish Prison Service in the round robin series, and won the gold medals by defeating the Irish Prison Service in the final. The Donegal ladies won the bronze medal.

The Donegal Garda contingent at the World Police and Fire Games, 2013
Back row, from left:
Rob Doyle, Niall Maguire, James Doran, Joe McManus, Charlie Gallagher, John Gallagher,
Adrian McGettigan, Adrian Lyons, Neil Cox, Ronan Steed, Rosemary Rooney,
Kevin McGettigan.
Front row, from left:
Sean McLaughlin, Grainne McCloone, Michelle McLaughlin, Michelle Kelly, Siobhan Tighe,
Brenda Healy, Carina Finn, Jenna Moynagh, Kathy Rabbitt, Denise Casserly,
Goretti Sheridan, Siobhan Campbell

Donegal ladies' panel of players

Grainne McCloone (Donegal), Michelle McLaughlin (Donegal), Michelle Kelly (Leitrim), Siobhan Tighe (Mayo), Brenda Healey (Sligo), Karina Finn (Cork), Laura Hynes (Roscommon), Jenna Moynagh (Tyrone), Kathy Rabbitt (Roscommon), Denise Casserly (Roscommon), Goretti Sheridan (Donegal), Siobhan Campbell (Donegal).

Over 35 Masters results, WPFG 2013
Round robin: Irish Prison Service 4-3, Donegal Gardía 4-2
Round robin: NIFRS 'A' 5-2, Donegal Gardaí 6-5
Round robin: NIFRS Stars 2-6, Donegal Gardaí 1-10
Final: Irish Prison Service 2-12, Donegal Gardaí 3-7

Garda Masters panel: Rob Doyle (Galway), Niall Maguire (Tyrone), James Doran (Leitrim), Joe McManus (Sligo), Charlie Gallagher (Donegal), John Gallagher (Donegal), Adrian McGettigan (Donegal), Adrian Lyons (Mayo), Neil Cox (Fermanagh), Ronan Steed (Galway), Kevin McGettigan (Donegal). Manager: Declan McFarland (Monaghan).

Chapter 14

Members who have represented Ireland in Compromise Rules and Shinty

Compromise Rules:

1984

Matt Connor (Offaly)

1987

Colm Browne (Laois)

1999

Declan O'Keeffe (Kerry)

2001

Johnny Crowley (Kerry)

2006

Aidan O'Mahony (Kerry), Kieran Fitzgerald (Galway)

2008

Aidan O'Mahony (Kerry), John Miskella (Cork)

2010

James Kavanagh (Kildare), Brendan Murphy (Carlow)

2011

Brendan Murphy (Carlow), Eamonn Callaghan (Kildare)

2013

Colm Boyle (Mayo)

2014

Colm Boyle (Mayo)

Caps for Ireland:

Brendan Murphy (Carlow), 4

Aidan O'Mahony (Kerry), 4

Colm Boyle (Mayo), 3

James Kavanagh (Kildare), 3

Declan O'Keeffe (Kerry), 2

Johnny Crowley (Kerry), 2

Stephen Kelly (Limerick), 2

Colm Browne (Laois), 1

Cathal Daly (Offaly), 1

John Miskella (Cork), 1

Kieran Fitzgerald (Galway), 1

Eamonn Callaghan (Kildare), 1

Matt Connor (Offaly), 1

Shinty

Garrett Howard (Dublin)

Brian O'Dwyer (Tipperary)

Eddie Brennan (Kilkenny)

David Kennedy (Kildare)

Shane Fennell (Louth)

Shane Cooke (Dublin, U21)

Ken Hogan (Tipperary, manager)

Chapter 15

Garda Participation in the Dublin, Cork and Limerick Interfirms Competitions

Galway
Courtesy of John Gray

Galway Garda dominated the interfirms GAA scene in recent years, winning three All-Ireland senior football titles (2010-2012), with Seamus McDonnell at the helm.

Their first success came in 2010. Defeating Mayo Teachers in the Connacht final, they set up an All-Ireland semi-final with Cork Garda in Pearse Stadium, Salthill. After an entertaining hour's football, the Galway men triumphed by four points. This led to an All-Ireland decider with the Dublin GAA Coaches in Westmanstown (Lucan). In an accomplished display, with Shane Waldron and Brendan Ryan pulling the strings at midfield and Cormac Bane kicking points from all angles (10 points in total), the Galway men ran out 1-17 to 2-6 winners. Neil Lydon scored the Galway goal.

The Garda team and scorers in the 2010 final was: Alan Keane, Pádraig Kelly, Barry Burke, Sean Durcan, Rowland McIntyre, Pat Kelly (0-1), Colm Boyle, Brendan Ryan (captain), Shane Waldron (0-1), Neil Lydon (1-2), Pádraic O'Connor (0-2), Brian Meaney (0-1), Declan Fawl, Mark Walkin, Cormac Bane (0-10). Subs: Shane Prendergast, Paul McBride, Shane Igoe, Niall Lennon, Mark O'Sullivan.

In 2011, the Mayo Teachers again provided the opposition in the Connacht final. Again, the Galway Garda were victorious. This set up another clash with the Cork Garda in the All-Ireland semi-final, which was played in Ballincollig, Co. Cork. Second half goals from Emmet

133

Galway, All-Ireland Interfirms Senior Football Champions 2010.
Standing, left to right:
Mark Caffrey, Shane Fitzmaurice, Emmet Rocke, Shane Igoe, Mark O'Sullivan,
Mark Walkin, Shaun Durkin, Shane Waldron, Alan Keane, Pádraic O'Connor, Pat Kelly,
Neil Lydon, Declan Fawl, Paul McBride, Dermot Hardiman, Derek Mullen,
Shane Prendergast, Don Connellan.
Front, from left:
Jason Kelly, Sean McHugh, Charlie Cawley, Pádraig Kelly, Nicholas Delaney,
Rowland McIntyre, Brendan Ryan (captain), Kian Flanagan (mascot), Barry Burke,
Brian Meaney, Colm Boyle, Niall Lennon, Cormac Bane, Conor Barrett,
Seamus McDonnell (manager).
Absent from photo:
David Clarke, Shane Nallen and Fergal Kilbane.

Rocke and Shane Prendergast paved the way for an eight-point victory for the Westerners. The Mountjoy Prison Officers provided the opposition for the Galway Garda in the final, which was played in the Na Fianna GAA Grounds. The Galway men were out of the traps the faster, and with Brendan Ryan in fine form at midfield they built up a nine point interval lead. The second half was a tighter affair after which they ran out 0-16 to 0-7 winners.

The Garda team and scorers in the 2011 final was: Alan Keane (0-1), Anthony Pender, Pádraig Kelly, Sean Durcan, Pat Casey, Pat Kelly, Shane Waldron (0-1), Brendan Ryan, Emmet Rocke, Pádraic O'Connor, Mark Caffrey (0-1) Neil Lydon (captain, 0-2), Declan Fawl, Mark Walkin (0-2), Cormac Bane (0-9). Subs: Nicholas Delaney, Shane Igoe, Shane Nallen, Jason Kelly and Brian Meaney.

2012 was the year for three-in-a-row in both Connacht and the All-Ireland. The Castlerea Prison Officers provided the opposition in the Connacht final, in which the Galway Garda finished ten-point victors. This set up an All-Ireland semi-final clash with the Mountjoy Prison Officers,

Galway Garda, All-Ireland Interfirms Senior Football Champions 2011.
Standing, from left:
Don Connellan, Emmet Rocke, Brendan Ryan, Shane Waldron, Mark Caffrey, Shane Nallen,
Alan Keane, Shane Igoe, Pat Kelly, Pádraic O'Connor, Anthony Pender, Shaun Durkin,
Seamus McDonnell (manager).
Front, from left:
Declan Fawl, Mark Walkin, Jason Kelly, Nicholas Delaney, Niall Lennon, Brian Meaney,
Neil Lydon (captain), Pat Casey, Cormac Bane, Pádraig Kelly.
Absent from photo:
Dara Bolton, Conor Barrett, Dermot Hardiman, Charlie Cawley, Michael Gallagher,
Colm Boyle, Shane Prendergast and Shane Fitzmaurice.

which was a repeat of the 2011 decider. In a match played in Tuam Stadium, the Galway men had to dig deep to carve out a two-point victory. It was a Limerick amalgamation of Analogue/Stryker/Gencell which provided the opposition in the final, a match which played in Corofin GAA Grounds. While the final scoreline of 1-19 to 1-4 may have flattered them in the end, this was an accomplished performance from the Galway boys. Once again, Cormac Bane played a captain's part and ended up with a personal tally of 1-10. It was far from a one-man show, however. Anthony Pender worked very hard in defence and covered a lot of ground, while attacking wing backs Pat Casey and Pádraic O'Connor scored three points between them. Don Connellan had an excellent game at midfield, while in a lively forward line, Mark Walkin helped himself to four points.

The Garda team and scorers in the 2012 final was: Shane Nallon, Anthony Pender, Pádraig Kelly, Sean Durcan, Pat Casey (0-1), Robert Molloy, Pádraic O'Connor (0-2), Shane Fitzmaurice, Don Connellan, Emmet Rocke, Mark Caffrey (0-1), Shane Prendergast, Cormac Bane (captain, 1-10), Mark Walkin (0-4), Brian Meaney (0-1). Subs: Nicholas Delaney, Padraig Moran, John Gallagher, Jason Kelly, Declan Fawl.

Galway Garda, All-Ireland Interfirms Senior Football Champions 2012.
Standing, from left:
John Gallagher, Pádraig Moran, Alan Keane, Mark Walkin, Rob Molloy, Shane Nallen,
Emmet Rocke, Shane Fitzmaurice, Shaun Durkin, Neil Lydon, Anthony Pender,
Pádraic O'Connor, Paul McBride, Pat Kelly, Seamus McDonnell (manager).
Front, from left:
Mark Caffrey, Nicholas Delaney, Don Connellan, Jason Kelly, Brian Meaney, Pádraig Kelly,
Pat Casey, Cormac Bane (captain), Shane Prendergast, Declan Fawl.
Absent from photo:
Colm Boyle, Niall Lennon, Marvin Lee, and Brendan Ryan.

Galway Gardaí were beaten finalists in the All-Ireland Interfirms junior football championship in Bishopstown, Cork on 3 February 1999. Result: Galway Gardaí 1-10, Cork National Teachers 3-9.

Team: S Glynn, J Lovett, D Fahy, D Raftery, F Larkin, T Moran, S Burke, M Coleman, G Burke, F Makin, D McGrath, P Fahy, P Burke, T Morris. Scorers; M Coleman (1-5), G Burke and P Burke (0-2 each), D McGrath (0-1).

Limerick Garda's Interfirms Story
Courtesy of Michael O'Neill

The Limerick Interfirm GAA board was formed on 20 November 1954 in the Gaelic League Hall. The first board included Mick O'Mahony (Limerick Gardaí) as its vice-chairman. The Gardaí only entered a football team, and their team was very strong. Denis Moran, father of the former well known Kerry star Denis 'Ogie' Moran, donated the cup for the senior football championship to the Limerick board. The Gardaí won the championship four years in succession: 1955, 1956, 1957 and 1958. The following players were involved in these wins: Gerry O'Sullivan (Kerry, captain, 1955, x 1958), Pat Silke (Galway, captain, 1956), Leo Duffy (Roscommon, captain, 1957), Paddy Donnellan, John Whelan, John J. Masterson, Michael Masterson, J. Frank Lyons, Tom Coleman, Maurice Jones, Tom Roche, John Hynes, P. J. McDonagh, Andy Scannell, Jim O'Brien, J. Mangan. Note: Andy Scannell's father was chairman of Cork County Board for many years.

Eleven of the Garda panel in those finals were members of the Garda team which won the Limerick County Championship proper in 1958 (see above highlighted), when they beat Pallasgreen 0-7 to 1-1 in final.

Interfirm activities came to a standstill in the 1960s and early 1970s. The Gardaí appeared on the scene again in 1984:

1984 Won senior football – championship and league double
1994 Won Limerick JFC and Munster championship
1995 Won Limerick JFC and Munster championship
2001 Won Limerick JFC and Munster championship. All-Ireland final: beat Meath champions 2-10 to 0-10.
2004 Won Limerick JHC and Munster championship. Won the All-Ireland, beating Procter and Gamble, Munster, and beat Thermo King (Galway) in the All-Ireland final.

At this time the Gardaí and teachers had joined together.

2006 Won Limerick JFC and Munster championship; the Armagh champions beat them in the All-Ireland final.
2008 Won Limerick JFC, Munster and All-Ireland. Beat Ulster champions Donegal County Council in the final. Beat Cork champions CITCO in the Munster final.
2009 Won Munster SHC final; beat Tipperary Gardaí/teachers.

Roll of honour
Limerick JHC, 2004
Limerick JFC, 1994, 1995, 2001, 2006, 2008
Limerick SHC, 2009
Limerick SFC/SHC, 1984
Limerick SF League, 1984
Munster JHC, 2004
Munster JFC, 1994, 1995, 2001, 2006, 2008
Munster SHC, 2009
All-Ireland JFC, 2001, 2008
All-Ireland JHC, 2004

Cork Gardaí Participation in Interfirms
Courtesy of Peter Dennehy

Cork Gardaí have won the All-Ireland Interfirms senior football title on five occasions.

1978: Cork Garda 1-7, Tara Mines (Meath) 0-4
Team: Paul Downey, K Clancy, Michael Lillis, John Cremin, J Byrne, Maurice O'Connor, Tom Hayes, Teddy Holland, D O'Connor, D Stapleton, Ned Kirby, Eugene O'Connor, Noel Ranahan, Joe Tubridy, P Doyle. Subs: Eddie Rock, J Buckley, Mick Kirwan, W Murphy.

1986: Cork Garda 1-11, Tara Mines (Meath) 1-7
Team: E McCarthy, Pat Lehane, Timmy O'Sullivan, John Quilter, John Kerins, Tom Hayes, K Gallagher, Tony Davis, Ned Dorney, Rory O'Dwyer, Teddy Holland, Ned Kirby, Eugene O'Connor, John Egan, Eoin O'Mahony. Subs: Eamonn O'Connor, John Grogan, C Noonan.

En route to the final in 1986, Cork Gardaí defeated Limerick Gardaí in the Munster Interfirms final in Buttevant, Co. Cork. Cork team: E McCarthy, C Noonan, J Quilter, P Lehane, J Kerins, T Sullivan, K Gallacher, A Davis, T Hayes, N Kirby, T Holland, R Dwyer, J Egan, E Hickey, E O'Mahony. Subs: M Dorney for Kerins, J Grogan for Hickey. Scorers: E O'Mahony

Cork Garda win All-Ireland

The Cork Garda Inter-firm senior football team created their own piece of history on Saturday at Athy when they won the Interfirm Senior Football All-Ireland final by beating Tara Mines 1-7 to 0-4. By doing so they became the first Cork team to win the competition. The Garda team were the first to settle down to the hard conditions and were soon on the scoreboard with a point and a goal. They added another point before Tara Mines could get on the scoreboard with a point. The Garda replied with two more points before half-time to lead at the interval 1-4 to 0-1.

On the resumption Tara Mines made a very determined attack on the Garda defence and were rewarded with three points. The Garda rallied and added three points to their own score and after that the end result was never in doubt.

Scorers for the Garda were: Garda Molone 1-1, Garda Holland 0-4, Garda Hayes 0-1, Garda O'Connor 1.

(Front L-R) B. Murphy; Wallace; T. O'Connor, M. Lillis, O'Connor; J. Cremins (Capt); O'Connor, N. Ranahan; M. Kirwan P. Ferrelly.

(Back L-R) D. Cullinane; Madden; T. Hayes, J. Turbidy, Stapleton, C. Clancey, F. Doyle, Kirby, P. Downey, J. Byrne, Connor, T. Holland, E. Roc.

(1-6), E Hickey (1-0), R Dwyer, T Holland, A Davis, N Kirby (0-1) each. Limerick Gardaí: D O'Neill, J Browne, P Ives, J Houlihane, P Begley, N Maxwell, J B O'Connor, L Kerins, S O'Neill, M McHugh, G Burke, T Dee, J Meaney, T Maher, J Leonard. Scorers: J Leonard and T Maher (1-1 each), G Burke (0-3), S O'Neill and L Kerins (0-1 each).

1987: Cork Garda 1-13, Dublin Garda 1-7

Cork Gardaí: John Kerins, C Noonan, Timmy O'Sullivan, Tom Hayes, Seamus Callinan, Tony Davis, K Gallagher, Pat Lehane, Mick Comyns, Gerry Ryan, Rory O'Dwyer, Eoin O'Mahony, Ned Kirby, John Egan, Teddy Holland. Sub: J Grogan for Ryan. Scorers; E O'Mahony (0-8), T Holland (1-0), R Dwyer (0-2), A Davis, N Kirby and G Ryan (0-1 each).

Dublin Gardaí: J Somerville, G O'Brien, J Culkin, D Brennan, L O'Callaghan, D Healy, G Connolly, J McGrath, J Sheedy, A O'Sullivan, W Hughes, T Flanagan, L Conlon, S Bonner, F White. Sub: K Dempsey for Brennan. Scorers: W Hughes (0-3), L Conlon (1-0), S Bonner, J Sheedy, T Flanagan and A O'Sullivan (0-1 each).

By PAT KEANE

**CORK GARDA 1-13
DUBLIN GARDA 1-7**

NSPIRED by a masterly display from Eoin O'Mahony, Cork Garda won the All-Ireland Inter-Firm Football title when easily beating the Dublin Garda in the final at Bishopstown on Saturday.

The foundations for the Cork victory was laid in a very one-sided first period. Playing with the stiff breeze and inspired by O'Mahony and excellent centre forward Rory Dwyer, the Cork team were well on top. They scored some marvellous points, and Ted Holland rammed home a goal after ten minutes. As a result, Dublin were left with a mountain to climb, and were ten points adrift at the break.

In a bad-tempered second-half, Dublin never looked like getting back on terms. Their main tormentor, O'Mahony, scored the opening two points of the half, and that ended the game as a contest.

Dublin's full-forward Seamus Bonner was dismissed nearing the end, and though Dublin did finish with a flourish, it was too little too late. Fittingly, O'Mahony scored the final two points in injury time to leave his side comfortable winners.

Scorers: Cork. E. O'Mahony 0-8, T. Holland 1-0, R. Dwyer 0-2, A. Davis, N. Kirby and G. Ryan 0-1 each.
Dublin. W. Hughes 0-3, L. Conlon 1-0, S. Bonner 0-1, J. Sheedy 0-1, T. Flanagan 0-1, A. Sullivan 0-1.
Cork: J. Kerins, T. Hayes, T. O'Sullivan, S. Calnan, C. Noonan, A. Davis, K. Gallagher, M. Comyns, P. Lehane, G. Ryan, R. Dwyer, E. O'Mahony, N. Kirby, J. Egan, T. Holland. Sub. J. Grogan for G. Ryan.
Dublin: J. Somerville, G. O'Brien, J. Culkin, D. Brennan, L. O'Callaghan, D. Healy, G. Connolly, J. McGrath, J. Sheedy, A. Sullivan, W. Hughes, T. Flanagan, L. Conlon, S. Bonner, F. White. Sub. K. Dempsey for D. Brennan.
Referee: T. Maher, Waterford.

1996: Cork Garda 2-15, Digital, Galway 1-8
Team: John Kerins, David Crotty, B McCarthy, John Kingston, James Bugler, Rory O'Dwyer, Jason Lynch, Brian O'Donovan, Mark McElhinney, Don Davis, Mick Comyns, Gary McPolin, J O'Shea, Eoin O'Mahony, Paul Holland. Subs: Ivan O'Callaghan, Pat Lehane, Stephen Dennehy.

Similar to 1986, Cork Gardaí defeated Limerick Gardaí in the Munster Interfirms final on 10 October 1996 at the Monaleen Grounds, Limerick on a scoreline of 0-11 to 0-8.

Cork Gardaí: J Kerins, R O'Dwyer, P Lehane, J Bugler, B McCarthy, J Lynch, J Kingston, M Comyns, B O'Donovan, P Hegarty, C O'Flaherty, S O'Donovan, S Dennehy, P Holland, D Davis. Subs: G McPolin for Lehane, D Crotty for O'Donovan. Scorers: P Holland, D Davis, G McPolin and M Comyns (0-2 each), C O'Flaherty, P Hegarty and B O'Donovan (0-1 each).

Limerick Gardaí: J Heaney, T Daly, P Ives, J Reddington, P Browne, M McCauley, O O'Sullivan, B Rouine, S O'Donovan, P Garland, S Fitzpatrick, J O'Neill, A McCarthy, A O'Sullivan, J Murphy. Scorers: A McCarthy (0-3), B Rouine and G O'Neill (0-2 each), O O'Sullivan (0-1).

2010: Cork Garda 0-14, Ballina Beverages (Mayo) 0-7
Cork team: Stephen O'Sullivan, Bryan Murphy, Tom Aherne, Michael Dennehy, Daniel Lucey, Aidan O'Mahony, John Daly, Chris Daly, Daniel O'Donovan, Eamonn Jer O'Sullivan, David Hickey (captain), Kieran Barrett, Brendan Hanafin, Sean Murray, James O'Shea. Subs: Mark Harrington, Jimmy Smiddy, Kevin McCarthy, Ollie O'Sullivan, Paul Gleeson, Danny Culloty, Karl Griffin, Denis O'Sullivan, Graham Baylor, Tom Browne. Player/manager: James O'Shea. Players/selectors: Ollie O'Sullivan and Danny Culloty.

1998 defeat
Cork Gardaí were defeated in the 1998 Interfirms All-Ireland final by Allergan on a scoreline of 1-12 to 2-8.

Cork team: K O'Dwyer, J O'Shea, B McCarthy, J Kingston, P Murphy, G McPolin, J Lynch, M Comyns, P Hegarty, D Lynch, O O'Sullivan, D Davis, J O'Shea, R O'Dwyer, M McIlhenney. Sub: J O'Sullivan. Scorers; D Davis (1-1), M McIlhenney (1-0), D Lynch (0-3), J O'Shea (0-2), R O'Dwyer (0-1).

Dublin Interfirms – Hurling
Courtesy of Tony Donoghue

Dublin Gardaí won the All-Ireland Interfirms title on one occasion in 2000, and won the Dublin Interfirms competition on four occasions: 1998, 1999, 2000 and 2001. They won Leinster Interfirms in 2000 and 2001, and were All-Ireland Interfirms runners-up in 1998 and 2001.

5 December 1998, Westmanstown:
Suir Engineering 0-10, Dublin Garda 0-5
Dublin Garda: C Jordan, J Shorthall, T Dwyer, D McCormack, G Kennedy, C Gleeson, D Sane, T Kennedy, T Kavanagh, S Moyles, M Morrissey, N Carey, J Finnegan, S Cooke, N Maloney. Subs: S Collum for Morrissey, M O'Rourke for Kennedy. Scorers: N Maloney (0-3), J Finnegan and S Moyles (0-1) each.

In 2000 they beat EMC Ovens in Bishopstown.

The Dublin Garda team also played in 1993, when they were beaten by Avonmore in the Leinster final.

Dublin Garda, All-Ireland Interfirms Senior Hurling Title Winners 2009.
Back row, from left:
Colm Matthews, Austin Larkin, Sean Fallon, Padraig Coone, Donal Tully, Tony Tighe,
Ger Mullins, Eddie Brennan, Shane Cooke, Tony O'Donoghue.
Front row, from left:
Chris Bonner, Seamus Delaney, Paul O'Shea, Liam O'Reilly, Noel Nash, John Finnegan,
Ger Flanagan, Brendan Corcoran, Tom Killion.

Dublin Interfirms – football
Dublin Gardai won the All-Ireland Interfirms SFC title on one occasion, beating Shannon Diamonds, Limerick in the final. They were beaten in the 2006 final by the Quinn Group, Fermanagh on a scoreline of 1-9 to 1-8.

30 July 1987: Dublin Gardai 2-7, Prison Officers 0-8
Scorers: L Conlon (1-2), E Walsh (1-0), E Keane anD. J. Newton (0-2 each), J Sheedy (0-1).

Chapter 16

Limerick Honouring the Greatest all time Garda Gaelic Football and Hurling Teams

With kind permission of Weeshie Fogarty and John Leamy

Garda announce their best ever football team at a gala function

by Weeshie Fogarty, 5 April 2005

It was certainly a night to remember at the Garda Club, Sexton Street, Limerick on 4 March 2005, when close to three hundred guests gathered to honour the greatest Garda hurling and football teams of the force since the first Garda club was formed in Dublin by Commissioner Eoin O'Duffy in 1923.

Among the huge attendance was the Mayor of Limerick, Michael Hourigan, GAA President Sean Kelly, Garda Assistant Commissioner Gerry Kelly, Eddie Woode Chairman of Limerick County Council, and the chairman of the Limerick county board, Denis Holmes.

An Garda Síochána and the GAA have enjoyed a wonderful relationship for close to 80 years and many famous players have served and will continue to serve in An Garda Síochána and the evenings event was a great opportunity to honour the awards recipients. It also afforded the opportunity to acknowledge the great area of administration. Indeed here in Kerry, the members of the force have always been to the fore in playing, promoting, and in the training of teams down through the years. One of Kerry's favourite sons, Michael Ó Muircheartaigh, was the chairman of the selection committee of Pat Coleman, Flan Wiley, and Martin Fitzpatrick. It is obvious that a great deal of thought was put into the selection process and the selectors came up with two great teams.

While the event honoured the great players well known to followers of the game, there is of course a huge number of Gardaí who have literally given all their spare time to the games, and here in Kerry especially, they have served the association with great loyalty. There are too many of course to mention, but in my involvement I have played with and met up with a huge number of the force as the loyally serve club and county.

Jack McGrath of Beaufort has been a Trojan worker; John Evans of Laune Rangers is one of the best known, and he is the man who trained his side to county, Munster and All-Ireland honours; Eamon O'Sullivan of Ballyduff was one of Kerry's great hurlers; P. J. McIntyre of Kenmare has given magnificent service to this county and sadly his fine young son Seamus, a great footballer and inter-county hurler, died in a tragic accident while on duty. Mick Fitzgerald, now retired in Castleisland, has been another exemplary servant of the GAA, and he was recently and rightly so honoured for his tremendous service to ladies' football – not alone here in Kerry but also through the 32 counties. It is safe to say that without Mick, ladies' football in Kerry would not be in a strong position it enjoys to day.

My own club, Killarney Legion, had many the Gardaí playing with them down the years. Jimmy Redpath comes to mind straight away. Jimmy was a superb midfielder and played league and championship with Kerry, and transferred to Kildare where he starred with the Lilywhites. My great friend Louis Nolan spent many years stationed in Kildorrery and played minor, junior and senior with the Kingdom. Yet another Garda who wore the green and gold was Paddy Culligan. Reared in lower New Street, Killarney, who went on to become Commissioner of the Force. Paddy also played with Cork when posted there, and was one of the first great basketball players of this county, winning county championships with Tralee EBS, an All-Ireland with Kerry and might have been the first Kerryman to play for his country in that sport. Let's not forget the great Jas Murphy and Pat Griffin, who starred as Kerry won in 1969-70.

Kerry, of course, would be to the fore when it comes to Garda footballing stars, and talking about stars, what about the men who were selected for the All Star teams, bringing further honour to the force? John Egan, Páidí Ó Sé, Connie Murphy, Declan O'Keeffe, John Crowley, and Tom O'Sullivan. Liam Kerins trained Limerick, and Michael McDonagh, a well-known Clare Garda, is currently chairman of the Clare County Board, while Mick Curley, Galway, and Liam Maguire of Cavan have refereed All-Ireland football finals. It goes without saying that we could go on and on recalling the men and woman of the force who given so much.

So back to that memorable night, and seeing that it's in the football that Kerry are so represented, we will stick to the team of that big round ball.

What a lineout was honoured – surely this is a lineout that itself would win an All-Ireland, the greatest Garda football side?

John Kerins (Cork), Páidí Ó Sé (Kerry), Paddy Prendergast (Mayo), Paddy Driscoll (Cork), Paul Russell (Kerry), Bill Carlos (Roscommon), Tony Davis (Cork), Paddy Kennedy (Kerry), Larry Stanley (Kildare), Pat Griffin, (Kerry), Mick Higgins (Cavan), Matt Connor (Offaly), John McCarthy (Dublin), Tom Langan (Mayo), John Egan, (Kerry).

The hurling team was selected by Micheál Ó Muircheartaigh, Flan Wiley and Pat Coleman.

Ken Hogan (Tipperary), Brian Murphy (Cork), Pat McInerney (Clare/ Dublin), John Mitchell (Wexford), Pete Finnerty (Galway), Mick Gill (Galway/Dublin), Garrett Howard (Limerick/Dublin), Frank Cummins (Kilkenny), Ollie Baker (Clare), Mossie Walsh (Waterford), Joachim Kelly (Offaly), Seamus Quaid (Wexford), Mattie Power (Kilkenny/ Dublin), Noel Casey (Clare), Eddie Brennan (Kilkenny).

The following is taken from the programme which was published for the occasion:

From the foundation of An Garda Síochána in 1922 to the present day there is a very close connection between the GAA and An Garda Síochána. In many clubs throughout the country Gardai are to be found whether it is playing, coaching, referring or involved in administration side of the GAA. Many players have gained national recognition through their involvement with county teams over the years.

In the Twenties, the names of 'Fowler' McInerney, Mick Gill, Mattie Power, Tom Burnell, Willie Phelan, Garrett Howard, Tom Barry, Martin Hayes, Mick Finn, Jack Conroy, Paddy Browne, the Graces, the Mullanes, and Tom O'Rourke were famous for their exploits on the hurling field. Several of them starred in the still remembered Dublin side that swept holders, Cork aside in the astounding All-Ireland final of 1927. Many of the above continued to play for long periods, in some cases winning All-Ireland medals with different counties and winning Railway Cup medals with different provinces.

In 1956, Terry Kelly was part of a great Cork team that failed so narrowly to Wexford in that never-to-be-forgotten All-Ireland final, where Art Foley's great save proved the difference between the teams. In 1960, a Wexford team powered by John Mitchell and the late Seamus Quaid – who was so tragically killed in the course of his duties – swept Tipperary aside to claim the All-Ireland title. In 1969, Frank Cummins started his great career with Kilkenny, winning seven All-Ireland medals in the process, playing at midfield in all seven finals. A serious injury prevented Jim O'Donnell from being part of Limerick's great triumph in 1973. The great Cork three-in-a-row team of the seventies contained at corner back the outstanding Brian Murphy, who has the unique honour of winning minor, U21 and senior All-Ireland medals in both hurling and football. Pat Cleary figured in Offaly's great triumph in 1985, while Pete Finnerty and Ken Hogan each won two All-Ireland medals with their respective counties in the Eighties and Nineties. Joe Hayes won an All-Ireland medal in 1989, while Mike Nash was most unlucky to be on Limerick's losing sides of 1994 and 1996.

In football there were many notable players right around the country. In the Twenties and Thirties, Jim Smith from Cavan, Paul Russell, Kerry and Paddy Kilroy, who won provincial medals with Monaghan, Wexford and Galway, were to the fore. Paddy Colleran of Sligo fame, Paddy Kirwan, a Cavan man who helped Dublin to three successive All-Irelands, and Larry Stanley were household names. George Comerford from Clare had the honour of playing with both Munster and Leinster. Tom Keogh, who won All-Irelands with both Kildare and Laois, and Tim O'Donnell of Kerry were also famous players. Then came Chris Delaney of Laois, Frank Cunniffe, of Galway, Kerry's Paddy Kennedy, and Charlie O'Sullivan, followed by the great Roscommon trio of Bill Carlos, Brendan Lynch and Liam Gilmartin. The Cavan duo of Phil 'Gunner' Brady and Mick Higgins were to the fore in their county's great triumphs of the Forties and Fifties, while Liam Quigley of Carlow, Tom Langa of Mayo, Jas Murphy of Kerry and Cork, Con McGrath Cork, Hubert Reynolds, Leitrim, and Louth, the Cavan Maguires, Liam and Tom, Tony Morris, Gerry Daly and Frank Eivers of Galway. Paddy Driscoll, Paddy Harrington and Eric Ryan of Cork, Dan O'Neill and Seamus O'Donnell of Louth, Con Crowley Waterford were all famous players. Another noted player of that era was Jim Rogers of Wicklow, who won four Railway Cup medals with Leinster. The Sixties brought more famous players – Sean Ferriter of Donegal, Tom Browne of Meath and Laois, and Mick O'Loughlin of Cork, Paddy English of Roscommon, Greg Hughes of Offaly, Mick McDonnell of Laois, Mick Carolan of Kildare, Cathal Cawley of Sligo, Ollie Shanley of Meath, J. J. O'Reilly of Leitrim, D. J. Crowley and Pat Griffin of Kerry, Kieran Brennan and Harry Mulhaire of Laois, and Noel Colleran of Galway.

The Connacht Railway Cup-winning team of 1969 contained those three Mayo greats, Johnny Carey, Willie McGee, and John Morley, who was tragically killed in the course of his duties. In the Seventies, we had Jack Cosgrove, Galway, Brian Murphy and Ned Kirby of Cork, John McCarthy of Dublin, Páidí Ó Sé, John Egan and Ger O'Driscoll of Kerry,

Seamus Bonner of Donegal. The Eighties produced men like Matt Connor of Offaly, Mattie Coleman, Peter Lee and Stephen Kinneavy of Galway, the late John Kerins, Cork, Tony and Don Davis also of Cork, and Colm Browne of Laois. The Nineties saw Brian Murray, Donegal, Jack Sheedy and Dermot Deasy of Dublin, Cathal Daly, Offaly, Kevin Walsh, Galway, Declan O'Keeffe and John Crowley of Kerry. In the present decade, John Crowley and Tom O'Sullivan were part of Kerry's All-Ireland winning team of 2004 and Kieran Fitzgerald, Kevin Walsh and Alan Keane were involved with Galway.

The above list of hurlers and footballers contains some of the players who were famous for their exploits on the playing field, there are many others who also contributed to the great connection between the Gardaí and the GAA.

In later years, Gardaí have become involved in managing inter-county teams, including Pat Begley, Clare, Liam Kearns, Limerick, Tom McGlinchey Tipperary, Colm Browne, Laois, Paul Caffrey, Dublin, Seamus Bonner, Leitrim, James Kerins Sligo, Michael McCormack Longford, Gerry Fahy, Offaly, Páidi Ó Sé, Kerry and Westmeath. There is Barnes Murphy in Sligo, while Ken Hogan is currently manager of the Tipperary hurling team and Joachim Kelly has managed the Wexford hurling team. Mick Curley, Galway and Liam Maguire of Cavan, have referred All-Ireland football finals, while on the administration side, Michael McDonagh, a well-known Clare Garda, is currently chairman of the Clare County Board.

Chapter 17

An Fear Rua's Greatest Garda Hurling XV (2008)

Well known GAA website, *An Fear Rua "The GAA Unplugged"* posted its greatest Garda hurling XV of all time in 2008. It is reproduced below with kind permission of Liam Cahill of *An Fear Rua*.

Goalkeeper:
Ken Hogan (Tipperary)

Ken was a reliable keeper in Tipperary's senior hurling successes of 1989-91. Ken joined An Garda Síochána in 1983.

Right Corner Back:
Brian Murphy (Cork)

The only player to win minor, U21 and senior medals in hurling and football. Brian joined An Garda Síochána in 1971.

Full Back:
Pat 'Fowler' McInerney, RIP (Clare)

The legendary 'Fowler' McInerney had a long career, winning All-Ireland medals with both Clare and Dublin. Pat joined An Garda Síochána (then the Civic Guard) in 1922, and retired in 1944. His daughter, Mary, collected the award.

Left Corner Back:
John Mitchell (Wexford)

John Mitchell was a tight-marking corner back on the great Wexford team of 1960, which won the All-Ireland senior hurling title. John joined An Garda Síochána in 1953 and retired in 1993.

Right Half Back:
Peter Finnerty (Galway)

Peter was part of an outstanding half back line of the 1980s. He joined an Garda Síochána in 1984 and served in Henry Street, Limerick. He resigned in 1990 to go into private business.

Centre Back:
Mick Gill, RIP (Galway/Dublin)

Mick Gill has a unique honour in GAA annals in that he won two All-Ireland senior hurling medals in 1924. He won one with Galway and the other with Dublin; the 1923 final was played in 1924. Mick joined An Garda Síochána in 1923 and retired in 1962. Grandson Austin Gill received the award on behalf of Mick.

Left Half Back:
Garrett Howard, RIP (Limerick/Dublin)

Garret Howard achieved fame with both Limerick and Dublin, and with Leinster and Munster. Garret joined An Garda Síochána in 1923 and retired from Feakle, Co. Clare in 1962. Daughter Liz collected the award.

Midfield:
Frank Cummins (Kilkenny)

Frank Cummins was a stalwart midfielder in the great Kilkenny team of the 1970s and 1980s. Frank joined An Garda Síochána in 1969 and resigned in 1978 to go into private business.

Midfield:
Ollie Baker (Clare)

Ollie Baker was a vital cog in Clare's great successes of the 1990s. Ollie joined An Garda Síochána in 1998 and continues to serve.

Right Half Forward:
Mossie Walsh (Waterford)

Mossie gave sterling service to Waterford over a long period of time. Mossie joined An Garda Síochána in 1972 and retired in 2008.

Centre Forward:
Joachim Kelly (Offaly)

Joachim Kelly was part of Offaly's team of 1981, which made history by winning Offaly's first All-Ireland senior hurling title. Joachim joined An Garda Síochána in 1977 and retired in 2007.

Left Half Forward:
Seamus Quaid, RIP (Limerick/Wexford)

Seamus Quaid was part of Wexford's great team of 1960, which won the All-Ireland senior hurling title. He also played for his native Limerick, and was on the losing side to Wexford in the National League hurling final of 1958. Seamus joined An Garda Síochána in 1957, and was murdered in the line of duty in 1980. His wife Olive collected the award.

Right Corner Forward:
Mattie Power, RIP (Kilkenny/Dublin)

Mattie Power had a long career, winning All-Ireland hurling medals with both Dublin and Kilkenny. Mattie joined An Garda Síochána in 1925 and retired in 1962. Daughters Ann and Catherine collected his award.

Full Forward:
Noel Casey (Clare)

Noel Casey was part of an outstanding Clare team of the 1970s which won two National League titles and narrowly failed to make the breakthrough in Munster. Noel joined An Garda Síochána in 1974 and retired from Bruff, Co Limerick in 2004.

Left Full Forward:
Eddie Brennan (Kilkenny).

Eddie Brennan is a member of the Kilkenny team that won back to back All-Ireland titles in 2002 and 2003. Eddie joined an Garda Síochána in 1999.

Chapter 18

A salute to the greatest Gardaí in Irish Sport

Written March 2013
reproduced with kind permission of Adrian Russell of The42.ie

Kilkenny hurler Eddie Brennan with Garda colleagues in 2007.
Photo: INPHO/Lorraine O'Sullivan

AN GARDA SÍOCHÁNA has a long history of members excelling at a range of sports. Here is a list of some of the finest gardaí to put place their badge in a locker, lace up and pursue sporting glory. "Bad boys, whatcha want, watcha want, whatcha gonna do…"

Gaelic Games

We begin our tribute to the men and women in uniform on the Gaelic pitches across the country. A host of gardaí have represented their counties with honour and driven them towards success.

In 1927, nine members of An Garda Síochána, including Tommy Daly and Mick O'Connell, were in the Dublin team that beat Cork in the All-Ireland Hurling Final. Garda Ken 'Killer' Hogan won All-Irelands with Tipperary's hurlers in 1989 and 1991, while Phil 'The Gunner' Brady won three All-Ireland Football titles with Cavan between 1947 and '52. While we can't list the hundreds upon hundreds of gardaí that have represented their counties with distinction, here are some of our favourites:

Páidí Ó Sé (Kerry - football)
Eleven Munster titles, eight All-Ireland medals and five All Star awards, Ó Sé was an undoubted Kerry legend. Captained the Kingdom to the 1985 All-Ireland title. He turned his hand to rugby, with Young Munster, in his early sporting years.

Paidí Ó Sé is held aloft by Kerry supporters after the 1985 All-Ireland win.
Photo: INPHO/Billy Stickland

Jerry O'Connor (Cork – hurling)
The midfielder has won two All-Irelands with The Rebels and made it onto three All Star teams. He has also claimed an All-Ireland club title with Newtownshandrum.

Aidan O'Mahony (Kerry – football)
Seven Munster titles, four All-Ireland medals and two All Star nods for the Kerry back. One of the most remarkable tales from O'Mahony's career is his 40-minute stint on a broken leg in a club final. They breed them law-abiding and talented in The Kingdom.

Eddie Brennan (Kilkenny – hurling)

'Fast Eddie' is one of the finest hurlers of his generation and part of a dominant Cats team that will go down as one of the best of all time. Brennan has 10 Leinster titles, eight All-Irelands and four National Hurling League medals in his coffers. The left-corner forward is also a four-time All Star.

Josie Dwyer (Wexford – camogie)

The midfielder has two All-Ireland winners' medals following victories in 2010, when she was nominated for an All Star, and 2011. Four Leinster titles in the [memory] bank too for the talented Wexfordian.

Eight years ago, the GAA named their Greatest Garda Football and Hurling teams (for members serving 1922 to 2005). Here are the line-ups: Football XV: John Kearns (Cork); Páidí O'Sé (Kerry), Paddy Prendergast (Mayo), Paddy Driscoll (Cork); Paul Russell (Kerry), Bill Carlos (Roscommon), Tony Davis (Cork); Paddy Kennedy (Kerry), Larry Stanley (Kildare); Pat Griffin (Kerry), Mick Higgins (Cavan), Matt Connor (Offaly); John McCarthy (Dublin), Tom Langan (Mayo) and John Egan (Kerry).

Kilkenny senior hurling manager Brian Cody gets a ride with a Garda escort to Crumlin Children's Hospital.
Photo: INPHO/Cathal Noonan

Hurling XV: Ken Hogan (Tipperary); Brian Murphy (Cork), Pat McInerney (Clare/Dublin), John Mitchell (Wexford); Pete Finnerty (Galway), Mick Gill (Galway/Dublin), Garrett Howard (Limerick/Dublin); Frank Cummins (Kilkenny), Ollie Baker (Clare); Mossie Walsh

(Waterford), Joachim Kelly (Offaly), Seamus Quaid (Limerick/Wexford); Mattie Power (Kilkenny/Dublin), Noel Casey (Clare), Eddie Brennan (Kilkenny).

Here are some Gardaí that are currently serving on the force and for their county: Eamonn Callaghan (Kildare – football), David Clarke (Mayo – football), Aaron Hoey (Louth – football), Emlyn Mulligan (Leitrim – football), Seanie Buckley (Limerick – football), Denis Glennon (Westmeath – football), Hugh Coghlan (Tipperary – football), Conor O'Brien (Tipperary – hurling), John Marley (Mayo – football).

18 September 2011
Bernard Brogan celebrates with former Dublin Manager Garda Paul Caffrey
and former Selector Dave billings (left)

Chapter 19

"May the force be with you": the Gardaí and the GAA

by Liam Ryan, August 2001;
with kind permission from Paddy Smith of the Irish Times

For Wexford on Saturday, it was a case of I Fought the Law and the Law Won. Unsurprisingly, given the Garda training college's location in Templemore, Tipperary have quite a connection with the force.

Current Tipperary selector Ken Hogan, an All-Ireland winner in 1989 and 1991, joined up in 1983 when the training period was just six months. During the height of his inter-county career, he was stationed in Pearse Street station in Dublin before moving back to serve as a PE and swimming instructor at the training college in 1989.

Centre back David Kennedy joined up last year after giving a couple of years as a national school teacher in Dublin. Now in the second phase of his training, he is currently based at Store Street station in Dublin.

Another panellist, Conor Gleeson, who captained the Tipperary side when they lost the All-Ireland in 1997, is a Garda since 1995. Based at Harcourt Street for the first few years of his career, Gleeson is back at Templemore since April where he is working alongside Hogan as part of the PE instructor team. In interviews this season, he believes the return to base has been instrumental in the recapturing of his form, particularly in the latter stages of the league.

Hogan believes the life of a Garda is difficult to square with the demands of an inter-county hurler.

"Certainly during my time in Pearse Street between 1983 and 1989, I found the travelling up and down to be very difficult, what with the shift work as well. Getting back to Templemore obviously made things easier, with more regular hours and being close to home for training."

Tipperary are not the only county with Garda among their ranks. Kilkenny and Graigue-Ballycallan forward Eddie Brennan is based in

Tallaght. Denis Byrne, introduced with Brennan during yesterday's game against Galway, also served for the boys in blue but has left the force in recent years to return to the family construction business. Niall Maloney, a Kilkenny panellist up to a couple of years ago, and Waterford's Peter Queally are also serving Gardai. Limerick's Brian Begley is currently undertaking phase two training alongside David Kennedy.

Since the Garda College qualified for the Fitzgibbon Cup in 1996 their sides have featured numerous inter-county players, Clare's Ollie Baker playing his part in a couple of finals tournaments.

The team was also captained by Seamus MacIntyre in 1998 (an outstanding hurler, says Ken Hogan), the young Kerry Garda who died with a colleague in a car crash earlier this year.

Other notable GAA figures work alongside Hogan and Gleeson as part of the instruction team in Templemore. Former Offaly hurler and Wexford manager Joachim Kelly has been based at the training college for some years while Laois manager Colm Browne, who also had a stint with Tipperary, works in research at the college.

Wexford's hurlers may have no representatives, but footballer Jason Lalor, previously on the hurling panel is in the force.

Golden Gaelic Memories

by Brendan Walsh, Coiste Siamsa

Of all the sports affiliated to Coiste Siamsa, Gaelic Football is probably the one which has made the most indelible mark in the history of both Gaelic Athletic Association and An Garda Síochána.

Indeed to go through the attached list of Garda All Ireland medal winners is to embark on a magical journey through the rich folklore of Gaelic games. Every decade from the 1920s to the present has thrown up a crop of famous names and games that recall memories of famous September days.

A quick run through the decades shows names like Tim O'Donnell, four in a row winner with Kerry from 1929-1932 and of course winner of the Coiste Siamsa Hall of Fame in 1997.

Jim Smith captained Cavan when they claimed their first All Ireland title in 1933 and was also on the winning side in 1935.

George Ormsby won his All Ireland medal in 1936 with Mayo and also won a record six league titles in a row from 1934 - 1939. The 1940's began with the one and only Paddy Kennedy claiming his second of four All Ireland medals having previously won in 1939, he also went on to win in 1941 and 1946.

Bill Carlos, legendary centre half back of the Roscommon team that

three in a row in 1964, 1965 and 1968 while DJ Crowley and Pat Griffin both won in 1969 and 1970 with Kerry.

The 1970's of course are firmly fixed in the public mind with Dublin and Kerry but Ned Kirby and dual star Brian Murphy were on the winning Cork team in 1973. Brian Murphy was the recipient of the Coiste Siamsa Hall of Fame award in 1996. John McCarthy won the first of his three All Ireland medals in 1974 while 1988 Hall of Fame winner John Egan collected the first medal of his haul in 1975.

That brings us to another Hall of Fame winner with Matt Connor playing a starring role in the Offaly team that stopped the Kerry five in a row bid in 1982.

The 1980's has again proved to be fruitful with Brian Murray making history with Donegal in 1992 as Donegal won the Sam Maguire for the first time.

Kevin Walsh won with Galway in 1998 which neatly brings to the present with Kerry supplying three Garda winners as the new millennium begins, the first of many future Garda winners who bring glory to themselves, their county and, of course, An Garda Síochána.

"In Safe Hands" Left to right: Jack Sheedy, Dublin, Leinster Champions '92, '93, '94, '95; Ashley O'Sullivan Wicklow, All-Ireland B Champions; Brian Murray, Donegal, All-Ireland winners, 1992; Garvan Ware, Carlow, Leinster Club Champions, Éire Óg, 1992.

All four provinces are represented on the list with over a hundred members of An Garda Síochána belonging to the elite band of sports men who own the most prized possession in Irish sport, the winners medal from an All Ireland final.

From Larry Stanely, John Sherlock and Paddy Kirwan in 1923 to this year's crop of All Ireland winners with Kerry's, Declan O'Keeffe, John Crowley and Tom O'Sullivan. An Garda Síochána can reflect with pride on its contribution to Gaelic football.

also included Brendan Lynch and Liam Gilmartin that won back to back titles in 1943 and 1944.

In 1947 Phil 'The Gunner' Brady and Mick Higgins made history as part of the Cavan team that beat Kerry in the Polo Grounds in New York, the list of three All Ireland wins for both men.

Dan O'Neill and Seamus O'Donnell were the only Louth team to win the All Ireland when they beat Cork in the 1957 final.

Tom Sands was on the panel of the great Galway team that won the

Members of An Garda Síochána who hold all Ireland Senior Football medals

1923 Paddy Kirwan, John Sherlock, Larry Stanley (Dublin).
1924 Jack Murphy, Paul Russell (Kerry).
1925 Frank Benson (Galway).
1926 Paul Russell (Kerry).
1927 Tom Keogh (Kildare).
1929 Paul Russell, Tim O'Donnell (Kerry).
1930 Paul Russell, Tim O'Donnell (Kerry).
1931 Paul Russell, Tim O'Donnell (Kerry).
1932 Paul Russell, Tim O'Donnell (Kerry).
1933 Jim Smith (Cavan).
1934 Martin Kelly (Galway).
1935 Jim Smith (Cavan).
1936 Peter Lalley, George

17

Chapter 20

The 1927
All-Ireland Hurling Final

by Pascal Brennan

This level of participation is not a modern phenomenon. Since the establishment of An Garda Síochána. its members have a significant contribution to the GAA. When we turn back the pages of sporting history nearly ninety years to the All-Ireland hurling final of 1927 we will discover that ten serving Gardaí were in the starting line up for the participating teams.

The 1927 final brought a clash between the previous year's winners, Cork, and Leinster champions, Dublin. The Dublin team was largely composed of Gardaí attached to the Garda GAA Club in the city. These were men drawn from the traditional hurling heartlands of Leinster, Munster and south Galway. They were the recruits who joined the new police force, the Civic Guard, following the establishment of the Irish Free State. The Garda GAA Club was the strongest club in the city and having won the Dublin Senior Hurling Championship in 1925 and 1926, they would go on to win the next three titles.

The Garda club was dominant for a number of reasons. Commissioner Eoin O'Duffy had placed an emphasis on recruiting active young sportsmen to the new force, many of whom were allocated to Dublin stations. Lack of transport, irregular working hours and primarily the GAA residency rules restricted opportunities for these Dublin-based players in lining out for their native counties. In addition, the gym facilities at Garda Headquarters and the pitches of the Phoenix Park allowed a near-professional approach to training.

Road To The Final

Prior to 1927, Dublin had already won four senior titles, the latest of which was in 1924. Dublin had reached the 1927 decider courtesy of a Leinster final victory over a Kilkenny team which included the rising star Lory Meagher. In that game Dublin scored an amazing seven goals and seven points – a far cry from the amount of goals that the current Kilkenny defence would concede!

Cork had powered their way through Munster to the final with an average of 23 points per game. The backbone of the team was a strong contingent of Blackrock clubmen such as brothers Paddy and Mick Ahern, Eddie Coughlan and Seán Óg Murphy, all of whom would win many All-Ireland medals. Coming into the final, on the back of a 1926 success, they were a formidable outfit.

The Boys In Blue

The starting fifteen for Dublin included nine Gardaí, with a further five members of the force on the substitutes bench. The Garda members were: Pat 'Fowler' McInerney (Clare), Ned Tobin (Laois), Bill Phelan (Laois), Mick Gill (captain, Galway), John Gleeson (Tipperary), Tom O'Rourke (Clare), Garrett Howard (Limerick), Ned Fahy (Clare), Mattie Power (Kilkenny). Substitutes: Willie Meagher (Kilkenny), Bob McGann (Tipperary), Mick Finn (Galway), Tom Burnell (Clare), Paddy Browne (Tipperary).

The balance of the Dublin team was drawn from the Faugh's club: Tom Barry, Dinny O'Neill, Jim Walsh, army men Joe Bannon, Martin Hayes and goalkeeper Dr Tommy Daly of UCD. Though hurling was popular in the city, there was no Dublin native on the panel and to this day, only one Dublin native, Jim Byrne, has won an All-Ireland senior hurling medal (vs Waterford, 1938).

While Gardaí dominated the Dublin team, it would be remiss not to mention the Garda connection on the Cork side with the sole serving Garda, Jeremiah Burke, lining out in goal for Cork. Playing centre back for

Cork was an ex-Garda, Jim Regan of Kinsale. Jim's senior hurling career actually started with Dublin in 1925 as a member of the Garda GAA Club, while serving in the city. Having resigned after nine months' service to pursue a teaching career, he went onto play for Cork, winning four All-Ireland senior medals. Pairc Uí Riagain, the home of Courcey Rovers in south-east Cork, is named in his honour.

The 1927 Final

On the first Sunday in September 1927, 23,824 hurling supporters, paying a total in gate receipts of £2,350, crowded into Croke Park. Special excursion trains deposited supporters at Kingsbridge, Amiens Street and Broadstone stations. Thousands more travelled by bicycle and motor car. Newspapers of the day reported that a "large force of Gardaí, under Inspector Cuddihy regulated traffic splendidly". Pre-match entertainment was provided by the ITWU Band and the Cork Volunteers Pipe Band, led by the son of murdered Lord Mayor of Cork, Tomás Mac Curtain.

Following the throw-in, Dublin took the initiative and dominated early proceedings. Though Cork were slow to show their form of early summer, the *Irish Times* reported "they were struggling like champions". After a relatively low-scoring first half, Dublin went in at half time leading 2-3 to 0-1. Goals by Tom Barry and Mattie Power had strengthened the Dublin performance.

The second half continued with Dublin in control, and while Cork fought hard, they were unable to close the scoring difference. A second goal by Tom Barry and a Ned Fahy goal sealed victory for Dublin, making a final score of 4-8 to 1-3.

The hurling had been hard with Tom Barry, Dublin free taker, knocked unconscious twice. Referee Dinny Lanigan, a double All-Ireland senior hurling winner with Limerick, kept control, but then as now, the referee's performance came under scrutiny. An *Irish Independent* report stated: "There were a few incidents that appeared to call for more vigorous treatment then awarding a free", and "there were a few heated incidents which should be foreign to any form of sport".

Over eight decades later, many of the 1927 Dublin team are included among the greats of the games.

Garrett Howard had an eventful senior inter-county career, winning three All-Ireland senior medals with his native Limerick, two with Dublin, and also lining out for Tipperary. At club level he won senior county medals with Croom of Limerick, Garda of Dublin and Toomevara of Tipperary. In 1982, he received the GAA all-time All Star award. Coincidentally, his teammate, Pat 'Fowler' McInerney – an All-Ireland winner with Clare (1914) and Dublin (1927), received an all-time All Star award the following year in 1983.

Mick Gill is remembered as the player who played two senior finals in the same year and emerged victorious on each occasion. The 1923 final was delayed due to a Civil War-related dispute, and was not played until September 1924, with Gill playing on the successful Galway team versus Limerick. Three months later, he featured on the Dublin team which defeated his native Galway in the 1924 decider.

Mattie Power of Kilkenny was one of the greatest forwards of the 1920s and 1930s, winning All-Ireland medals with both Dublin (one) and Kilkenny (four), National League and Railway Cup medals, and several Dublin championship medals with the Garda club.

Dr Tommy Daly of Tulla, Co Clare, as goalkeeper, won his fourth senior All-Ireland medal in the 1927 final, having won previously with Dublin in 1917, 1920 and respectively. Following his playing career, he took up refereeing duties and was the referee in the 1935 All-Ireland senior hurling final.

Cork recovered from the defeat of 1927, and went on to success in 1928 and 1929. Dublin, though reaching the 1930 final, were not successful again until 1938.

Changes in the GAA residency rules in 1928 allowed the Dublin-based players to declare for their native counties. A number of the 1927 team did so, and achieved much success. This signalled the end of the Garda club's hurling dominance. While the club did win further hurling titles in the late 1920s, their stranglehold on the Dublin team came to an end. There was to be no repeat of that memorable Sunday in September 1927, when the "Boys in Blue" took over Croke Park.

Chapter 21

Mick Gill's Unique Double

When Mick Gill walked off the pitch at Croke Park on Sunday, 14 December 1924, at the end of an entertaining All-lreland hurling final against his native county, Galway, he had, without realising it at the time, collected a unique record in the history of the GAA and Gaelic games.

He had, in fact, become the first man and indeed, still the only man to win All-Ireland senior hurling medals twice in the one year.

And to add piquancy to that extraordinary feat, he had won his second medal playing against the county with whom he had won the first just three months earlier.

Gill, one of hurling's greatest personalities in the era between the two World Wars, was one of Galway's outstanding men in the early 1920s, and played a major role in taking his native county into the All-Ireland final of 1923 against a fancied Limerick side.

Galway, who had earlier beaten Kilkenny in the All-Ireland semi-final, really upset the odds in the decider with a magnificent victory by 7-3 to 4-5. These, of course, were unsettled days in Ireland and the championship programmes, often run under difficult circumstances, were sadly in arrears.

And it happened that this 1923 final was not played until 14 September 1924. During the running of that 1923 championship, Mick Gill, then a member of the Gardaí in Dublin, had declared for Dublin in the championships of 1924.

Dublin had swept all before them in Leinster, and just two months later, he had won his All-Ireland medal with Galway. He qualified for his second final that year when Dublin swept Antrim out of the race with an effortless semi-final win, 8-4 to 3-1 at Croke Park.

On 14 December, Gill took the field at Croke Park against his native Galway, and turned in a superb performance as the Metropolitan side held out to win by six points, 5-3 to 2-6. That brought him his second All-Ireland senior hurling medal of the year – an achievement which now ensures him a place all of his own in the colourful history of Gaelic games.

But there was to be another wonderful day in Mick Gill's career – and it probably brought him a greater satisfaction than those two medals of 1924.

In 1927, then with the all-conquering Garda Hurling Club, he took over the captaincy of the Dublin side which won out in Leinster and qualified to meet Cork in the All-Ireland final.

Dublin won by 4-8 to 1-3 and, even today, that victory is recalled as one of the major upsets in the history of All-Ireland finals.

Mick Gill remained in hurling for many years and before he finally called it a day, he had added six medals to his collection, the last with Faugh's in 1930.

A CEILIDH MOR, which was held in the Depot, Phœnix Park on Saturday night, 4th inst., in honour of the All Ireland's Hurling Champions, when Commissioner Gen. O'Duffy presented medals. Flashlight photo taken on the occasion. Names (reading from left to right):—
Sitting—Sean Ryan (Chairman, Dublin Co. Board); Commr. Gen. O'Duffy; Mr. L. O'Toole (Sec. Central Council, G.A.A.); Assist. Commr. Murphy.
Back Row—Capt. Howe (Vice-Chairman, Dublin Co. Board); Gd. M. Gill (Capt. Dublin Co. Team); Supt. Sean Gantly (i/c Hurling at Depot; Sean O'Neill (Dublin Co. Board); Sean O'Hanlon (Hon. Sec., I.A.H.A.).
Photo] [J. Merriman.

In 1928 Sean Gantly, a native of Roscrea, Co Tipperary was captain of the Garda intermediate hurling team which beat the Civil Service in the final. Twenty years later, in January 1948, he was shot dead in the Hammond Lane Foundries, Dublin, while confronting escaped armed criminals.

Chapter 22

The Legendary Paddy Colleran

'Great' is a word too often abused in sport. There can be little doubt, however, that it is a fitting description of Paddy Colleran – a man whose Gaelic football powers earned for him inter-county honours with six counties, as well as Tailteann Games awards, and inter-provincial jerseys with three provinces.

Few players, in fact, packed so much football and such a wide variety of teams into a career. as this talented son of County Sligo, who retired with the rank of Chief Superintendent. In the 1920s and early 1930s, he paraded his skills around midfield in a majestic style that was not matched by many – and that was an era of some superb footballers.

Just two of the famed names that immediately spring to mind from those years are Con Brosnan and Bob Stack of Kerry, whom Paddy Colleran rate as the greatest outfield players he met.

So, it could be fairly said of Colleran that he is the greatest footballer never to win an All-Ireland medal. Indeed, with better fortune, he might have landed that elusive award early in his career.

In 1923, he and three of his brothers were prominent in a Sligo team that beat Tipperary in the 1922 All-Ireland senior semi-final. But the Western county did not contest the final. Instead, following an objection, Sligo and Galway met in Connacht; Galway won that clash, and then lost the All-Ireland final.

Five Colleran brothers played with Sligo in the 1920s. They were also mighty bulwarks of the Curry club, and Paddy, himself, collected five county senior football medals in a row with the club in those years.

He was back in the All-Ireland senior championship scene in 1928, when Sligo won their first Connacht senior title, and lost the national semi-final to Cavan. Three years later, Paddy, ironically enough, was in the Cavan side that lost the All-Ireland semi-final to Kildare.

His inter-provincial career was a truly remarkable one. In 1924, while stationed in the South, he played with Munster in the Tailteann Games.

In 1927, he was the only Sligo man in the Connacht team that lost to Munster in the first Railway Cup final, and in the following years, he made a number of appearances with Ulster.

Nor does the representative story end there. In the second Tailteann Games, in 1928, Paddy was a team-mate of such as Johnny McDonnell (Dublin), Con Brosnan (Kerry). Jim Smith (Cavan) and Martin O'Neill (Wexford) in the Irish team which beat America.

This varied representative career is matched by Colleran's appearances on the inter-county and the club fronts. In addition to Sligo, he distinguished himself in the county jerseys of Galway, Mayo, Tipperary, Waterford and Cavan. A Sigerson Cup player with University College Galway, he added Waterford and Cavan county senior championships medals to his Sligo county awards. and also gained league mementos in Dublin with Garda.

Paddy captained Garda for a number of years in Dublin, at a time when the club had some great players and great teams. Under his captaincy, Garda figured in some stirring battles with all-powerful O'Tooles selections.

This extremely dedicated and enthusiastic performer also found time in his active career to swing a hurley. During a period of duty in Dungourney, in Cork, he played competitive hurling.

Colleran had a preference for midfield in football, but he also played in defence and attack.

His great career came to an end in 1933. Finding, understandably enough, that his old sharpness was just not as razor-edge keen as before, he decided that it was time to hang up his boots. There was a strange twist to his retirement. After his very last game, his football boots were stolen! Colleran had used the same boots for some years.

One wonders if the boots were stolen for their commercial value, or if they were secreted away by an ardent, or over-zealous, admirer, as souvenirs – as tangible links with an outstanding player. Whatever about that, this remarkable career of a truly remarkable player was probably best summed up by Paddy himself as he reminisced about past events: "I spent my whole life playing football."

But then, this brilliant ace from the west coast had a great love of the game. There was certainly a tradition of football in his family. However, Paddy himself was so attached to the game that, as he put it: "I was always sorry when any match was over."

Not surprisingly, he was dedicated in training. He spent many hours with a football, outside of the competitive scene, and he recalls that seven-a-side and five-a-side matches made the Curry players sharp and extremely fast runners during the club's great era of five Sligo county senior championships in succession.

In these days when substitution is such a feature of nearly all field games, the former great recalls that in his time it was almost regarded as a disgrace for a player to be taken off the field.

A man apart, then, in many ways – that's Paddy Colleran, and a man whose outstanding football career will ensure that he will always have a very prominent place in any gallery of greats of the game.

Chapter 23

The Thomas St George MacCarthy Cup: Garda V PSNI

Thomas St George MacCarthy (1862-1943) was an Irish rugby union international and founder member of the Gaelic Athletic Association, being present at Hayes Hotel, Thurles, Co Tipperary, Ireland at the Association's inaugural meeting on 1 November 1884. He was born at Bansha, County Tipperary, though he was often erroneously described as being a native of Kerry. This was due to the similarity of name with his father, George MacCarthy (1832-1902), Lieutenant of the Revenue Police, County Inspector of the RIC and a resident magistrate who was from

County Kerry, though working in Tipperary and residing in Bansha. The family used the rarer MacCarthy spelling of their surname, which appears more commonly as McCarthy.

At the time of the founding of the GAA, MacCarthy was a District Inspector of the Royal Irish Constabulary based at Templemore, County Tipperary. He moved to Dublin in 1877 and became a friend of Michael Cusack, who had a cramming school. He was coached by Cusack for an RIC cadetship examination in 1882, in which he took first place. In 1881, he joined Dublin University Football Club and was capped against Wales in 1882. Later in 1882, he was a member of the Dublin University team which won the Leinster Senior Cup, the inaugural year of this competition. He also played soccer with Limavady FC when he was stationed in the town in 1889, captaining the club in 1889.

His involvement in the GAA is notable, because in a later period there would be a ban for many years in the GAA on people who played rugby and soccer joining the Association, and this ban also applied to members of the British police and armed forces.

He had a great love of the game of hurling, which he witnessed being played in his native village by the local enthusiasts who were later to form the Galtee Rovers GAA Hurling and Football Club. He was a regular attendee at matches in Croke Park, to where he travelled from his home is Oakley Road, in the Dublin suburb of Ranelagh. He died in 1943, and was buried without fanfare in an unmarked grave in Deansgrange Cemetery, Dublin, though there is a family plot in the old graveyard at Bansha village, where his sister Kathleen MacCarthy is interred. Unlike the other six founding members of the GAA, very little has been done to commemorate MacCarthy, presumably due to his position as a member of the Royal Irish Constabulary. However, the GAA authorities erected a commemorative gravestone at Deansgrange, where it was unveiled on Wednesday, 18 November 2009 as part of the "re-dedication of Founder's Graves" programme to mark the 125th Anniversary of the founding of the GAA. There have also been calls for more recognition of his contribution to the GAA.

The two police forces in Ireland, An Garda Síochána and the Police Service of Northern Ireland (PSNI), have already honoured him by presenting the Thomas St George MacCarthy Cup for competition by members of the Garda GAA (Garda Thirds) and the Police Service of Northern Ireland. The first match was played in 2002. (*Source: Wikipedia*).

Chapter 24

"Did You Know?"

1. A special mention to Dan Stapleton, who joined An Garda Síochána in 1936. Dan won All-Ireland senior hurling medals in 1904, 1905 (captain) and 1907 with Kilkenny. At that time, the county club champions represented their county in the All-Ireland. Dan's club was Erins Isle, Castlecomer
2. Joe Kelly was born in New York, came to Ireland at a young age and played hurling for Galway in the 1920s.
3. Tony Davis (Cork) is the only player in the history of the GAA to hold an All-Ireland medal in all codes – senior (1989 and 1990), minor (1981), U21 (1983 and 1984) junior (1984) and club (1993).
4. Brian Murphy is the only member to win All Star awards in both Gaelic football (1973 and 1976) and hurling (1981), and is only one of eighteen players to have won both All-Ireland hurling (1976, 1977 and 1978) and football medals (1972).
5. The three Davis brothers, the aforementioned Tony, Don and Pat, all played senior football for Cork in the 1980s and 1990s.
6. The three Brennan brothers, Leo, Kieran and Dessie, all played senior football for Laois in the 1970s and 1980s.
7. The three Farrell brothers, Sean, Seamus and Kieran, all played senior hurling for Roscommon and played together in the 1970s and 1980s.
8. The three Brennan brothers, Leo, Kieran and Dessie, all played football for Laois in the 1960s, 1970s and 1980s, and David Brennan, son of Dessie, played football for Laois in the 2000s.
9. The three Connolly brothers: Martin and Gerry played football for Monaghan in the 1970s and 1980s, and their brother Sean played football for Leitrim in the 1960s.
10. Brothers Jack and Matt Kilroy were on the Tremane hurling team from Roscommon who won a Connacht club championship in 1977.
11. Brothers Des and John Kiernan played at midfield for the Westmeath hurling team in the mid-1960s.

12. Brothers Ollie and Greg Baker both played hurling for Clare in the 1990s.

13. Brothers Cathal and Nathy Cawley played football for Sligo in the 1960s.

14. Brothers Martin and Willie Hogan played for Carlow in the early 1960s. They played together in a National League match against Cork, with Martin marking the great Christy Ring.

15. Brothers Noel and Terry Blessing played football for Leitrim in the 1950s and 1960s.

16. Brothers Leo and Paddy English played football for Roscommon in the 1950s.

17. Brothers Luke and Patrick Colleran both played football for Sligo in the 1920s.

18. Brothers John and Dick Keating played football and hurling for Tipperary in the 1950s and 1960s. Dick also played hurling and football for Roscommon.

19. Sisters Linda and Sarah O'Connell played football for Cork in the 1990s and 2000s.

20. Liam and Des Maguire played football for Cavan in the 1950s, and their brother Brendan played for Meath also in the 1950s. They played against each other in the 1952 All-Ireland final.

21. Brothers Derek and Ken Duggan played football for Roscommon in the 1990s.

22. The Loughnane brothers: Colman Loughnane played hurling for Offaly in the 1970s, while Donal played hurling for Waterford in the 1980s.

23. Brothers Jack and Frank Reynolds played football for Leitrim and Westmeath respectively in the 1950s and 1960s.

24. The McHale brothers: Eugene McHale played football for Mayo in the 1970s and 1980s, and Eddie McHale played football for Mayo, Leitrim and Sligo in the 1970s and 1980s.

25. Garrett Howard played hurling for Tipperary, Limerick and Dublin in the 1920s and 1930s, and his granddaughter played camogie for Tipperary in the 2000s.

26. Joe Delaney played hurling for Louth in the 1960s and 1970s, and his son Aidan Delaney played football for Louth in the 1990s.

27. Danny Boyce played football for Donegal in the 1960s and 1970s, and his son Padraig played football for Galway in the 1990s.

28. John Bourke played hurling for Dublin in the 1970s, and his son Willie also played hurling for Dublin and Fingal in the 2000s.

29. Tim Doyle Snr played hurling for Kerry in the 1960s and 1970s, and his son Tim Jnr played football for Dublin in the 2000s.

30. John McGrath played football for Clare in the 1970s and 1980s, and his son Shane played football for Dublin and Clare in the 2010s.
31. P. J. McIntyre played football and hurling for Offaly and Kerry in the 1960s and 1970s, and his son P. J. played hurling for Kerry in the 1980s and 1990s.
32. Jim Quinn played football for Roscommon and Mayo in the 1940s, and his son Cormac played hurling for Wexford in the 1980s.
33. Pierce Freaney played hurling for Carlow, Kilkenny and Kildare in the 1960s, and his son Enda played football for Kildare in the 1990s and 2000s.
34. John O'Brien played hurling for Leitrim in the 1970s and his son Dermot played football with Clare in the 1990s and 2000s.
35. Pat Begley played football for Clare in the 1970s and 1980s, and his son Brian played hurling and football for Limerick in the 1990s and 2000s.
36. Christy Grogan Snr played football for Roscommon and Westmeath in the 1960s, and his son Chris Grogan Jnr played football for Roscommon in the 1980s.
37. Niall Moloney played hurling for Kilkenny in the 1990s, and his brother John played football for Kilkenny in the 1970s.
38. Seamus Keevans played football for Sligo, Wexford, Cavan, Waterford and Cork in the 1950s and 1960s, and his son Michael played for Wexford in the 1980s.
39. Brother and sister Enda Kenny and Ursula Kilcoyne both played for Roscommon in the 2000s.
40. Ex-Garda Peter Earley is a brother of the late Dermot and Paul Earley of Roscommon football fame.
41. Martin Langton played senior inter-county hurling for Kilkenny prior to joining the force in the early 1920s.
42. Brian Carroll became the first member to become a GAA county board secretary (Roscommon).
43. Tom Dee captained the Kerry minor football team to All-Ireland success in 1980, prior to joining the force. The same is true of Westmeath's Damien Gavin (1995).
44. Only two players in GAA history won two Tailteann medals: Jim O'Regan in 1928 and 1932 and Garrett Howard in 1924 and 1928.
45. In 1980, two Gardaí, Joachim Kelly (Offaly) and Mossie Walsh (Waterford) were selected at midfield in the All Star hurling team.
46. Three Gardaí were on the Kilmacud Crokes team which defeated St Columba's in the 1966 Dublin senior hurling final. They were Brian

Cooney (captain), Mick Regan (from Galway, who scored 2-2), and Jerry Keane (Dublin and Limerick, who scored 1-3, including the winning point in the dying seconds).

47. Three former inter-county players rose to the rank of Commissioner of the Force: Paddy Culligan (although from Kerry, played for Cork), Paddy McLoughlin (although from Donegal, played for Monaghan) and Fachtna Murphy (Cork).

48. Tribute has to be paid to the members of the force who were killed on duty and were stalwart GAA members: Detective Garda John Morley, who was murdered on 7 July 1980 played senior football for Mayo; Detective Garda Seamus Quaid, who was murdered on 7 October 1980, played senior hurling for Wexford; Garda Seamus McIntyre, who was killed in a car crash while on duty on 22 April 2001, played senior hurling for Kerry; Garda Ciaran Jones, who drowned trying to rescue people on 24 October 2011, played senior football for Wicklow. A special mention must also go to two members who were murdered on duty, and who although did not play inter-county at senior level, were exceptionally involved in the GAA: Garda Robert McCallion, who was murdered on 26 March 2009, was involved with Swinford GAA club and played U21 football with Mayo; Detective Garda Adrian O'Donohue, who was murdered in Bellurgan on 25 January 2013, played U21 football with Cavan.

49. The following members who were killed on duty are in An Garda Síochána's Roll of Honour with special mention of their connection with the GAA:

Harry Phelan (Laois) was murdered on 14 November 1922. On the day he was murdered, he was in a shop in Mullinahone, County Tipperary purchasing hurleys for a team he was starting.

John Roche (Limerick) was murdered on 3 January 1940. He was a keen Gaelic footballer.

James Downey (Cork) was killed in a traffic accident on 12 February 1972. He played Gaelic football and hurling with St Finbarr's.

John Lally (Mayo) was killed in a traffic accident on 5 March 1973. He played Gaelic football.

Walter Hennelly (Mayo) was killed in a traffic accident on 13 May 1974. He played Gaelic football.

Nathy Cawley (Sligo) was killed in a traffic accident on 24 February 1982. He played senior inter-county for Sligo and was a noted referee.

Pat Ruttledge (Sligo) was killed in the same accident on 24 February 1982. He was a member of the Monaghan Town hurling team.

J. J. Brennan (Wexford) was killed in a traffic accident on 4 August 1982. He played Gaelic football and hurling.

Tom Lawn (Donegal) was killed in a traffic accident on 27 April 1983. He was a keen GAA enthusiast.

Declan O'Connor (Dublin) was killed in a traffic accident on 17 May 1983. He played Gaelic Football.

Recruit Garda Gary Sheehan, who was murdered on 23 November 1983, was from Monaghan and played football with Carrick Emmetts.

Denis Connolly (Tipperary) was killed in a traffic accident on 11 July 1983. He played Gaelic football and hurling.

David Dowd (Longford) was killed by a train on 18 February 1989. He played Gaelic football.

Declan Roe (Offaly) was killed in a traffic accident on 13 July 1992. He played Gaelic football.

William Roche (Laois) was killed in a traffic accident on 1 August 1992. He played Gaelic football and hurling.

Richard Nolan (Carlow) was killed in a traffic accident on 26 September 1999. He played hurling.

Conor Griffin (Dublin) was killed in a traffic accident on 15 May 2000. He played hurling and was a member of Lucan Sarsfields.

George Rice was killed in a traffic accident along with Seamus McIntyre on 22 April 2001. He played Gaelic football and hurling.

John Eiffe (Meath) was accidentally killed on 7 December 2001. He played Gaelic football and hurling. Sean Eiffe Park in Ratoath was named in his honour in 2004.

Michael Padden (Mayo) was killed by a stolen vehicle at a checkpoint on 14 February 2002. He played Gaelic football for Belmullet.

Brian Kelliher was killed by a vehicle at the scene of a traffic accident on 25 February 2007. He played Gaelic football.

50. On 30 September 1955, a Garda football team played a New York selection in Croke Park in an exhibition match. The Garda team included Tom Langan and the New York team included Bill Carlos.

51. A senior football challenge match was played between Dublin and Sligo in Tubbercurry in the mid-1950s. Thirteen players on the "Dublin" team were Gardaí, all of whom were inter-county players. The line up was as follows: P. Duff, K. Scally, B. Byrne, J. F. O'Sullivan, T. O'Sullivan, D. O'Sullivan, C. O'Sullivan, T. Maguire, P. Harrington, J. Chatten, T. Langan, P. Irwin, O. Freaney, D. O'Neill, K. Heffernan. Substitutes: M. Moriarty, G. Spillane, A. Burke, G. McNadle, K. McDonough.

52. A Garda club team that played in the Dublin senior championship in the mid-1950s contained the following twelve inter-county players: D. O'Sullivan (Kerry and Dublin), T. Langan (Mayo), W. Shannon (Mayo), D. McCaffrey (Mayo), G. Daly (Galway), P. Harrington

(Cork), P. McCarthy (Clare), T. Maguire (Cavan), C. Godkin (Cork), J. Connell (Mayo), F. Evers (Galway) and T. O'Sullivan (Kerry).

53. A Garda team which played Geraldines in a league game in Croke Park in the early 1950s contained the following twelve inter-county players: Con O'Sullivan (Cork), Pat McGrath (Longford), Tim Ferguson (Roscommon), Mick Moriarty (Kerry), Gerry McArdle (Meath), Paddy Irwin (Mayo), Dan O'Sullivan (Kerry and Dublin), Kevin Scally (Offaly), Teddy O'Sullivan (Kerry), Tom Langan (Mayo), John F. O'Sullivan (Kerry), Paddy Harrington (Cork), Jack Duff (Kerry). Ger Spillane, who played minor for Kerry, was also on that team.

54. The 'C' Inter-District Champions in the mid-1950s featured the following ten inter-county players: Paddy Irwin (Mayo), Pat McGrath (Longford), Tom Langan (Mayo), Pat McCarthy (Clare), Pat Daly (Kildare), Mick Guthrie (Clare), Tom Maguire (Cavan), Jack Chatten (Sligo), Dan O'Sullivan (Dublin and Kerry).

55. The Donegal team that won the Ulster Hurling Championship in 1923 featured eleven Gardaí: Dan Lenihan (Limerick), James Clooney (Wexford), P. McMahon (Clare), J. Carroll (Limerick), M. Mulhall (Kilkenny), P. Tobin (Clare), M. Kelleher (Clare), Dan Taylor (Tipperary), Twomey (Limerick), E. White (Kerry), M. Ryan (Limerick).

56. An inter-provincial hurling final was played on 31 May 1967 at O'Toole Park, Kimmage between DMA and Munster.
DMA: P Verdon (Pearse Street), P Harte (Kevin Street), S Walsh (Pearse Street), E Coogan (Kevin Street), J O'Donnell (Blackrock), J Hearne (Chapelizod), N Power (Traffic Dept), J Doran (Blackrock), V Duffe (Kevin Street), M O'Brien (Cabra), P Daly (Donnybrook), M Regan (Store Street), T Purcell (Dun Laoghaire), M Hayes (Dalkey, captain), W Murphy (Store Steet), C Minnock (Rathfarnham), D Fenton (Pearse Street), B Cooney (Store Street), E Carey (Dublin Castle), P Enright (Chapelizod).
Munster: C Doocey (Waterford/Kilkenny), J Lordan (Clare), W Maloney (Kerry), N Quill (Kerry), S English (Tipperary), N Power (Kerry), J Keating (Cork East), G Lohan (Clare), M O'Loughlin (Cork East), N Lane (Clare), P McGovern (Waterford/Kilkenny), P Freeney (Cork East), T Kelly (Cork East), M Barry (Cork East), J Cullinane (Tipperary), P Kearns (Tipperary), M Quinn (Kerry), J O'Sullivan (Waterford/Kilkenny), J Dowling (Tipperary), P Flanagan (Limerick), E Doyle (Waterford/Kilkenny), J Murphy (Limerick), K Mannion (Limerick).

57. An inter-provincial football final was played on 30 May 1967 in Croke Park between DMA and Connaught/Ulster.

DMA: J McGuinness (Clontarf), B O'Connor (Cabra), N Colleran (Chapelizod), F McArdle (Bridewell), P King (Pearse Street), J. J. O'Reilly (Store Street), W Molloy (Store Street), P Hallinan (Dublin Castle), T Blessing (Bridewell), A Breslin (Fitzgibbon Street), F Kennedy (Tallaght, captain), P Lawlor (Cabra), T Scanlon (Pearse Street), H Hammil (Pearse Street), J McMenamin (Dundrum), T King (Dalkey), J Healy (Kilmainham), A Breen (Harcourt Terrace).
Connaught/Ulster: D Kelly (Roscommon), J Kenny (Roscommon), J Manicle (Galway), B Tighe (Cavan), J Cassidy (Sligo), F Reynolds (Mayo), P Mockler (Galway), C Cawley (Mayo, captain), D Thomas (Cavan), P Dolan (Roscommon), P Clancy (Cavan), S Ferriter (Donegal), P Dolan (Mayo), S McMenamin (Roscommon), J MCNelia (Roscommon), S Durkan (Donegal), J Weir (Galway).

A Garda Team of All-Ireland Medal Holders …

The following team of All-Ireland medal holders was supplied by Tony Burke, who played senior football for Kildare between 1943 and 1953 and won a Dublin senior championship medal with the Garda team in 1948:

1. John Kerins (Cork), 2. Jas Murphy (Kerry), 3. Jim Smith (Cavan), 4. Brian Murphy (Cork), 5. Paul Russell (Kerry), 6. Bill Carlos (Roscommon), 7. Brendan Lynch (Roscommon), 8. Larry Stanley (Kildare), 9. Paddy Kennedy (Kerry), 10. Pat Griffin (Kerry), 11. Mick Higgins (Cavan), 12. Charlie Sullivan (Kerry), John McCarthy (Dublin), 14. Tom Langan (Mayo), 15. John Egan (Kerry). Subs: Paddy Prendergast (Mayo), Liam Gilmartin (Roscommon), Phil 'Gunner' Brady (Cavan), Tim O'Donnell (Kerry), Gerry Daly (Galway), Tom Keogh (Kildare) and Paddy Irwin (Mayo).

Garda inter-provincial competition, 1984

The GAA celebrated the centenary of its foundation in 1984. To mark this special milestone, a Garda inter-provincial Gaelic football competition was played. In the semi-finals, Leinster defeated Connaught/Ulster and Munster were victorious over the DMA from Dublin.

In a high quality final, Leinster overcame the men from Munster after a hard fought game. The winning Leinster team panel, containing fifteen inter-county players, was

as follows: Aidan McHugh (Roscommon), Seamus Reynolds (Mayo),

Jimmy McManus (Roscommon), John Keane (Tipperary), Michael O'Riordan (Tipperary), Pat Spollen (Offaly), Eddie Tynan (Westmeath), Noel O'Dowd (Roscommon), Philip Kiernan (Longford), Gerry Sheridan (Cavan), Michael Keevans (Wexford), Matt Connor (Offaly), Ben Tansey (Roscommon), Stephen Kinneavy (Galway), Mick Lowry (Westmeath), John Walsh (Westmeath) and Pascal Hanrahan (Tipperary).

An intrepid GAA career:

Superintendent Joseph Murray joined the GAA in 1906, with future Garda Commissioner Eoin O'Duffy's club, Monaghan Harps, and from there built up a long record of service to Gaelic games. In 1909-10, he was a member of Monaghan County Board, and from 1910-12 was the honorary secretary and secretary of the North Monaghan (Toal) League. He was an organiser, a playing member of the St Tiernach's club in Clones, and a member of Ulster Council. In 1913, he was acting secretary  of Ulster Council, and from 1913-14 honorary secretary of Erin's Own hurling club, St Patrick's Training College, Drumcondra (winners of the Co. Dublin junior championship and All-Ireland Colleges Championship), and delegate to Dublin junior county board. In 1915, he was appointed honorary secretary of Loughrea GAA in Galway, and successfully established a new Kickham Association of GAA in Co. Galway. From 1918 to 1922, as the Irish Revolution played out, he assisted in organising the GAA in Donegal and became a member of the county's first county board; he also became a Donegal representative on Ulster Council and a delegate to Congress, a club player (1921-22) and a member of the Donegal senior football team in 1922. Rising to the rank of Superintendent in the fledgling Garda force in the mid-1920s, he was subsequently involved in organising football and hurling teams in west Waterford (1924-25), became a member of Waterford County Board, and a delegate to the Munster Convention, 1925.

The Seamus O'Reilly Memorial Cup, 2001-2013

The Seamus O'Reilly Memorial Cup Tournament was run from 2001 to 2013 as a tribute to Seamus. This tournament comprised each region fielding their best Gaelic football players, culminating in a final. The tournament would have featured the cream of inter-county players from every region. The competition was sponsored annually by St Paul's Garda Credit Union, Cork. The following is taken from a programme issued to mark the final:

"The late Seamus O'Reilly is fondly remembered by his many colleagues and friends for many reasons. A native of Lacken in Co. Mayo, he joined An Garda Síochána in 1974. After his graduation from Templemore, he was posted to Co. Donegal, where he worked for many years.

"Seamus was a devoted GAA man. He played with considerable distinction for Mayo at both minor and under 21 level. Following his posting in Donegal, he immediately became involved in the GAA in his adopted county. He joined Bundoran GAA club, and in the years that followed enjoyed considerable success. It was a tribute to his talent that he also went on to represent Donegal at senior level. During these years he became an extremely well known player across the North east and beyond.

"It says much for the type of man that Seamus was that he did not end his involvement with the GAA after his retirement from playing. He became involved in the management of various teams. He also served as a club official and was involved in the administrative side of things.

"Overall, Seamus was a talented sportsman who could have thrived in many sports; it just happened that GAA was his first love. For example, Seamus was a fine golfer who played to a very respectable handicap.

"Until his death Seamus worked tirelessly for the good of the community.

"He was renowned as a very kind and considerate man. It was while taking part in a charity cycle in April 1999 that his sudden death occurred. It was a huge loss to friends and colleagues, but, of course, a much greater one to his family. Seamus is survived by his wife, Rosalee, and his four children Lauren, Rebecca, Stephen and Michaela.

"Ar dheis Dé go raibh a anam."

Photographs of teams taking part in the Seamus O'Reilly Memorial Cup:

Seamus McIntyre
Garda Hurling Tournament

The Seamus McIntyre Memorial Garda Hurling Tournament takes place every year by way of a tribute to the late Seamus McIntyre, who was tragically killed while on duty on 22 April 2001. To commemorate his life, the McIntyre family donated a cup to the Garda College GAA club, and every year, Garda hurlers participate in an annual tournament. The tournament is an eleven-a-side blitz.

The competition started in 2002, and is still being played on an annual basis, with Mick Morrissey hugely influential in its longevity.

Seamus McIntyre Tournament 2012
Back row, from left:
Paul Aherne, Declan Healy, Paul Shanahan, Denis O'Sullivan, Tom Delaney, Jimmy Smiddy, Jerry O'Connor, Vincent Hurley, Brian Smiddy.
Front row, from left:
Danny Culloty, Ger Melvin, Shannon Ryan, Damien Ring, Ger O'Leary, Jeremy Hurley.

Seamus McIntyre Tournament 2012
Back row, from left:
Liam Phillips, Philip Hayes, Shane Kelly, Tim O'Donovan, Dave Slattery, John Horgan,
Ken O'Donovan, John Fitzgerald, Willie Tobin, Pa Finnegan, Dave O'Shea, Tom Tobin,
Kieran Lynch.
Front row, from left:
Mick Dowling, Pat Sexton, Tony O'Connor, Ray Massey, Shay Lyons.

Seamus McIntyre Tournament 2014
Back row, from left:
Danny Culloty, Ger O'Leary, David Cuthbert, Shane Fitzgerald, Diarmaid Lane,
Cormac Dineen, Shannon Ryan, Philip Taylor, Brian Smiddy, Ger Melvin, Jimmy Smiddy.
Front row, kneeling:
Tom Delaney, Jeremy Hurley.

Seamus McIntyre Tournament 2014

Photo includes:

Barry O'Donnell, Dave Givens, Brian Begley, Kevin Mulryan, Kevin Dilleen, Sean Kennedy, Niall O'Connor, Barry O'Grady, Niall Donovan, Conor McNamara, Michael Fitzgerald, Noel Nash, Jamie O'Connor, Dave Boland, Brian O'Dwyer, Bryan Darcy, Pat Brennan.

Missing from photo:

Caimin Treacy.

Seamus McIntyre Tournament 2015

Back row, from left:

Paul Aherne, Jimmy Smiddy, David Hickey, Diarmaid Lane, Ger Whelton, Shane Fitzgerald, Brian Maher, Brian Smiddy, Ger O'Leary, David Cuthbert.

Front row, from left:

Liam Ryan, Jeremy Hurley, Danny Culloty, Shannon Ryan, Denis O'Sullivan, Ger Melvin, Niall Hayes.

Seamus McIntyre Tournament in 2008
Back row, from left:
Pat Whelan, A. N. Other, Kevin Hoban, Sean Kennedy, Dave Kelly, Brian Culbert.
Front row, from left:
Paul Flynn (RIP), Niall Donovan, Barry O'Donnell, Damien Kennedy, A. N. Other,
Caimin Treacy.

Garda Referees and Managers

There have been many inter-county referees who have served in the Force over the years. Former county footballers and hurlers who went on to become referees after their playing days were over are documented in their profiles in previous chapters. The members listed below were/are noted inter-county referees.

Referees

Michael Curley: a native of Galway who played minor football for Galway; Refereed All-Ireland minor finals in 1995 and 1998; refereed All-Ireland senior final in 1999; refereed the 1998 International Rules match, Ireland v Australia.

Others were: Christy Browne, Con Crowley, Michael Daly, Shane Farrell, Willie Feeley, Pierce Freaney, Denis Harrington, D. M. A. Helferty, Mick Higgins, Declan Hunt, Mick Keane, Alan Kelly, Joe Kelly, Harry Lamb, Liam Maguire, Eugene McHale, Pat McKenna, Sean McManamon, Mick O'Neill, Jim O'Regan, Peter Roberts, Pat Silke, Adrian Walsh, Francie Ward, Sean Whelan. Of these, Pat McKenna refereed two All-Ireland finals; Liam Maguire refereed the All-Ireland final in 1961; Pat Silke refereed the 1958 All-Ireland minor final and won a senior championship medal with the Limerick Garda team in 1958.

Inter-County Managers

There are other members who, although not representing their counties at senior level, have become accomplished managers:

Tom McGlinchey, a native of Cork (football). Manager of the Tipperary senior team 1999-2003, Limerick minor team 2010-2012, Limerick junior team 2013, and Waterford senior team 2014-present.

Peader Healy, manager of the Cork senior football team 2015 to 2017.

Billy Blackwell, who trained the Laois senior football team which reached the All-Ireland final in 1936.

Pat Nally trained the Athenry team that won the All-Ireland Club Championship in 2000 and 2001.

There have also been many members who became inter-county managers. Former players who were managers can be found in their profiles: Ollie Baker, Eamonn Barry, Pat Begley, Mick Behan, Seamus Bonner, Willie Bourke, Eddie Brennan, Kieran Brennan, Noel Brett, Colm Browne, Paul Caffrey, Nigel Carey, Mark Carroll, John Evans, Gerry Fahy, Sean Farrell,

Willie Feeley, Pete Finnerty, Mick Galvin, Joe Hayes, Dick Hearns, Mick Higgins, Ken Hogan, Teddy Holland, Garrett Howard, Jim Hughes, James Kearns, Liam Kearns, Joachim Kelly, Kevin Kennedy, Jack Kilroy, Mick Lillis, Liam Maguire, Michael McCormack, Gerry McManus, Barnes Murphy, Fergal O'Donnell, Seamus O'Reilly, Páidí Ó Sé, Peter Queally, Paul Russell, David Ryan, Jack Sheedy, Kevin Walsh.

The Gloucester Diamond episode

All those members of An Garda Síochána who served in Store Street and Fitz Garda Stations will certainly remember the Gloucester Diamond area of Dublin, particularly during the 1950s, 1960s and 1970s.

One such member is Mick Behan, who played senior GAA football for Dublin between 1973 and 1976. Mick was based in Store Street, and was summons server for the 'C' District. At the time, the Gloucester Diamond were running a five-a-side soccer tournament to acquire money to purchase sporting equipment to help the youth in the inner city area, and encourage them away from crime. Mick was approached by a Gabriel Murphy from St Bridget's Gardens, North Wall, a tremendous organiser, enquiring if he would be interested in entering a Garda team for this tournament. Mick was certainly agreeable, and got his team of players together with the great Tom Troy as their manager. Apparently there was a certain trepidation among the upper echelons of An Garda Síochána as to whether this was a good idea or not.

However, Mick went ahead in the summer of 1975. They togged out in Store Street Station and the whole team jogged out across Talbot Street down Foley Street and on to the Gloucester Diamond, where they were greeted with clapping and a standing ovation from the supporters of the tournament. Some of the well-known companies from around the city had teams entered, including one by the great Johnny Giles. At half time some of the younger people attending asked Mick, "Who is the guy in the backs?" – they did not recognise him as being from Store Street or Fitz Street. He was a brother-in-law of Mick who invited him to play with the team. Mick whispered to them that he was from the Special Branch – they whispered back, "We wont tell anyone!".

As a result of this very innovative gesture by Mick Behan, the manager of their team, Tom Troy, became one of the first Community Officers to be appointed for the inner city area. Mick Behan resigned from An Garda Síochána in 1977 and studied to become a sports therapist as well as a cranio-sacral therapist in Carlow. He also conducts counselling and hypnosis sessions. In his spare time, he can be seen floating like a butterfly

Gloucester Diamond Soccer Team – C District
Front Row:
Liam Doran, Mick Behan, Brian Fenton, Mick McKenna
Back Row:
Tadgh Harrington, Mick O'Connor, Pat Corry, John Costello, Mick Killeen, Tony P,
Tom Troy, Manager,

Tadgh Harrington played senior football with Cork. Brian Fenton is the father of the current
Dublin football centre field player – also named Brian.
Mick Behan played senior football from Dublin from 1973 to 1976 and won leinster football
and hurling championships medals with St Vincent's Club in Dublin

around many ballrooms, particularly in Dolmen's Hotel, Carlow and Tougher's Ballroom in Naas, as a very accomplished dancer – akin to poetry in motion. Like many members of our esteemed body known as An Garda Síochána, Dr Michael Behan has many strings to his bow.

Crossing the Line – from GAA to Rugby
Noel Hynes.

In the late 1960s, Jerry McManus, then playing senior football with his native Sligo and an esteemed member of An Garda Síochána, was approached by an experienced Garth Rugby player who had attended a Rugby School in his day, inviting him to play with the Garda Rugby team.

Jerry explained to him that he had never kicked a rugby ball. The colleague retorted that if he could kick a GAA football he could also kick a rugby ball. The Garda Rugby team were due to play a game that evening and this Rugby mentor pointed out to Jerry that he was short a few players due to injury etc, hence his request. As Jerry was free and a type of an obliging individual he agreed and duly turned up for the match complete with boots and togs and was handed the no 15 jersey.

He was given brief instructions as to how he should play - call a mark, kick to touch, wrap around tackle etc. Jerry enjoyed the experience and could visualise International Caps looming. He attended training sessions and continued being selected at no 15 for subsequent matches. At the end of the season the highlight was always the game v the RUC which was played in Donnybrook and Jerry was selected to play retaining his place at no 15. The game was given subslantial media coverage in the newspapers the following day, including photos of the teams. Shortly after that our Jerry was notified by the Sligo GAA County Board that as a consequence of having played a foreign game he was being suspended under rule 27. As Jerry was nearing the end of his GAA career any way he decided to make the suspension permanent and certainly had no regrets. He subsequently coached the seniors hurlers of Ballyduff in Kerry while based there, winning a few County titles as well as coaching the Kerry senior hurlers. Not many ex county footballers, if any, have taken on the task of coaching hurlers. (It is known as mixing the codes)

Eoin O'Duffy, Commissioner of An Garda Síochána and long time GAA Official
Noel Hynes

If Eoin O'Duffy had not become Commisioner of An Garda Síochána in September 1922 it could be stated that the link between An Garda Síochána and the GAA would be quite different to day. He was a man of indefatigable energy a born organiser and a tireless worker. He placed strong emphasis on sport recognising that the RIC had never integrated culturally with the people consequently ensuring that Gaelic games were fostered with great enthusiasm in the force. O'Duffy ensured that the Garda Síochána became a focal point throughout the country resulting in many young people being coached as hurlers, footballers and handballers by friendly members of An Garda Síochána. Indeed Garda support provided a badly needed stimulus in areas where native games had previously not gained local acceptance.

He had been involved in administrative positions with the GAA as far back as 1910 and was elected as Sec of the Monaghan Co. Board in 1912 at the young age of 20 and as Sec of the Ulster Council the following year holding that position up to 1923. As far as can be ascertained O'Duffy never played football or hurling but used his administrative talents to great effect in fostering Gaelic games particularly among the new Garda force after he became Commissioner of An Garda Síochána in 1922. He is given much of the credit for the emergence of a respected non political and unarmed Police Force. He insisted on a Catholic nationalist ethos to distinguish his force from their RIC predecessors and importantly instructed all members to avoid the use of alcohol of which he was a vocal opponent.

Eoin O'Duffy was born in Laragh, Castleblayney, Co. Monaghan in October 1890 and died in a Nursing Home in Ballsbridge in 1944 at the age of 54. He received a State Funeral and was buried in Glasnevin Cemetry not far from Michael Collins, after Mass in the Pro Cathedral In his retirement years he is reported as stating that he had made two mistakes in his life - he had not married and that he had entered politics. He is the only native of Monaghan given a State funeral.

In 1926 Eoin O'Duffy attended an International Police Conference in New York where he was interviewed by the Editor of the New York Evening Post who stated in his subsequent article that "O'Duffy was one of the most popular Police Chiefs attending the Conference. Although he proved one of King George's most rebellious subjects, together with Michael Coffins and Arthur Griffith, General O'Duffy has brought peace and quiet to Ireland in the two years since he headed the Police Force. Although no man was more ready than General O'Duffy to seize a gun and fight for the cause of Ireland in the days of guerrilla warfare against the King's men, to-day not one of his Policemen, 7,000 in all, carries a gun of any description". That Editor goes on to give the following most unusual description of our Eoin O'Duffy. "General Eoin O'Duffy has just turned thirty two and the average age of his Civic Guard is twenty three. This man who carried a price on his head for three years, never lost the smile in his blue eyes nor the lightening power of his right arm. He has a laugh for a friend, a blow for a foe, and looks the world straight

in the eye. Standing straight as an arrow, lean and strong, and looking remarkably well set up in his blue tunic and slacks, black Sam Brown belt and scarlet insignia of rank, General O'Duffy inspires confidence in his ability to keep turbulent Ireland in the palm of his hand. He knows his Irish and has shed his blood for them in the conflict with England. Three times he was wounded.

You will look in vain for the index finger of his right hand, shot off in one of his numerous engagements. He was with Michael Collins earlier in the day when the leader was shot down in ambush, and escaped three times himself from ambuscades. His words stream out in a sharp crackle, like a machine gun burst. When his thin lips are unsmiling they make a firm hard line at right angles to a thin hawk nose. His Irish blue eyes freeze suddenly into two points of ice". During that interview O'Duffy stated as follows - "I had no special qualification for a Policeman. Organisation was my forte. The Guard needed that. The members of the RUC. could'nt be taken back because of the part they played in the war with England. The Irish had been looking long for an unarmed, non sectarian, non political Police. We gave them that. We'll serve any government chosen by the Irish people. I have no interest in or time for politics. I work seventeen hours a day. The only holidays I have taken have been to attend the 1923 Conference and this one. We have an efficient Police Force in Ireland. The men are young, very hard worked, and have the confidence of all sections of the people. They are known for their courtesy and efficiency". O'Duffy's assertion that he was non political is contradicted by Fearghal McGarry in his Autobiography - "Eoin O'Duflr: A Self Made Hero" - where he poses the question "Was this simple fighter genuine in O'Duffy's case? Or was he always a politician at heart".

General Eoin O'Duffy, although a controversial figure in Irish society, must be given credit for the part he played during the ten years he was Commissioner of An Garda Síochána and the great involvement of that organisation with the GAA. As stated by Conor McMorrow in his book -Dail Stars, published in 2010, "O'Duffy left a legacy in the GAA and Irish sport that should not be forgotten".

It has to be acknowledged that due to his encouragement and guidance there are now 127 Garda footballers holding senior All Ireland medals and 89 members holding senior All Ireland hurling medals. No other single organisation in this State can boast such a tremendous collection.

Sources

Guardians of the Peace by Conor Brady, 1974.
Dail Stars by Conor McMorrow, 2010.
The GAA - A history of the Gaelic Athletic Association by Marcus de Burca.
Eoin O'Duffy: A Self Made Hero by Fearghal McGarry, 2005.
Garda Times, Winter 2000.
RBISS Year Book and Diary, 1977.
Ireland's Eye, July 2004.

The Ancient Game of Hurling
Noel Hynes.

Back in 1923 the following article appeared in *Iris An Garda* in their April edition, written by Crawford Neil under the heading "Plea for Hurling". At that time members of An Garda Síochána were ruling the roost on the hurling playing fields of Ireland under the guidance of the Garda Commissioner, General Eoin O'Duffy, culminating in the winning of the Senior All Ireland Hurling Final in 1927. The following is an edited edition of that article.

"Those who were fortunate enough to be present at the thrilling contest in Croke Park on Sunday 25th of March, between the Limerick and Kilkenny hurlers will be keenly anxious to know if the GAA intends taking steps to see that the premier national pastime is in future given the attention which is its due. No matter what may happen in regard to other games and branches of sport in this country, it is incumbent on all to keep hurling going with greater vigour in the years before us than in the past. This because of the pride of place it has ever held amongst all other forms of athletic prowess in Ireland.

It is the Irishman's game, and as such, must be given every encouragement by those whose first duty is to propagate and foster the pastimes that are racy of the soil. From a health giving viewpoint it has no equal, bringing, as it does every nerve and sinew of the body into action, and requiring great judgement of the eye and skill and strength of arm that cannot but be beneficial. People who have not played it will tell you it is dangerous. This is admitted by the hurler, and an accurate record would, I am sure, uphold his contention that there are far more injuries of a serious nature sustained at football, whether under the Gaelic, Soccer, or Rugby codes. There is no game that will give more pleasurable excitement and enthusiasm to a crowd of spectators than a good hurling match. And with truth, indeed, it has been said that *"the swish of the caman is as music to the ear"*.

Hurling is, beyond a shadow of doubt, the most ancient of the Irish games. We read in history that it was played by the prince and kings of Ireland even before the birth of Christ. It has outlived the trials and persecutions that visited us, until to day we find it is still foremost amongst the games of the Gael. With our exiles in America (North and South), Australia, South Africa, England, Scotland and Wales, it is, in the absence of the language, a hallmark of our nationality more distinctly Irish than anything else of which I know".

Ninety-five years after the above article appeared, the ancient game of hurling is still thriving and will certainly continue to do so. Like the said author, I also contend that it is definitely the most exciting game in the world - without a shadow of doubt it is music to the ear akin to Rachmaninov's Rhapsody on a Theme of Paganini. Indeed Tom Humphries aptly sums up the game of hurling when writing in Hibernia in the Winter 2000 edition as *"Hurling isn't merely a patch of grass, two goal posts and thirty players in search of a ball. The game is the most common expression of our hunger for poetry, the truest expression of Ireland's wild beauty. Hurling is art wrapped up in sport"*. Similarly, Paul Healy writing in his book *"Gaelic Games and the Gaelic Athletic Association"* published in 1998, states that *"There are many Irishmen and women who have reason to link God with the game of hurling when it has been seen at its most exhilarating"*. Paul goes on to state that *"What magic the great hurlers possess. The hurler in full flight silences the whispered protests of pretenders. No soccer or rugby player, or Gaelic footballer either, finds it easy o state his case when confronted with the hurler in motion. It is awesome, gracious and sublime "*.

It is very gratifying then that the Garda Síochána organisation have played a leading role with the GAA in ensuring that this great game of hurling will continue to survive for ever. I salute all my Garda comrades who have contributed magnanimously in demonstrating their skill with the caman from 1922 up to the present day Mick Gill, Garrett Howard, "Fowler" Mclnerney, Mattie Power, Terry Kelly, Mick Regan, Frank Cummins, Peter Finnerty, Ollie Baker, Joachim Kelly, Seamus Quaid, Mick Morrissey, Noel Casey, Eddie Brennan, Brian Murphy, Ken Hogan, Mossy Walsh, Jim Doran, Moses Morrissey, Jerry O'Connor, Peter Quelly, and many more, all of them echoing the words of that famous Cork hurler Jack Lynch, when he stated back in 1968 that *"The true hurler is a man of dignity, proud of his heritage, skilful, well disciplined and a sportsman"*.

Contrast Jack's view with that of the Rev Seathrun Ceitinn (Geoffrey Keating c.1569-c1644) a 17th Century Historian, born in Co. Tipperary, who was scathing of the activities of the young men of his time, referring to them as *"foolish young men leading a wild life, playing hurling, shooting darts and arrows, drinking and playing, swearing and bubbling"*. He saw these activities including hurling, *"as an occasion of sin and devoid of decency, diligence., gravity, modesty, orderliness, prudence,reason, self control, sobriety and thrift"*.

Like Jack Lynch, P. D. Mehigan (1884-1965) a GAA Correspondent for the Cork Examiner writing under the pseudonym "Carbery", also had a contrasting view to the Rev. Geoffrey Keating, when referring to the great game of hurling, stating that *"It teaches reckless courage, initiative, speed of thought and action; it encourages collective effort, mutual respect, gallant sportsmanship, discipline, fair play, self control, agility and uniform development".*

In my opinion it would be very appropriate indeed to conclude this article by quoting Michael Cusack (1847-1906) the founding member of the GAA in 1884, with his views on our wonderful ancient game of hurling. *"When I reflect on the sublime simplicity of the game, the strenght, the swiftness, of the players, their appararentlyangelic impetuosity, the apparent recklessness of life and limb, their magic skill, their marvellous escapes and the overwhelming pleasure they give their friends, I have no hesitation in saying that the game of hurling is in the front rank of the fine arts"*

A poignant letter written by Kerry footballer Jack Murphy in 1926

with kind permission of Weeshie Fogarty

What follows is an historic letter written by Kerry footballer, Garda Jack Murphy following the 1926 All-Ireland drawn final. He died before the replay. Our thanks to his great grand nephew Joe McGill for allowing us to make it available to followers.

Jack Murphy was a native of Ballycarbery. He joined the Gardaí and won his first All-Ireland in 1924. He played in 1925 and again in 1926 when Kerry drew with Kildare in the All-Ireland final. Jack was the hero in the drawn final with a man of the match display. He organised collective training in Tralee for the replay. The *'Over the Water'* man was put up in a bed and breakfast in Tralee where he developed pneumonia, perhaps from wearing wet clothes after training. Jack was very ill when Kerry won the replay, and he died eleven days later at the tender age of twenty-two. A cup in honour of Jack was donated in 1969 by his family to the St Mary's club for an inter-county tournament on Whit Sunday. When the county leagues put paid to these tournaments, it was given to the South Kerry GAA board for the South Kerry championship. It was first presented by chairman Micheal Lyne (grandnephew of Jack) to Joe Joe O'Sullivan, winning captain for Renard in 1975.

Jack's sister Nell gave the letters to her nephew Denis Lynch, who in turn gave them to Mary Ann McGill, grandniece of Jack Murphy. Below is the letter to Nell Flahive, Jack's sister, who later retired from America to Ballybunion with her husband Jim.

Phoenix Park Depot,
Dublin
14/9/26

My Dear Nell,

*We lined out against Kildare at 3:30 before a gathering estimated at over 40,000. It was some crowd indeed. We were really lucky to make it a drawn game as we were outclassed for at least 40 minutes of the game but the boys make a grand rallying in the last quarter of an hour and equalised. Nevertheless I think we were unlucky in the closing stages in not winning by the smallest of margins. However we will have another day to decide the issue. The crowd went frantic with excitement when we drew level can still picture headgear floating in the air. I met Denny **[Jack's brother]** on our way to Barry's and he was scarcely able to speak, you can imagine the excitement that prevailed. We spent a most enjoyable evening in Howth and got back at 2am but did not get to bed till 6am, absolutely fagged out. The replay may take place on the 10th of October and all are looking forward to the keenest of struggles, which will I am sure will surpass any of the old time encounters with Kildare. The match was broadcasted during the play so that many had full details without going to see it. Phil Sullivan was injured but may be fit for the replay. I am sending you a couple of press cuttings just to give you and Jim an idea of the match though I'm afraid one of them is rather flattering in the extreme. However, it will make good reading for you too who will be interested. I am sure we may go to Tralee again for training at the end of the month. My letters will be forwarded, however, so I will be eagerly awaiting a line from you and Jim.*

With best wishes to yourself and Jim from your affectionate brother,

Jack

Sigerson Clifford wrote The Ghost Train for Croke Park ballad about this drawn All- Ireland Final with Kildare. The last two verses are as follows:

Then the soft grass and the sunshine and the marching of the bands
With the green and gold flag fluttering over all
There's Con Brosnan running swiftly and our Sheehy shooting low
And Larry Stanley jumping skyhigh for the ball.
It put the heart across me when the leather grazed our goal,

And my throat with shouting tattered like a scraw
There was never sweeter music than that final whistle blown,
And the board said, let me whisper, 'twas a draw.

Loud and long we held the inquest steaming home from Dublin town
And we wrote down who kicked well and who played poor
But John Pete agreed with me that all the luck was with Kildare
And Bob Doyle maintained we'd win the next time sure.
We still chalked up the scoreboard and the chalk was green and gold,
Said the Tailor, white teeth grinning like a shark,
Sure we only took their measure and we'll cut the cloth to scale
When we take the Ghost Train three weeks for Croke Park.

Garda Sportsmen
by Liam Hayes

Contributed to Sport in the Garda:
a Souvenir of the Silver Jubilee of Coiste Siamsa, 1962-1987

The immediate difficulty in reviewing the immensely successful history of the Garda Athletic Association is choosing where to start. How can twenty five years, the work of thousands of men and women, and the impressions which they have made in every walk of sport be adequately covered in one article, or one book. The thought would leave me weak at the knees if I wasn't already sitting down. Luckily, the truth of the matter is that it cannot be done.

Where could you start? On a personal note, by choosing an acquaintance, say Matt Connor or Paul Reyfus? By opening with an historical blast and lavishing praise on the pioneers of Garda sport? Or by breathing life into the legendary careers of men like Larry Stanley and Ned Tobin? Or instead should the present day members who have strengthened the Garda Athletic Association into a powerful body comprising 26 different sports be promptly awarded pride of place? It's safer and much more sensible to mention them all, in a single paragraph. It's done.

Of the many hundreds of Gardaí who have excelled as sportsmen over the last sixty years, and including the men who were honoured with silver jubilee awards at a gala banquet in Dublin last November, it is difficult to find anyone who was more readily identified as a Garda and an outstanding athlete as Matt Connor. The tragic conclusion to his career shocked so many of his fellow members in the Force and many thousands of football fans throughout the country. They had watched his beautiful and artistic

199

skills as Offaly spent six years waiting to be crowned All-Ireland champions in 1982, and they witnessed him as a Garda on duty inside Croke Park on many major occasions.

In this writer's opinion he was perhaps the most brilliant footballer in the history of the GAA. Certainly his scoring exploits devoured most of the records which had existed. The re-written history books now record him as someone who once scored two goals and ten points in an All-Ireland semi-final, and a recipient of two All-Star awards, three Leinster medals and one All-Ireland. They really only serve as an injustice to the man, and fail to take into account his natural brilliance as an athlete and what he certainly would have achieved had he not suffered such severe injuries in a car accident. And most unfortunately they are unable to recall his complete honesty and fairness which were always obvious whether he was a 'footballer' or a 'Garda'.

But how can anyone attempt to compare Connor with someone like… say, Larry Stanley, who sadly died last year. It's simply impossible.

For some reason I have always been intensely sceptical of the numbers of 'great' sportsmen of former generations. It's very easy to say "they don't make them like they did in the good old days", but it's seldom true. It so happens that athletes do improve with time. Men and women have become faster, stronger and tougher mentally. In many sports they have become more skilful. It is, as it should be. But of course there are exceptions, and from amongst the galaxy of 'greats' in the GAA for instance, there exists a tiny number of players who escaped the limitations of their era. Men who could fit comfortably into any generation of Gaelic football. It seems safe to say that Larry Stanley was one such individual.

Very few sports fans of today also had the satisfaction of watching someone like Stanley at his prime. It was sixty years ago. But the memory of those who did see him, rather than just hear about him, marks the Kildare man down as 'genuinely great'. He was a supreme footballer and high jumper, and was actually selected to represent Ireland at the Olympic Games in Paris in 1924. An Olympics which has since gained additional fame in the Academy Award-winning movie "Chariots of Fire" which captured the legendary battle between rival sprinters Eric Liddel and Harold Abrahams. It's Fascinating to think that Stanley would have witnessed these men at first hand. Or perhaps he was too concerned with his own event to consider the Scot and the Englishman. He probably took a passing interest in them and no more.

Looking back through the history books can be a dangerously deceptive hobby. It's very difficult to judge former generations, and it's extremely easy to be misguided by the opinions and emotions of others. Television, radio and newspaper reporters of the past allowed themselves to be engulfed by the occasion and the performance, and frequently acted like fanatical supporters who coincidentally happened to be sitting in front of a microphone or had to scribble away on a notebook.

Of course there are still some sports reporters around today who are incapable of removing themselves from a memorable even, and thereby making an unemotional and incisive judgement. But there are only a few. In fact, most reporters in this day and age much prefer to be critical rather than praiseworthy. Their argument is that a 'hard to please attitude' will sell more newspapers (or television and radio programmes) and has a greater chance of building the reporters reputation.

It's not surprising that this should be the case. During the last ten or twenty years the entire world of sport has grown sophisticated and cynical. Nowadays it's incredibly difficult for so called 'greats' to emerge from professional or even amateur games. It's especially obvious in soccer, golf, tennis and athletics, where there is so much money available, and where no matter how magnificent a performance might be, there is always a great possibility that the actual skills of the sportsman can become a side-issue to a financial story or a personal scandal. We read it all the time "X wins the Open … He has now made 2.6 million this season … He has also walked out on his wife and 12 kids … And by the way, next month he attempts the grand slam." We do not read it all in the same story but we do read it.

It will not be as simple or straightforward as the 'good old days'. How will the history books momorise Mr. X's career? Will he be automatically categorised as a 'great' alongside Henry Cotton and Jack Nicklaus?

The situation is much different when we compare modern Irish sportsmen with legendary Irish sportsmen. But the same sophistication and cynicism arises. There just does not seem to be so many 'greats' in sport any longer, even though sportsmen are much, much greater than ever before.

We should accept that it is incredible difficult to compare different generations, but sometimes it has to be done. The men who were handed the task of choosing the Garda silver jubilee award winners had a thankless job. Somehow they managed to sort through thousands of sportsmen, and retraced their achievements for the last 25 years. The result of their work is a considerable and impressive list of men, some of whom have served as foundation stones for the athletic association and individual sports, others who seem to have sacrificed every spare minute in their lives in recent seasons, and a few who have reached the very top of their sport in this country.

It's not too surprising that Gardaí have left an indelible mark on the GAA, a much deeper imprint than they have made on any other sport. As the largest association in the country, and with a membership of over 750,000 the GAA is a perfect vehicle for the Gardaí to become acquainted with communities in towns and villages throughout the country, and also serve as an example to the people themselves. What an example that proved to be!

We have already considered Larry Stanley and Matt Connor, but in the intervening period between the careers of these two great men there are lists of names which are familiar to any GAA fan. I'll stick to those whom I have watched myself. The easiest to recall are John Egan and Paudie O'Shea, the Kerry pair who played such diverse roles in the story of the greatest team in the history of the game. Egan will be best remembered for his amazing and inspiring ability to score goals during the most crucial period of a game. He was elusive and smart, and had the ability to recognise in a match the exact moment when a single score can decide the issue. He hadn't the style of Pat Spillane or the poise of Mickey Sheehy but his contribution was always of equal importance.

O'Shea could never be credited with style or poise either. But why would one of the powerful defenders – and I mean Power – be bothered by looking good. Unlike Egan, his career has somehow outlasted most of his teammates and certainly all his rivals of the mid-70's, other familiar names of Gardaí like Ger O'Driscoll and John McCarthy, and next summer he should still be a part a nd a vital parcel of the Kerry machine.

At present there is still a plentiful supply of Gardaí appearing at inter-county level – although I must admit that in Meath the only member of our All-Ireland winning squad, Donal Smith from Navan, is a member of the force. Elsewhere in the '80s there has been Mattie Coleman, Peter Lee and Stephen Kinneavy from the Galway team which reached the All-Ireland final in '83, Donegal's Seamus Bonner, Richie Culhane of Louth, who is one of the most under-rated forwards in the country, and the brilliant Laois duo of Colm Browne and Tom Prendergast.

And in the '70s there was Brian Murphy from Cork, who won many All-Star awards during his career, and was the silver jubilee award winner for hurling last November. He is the only player in history to have won All-Ireland medals at minor, U21 and senior level in both codes. If the GAA ever does decide to register its really 'great' players then Murphy will certainly be amongst them.

Again many brilliant players have represented the force and their counties on the hurling fields, including Pat Cleary, Frank Cummins, Joachim Kelly and Mossie Walsh during the last decade. But perhaps 1987 was the most memorable year yet. Cleary and Kelly played for Offaly in the Leinster final. Ken Hogan and Joe Hayes were central figures in the Tipperary team which won the Munster Championship for the first time in 16 years, and much more importantly won it in magnificent style. While Peter Finnerty was, in the opinion of this writer, the most important man on the Galway team which won the All-Ireland at a third, gasping, successive attempt. Two weeks later John Kerins and Anthony Davis were on the Cork team which lost in the All-Ireland Football final. 1987 was one hell of a year!

For the love of the game …

It's amazing how the youth of Ireland of all generations gravitate towards the GAA, in some cases to the total abandonment of more important tasks in life.

One such youth, Hugh O'Donnell, son of Tom O'Donnell – a revered member of An Garda Síochána stationed in Store Street in the 1950s, and a member of the Garda Male Choir – has penned the following poem, which illustrates how the lure of a GAA game took precedence over his piano lessons.

That youth is now Fr Hugh, a member of the Salesian Order in Ireland based in Sean McDermott Street, Dublin, who care for homeless boys in that area. Hugh's brother, Dermot, is a retired member of An Garda Síochána and was a past President of the Garda Representative Association and the founding member of the Garda Survivors' Support Association in 2006.

Here is Hugh's poem, short and to the point, which is the hallmark of many memorable poems:

I always tried to be away
on Saturdays, preferring
sticky pitches and stinging
rain to a piano lesson;

for thoughts of fielding
a greasy ball, defending grimly
defied a classic score.

My music was a whistle in the wind.

Rule 42 and the Garda Connection
Noel Hynes.

When General Eoin O'Duffy became Commissioner of An Garda Síochána in 1922 I am sure he never envisaged the impact that so many members of his illustrious force would have within the GAA, both as playing participants and Delegates to conventions. One such member, Jerry Flanagan, rocked the GAA world back in 1983 when ha addressed the GAA Convention as Chairman of Dunshaughlin GAA club with their motion "That the Central Council be advised to exercise its discretion under rule 31 to permit if so requested the use of Croke Park for field games without discrimination and subject at all times to the convenience of Cumann Luthchleas Gael". The motion was defeated by 80 votes to 25. Fast forward to the Annual GAA Congress of 2005 attended by 350 delegates when that same motion was carried by 227 to 97. Jerry Flanagan, now a retired member of An Garda Síochána, residing in the Royal County, had indeed been vindicated and given recognition by no less than Sean Kelly a past President of the GAA from 2003 to 2006, when he stated in his book published in 2007 - Rule 42 And All That - under the chapter The Long Road to Change - "In 1982 a man called Jerry Flanagan asked the Meath County Board to examine the possibility of making more extensive use of Croke Park, but his appeal fell on deaf ears and that was the end of that". Let us all salute Jerry for his foresight in introducing this now famous motion back in 1982 on behalf of the Dunshaughlin Hurling Club at the Meath Annual Convention. It was the first time that such a motion was put forward by any club in this country. General Eoin O'Duffy, who himself was involved in administrative positions with the Monaghan County Board between 1912 and 1923 would indeed be very proud of our Jerry. You can view Jerry Flanagan's impressive GAA playing career for Roscommon in our alphabetical list in this book.

Chapter 25

New York and Boston Police Departments and the GAA

Our sister police forces in New York and Boston have a long affiliation with the GAA. In the 1950s and 1960s, the Lydon family started a chapter of the Connemara Gaels in Boston. The NYPD Gaelic football team was originally founded in 1968. In 2004, NYPD Paul McCormack and Steve Morrissey (both Irish born) contacted Colm Lydon about playing a game between Boston and New York Police Departments.

Kieran Cox of the Connemara Gaels (who is now a US youth co-ordinator for Gaelic games) along with other Gaels and Boston PD's own Tim Horan (past player), began to train American-born cops to play Gaelic football.

After a few scrimmages, the first game was on 24 September 2004 between Boston PD and NYPD. Boston lost to New York in a game at the Irish Cultural Centre in Canton, Massachusetts.

In October 2004, a Garda team came over travelling with team manager Eugene O'Sullivan, and played in Moakley Park, in South Boston. Robbie Harrison may have also travelled with this team. In June 2005, Boston PD travelled to NYPD Gaelic Park in the Bronx, and played for a Pettit-Hurley trophy (named after Glenn Pettit, an NYPD officer killed in 9/11, and Jerry Hurley, who was killed by a bomb in Boston). Boston PD won.

Boston PD played another Garda team combination in 2007, and also played the Mayo Gardaí in September 2009. They conceded the Pettit-Hurley Cup to NYPD again in 2011, and games have not been played since.

Through all these games, we made many friends within the Boston Police Department and the Irish immigrant community. Every Thanksgiving for the past fifteen years, they play a flag football game in Dorchester called the Turkey Bowl, where the Boston PD plays against a team made up of local Gaelic football players.

According to Colm Lydon, a Deputy Superintendent of the Boston Police Department, American cops can "run like deer, jump like gazelle, are strong as a horse, have hands like Michael Jordan, and can kick a football through the uprights from fifty yards from any corner of the field."

But it will be a thousand years before they can learn how to throw such an oddly shaped ball in accuracy. In the third year, they brought in their Irish quarterback, and won handily!

Boston police commissioner Kathleen O'Toole with the Pettit-Hurley Cup.
Left to right:
Mark Stokes, Tim Horan, Jim Giardina, Gerard Bailey, Mike Devane and son, Kieran Cox,
Colm Lydon, Pat McNicholas, Commissioner Kathleen O'Toole with the Pettit-Hurley Cup
in Boston PD Headquarters.

Photographic Memories

A District Hurling Team c.1961

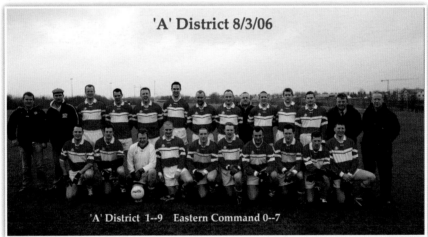

'A' District 8/3/06

'A' District 1--9   Eastern Command 0--7

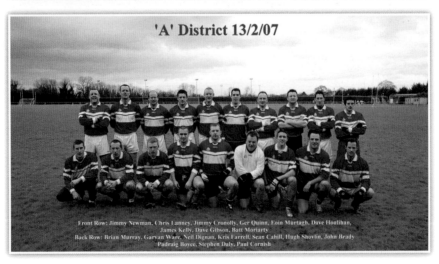

'A' District 13/2/07

Front Row: Jimmy Newman, Chris Lanney, Jimmy Cronolly, Ger Quinn, Eoin Murtagh, Dave Houlihan,
James Kelly, Dave Gibson, Batt Moriarty
Back Row: Brian Murray, Garvan Ware, Neil Dignan, Kris Farrell, Sean Cahill, Hugh Shovlin, John Brady
Padraig Boyce, Stephen Daly, Paul Cornish

B District Hurling Team 1963

Blast from the past
Garda Hurling Team

Presentation to Eddie Brennan and Edel Hanley at Portlaoise Garda Station,
with Jim Doyle, Brian Willoughby and Mick Morrissey

Co-authors Noel Hynes and Brian Willoughby
with Offaly GAA Legends Matt Connor, Joachim Kelly, Pat Cleary and Cathal Daly

Páirc an Chrócaigh   9/11/1980

Cluiche Ceannais
An Cheannárais
(Sponsored by Clerys)

CIARRAÍ
V
UIBH FHÁILÍ

Réiteóir: C. Mac Cathmhaoil (An Mhí) 3.00 p.m.

Cluiche Ceannais an Cheannárais (Club)
(Sponsored by Surgical Distributors Ltd.)

NA GARDAÍ
V
NA SEIRBHÍSÍ
PRÍOSÚIN

Réiteóir: P. Ó Ciaráin (Áth Cliath)

Clár
Oifigiúil
Luach 20p

Liam Ó Maolmhichíl

GÁRDA
Dáthanna: **Bán agus Gorm** (White and Blue)

1
S. Ó Cadhain
(Gaillimh)

2
S. Mac Róibín
(Gaillimh)

3
S. Ó Mairtín
(Cabhán)

4
D. Ó Braonáin
(Laois)
Des Bachman

5
B. Mac Giolla Phádraig
(Cill Mhantáin)

6
P. Ó Cafrai
(Áth Cliath)
Pillar Caffrey

7
E. Mac Einrí
(Cill Dara)

8
R. Ó Raghallaigh
(Áth Cliath)

9
D. Ó Briain
(Áth Cliath)

10
Seán Ó Briain
(Áth Cliath)

11
S. Mac Craigh
(An Clár)

12
C. Cuirtéis
(Áth Cliath)

13
E. de Barra
(An Mhí)
Eamonn Barry

14
S. Mac Cnáimhsí
(Dún na nGall)

15
S. Mac Carthaigh
(Áth Cliath)

FIR IONAID: 16. E. Ó Catháin (Áth Cliath); 17. M. Mac Giolla Bháin (Maigh Eo); 18. M. Mac Craith (Gaillimh); 19. S. Mac Uilcin (Maigh Eo); 20. S. Ó Díomsaigh (Cill Dara); 21. L. Mac Aodha (Áth Cliath).

NA SEIRBHÍSÍ PRÍOSÚIN
Dáthanna: **Gorm agus Bán** (Blue and White)

1
M. Ó Conaire
(Laois)
Martin Farrelly

2
P. Mac Giolla Chanáin
(Sligeach)

3
P. Ó Loinsigh
(Ros Comáin)

4
T. Ó Raghaillaigh
(Maigh Eo)

5
M. Ó Murchú
(Uibh Fháilí)

6
T. Ó Conaire
(Laois)
Tom Conroy

7
B. Ó Conbhui
(Liatroim)

8
P. de Bróite
(Laois)
Pat Brophy

9
C. Seoighe
(Laois)

10
T. Mac Machúna
(Sligeach)
Seán Dempsey

11
S. Ó Dionsaigh
(Laois)

12
S. Ó Leathlobhair
(Laois)
Seamus Walsh

13
L. Ó Duinn
(Uibh Fháilí)

14
S. Ó Loingsigh
(Cill Mhantáin)

15
M. Ó Brádaigh
(Cabhán)

FIR IONAID: 16. C. Mac Dhonncha (Laois); 17. C. Ó Cafrai (Cabhán); 18. M. Mac Gilla Phádraig (Uibh Fhail), 19. S. Ó Murchú (Ceatharlach); 20. S. Ó Brádaigh (Cabhán); 21. M. Ó Seasnáin (Cabhán); 22. P. Ó Ceallaigh (Cill Mhantáin); 23. S. Ó Murchú (Loch Garman); 24. S. Ó Treasaigh (Gaillimh); 25. G. Ó Gearlann (Áth Cliath); 26. M. Ó Gallchóir (Gaillimh); 27. C. Ó Dochartaigh (Corcaigh); 28. Seán Mac Aogáin (Áth Cliath).

GÁRDA	Cúl	Cúilíní	Seachtar	45m	Saor-chiceanna
1 adh Leath					
2 adh Leath					
Iomlán					

NA SEIRBHÍSÍ PRÍOSÚIN	Cúl	Cúilíní	Seachtar	45m	Saor-chiceanna
1 adh Leath					
2 adh Leath					
Iomlán					

GARDA SIOCHANA HURLING TEAM 1964
BACK ROW: M. Regan, J. Kennedy, N. Coogan, P. McGovern, B. Cooney, J. Nealon, J. Prendergast.
FRONT ROW: W. Walsh, M. Hayes, S. Quaide, E. Carey(Capt.), J. Conroy, M. Regan, N. Power, P. Verdon.

County Stars; Garda were well represented in the 1956 All Ireland Football Final.
Here they are greeted by Chief Superintendent R.F. Creagh,
then Chairman of Coiste Siamsa and Commissioner D. Costigan.
Pictured are Left to Right
Chief Supt Creagh, Gerry Daly (Galway), Frank Eivers (Galway), Commissioner Costigan,
Paddy Harrington (Cork), Eric Ryan (Cork) and Paddy Driscoll (Cork).
Daly, Eivers and Harrington played with the Dublin Garda Club.

213

G.A.A.

Hurling Exhibition

Dublin Garda v. Army Metro

Co. Champions, 1932.   Co. Champions, 1922.

at

Mourne Park, Strabane

on

SUNDAY, 15th JULY, 1934.

THROW-IN at 3.30 p.m.

Team Colours : Garda—Blue ; Army—Yellow.

Referee - - - - - Mr. James Hehir, Dublin.

Selections by St Eugene's Silver Band, Strabane, from 3 p.m.

PROGRAMMES - - - - ONE PENNY

Visiting Teams will be guests of STRABANE CAMOGIE CLUB

— at —

A CEILIDHE

— in —

LYRIC HALL, LIFFORD

Commencing at 9 p.m.—1 a.m.

Music by —— SAVOY CEILIDHE ORCHESTRA

ADMISSION - - - - ONE SHILLING

—— COME IN YOUR THOUSANDS ——

C.L.C.G.
OFFICIAL
OPENING

of TURLOUGHMORE FIELD & SOCIAL CENTRE
on SUNDAY 17th JUNE 1990

Pat Hurney Memorial Tournament

GARDAI v TURLOUGHMORE

5.30 p.m.   *Referee : John Coady*

**Official Opening by G.A.A. President Elect Peter Quinn
& Blessing by Rev. Michael Lyons, P. P.**

Senior Hurling Challenge

CORK v GALWAY

7.00 p.m.   *Referee : Gerry Long*

GARDAI

1
FRANK LARKIN
(Liam Mellows)

2	3	4
BRIAN BRENNAN (Gort)	**GERRY MAHER** (Oughterard)	**KEVIN KENNEDDY** (Killenana)

5	6	7
JOHN HYNES (Portumna)	**PETER FINNERTY** (Mullagh)	**GABRIEL KEATING** (Wolfe Tones)

8	9
MATTIE COLEMAN (Abbeyknockmoy)	**DAMIEN FLANAGAN** (Oranmore-Maree)

10	11	12
MARTIN O'SHEA (Castlegar)	**PAT BURKE** (Castlegar)	**GERRY FAHY** (Oranmore-Maree)

13	14	15
LIAM CREAVAN (Killimordaly)	**PADRAIC HESSION** (Cappataggle)	**GERRY CURTIN** (Kinvara)

SUBS:
16. John Glynn (Menlo Emmetts), 17. Michael Ryan (Ennis),
18. Gerry Hogan (Mill St.), 19. John O'Donnell (Mill St.),
20. Joe Salmon (Menlo Emmetts), 21. Seamus Lydon (Mill St.)

TURLOUGHMORE

1
MICHAEL SHAUGHNESSY
(Cregmore)

2	3	4
GERRY DOHERTY (Bawnmore)	**MARTIN HURNEY** (Cregmore)	**DENIS BURKE** (Corbally)

5	6	7
PAUL HURNEY (Cregmore)	**JIMMY BURKE** (Corbally)	**JIMMY McGRATH** (Cregmore)

8	9
BOSCO HURNEY (Cregmore)	**MARTIN NAUGHTON** (Lisheenavalla)

10	11	12
GERRY BURKE (Coolarne)	**GERRY HOLLAND** (Waterview)	**PAT BURKE** (Lackagh)

13	14	15
TOMMIE BURKE (Cregmore)	**FRANK BURKE** (Knockdoe)	**PADRAIG BURK** (Corbally)

SUBS:
16. Willie Burke, 17. Seamus Qualter, 18. Pat Forde,
19. Richard McNicholas, 20. Gerry Linnane, 21. Pat Costello,
22. Patsy Clark, 23. John Fallon, 24. Declan Hurney,
25. John Fahy, 26. Noel Duffy, 27. Michael O'Brien,
28. Kevin Cullinane.

All Ireland Football Final Croke Park 1976
Kerry V Dublin.

Kevin Heffernan, Manager of the Dublin Team whose father was a Garda Inspector in Store St in the late 1950's keeping a close eye on his Dublin charges. On the extreme left in uniform is Mick Behan, who played for Dublin between 1973 and 1976. Next to Mick is Lorcan Redmond Dublin Selecctor, Donal Colfer, partly hidden and wearing spectacles Also a Dublin selector two unknown recruit gardai, garda Willie Ryan, Limerick and a Croke Park steward. Dublin Beat Kerry 3-8 to 0-10. It was the second 70 minute final. Four members of An Garda Siochana participated in that final - John McCarthy corner forward for Dublin, father of the current Dublin senior player James McCarthy. John senior played for Dublin between 1970 and 1981. Paudie O'Shea played at right halfback for Kerry and John Egan played at full forward. Ger O'Driscoll came on as a sub. Paudie played for Kerry betweer 1974 to 1988, John Egan, between 1975 and 1984 and Ger O'Driscoll between 1975 and 1982

- **LAOIS/OFFALY HURLING TEAM (1960)**
The Laois/Offaly Divisional Hurling Team from the 1960s. Pictured (l-r): S. Francis, M. O'Brien, J. Molloy, T. Canavan, S. Giles, J. Donovan, D. Dunne, P. Cloke, E. Begley, D. Wheelan, F. Garvey, M. Coughlan, M. Manley and B. Gleeson with trainer Supt Ned Kennedy.

- **GARDA TRAINING CENTRE, TEMPLEMORE (OCTOBER 1964 FOOTBALL TEAM)**
Front Row: (l-r): Eamonn Coleman (Carlow) Eamonn Giles (Meath) Noel O'Connor (Clare) Tom Mongey (Meath) Brendan Gilmore (Longford) Seamus Keevans (Wexford) Tony Sourke (Dublin) Gabriel McCarthy (Cork) Basil Johnson (Offaly) Noel Smith (Cavan).
Back Row (l-r): Mick Murphy (Westmeath), Willie Molloy (Offaly) Brendan McDonnell (Mayo) Colm Ridge (Galway) Dan Duffin (Offaly) Noel Mulhern (Leitrim) Tom Byrne (Laois) Maurice O Connor (Kerry) Danny Thomas (Donegal) John Dan McMenimon (Donegal)

Photo courtesy of Eamonn Coleman,

- **CORK COISTE ROINNE MEDAL CEREMONY 1967**
Pictured at the Coiste Roinne function at Cork's Metropole Hotel in 1967 for Cork ER hurling and football teams – the winners in Munster Division Coiste Roinne championships:
Front Row (l-r): John P. Conrick (RIP), E.J. Doherty (RIP), P. Malone (RIP), P.G. Power, T.J. Kelly, M. McQuinn, J. Keating, E. Howard, and F. Cotter.
Middle Row (l-r): John Sheehy, Paddy Casey, John F. O' Riordan, Morgan Lahive, John F. O Brien, unknown, Moss O' Connor, Paul Downey, John O Brien (RIP), Noel Kirwan, Cormac Moroney, and J. B. Long.
Back Row (l-r): H. Moynihan (RIP), unknown, Batt Kirby (RIP), P. Freeney, J. Dillon, M. Keane, T.C. Kirby (RIP), M. O' Loughlin, J.B. Griffin, J. White (RIP), B. Feeney, M.J. Griffin, and J. Hickey.

Photo courtesy of J.B. Long, Cork City Branch.

The Waterford/Kilkenny team that played Cork East in the Coiste Siamsa Football Championship at Fermoy, 1962. This is the 50th anniversary of that match. Cork East were victorious on the day.
Back Row: Mick Delaney (Carlow); Peter McGovern (Carlow); Pat Ferris (Tipperary); Chris Doocey (Tipperary) RIP; Andy Hallissey (Kerry); Willie Walsh (Carlow); Martin Hogan (Carlow) RIP; Mick Delaney (Laois).
Front Row: Liam Condon (Tipperary); Willy Smith (Cavan) RIP; Peter O'Reilly (Leitrim); Hugh Donnelly (Tyrone); Mich Cronin (Kerry); Tom McDermott (Westmeath); Martin McQuinn (Kerry).

Photograph courtesy of Tom McDermott, 13957B, Waterford Branch.

GARDA SENIOR FOOTBALL TEAM – 1955
Front Row (l-r): Paddy McCarthy (Clare. RIP); Tom Maguire (Cavan. RIP); Chris Godkin (Cork. RIP); Unknown; Joe O'Connell (Mayo); Frank Eivers (Galway); Teddy O'Sullivan (Kerry. RIP)
Back Row (l-r): Dan O'Sullivan (Kerry and Dublin. RIP); Tom Lan-gan (Mayo. RIP); Bill Shannon (Mayo and Sligo. RIP); O'Shea (Kerry); Unknown; Dan McCaffrey (Cavan); Gerry Daly (Galway); Paddy Harrington (Cork. RIP).

B DISTRICT FOOTBALL TEAM, 1960
Back row, L-R: Mick Waters (RIP), J Nugent (RIP), J Rafter (RIP), P Halloran, Joe Campbell (RIP), B Kennedy, J Carey, P Slyon (RIP), D Nocton (RIP), Unknown, Oliver Nugent (RIP), John Keating (brother of Dick).
Front row L-R: J Murphy, T Grimes, O Nolan, J Mahoney (RIP), P O'Shea, M Needham, J Coggins, D McCormack, Dick Keating (RIP).

Photo courtesy of John Carey, Dublin North Branch.

DEPOT WINNERS: *The Class 4 team, winners of the Garda Depot League in 1954. Front row (l to r): Hugh Donnelly, Gerry Keane, Phil O'Mara, Dan O'Neill (capt.), Tom Muldoon, Eamonn Cleary, PJ Daly; Second row (l to r): John Hamill, Charlie McElwain, Michael Murphy, Tony Solon, John Hickey, John Lavin, Bertie Marren; Back row (l to r): Michael Campbell, John Keogh, Kevin McNicholas, Bernard Brennan.*

A DISTRICT FOOTBALL TEAM 1967/8

WINNERS OF THE DMA CHAMPIONSHIP

Back Row – L to R
      Ned Coogan, Kilkenny; Pat O'Donnell. Donegal; Fergus Doggett, Louth; Charlie McGinley, Donegal; Myles Fitzgerald, Dublin; Pat McDaid, Donegal; Watters, Sligo; Moses Morrissey, Wexford; Gabriel McCarthy, Cork; Bill Dwyer, Laois; Jim Flynn, Team Manager;

Front Row – L to R
      Tom McArdle, Louth; Mick Carolan, Kildare; John Maloney, Mayo; Harry Murphy, Louth; John Healy, Sligo; Seamus Mellett, Meath; Peter Roberts, Carlow; Jerry Flanagan, Roscommom; Pat Kenny, Roscommon; Tom McKeown, Leitrim; Denis McBride, Donegal;
Team Selectors Phil Cahill, Kerry and John Ford, Mayo, missing from photo.

Photo supplied by Jerry Flanagan.

RECENT RE-UNION OF FORMER ALL-IRELAND GARDA HURLERS, FOOTBALLERS AND ATHLETES AT THE CENTRAL HOTEL, DUBLIN

FRONT ROW (left to right): Sergeant Finucane, Paddy Reid, Chief Superintendent R. Creagh, Pádraig Ó Caoimh, General Secretary, G.A.A.; the Commissioner, Mr. D. Costigan; Rev. Fr. Kelly, Deputy Commissioner G. Brennan, T. Soye, P. Pringle, T. O'Donnell, Martin Kelly. CENTRE ROW: Jas. Murphy, Ned Tobin, P. McInerney, P. Perry, Larry Stanley, Ned Tobin (Depot), P. Kenneally, E. Fahy, Tom Cunniffe, Dan Canniffe, Inspector R. McGann, Ml. Gill. BACK ROW: Jim Kirwan, M. Power, W. O'Brien, John Doherty, W. Shannon, J. Brannigan, M. Kelly, J. Brennan, F. Cunniffe.

Dublin Metropolitan Area football team taken in Croke Park probably late sixties or early seventies. Many represented their native counties and some held provincial and All-Ireland medals, most notably Fachtna Murphy, Ned Kirby, Ray Prendiville, Willie Magee and Gerry Flanagan who won two All Ireland Junior Hurling medals with Roscommon.

Back Row L to R: Billy Dwyer (Laois) selector; Mick Mulhaire (Laois); John Clarke (Mayo); Kieran Brennan (Laois); Mick Mitchell (Meath); Noel McDermott (Sligo); Ned Ryan (Mayo) Ray Prendiville (Kerry); Tom Flanagan (Roscommon); Mick Woods (Clare); Vincent O'Donnell, RIP, (Tipperary); Jim Murphy, (Mayo) Manager.

Front Row L to R: Fachtna Murphy (Cork); Jim Hallinan, (Dublin); Willie Molloy (Offaly); Willie Magee (Mayo); Ned Kirby (Cork); Tom Hearty (Louth); Gerry Flanagan (Roscommon); John Mulligan.

Above photograph was taken at Rathmines Garda Station after the 1942 All-Ireland Final when the Captain of the winning Dublin team, Joe Fitzgerald, a Kerryman attached to Rathmines Station, brought the Sam Maguire Cup to his comrades at the old Rathmines Station. We think this was the last time an "outsider" played on the Dublin team. Photograph provided by Moss Walsh, kneeling in front.
FRONT: S.S. Deasy, R.I.P., Harry Conlon, R.I.P., Martin Walsh, R.I.P., Mick Brennan, R.I.P., Ml. McDonnell, R.I.P., Joe Fitzgerald, Captain, Desmond Mullally, R.I.P., Dick Nash, R.I.P. *Kneeling –* Moss Walsh. *BACK:* Bill Doherty, Tim Duignan, Dick Vaughan, R.I.P., Andy Higginbotham, R.I.P., Insp. D. Buckley, R.I.P., John Ford, R.I.P.,Matt Donovan, R.I.P.

"C" District G.A.A. Football Team — 1955

Winners of Inter-District League. Ten of the team were Inter-County players

BACK ROW: *Jack Hickey (Manager) Martin O'Hora, Paddy Irwin, Tom Callinan, Pat McGrath, Tom Langan, Pa McCarthy, Jim Enright, Bill Doherty and Barney Mullen.*
FRONT ROW: *Pat Daly, Mick Guthrie, Mel McGarry, Mick O'Reilly, Tom McGuire, Jack Chatten, Dan O'Sullivan an Jer Spillane*

GEORGE RANKINS, Bunclody

Clár

Oifigiúil

24 - 3 -'63

i bPáirc an Chrócaig

2 p.m.

An tArm v. Gárdaí Síocána

Réiteoir : S Ó Máirtín (Ros Comáin)

*

3-15 p.m.

Ciarraí v. Roga na nIolscoil

Réiteoir : P Ó Ceallaig (Áth Cliat)

Luac - - 3p

Cló-Oiris Uí Caoilte, Tta.

An tArm

Dáṫanna : Ḡlas is bán
(Green and White)

(1)
n. mac amlaiḋ
(R. Cawley) Corcaiġ 7 Currać

(2)
p. ó coiléin
(P. Collier) An Mí 7
Aer-Cór

(3)
t. ó maoltuile
(T. Flood) Cill Dara 7 W. Comd.

(4)
n. ó luasa
(N. Lucey) Ciarraí 7
Aer-Cór

(5)
m. ó coclám
(M. Coughlan) Cill Dara 7
Aer-Cór

(6)
m. ó buacáin
(M. Bohane) Áṫ Cliaṫ 7 Currać

(7)
p. ó cillġeanáin
(P. Kilgannon) Sligeaċ 7
W. Command

(8)
n. ó suain
(R. Swan) Cill Dara 7 Currać

(9)
s. ó luasa
(J. Lucey) Ciarraí 7 Currać

(10)
n. ó madaġáin
(N. Madigan) Cill Dara 7
Aer-Cór

(11)
u. ó luasa
(V. Lucey) Aer-Cór

(12)
t. ó seacnasaiġ
(T. Shaughnessy) Aer-Cór

(13)
p. mac cafraiḋ
(F. Caffrey) Cill Dara 7
Aer-Cór

(14)
t. ó murcú
(T. Murphy) Corcaiġ 7 Aer-Cór

(15)
a. ó donġaile
(H. Donnelly) Ua bfáilí
7 Aer-Cór

Fir ionad : (16) m. mac Searlóg (M. Sherlock) Aer-Cór ; (17) p. mac meanman (P. McMenamin) Currać ; (18) t. ḡoċ (T. Goff) Currać : (19) s. praġas (J. Price) Currać : (20) p. ó Dálaiġ (P. Daly) S. Command.

Gárdaí Síocána

Dáṫanna : Ḡorm is bán
(Blue and White)

(1)
s. mac aonġusa
(S. McGuinness) Muiġeo

(2)
p. ó húrdail
(P. Harrington) Corcaiġ

(3)
m. mac domnaill
(M. McDonnell) Laois

(4)
p. s. ó cinnéide
(P. J. Kennedy) An Clár

(5)
s. ó haoḋa
(J. Hughes) Laois

(6)
m. ó cearbálláin
(M. Carolan) Cill Dara

(7)
s. ó caoimín
(S. Keevans) Loċ Ḡarmón

(8)
t. de brún
(T. Browne) Laois

(9)
s. feiritéar
(S. Ferriter) Dún na nḠall

(10)
ḡ. ó raġallaiġ
(G. Reilly) Ros Comáin

(11)
p. ó cinnéide
(F. Kennedy) An Clár

(12)
t. ó raincín
(G. Rankins) Laois

(13)
t. ó monġaiġ
(T. Mongey) An Mí

(14)
e. ó riain
(E. Ryan) Corcaiġ

(15)
p. mac riobáird
(P. Roberts) Ceatarloċ

Fir ionad : (16) p. ó ḡioltáin (F. Gilton) Áṫ Cliaṫ ; (17) p. ó colgáin (P. Culligan) Corcaiġ ; (18) ḡ. ó Staircín (G. Starkin) Ua bfáil. ; (19) t. ó húrdail (T. Harrington) Corcaiġ ; (20) b. mac Canna (B. McCann) An Mí.

	An tArm					Gárdaí Síocána				
Cúil Goals	Cúilíní Points	Seacaí Overs	50 St. 50's	Saon- ċiceanna Free Kicks	Cúil Goals	Cúilíní Points	Seacaí Overs	50 St. 50's	Saon- ċiceanna Free Kicks

The O'Donovan Rossa squad who won the All Ireland Senior Club Championship in 1993
contained 8 Gardaí
Front Row second from left , Don Davis, third from left Pat Davis,
ninth from left, Gearoid Davis, eleventh from left, Martin Bohane.
Back Row sixth from left, Ian Breen, seventh from left Kevin O'Dwyer,
ninth from left, Brian O'Donovan and tenth from left Tony Davis

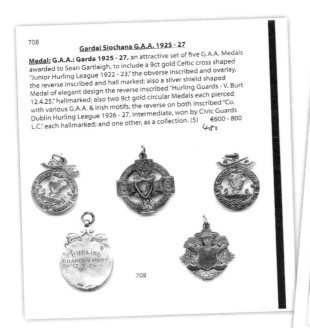

708

Gardai Siochana G.A.A. 1925 - 27

Medal: G.A.A.: Garda 1925 - 27, an attractive set of five G.A.A. Medals awarded to Sean Gartlaigh, to include a 9ct gold Celtic cross shaped "Junior Hurling League 1922 - 23," the obverse inscribed and overlay, the reverse inscribed and hall marked; also a silver shield shaped Medal of elegant design the reverse inscribed "Hurling Guards - V. Burt 12.4.25," hallmarked; also two 9ct gold circular Medals each pierced with various G.A.A. & Irish motifs, the reverse on both inscribed "Co. Dublin Hurling League 1926 - 27, Intermediate, won by Civic Guards L.C." each hallmarked; and one other, as a collection. (5) €600 - 800

708

New Perpetual Challenge Cup.

The Coiste Siamsa Committee desire to express most sincere thanks to Mr. Maxwell Arnott, Clonsilla, Co. Dublin, for his kindness in donating a Perpetual Challenge Cup value £30 to be competed for in Football between the Army and An Garda.

The Cup is of the Chalice pattern, with arms on either side extending to the base, and artistically ornamented in Celtic design. It will be on view during Garda Week midst the numerous other prizes presented for competition.

Mr. Arnott's generosity in making presentation of this magnificent Cup is but another practical example of his very practical sportsmanship, and it is this trait, combined with other sterling qualities, which has earned for him a place high in the estimation of racing and polo circles.

To Mr. Arnott and the donors of other valuable prizes we express our indebtedness, and assure one and all that the honour of winning such splendid trophies will be a sure incentive to competitors to put forward the best that in them lies.

Sergts. Grey, Tobin and Ryan, Gardai Hayes, Howard, Conway, Gill, Browne, Burnell, Phelan, McGann, McInerney, O'Rourke, Conroy and Grace.

• *Offaly Garda Football Team in the 1960s*
F/Row: J. Cooney, ——, J. McHugh, J. Donovan, M. Ashe, B. Keogh, J. Duncan, J. Coogan
B/Row: A. Brennan, M. Murphy, S. O'Connor, D. Carroll, V. Brennan, G. Sweeney,
M. Kearns, G. McGrath, ——.

• *1969 - Offaly Garda Football Team*
F/Row: D. Daly, T. Hannon, J. Hopkins, D. Dunne, J. Fahy, N. Cummiskey,
P. Prendergast, T. Brown
M/Row: J. Donellan, J. Dunne
B/Row: E. Kennedy, Ref. E. Giles, M. Carty, G. Campbell, G. Gavin, T. McNamara,
D. Prendergast, V. Moran, K. Moroney.

Portlaoise A v Portlaoise B 1978

ABX team, winners: back row left to right – J. Larkin, M. Lyons, S. Fitzgerald, S. Holden, J. Ryan, K. Wolfe. Front row, left to right – M. O'Hea, P. Doolin, E. Hayes, F. Ward (captain), J. Egan, T. Horgan.

1978

CD team, runners-up: back row left to right – B. O'Connell, M. Carthy, M. Keane, B. Redmond, P. Kelliher, G. McNamara, J. Durcan: Front row left to right – T. Donovan, J. Sheehan, D. Ahern, J. O'Gara (captain), J. Daly, S. Fitzgerald, E. Condon.

centenary regional winners

The G.A.A. celebrated the centenary of its foundation in 1984. To mark this special milestone a garda interprovincial gaelic football competition was played. In the semi finals Leinster defeated Connacht/Ulster and Munster were victorious over the D.M.A. from Dublin.

In a high quality final Leinster overcame the men from Munster after a hard fought game. This photograph of the winning team from Leinster is reproduced with each player native county in brackets and also their current station

Front Row: left to right, -
Aidan Mc Hugh (Roscommon) Tullamore Station
Seamus Reynolds (Mayo) Geashill station Co. Offaly
Jimmy Mc Manus (Roscommon) Portlaoise Station
John Keane (Tipperary) Tullamore Station
Michael O Riordan (Tipperary) Garda College
Pat Spollen (Offaly) Now retired and living in Kerry
Eddie Tynan (Westmeath) Clara Station

Back Row: left to right, -
Noel O Dowd (Roscommon) Kilbeggan Station
Philip Kiernan (Longford) Clara Station
Gerry Sheridan (Cavan) Carrigallen Station
Michael Keevans (Wexford) Nass Station
Matt Connor (Offaly) Tullamore Station
Ben Tansey (Roscommon) Now retired, living in Co. Meath
Stephen Kinneavy (Galway) Kilcullen Station
Mick Lowery (Westmeath) Tullamore Station

Other members of the panel not in Photo:
John Walsh (Westmeath) Tullamore Station
Pascal Hanrahan (Tipperary) Tullamore Station

Illustrations by renowned artist ex-garda Paul Downey

229

CORK GARDA FOOTBALL TEAM AT THE MARDYKE, CORK, 1956

Back Row, L-R
Paddy McLoughlin, Jerry Mullaney,
Eric Ryan, Kieran O'Donnell, Pat Brophy,
Terry Carthy, Bernie Feeney, George White,
Mick Browne, George Brophy, Paddy Culligan,
Frank Cotter.

Front Row, L-R
John Carey, Paddy Driscoll, Mick McCarthy, Dick
O'Callaghan, Mick Enright, Peter Fitzpatrick, Paddy Casey,
Pascal Cronin.

Courtesy of Pascal Cronin.

CORK GARDA TEAM -V- DELANEY ROVERS IN THE KELLEHER SHIELD AT THE CORK ATHLETIC GROUNDS ON MARCH 8TH 1964

Back Row, L-R
Jim Buckley (selector), Paddy Casey (Longford),
Christy Brosnan (Kerry), Gerry Mullaney (Roscommon),
Jack McGrath (Tipperary), Ben Coughlan (Waterford),
Tom Kirby (Kerry), Frank Corrigan (Monaghan),
Martin McQuinn (Kerry), Jim Griffin (Kerry),
Jerry Moran (selector).

Front Row, L-R
Jim Hayes (selector), John O'Brien (Kerry), Tim O'Leary
(Cork), Gerry O'Sullivan (Kerry), Joe White (Kerry),
Matt Dowd (Monaghan), Mick McDonald (Laois),
Kieran O'Donnell (Laois), Gerry Brennan (Clare).

Courtesy of Frank Corrigan.   SIOLHAIN - SPRING 2014

230

Dalkey Mitchells, Dublin junior hurling champions. 1967

(Back Row L to R)   H.Roberts, J.Branelly, A.Wallace, D.Byrne, J.Doran, P.Anders, B.Maher, T.Purcell, J.O'Donnell, J.Kerins, M.Gleeson, T. Ryan, M.Hayes, P.Murphy.

(Front Row L to R)   G.Wallace, J.McMonigle, S.Byrne, M.Kennedy, K.Dunphy, J.Delehunty, H.McCann J.Cahill, P.Gleeson, P.Byrne.

Eight players in this team were members of An Garda Siochana
They were Paddy Byrne, Mick Hayes, Jim O'Donnell, Pascal Anders, Jim Doran,
Murt Gleeson, Brendan Maher and Tom Purcell

- **DMA 'F' DISTRICT TEAM ON EASTER SUNDAY 1955**
The DMA 'F' District of Dublin Metropolitan Garda (DMG) team: pictured on Easter Sunday 10 April 1955:
Front Row (l-r): R.C. Curran, B. Madden, J.V. Donoghue, S.E. King, P.A. Hedderman, P. Reilly and E.A. Gunn.
Back Row (l-r): J.M. Doddy, J. McHugh, C.P. McCarthy, E.J. Doddy, L.C. Ferguson, D. McCaffery and W.P. O'Leary.

Photo courtesy of Sean Brennan, Limerick City Branch (on behalf of C.P. McCarthy's son)

Drogheda Garda Football Team which played in the first Cardinal O'Donnell Cup Final in Drogheda in 1927.

Included are: *P.J. Kirwan, Dublin & Wexford; James Reynolds, Leitrim; John Reynolds, Leitrim; John McMahon, Down; Wm. Bracken; John Smith, Cavan; Pat Curran, Westmeath; Jim Bergin, Kilkenny; Pat McKenna, Kilkenny; John McDonnell, Down; George P. Caville, Westmeath; Peter Blessing, Leitrim; John Ford, Mayo; Alfred Hayes, Galway; John Connoll, Laois; John McHugh, Goalie; J. J. Matthews; Jimmy Mullen.*

This fine photograph was sent to us by Ex-Sergeant Michael Conneally, Reg. No. 9252 who is in the centre of the picture as the team mascot holding the ball and whose father, Michael Conneally, Galway, Reg. No. 772, a team mentor, is situated at the right on the back row.

GARDA HURLING TEAM 1928

Winners of the Intermediate hurling league final V Civil Service.

Seated from left - J. Clarke, J. O'Neill, W. Brown, T. Quinlan, Supt. Sean Gantly, Captain, G. Mulcahy, G. Brown, L. McDonald.

Back Row from left - J. Reilly (Coach), W. Hackett, W. Tierney, J. Reeves, D. McHugh (Goalie), P. Clarke, T. Burke, J. Kirwan, P. Cusack.

Sergts. Grey, Tobin and Ryan, Gardai Hayes, Howard, Conway, Gill, Browne, Burnell, Phelan, McGann, McInerney, O'Rourke, Conroy and Grace.

Winners of the President's Cup
Sunday 6th July 1924

Dublin G.A.A. Club — Winners of Dublin Intermediate Championship, 1986.
Front Row, left to right: Frank White (Donegal), Larry Byrne (Wexford), Pat Cummaskey (Cavan), Ken Brennan (Cavan), Ashley Connolly (Monaghan), Larry Byrne (Galway).

Back Row, left to right: Declan Healy (Louth), Martin O'Connor (Mayo), Willie Hughes (Dublin), Michael Driscoll (Kerry), Liam King (Galway), John Newton (Roscommon), Tom Flanagan (Galway), David Byrne (Monaghan).

Garda All-Ireland G.A.A. Team — Winners of Inter-Services, Inter-Universities, G.A.A. Tournament, 1984.
Front Row, left to right: Mick Lillis (Clare), John Keane (Tipperary), James Kearns (Sligo), Eugene McHale (Mayo), Colm Browne (Laois), Peter Lee (Galway), Jim McManus (Roscommon), Jim Marshall (Wexford).

Back Row, left to right: Eamonn Barry (Meath), Des Brennan (Laois), Matt Connor (Offaly), Seamus Bonner (Donegal), Pat Forrestal (Meath), Mick Gallagher (Donegal), Des McGrath (Mayo), John Clarke (Mayo), Mick Lowry (Wexford), Ben Tansey (Galway), Mick O'Connor, Manager.

Celebration of Garda Medal Winners on the Centenary of the founding of the GAA 1984

Photo] GARDA FOOTBALL TEAM TO OPPOSE THE ARMY DURING AONACH AN GHARDA. [Garda Saol.
Top Row—Jas. Kirwan, M. Reidy, J. Smith, P. Flynn, J. Farrell, J. J. Scanlon, P. Colleran, P. Lynam.
Bottom Row—J. O'Toole, J. O'Reilly, J. Kirwan, P. Russell (capt.), D. Creagh, K. Kenny, F. Teeling.
Seated in front—M. McCoy and J. Sherlock.

A Brief History of Gaelic Football in An Garda Síochána

Gaelic Football has been played in An Garda Síochana since 1923. Commissioner Eoin O'Duffy formed the Garda GAA Club in Dublin the same year and instant success was achieved winning Dublin Championships in 1927 and 1929 and a three in a row 1933-34-35 with some of the best footballers in the Country at that time like Larry Stanley of Kildare - Dick Creagh Mayo and Paddy Corroran of Sligo.

The team was considered to be too strong so it was disbanded by transferring most of the members to various parts of the country.

It was reformed again in 1947 and again won the Dublin S.F.C. in 1948 and 1952 where the team had extraordinary talent in men like Paddy Kennedy of Kerry, Bill Carlos, Brendan Lynch, Liam Gilmartin and Tom Langan of Mayo.

There was no competition at this time for the members of the force as a team to compete against, and almost every county in the country had some members playing on its team.

In 1966 an InterDivisional Championship was organised between the 26 Divisions in the Country and this still continues to date with the Cavan/Monaghan Division being the winners in 1995 defeating the Garda College in the Final at Westmanstown.

The last twenty years has seen the force produce some of the greatest gaelic footballers in the history of Gaelic Games many of whom won All Ireland Medals and All Star Awards like John Egan and Paudie O'Shea of Kerry, John McCarthy of Dublin, Matt Connor from Offaly, Anthony Davis of Cork. While other famous players from that era include Willie Magee - Mayo, Mick Carola - Kildare, Sean Ferriter - Donegal, Seamus Bonne - Donegal, John Morley - Mayo and Tom Prendergast and Colm Brown from Laois.

Currently there are 30 members playing Senior Inter County Football, so if anything the force is getting stronger in Gaelic Games especially with new members playing with the Garda College in the higher education competitions like the Sigerson Cup where they were recently defeated by U.C.D. in the Final.

Some of our best players are still winning All Ireland Medals like Brian Murray of Donegal and Dermot Deasy of Dublin. Other well known current players who will be playing today are Niall O'Donnell from Louth, Brendan Rouine - Clare, John Newton and Dereck Duggan - Roscommon, Pat O'Donoghue and Liam Conlon - Leitrim and Kevin Walsh from Galway.

Each year An Garda Síochána look forward to competing in the Cumann Lúthchleas Gael Representatives Games and as in 1995 once again we are delighted to be hosts to the games (at our Sports Complex at Westmanstown where the facilities are top class.

Finally I would like to thank the Garda G.A.A. Club and its members for helping to organise this competition and I hope all players - mentors and visitors enjoy the competitions.

Eamon Barry.

10

GAA
REPRESENTATIVE
GAMES

12.00
GARDA V FITZGIBBON -
Hurling Semi Final
DEFENCE FORCES V COMBINED COLLEGES -
Hurling Semi Final

1.30
GARDA V SIGERSON -
Football Semi Final
DEFENCE FORCES V COMBINED COLLEGES -
Football Semi Final

3.00
Hurling Final

4.30
Football Final

Westmanstown 3rd April, '96

GARDA HURLING PANEL

Name	Club	County
Mick Cuffe	St. Pats Palmerstown	Dublin
Seamus McIntyre	Kenmare	Kerry
Gerry Kennedy	Roscrea	Tipperary
John Finnegan	Commercias	Dublin
Kevin Long	Newcestown	Cork
Pat O'Connell	Lisnan	Kerry
Padraig Tobin	Kilmallock	Limerick
Denis Byrne	Graigue-Ballycallan	Kilkenny
Peter Queally	Ballydurn	Waterford
Tom Kennedy	Thurles Sarsfields	Tipperary
Sean Colum	J. K. Brackens	Tipperary
James Aherne	Fermoy	Cork
Aidan Flanigan	Boherlahan	Tipperary
Seamus Maher	Borrisoleigh	Tipperary
Padraig Hession	Ballyboden-St. Endas	Dublin
Tom O'Dwyer	Holycross	Tipperary
Mick Nash	South Liberties	Limerick
Brendan Carey	Roscrea	Tipperary
Austin Cleere	Emeralds	Kilkenny
Chris Bonar	Eire Óg Nenagh	Tipperary
John Shortall	Harps	Laoise
Sean Moyles	Faughs	Dublin
John Twomey	Erins Isle	Dublin
Paddy Kelly	Kiltale	Meath
Seamus Delaney	J. K. Brackens	Tipperary
Ml. O'Sullivan	St. Bridgets	Dublin

Selectors:

Tony O'Donoghue, Ballyboden - St, Endas, Dublin
John O'Shea, Faughs, Dublin
Ken Hogan, Lorna, Tipperary.

Manager

John O' Shea.

GARDA FOOTBALL PANEL

Name	Club	County
Niall O'Donnell	Clanna Gael	Louth
Chris Grogan	Roscommon Gaels	Roscommon
Connie Murphy	Dr. Crokes	Kerry
Adrian Phelan	Portarlington	Laois
Brendan Rouine	Ennistymon	Clare
Fergal Reynolds	St. Marys	Leitrim
Peter McConnan	Round Towers-K	Kildare
Fergal Dardis	Round Towers - D	Dublin
Oliver O'Sullivan	Garnish	Cork
David O'Connor	Garda	Roscommon
Dermot Deasy	Ballymun	Dublin
Kevin McGettigan	Termon	Donegal
Brian Murray	Kilcock	Donegal
Pat Hegarty	Caragha	Cork
John Newton	St. Marys Leixlip	Roscommon
Kevin Walsh	Killannin	Galway
Pat O'Donoghue	Drumreilly	Leitrim
Greg McGovern	Garda	Fermanagh
Brian O'Donovan	O'Donovan Rossa	Cork
Martin Doran	Clontarf	Dublin
Dereck Duggan	Garda	Roscommon
Liam Conlon	Sean O'Heslins	Leitrim
Eamon McManus	Clanna Gael	Roscommon
James Kingston	Tadgh McCurtaghs	Cork
Garvan Ware	Eire Óg	Carlow

Managers
Eamon Barry
Paud Curran

Tipperary New York team

Panel of Players
Declan O Carroll, Bob Fitzsimons, Stuart Beatty, John Ivers, Mick O Keeffe,
James Tierney, Brian Murphy, Paul English, Johnny Power, Eoin Clifford,
Aidan IversKieran O Shea, Chris O Meara, Niall Tobin, Pa Gleeson, Padraic Lalor,
Larry Stapleton, Anthony Owens, Sean Brosnan, Kevin Ivers

Rising Stars
Some of the country's finest up and coming GAA footballers and hurlers gathered in Dublin for
the Ulster Bank Rising Stars Awards. Having been selected from the 2008 Higher Education
Championships, the best of the best were honoured at a reception held in Ulster Bank's Group
Centre, in Dublin, on the 9th June, 2008.
From the left Garda College players, John O'Brien (Dublin), Rory Guinan (Offaly)
and Cormac McGill, (Meath)

Wicklow / Wexford All Ireland Garda Team 1975

Back Row: Pat Sheehan, Tom Byrne, Pat Mulcahy, Pat Flynn, Tony Fagan, Declan O
Rourke, Bill Humprys.
Front Row: Mortie Ambrose, Tom Miller, Tom Flynn, Tom Dunphy, Liam Doyle,
David Lynch.

1962–63 Place Unknown Store St GAA Team

1967 23 Jul O'Toole Pk Garda Football Teams

Garda Dog Unit

Garda Mounted Unit

Garda Band

Garda Air Support

*Superintendent Gerard Murphy, Superintendent Dan Flavin, Chief Superintendent Seán Ward
and Assistant Commisioner Pat Leahy at the launch of the inaugural
Dublin North Central Garda Youths Awards on the 18th October 2017 in association with
Croke Park. These awards are being launched to celebrate outstanding young people throughout
the communities of Dublin North Central. Find out more at crokepark.ie/YouthAwards*

Chapter 26

Player Profiles

Featuring members of An Garda Síochána who have played
senior inter-county football, hurling, ladies' football and camogie

A

Aherne, Mick (football)

▶ *Native of Kerry; played for Kerry (1967-71), Waterford (1973-76).*
Career/honours: played club football for Currow.

Ashe, Michael (football)

▶ *Native of Kerry; played for Kerry (1952-54), Offaly (1954-59), Monaghan (1959-61).*
Career/honours: played minor for Kerry, 1951-52; Offaly junior championship with Rahan, 1955; Offaly senior championship with Daingean, 1958 and 1961.

B

Bailey, Jim (football)

▶ *Native of Kerry (Tralee); played senior football for Waterford.*
Career/honours: played against Kerry in the 1946 Munster final as a half back, and against Tipperary in the 1947 first round; a sub against Clare in 1949 (Munster JFC). Played with Dungarvan and helped them win four Waterford SFC titles in a row from 1945 to 1948.

Baker, Greg (hurling)

▶ *Native of Clare; played senior hurling for Clare (1995).*
Career/honours: **All-Ireland Club championship medal (1999) with St Joseph's Doora Barefield;** *All-Ireland Club finalist medal (2000); three senior club and two Munster senior club championship medals with St Joseph's Doora Barefield.*

Baker, Ollie (hurling)

▶ *Native of Clare; played senior hurling for Clare (1994-2004).*
Career/honours: **County – Two All-Ireland senior medals, 1994 and 1996; two All Star Awards, 1995 and 1998 (both at midfield***); three Munster senior championship medals, 1994, 1996 and 1998; one All-Ireland senior finalist medal, 2002; Railway Cup medal, 1996.* **Club –** *St Joseph's Doora Barefield – minor (1990), U21 (1993-94) county championship medals; three senior championship medals in hurling and football (1998, 1999, 2001); two Munster championship medals (1998, 1999);* **All-Ireland Club championship medal, 1999.** *Former inter-county manager with Offaly.*

Bambrick, Niall (football/hurling)

▶ *Native of Carlow; played senior football and hurling for Carlow during the 1990s.*
Career/honours: **County –** *hurling with Carlow, U14 to U21; played senior hurling with Carlow, winning* **All-Ireland 'B' championship in 1991***; played until 2002; played senior football with Carlow 1997-98.* **Club –** *senior hurling medal with Naomh Bríd, 2014*

Bane, Cormac (football)

▶ *Native of Galway; played senior football for Galway (2002-12).*
Career/honours: **County –** **All-Ireland U21 medal (2002);** *Connacht U21 medal, 2002; one Connacht junior championship (2005); one Connacht senior championship (2008); three Connacht FBD League medals.* **Club –** *One county intermediate championship and Connacht intermediate club championship (2006) with Caherlistrane.* **Three All-Ireland senior interfirms medals (2010, 2011, 2012) with Galway Garda.** *Intermediate Player of Year, 2006; Connacht Sports Personality of the Month, October 2006.*

Barber, Tom (football)

▶ *Native of Dublin; played senior football for Dublin (1982-84).*
Club: Erin's Isle.

Barden, Yvonne (ladies' football)

▶ *Native of Longford; played ladies' football for Longford.*
Career/honours: Leinster ladies' IFC medals with Longford, 2008, 2009, 2010, 2012; named on the Bord Gáis Energy Ladies' NFL Division 2 team of the league in 2009. **Club – Clonguish:** *IFC medal, 2002; senior league, 2003, 2006; SFC 2004, 2005 (captain), 2007, 2009; Leinster Club IFC, 2005 (captain); Leinster Club SFC, 2007, 2009; Clonguish Ladies Player of the Year, 2009.* **St Ultan's Ladies' GFC (Meath)***: Meath senior league, 2014; Meath ladies' SFC, 2015, 2016 (captain).*

Barrett, Paddy (hurling)

▶ *Native of Mayo; played senior hurling for Mayo (1998-2004).*

Barrett, Sean (football)

▶ *Native of Mayo.*
Career/honours: All-Ireland Vocational Schools medal, 1971.

Barrins, Gerry (football)

▸ *Native of Sligo; played football for Sligo (1975-79) and Longford (1979-85). Career/honours: Played played minor football for Sligo; captained Mayo Vocational to first All-Ireland success in 1971; three county championships with Longford Slashers; won Division 4 league title with Longford.*

Barron, Damien (hurling)

▸ *Native of Offaly; played senior hurling for Offaly (1992-98). Career/honours: Walsh Cup medal;* **All-Ireland minor medal, 1989***; Kilcormac/ Killoughey clubman.*

Barry, Eamonn (football)

▸ *Native of Meath; played senior football for Meath (1980-84). Career/honours: Centenary Cup medal in 1984 (captain); O'Byrne Cup medal in 1983; captain of Meath U21s in 1980. Walterstown clubman. Former inter-county manager with Meath.*

Baxter, John (football)

▸ *Native of Leitrim; played senior football for Leitrim in the 1970s. Career/honours: senior championship medal with Mohill, 1971.*

Baxter, Karen (ladies' football)

▸ *Native of Cavan; played for Cavan (2002-12). Career/honours: intermediate football with club (Templeport); Ulster championship medal, 2011; All-Ireland intermediate finalist medal, 2011.*

Begley, Brian (football/hurling)

▸ *Native of Limerick; played hurling (1999-2008) and football (1998-2004) with Limerick. Career/honours: U21 Munster medal – hurling and football; All-Ireland finalist medal, 2007; county intermediate football medal; junior hurling medal; city championship medals in hurling and football and county cup championship medals with Mungret.*

Begley, John (football)

▸ *Native of Waterford; played senior football for Kerry. Career/honours: played on the 1938 Dungarvan Waterford SFC-winning team.*

Begley, Pat (football)

▸ *Native of Clare; played football with Clare during the 1970s. Career/honours: played minor and U21 for Clare; two intermediate, two junior, one minor and one U21 championships in Clare; one intermediate championship in Leitrim. Interfirms* **All-Ireland with Limerick***. Beaten in five senior championship finals with club Ennistymon. Former inter-county manager of the Clare minor and U21 teams.*

Behan, Mick (football)

▶ *Native of Dublin; played football with Dublin (1973-76).*
Career/honours: one All-Ireland Club championship medal with St Vincent's,
1975; two Leinster and four senior football and hurling championship medals
with St Vincent's; two senior club championship medals with Éire Óg, Carlow,
1976-77; also played with Graiguecullen, Carlow. Former manager of Carlow
senior team and Dublin U21 team. A ballroom dancer of note!

Behan, Owen (hurling)

▶ *Native of Kilkenny; played for Kilkenny (2002).*
Club: Fenians, Johnstown.

Benson, Frank (Galway)

▶ *Native of Galway; played football for Galway in the 1920s.*
Career/honours: All-Ireland senior medal, 1925

Bergin, Shane (football)

▶ *Native of Cork; played for Waterford (1995-97).*
Career/honours: played minor football for Cork; junior football for Waterford,
1999; All-Ireland junior medal, 1999. Club: Gaultier.

Blake, Tomás (football)

▶ *Native of Meath; played inter-county football for New York (2000) and junior*
football for Meath.
Career/honours: two junior and one intermediate, Division 1 and 5 league and
U21 medals with St Brigid's/Ballinlough; Leinster junior medal with Meath,
2005; **All-Ireland Masters medal with Westmeath, 2015.**

Blessing, Noel (football)

▶ *Native of Leitrim; played for Leitrim, 1954-58.*
Career/honours: minor football, 1951-52; Railway Cup medal, 1957; London
championship, 1954; three senior county championships and one league with
Aughavas; one minor championship in 1952.

Blessing, Peter 'P. C.' (football)

▶ *Native of Leitrim; played for Leitrim in 1927.*
Career/honours: senior Connacht medal, 1927.

Blessing, Terry (football)

▶ *Native of Leitrim; played for Leitrim (1962-70).*
Career/honours: minor in 1957; ninor championship and league with Aughavas
in 1957; four senior championships with Aughavas, 1963-66.

Bohan, Frank (football)

▶ *Native of Leitrim; played football for Leitrim, 1975-82.*
Career/honours: U21 Connacht championship medal in 1977; two All-Ireland
Agriculture medals with Ballyhaise, 1975.

Boland, Andy (football)

▶ *Native of Sligo;*
Club: St Patrick's.

251

Bonner, Chris (football)

▸ *Native of Tipperary; Played football for Éire Óg, Nenagh.*

Bonner, Seamus (football)

▸ *Native of Donegal; played for Donegal, 1968-85.*
Career/honours: two Dr McKenna Cup medals; three Ulster senior medals, 1972, 1974 and 1983; one Dublin senior championship and league medal, 1980; one replacement All Star, 1975.
Featured in John Scally's All-Ireland Ambitions as follows: "I was playing against Monaghan one day in a league match in Ballybofey and I was soloing with the ball twenty yards out from the goal with the defence beaten. I had a goal on my mind, but I had my mouth open and a fly flew into my mouth and I swallowed it and nearly choked. I was clean through and came to a sudden staggering stop, and with nobody near me I let the ball fall out of my hands. The Donegal fans didn't know what happened. I'm not sure what they were thinking, but I'm sure it wasn't complementary. The moral of the story is that when you are on a football field, you should keep your mouth shut!"

Bonner, Sean (football)

▸ *Native of Donegal; played for Donegal (1983-91).*
Career/honours: Ulster senior championship medal, 1990; Ulster U21 and All-Ireland; one Donegal junior championship with Na Rossa, 1982; two Donegal intermediate championships with Na Rossa, 1989 and 1999.

Bourke, John (hurling)

▸ *Native of Dublin; played for Dublin (1972-73).*
Career/honours: Senior club championship medal with Craobh Chiaráin, 1971.

Bourke, Willie (hurling)

▸ *Native of Dublin; played for Dublin (2004-05) and Fingal (2008-10).*
Career/honours: Inter-county manager of Fingal; Division 3 National League title, 2012; Kehoe Shield.

Bowe, Tom (football)

▸ *Native of Laois; played for Laois (1991-2001).*
Career/honours: played minor and U21 football; All-Ireland 'B' medal in 1993; two O'Byrne Cup medals.
Legendary sports commentator Jimmy Magee referred to a point scored by Tom in the 1995 replay against Carlow as "one of the greatest scores ever".

Boyce, Danny (football)

▸ *Played for Donegal in the 1960s and 1970s.*

Boyce, Padraig (football)

▸ *Native of Galway; played football for Galway (1993-99).*
Career/honours: **All-Ireland senior medal, 1998**. *Connacht championship medal, 1998;* **All-Ireland U21 medal, 1992;** *Galway U21 1991, 1992, 1993, 1994 (captain); Galway minor 1989, 1990 (captain), 1991; Galway U16 1987, 1988, 1989.*

Boyle, Aidan (hurling)

▸ *Native of Kerry; played for Kerry (2004–14).*
Career/honours: Played club hurling for Ballyduff, winning five senior county championship medals.

Boyle, Colm (football)

▸ *Native of Mayo; played senior football for Mayo, 2006 to present.*
Career/honours: **Four All Star Awards – left half back 2013, 2014, centre back 2016, right wing back 2017; All-Ireland U21 medal, 2006**; *two All-Ireland finalist medals, 2012, 2013; five Connacht senior championship medals, 2009, 2011, 2012, 2013, 2014; minor and U21 football for Mayo.* **Represented Ireland in the 2013 and 2014 International Rules series.** *Connacht and county intermediate medals, 2011 (club: Davitts).*

Boyle, Conor (football)

▸ *Native of Laois; played senior football for Laois (2012–16).*
Career/honours: played minor football for Laois, 2007; Leinster minor medal, 2007; played U21 football for Laois, 2008–12; ten club championship medals with Portlaoise, 2007-2017; Trench Cup medal with Garda College, 2015; Laois player of the year, 2012.

Boyle, Patrick (football)

▸ *Native of Donegal; played senior football for Donegal (1994–97) and Dublin (1997).*

Boyle, Seamus (football)

▸ *Played senior football for Longford (1987–89 and 1995).*
Career/honours: one minor 1982, Masters 2005–10; All-Ireland Masters medal in 2005; played for Irish Masters team, 2006.

Boyle, Vincent (football)

▸ *Native of Donega; played senior football for Donegal (1945–46).*
Career/honours: Donegal League Democrat Cup, 1943. Club: Garda, Dublin.

Bracken, Aidan (football)

▸ *Native of Offaly; played senior football for Offaly (1987–97).*
Career/honours: **All-Ireland U21 medal, 1988**; *two O'Byrne Cup medals; two Division 3 National League medals; intermediate championship medal in 2004 with Ballymore; four senior league medals with Garda Club, Dublin. Club: Shamrocks.*

Brady, Eamonn (football)

▸ *Native of Cavan; played for Cavan (1995–96).*
Career/honours: three senior championship medals with Mullahoran, 1998, 2006, 2012.

Brady, Eoin (hurling)

▸ *Native of Dublin; played for Dublin (1981–82).*
Career/honours: two senior club championship medals with St Vincent's, 1981 and 1982

Brady, Ger (football)

▶ *Native of Mayo; played football for Mayo (2003-07).*
Career/honours: one Connacht senior medal, 2006; All-Ireland senior finalist medal, 2006; inter-provincial football for Connacht; **one All-Ireland Senior Club championship medal with Ballina Stephenites, 2005.**

Brady, Killian (football)

▶ *Native of Cavan;*
has played all grades for Cavan, senior 2013 to present.
Career/honours: U21 panellist in 2012, and Ulster medallist. Club: Mullahoran. Won a Cavan SFC medal in 2012, and was player of the year.

Brady, Phil 'The Gunner' (football)

▶ *Native of Cavan; played football for Cavan (1944-57).*
Career/honours: **three All-Ireland senior medals, 1947, 1948 and 1952 (1947 in Polo Grounds, New York);** *eleven club championship medals with Mullahoran; one Garda Cork National League medal, 1948; Railway Cup football with Ulster.*
Named at midfield in the *Sunday Independent's* 2017 'Football's Toughest Team'. Received a Scott medal in September 1970 from then Minister for Justice, Des O'Malley at the Garda Training College, Templemore, for disarming a man near Castleblayney in 1969.

Brady, Tom (football)

▶ *Native of Cavan; played senior football for Waterford in the late 1960s and early 1970s. Club: De La Salle.*
Career/honours: played at full back against Kerry in a championship match, 1969.

Brady, Yvonne (ladies' football)

▶ *Native of Meath; played for Meath (2002-03).*

Breen, Dinny (football)

▶ *Native of Galway; played football for Westmeath, 1931.*
Career/honours: **All-Ireland junior medal, 1929;** *two senior championship medal with Rochfortbridge Warriors, 1923 and 1925; four senior championship medals with Garda Club, Dublin; Railway Cup football with Leinster. Also played with Ardagh, Newbridge, Sarsfields and Maynooth.*

Brennan, Barry (football)

▶ *Native of Laois; played football for Laois (2005).*
Career/honours: played minor football for Laois; Leinster senior medal, 2003. Club: Graige.

Brennan, David (football)

▶ *Native of Laois; played football for Laois (2000-02, 2005, 2007).*
Career/honours: U21 football with Laois, 1999; Division 1 Dublin league medal with St Mary's of Saggart in 2004; one league medal with St Joseph's in Laois in 2011.

Brennan, Dessie (football)

▸ *Native of Laois; played football for Laois, 1973-83.*
Career/honours: O'Byrne Cup medal; seven senior championship medals with St Joseph's; five senior league medals; one junior medal and two minor medals; Laois Footballer of the Year, 1983. Leo, Kieran and Dessie were on the same Laois team together in 1976; David is a son of Dessie.

Brennan, Donal (football)

▸ *Native of Leitrim; played for Leitrim. Club: Cloone.*

Brennan, Eddie (hurling)

▸ *Native of Kilkenny; hurled for Kilkenny, 1999-2012.*
Career/honours: **County – eight All-Ireland senior hurling championship medals, 2000, 2002, 2003, 2006, 2007, 2008, 2009, 2011; four All Star awards – left half forward (2003, 2006), left corner forward (2007), right corner forward 2008; one All-Ireland U21 hurling championship medal,** *1999; ten Leinster senior hurling championship medals, 2000, 2001, 2002, 2003, 2005, 2006, 2007, 2008, 2009, 2010; four National Hurling League medals, 2000, 2003, 2005, 2009; four Walsh Cup medals, 2005, 2006, 2007, 2009; one Leinster U21 hurling championship medal, 1999.* **Club** *– Graigue-Ballycallan (senior), 2002-12; one Leinster senior club hurling championship medal, 2000; one Kilkenny senior club hurling championship medal, 2000. Manager of Kilkenny U21 team, 2015.*
Known as 'Fast Eddie', Brennan played shinty for Ireland in 2008. Was ranked at 109 on the 125 Greatest Stars of the GAA.

Brennan, James (football)

▸ *Native of Mayo; played for Donegal (1974-81).*
Career/honours: two Donegal intermediate and one junior championship medals; Division 1B Colleges medal with St Colman's, Claremorris. Managed Donegal junior team.

Brennan, Joe (football)

▸ *Native of Laois; played football for Laois, 1936-39.*
Career/honours: three Leinster senior championship medals.

Brennan, John (hurling)

▸ *Played senior hurling for Kerry, 1987-88. Club: Austin Stacks.*

Brennan, Kieran (football)

▸ *Native of Laois; played for Laois, 1966-78.*
Career/honours: Railway Cup player, 1970 and 1976; five senior championship medals with St Joseph's.
Has the distinction of playing league or championship against every other county in Ireland. Former inter-county manager with Laois.

Brennan, Laura (ladies' football)

▸ *Plays ladies' senior football for Westmeath.*
Career/honours: All-Ireland ladies' IFC medal, 2011; Ladies' NFL Division 2 medal, 2017. Club: Garrycastle.

Brennan, Leo (football)

▸ *Native of Laois; played for Laois (1971, 1976).*
Career/honours: Five Laois senior football titles with St Joseph's; played minor football for Laois; Leinster minor, 1966, junior, 1968 and U21, 1969.

Brennan, Michael (football)

▸ *Native of Wicklow; played football for Cavan.*
Career/honours: played U21 football; minor football and hurling; Dublin junior league medal with Garda in 1984.

Brennan, Rory (football/hurling)

▸ *Native of Sligo; played football for Sligo (1998-2002) and Mayo (2003), and hurling for Sligo (1998-2002).*
Career/honours: Played senior hurling for Sligo; ten senior hurling championship medals in a row with Tubbercurry; Connacht junior medal, 1998.

Brennan, Tom (football)

▸ *Native of Galway; played football for Galway during the 1960s.*
Career/honours: **senior All-Ireland medal, 1966; junior All-Ireland medal, 1965**; *two Connacht senior medals, 1966 and 1968; one Connacht junior medal, 1965.*

Breslin, Aidan (football)

▸ *Native of Meath; played football for Meath, 1960–64.*
Career/honours: Leinster junior medal in 1964; Feis Cup, Meath, 1959.

Brett, Noel (football)

▸ *Native of Sligo; played football for Sligo, 1978–80*
Career/honours: Junior football, 1985; county senior championship medal with Tourlestrane in 1978 and two senior leagues; **two All-Ireland over 40s medals, 1995 and 1997**; *minor football, 1971–72; county senior medal with Erris Gaels in 1988. Inter-county management: Mayo minors.*

Briggs, Niamh (ladies' football)

▸ *Native of Waterford; played with Waterford, 2003–10.*
Career/honours: All-Ireland minor and intermediate medals; Munster intermediate medal; **three All-Ireland Club 7s medals – two with Old Parish, one with Abbeyside.**
Captain of the Ireland women's rugby team which won the Grand Slam in 2013.

Broderick, Frank (football)

▸ *Native of Galway; played with Galway.*
Career/honours: three Connacht senior championship medals; four senior club championship medals with Annaghdown.

Brogan, Declan (hurling)

▸ *Played hurling with Galway during the 1970s.*

Brogan, Seamus (football)

▸ *Native of Leitrim; played football for Leitrim.*
Career/honours: Railway Cup football for Connacht.

Brosnan, Robbie (football)

▸ *Native of Cork; played for Cork, 1999-2008.*
Career/honours: McGrath Cup medal, 2007; Club: St Nicholas.
Played soccer for Waterford.

Brown, Aidan (football)

▸ *Native of Cork; played football for Dublin, 1958-59.*
Career/honours: Junior football for Dublin; Leinster junior championship medal, 1959; intermediate championship medal, 1958; senior league (Division 2) medal, 1960.

Brown, Jim (football/hurling)

▸ *Native of Cork: played hurling for Monaghan (1975-78) and football for Limerick (1983-88).*
Career/honours: five county senior championship medals with Claughaun (Limerick).

Brown, Tom (football)

▸ *Native of Meath; played football for Meath (1958, 1964-67) and Laois (1960-63).*
Career/honours: Leinster senior championship medals, 1964 and 1966 (Meath); Leinster junior championship medal, 1958 (Meath). Club championship medal with O'Dempsey's (1963) and Emo (1972). Railway Cup: 1962-66.
Made the Gaelic Weekly All Star team for 1963.

Browne, Colm (football)

▸ *Native of Laois; played for Laois, 1976-89.*
Career/honours: **One All Star award in 1986 at left half back; one All-Ireland Club championship medal with Portlaoise in 1986;** *ten senior club championship medals with Portlaoise; three Railway Cup medals, 1985, 1986 and 1987; played inter-provincial football for Leinster.*
Selected at wing back by an *Irish Independent* panel of media experts on a team of the fifteen best footballers of the 1980s who never won an All-Ireland medal. Inter-county management: Laois and Tipperary senior football teams. International Rules: played for Ireland vs Australia in the 1987 series.

Browne, Gerry (hurling)

▸ *Native of Roscommon; hurled for Dublin in 1933.*

Browne, Ian (football)

▸ *Native of Tipperary; played for Tipperary, 2003-07.*
Career/honours: Junior football, 2008-09; U21 (2005-07) and minor football (2003-04). Younger brother of All Star winner Declan Browne.

Browne, Michelle (camogie)

▸ *Native of Cork; played senior camogie with Cork, 2009-13.*
Career/honours: played first game in 1999; played U14, 2000-03, U16, 2003-04 (won an All-Ireland title in 2003); minor, 2005-06; junior/intermediate, 2007-08; **senior, 2009-13 (won All-Ireland title, 2009).** *Won a minor county medal with Mallow (2006) and a senior 'B' club medal (2016).*

257

Browne, Paddy (hurling)

▸ *Native of Tipperary; played hurling for Tipperary and Dublin in the 1920s. Career/honours: Munster senior hurling championship medal in 1922. Boerlahan–Dualla clubman.*

Browne, Peter (hurling)

▸ *Native of Louth; Hurled 1926-31.*

Brussels, Billy (hurling)

▸ *Native of Tipperary; hurled for Tipperary during the 1940s. Club: Roscrea.*

Buckley, Seanie (football)

▸ *Native of Limerick; played for Limerick, 2001–13. Career/honours: Six county senior football medals with Dromcollogher-Broadford, 2001, 2003, 2004, 2008, 2009 (captain), 2012 and 2013; one Munster senior club football medal, 2008.*

Bugler, Liz (camogie)

▸ *Native of Cork; played camogie for Cork. Career/honours:* **one All-Ireland senior 'B'** *and one Munster medal, 2006; junior and minor All-Ireland medals;* Represented Ireland at international level in 2004.

Burke, Brendan (football)

▸ *Roscommon.*

Burke, David (hurling)

▸ *Native of Limerick; hurled for Limerick, 1971. Career/honours: National League medal, 1971; Oireachtas medal, 1971; minor, U21 and junior hurling.*

Burke, Gerry (football)

▸ *Native of Galway; played for Galway. Career/honours:* **All-Ireland minor medal, 1976 (captain); All-Ireland Club championship medal with Corofin, 1998; man of the match in the final.** *Three Connacht SFC medals with Galway; five senior club and three Connacht club championship medals with Corofin.*

Burke, Jarlath (hurling)

▸ *Native of Sligo; Also played junior football for Sligo.*

Burke, Jeremiah 'Miah' (hurling)

▸ *Played for Cork, 1927-1929. Career/honours: Made thirteen appearances for Cork and won three Munster titles and* **two All-Irelands.** *Goalkeeper with the Collins club.*

Burke, Mick 'Blondie' (football)

▸ *Native of Laois; played football for Laois in the 1970s. Career/honours: played played U21 football for Laois, 1972, and his club football with Stradbally.*

Burke, Seamus (football)

▶ *Native of Galway; played for Galway in the 1980s. Club: Kilererin. Career/honours: two Connacht winners medals, 1982-83. All-Ireland runner-up medal with Galway, 1983; National League medal, 1981; All-Ireland JFC winners' medal, 1985. Two county titles with Kilererin, 1976, 1978.*

Burke, Tony (football)

▶ *Native of Kildare; played for Kildare, 1943-53. Career/honours: Railway Cup medals with Leinster, 1948 and 1949; Dublin senior championship medal with Garda, 1948.*

Burnell, Tom (hurling)

▶ *Native of Clare; played hurling with Dublin and Clare. Career spanned 1927-37.*

Burns, Barney (football)

▶ *Native of Mayo; active during 1950s. Played club football for Garda GAA Club, Dublin.*

Burns, W. M. (hurling)

▶ *Played senior hurling for Kerry in 1924.*

Butler, Gerard (football)

▶ *Native of Leitrim; played football for Leitrim, 1988-91.*

Byrne, David (football)

▶ *Native of Monaghan; played for Monaghan, 1983-96. Career/honours: two Ulster senior championship medals; two Railway Cup medals with Ulster; one National League medal (Division 3); Dublin senior league with Garda.*

Byrne, Denis (hurling)

▶ *Native of Kilkenny; hurled for Kilkenny (1999-2001) and Tipperary (2003). Career/honours:* **All-Ireland senior hurling championship medal with Kilkenny in 2000;** *runner-up medals, 1998, 1999 (captain);* **All Star award (right half forward), 2000. All-Ireland U21 hurling championship medal, 1994;** *runner-up, 1995; minor All-Ireland medal, 1991; Leinster senior hurling championship medals, 1998, 1999, 2000, 2001; runner-up 1995, 1996, 1997. Kilkenny senior hurling championship medals with Graigue-Ballycallan (1998, 2000); runner-up, 1999, 2001. AIB Leinster Club Player of the Year, 2000; Oireachtas medal winner, 1999; Walsh Cup runner-up, 2002; National Hurling League medals with Kilkenny, 1995, 2002.*

Byrne, Frank (hurling)

▶ *Native of Laois; hurled for Laois, 1964-72. Career/honours:* **minor hurling All-Ireland medal with Laois, 1964;** *senior football championship medals with Portlaoise, 1967, 1968 and 1970; senior football championship medals with Baltinglass, 1971 and 1972.*

Byrne, Michael (football)

▶ *Played senior football for Waterford, 2000. Club: The Nire. Career/honours:* **All-Ireland junior football medals, 1999 and 2004.**

Byrne, Rachel (ladies' football)

▸ *Plays senior ladies' football for Dublin.*

Byrne, Susan (ladies' football)

▸ *Native of Kildare; played with Kildare, 2012 to present.*
Career/honours: Played at all underage levels for Kildare; five senior club championship, three Division 1 and one Division 2 medals with Grangenolvin. Also played for St Laurence's.

Byrne, Tom (football/hurling)

▸ *Native of Laois; enjoyed stints with Wexford (1964, 1971-72) and Laois (1967-68).*
Career/honours: U21 football/minor hurling with Laois; U21 Hurling; senior football championship medal with Portlaoise.

Byrne, Tom (football)

▸ *Native of Mayo; played for Mayo (1982-84).*
Career/honours: **All-Ireland minor medal, 1978; came on as a sub in the final and scored two goals.**

C

Caffrey, Paul 'Pillar' (football)

▸ *Native of Dublin; played senior football for Dublin, 1986-88.*
Career/honours: National League medal, 1987; minor (1980) and U21 (1982-83) football; played senior football for Na Fianna for eighteen years. **Inter-county manager (Dublin): four consecutive Leinster titles (2005, 2006, 2007, 2008) as manager.**

Cahill, Martin (football)

▸ *Native of Dublin; played for Dublin (1999-2000).*
Career/honours: U21 Dublin championship medal with St Brigid's.

Cahill, Sean (football)

▸ *Native of Dublin; played for Dublin in 1995 and won an* **All-Ireland SFC medal** *that year.*

Callaghan, Eamonn (football)

▸ *Native of Kildare; played for Kildare, 2002 to present.*
Career/honours: Won intermediate championship in 2005 with Naas; past captain of Kildare. Club: Naas. Represented Ireland in 2011 in the International Rules;

Canavan, Mick (football)

▸ *Native of Clare; played for Clare, 1961-67.*
Career/honours: played minor and senior football for Clare; Senior League medal with Garda, 1966.

Canniffe, Dan (hurling)

▸ *Native of Dublin; hurled for Dublin in the 1930s.*
Career/honours: All-Ireland finalist, 1934; played centre half back.
Dan was the father of Donal Canniffe, who captained Munster in November 1978 in their famed rugby victory over the All Blacks. Dan died suddenly after the final whistle.

Carey, Brendan (hurling)

▸ *Native of Tipperary; played senior hurling for Tipperary, 1991-92, and U21 hurling for Tipperary, 1988.*

Carey, Eamonn (hurling)

▸ *Native of Limerick; hurled for Limerick, 1958-67.*
Career/honours: **minor All-Ireland medal, 1958**; *two senior club championship medals with Patrickswell, 1965 and 1966.*

Carey, Johnny (football)

▸ *Native of Mayo; played football for Mayo, 1962-73.*
Career/honours: **All Star 1971, right full back (inaugural team)**; *U21 and minor football with Mayo; National Football League medals, 1967 and 1969; two Connacht senior championship medals; Railway Cup, 1969.*

Carey, Mick (hurling)

▸ *Native of Westmeath; played senior hurling for Westmeath. Club: St Oliver Plunkett's/Pearses (Mullingar).*

Carey, Nigel (hurling)

▸ *Native of Limerick; played for Limerick in the 1990s and 2000s.*
Career/honours: minor and U21 hurling with Limerick; seven senior club championship medals with Patrickswell; two Munster club championship medals; **two All-Ireland 7-a-side medals.** *In total, six Carey brothers played for Patrickswell. Inter-county management: Mayo.*

Carey PJ (football)

▸ *Native of Mayo; played for Mayo, 1986-89.*
Career/honours: Intermediate championship medal with Kiltaine; intermediate league medal, 1979. Also played with Ballymun Kickhams and Fingallians in Dublin.

Carrigan, Denis (football)

▸ *Native of Dublin; played for Dublin in 2010. Club: St Mary's, Saggart.*
Career/honours: World Police and Fire Games gold medal, 2013.

Carley, Mark (football)

▸ *Native of Wexford; played for Wexford, 2001. Club: Glyn-Barntown.*

Carlos, Bill (football)

▸ *Native of Roscommon; played for Roscommon, 1940–44.*
Career/honours: **two All-Ireland senior medals, 1943 and 1944; two All-Ireland minor medals, 1939 and 1941 (captain)***; senior All-Ireland finalist, 1946; National League Division 3 medal with New York in 1950. County senior championship medals with Tarmon; senior club championship medal with Garda, Dublin, 1948.*
Named in John Scally's book as one of *"the GAA greats of Connacht".* The late Cardinal Tomás Ó Fiaich, when asked what he would like to have achieved as a sportsman, stated: "To play centre back like Bill Carlos."

Carmody, Tony (hurling)

▸ *Native of Clare; played for Clare, 2000–09 and 2012.*
Career/honours: **All-Ireland 2011 intermediate medal (as captain)***; All-Ireland finalist, 2002; Munster finalist in 2008; Munster intermediate medal, 2011. Nominated for an All Star award; Railway Cup medal for Munster, 2005. Club: Inagh and Inagh/Kilnamona.*

Carolan, Barry (hurling)

▸ *Native of Dublin; played for Dublin, 1989 and 1992.*
Career/honours: junior championship medal for Na Fianna, 1986; Dublin Blue Star Award, 1991; Dublin Interfirm medals.

Carolan, Mick (football)

▸ *Native of Kildare; played football for Kildare for eighteen years (1957-75).*
Career/honours: **Cú Chulainn (All Star) award in 1966***; four O'Byrne Cup medals; minor and intermediate championship medals with Athy; two Railway Cup medals with Leinster, 1961 and 1962.*
Garda Hall of Fame Award, 1999. Selected on the Kildare Millennium team.

Carr, Eddie (football)

▸ *Native of Louth; played for Louth, 1997 and 1998. Also played minor and U21 football for the Wee County.*

Carr, Thomas (football)

▸ *Native of Louth; played senior for Louth, 2005, and also played minor and U21. Career/honours: three senior club championships medals with Newtown Blues, 2000, 2001 and 2008.*

Carrie, Paddy (football)

▸ *Native of Meath native;*
Career/honours: **part of Meath's All-Ireland SFC-winning team in 1954.**

Carroll, J. (hurling)

▸ *Native of Limerick native;*
hurled for Donegal in the 1920s and won an Ulster SHC medal in 1923.

Carroll, J. (football)

▸ *Native of Kildare; played football for Kildare (1924) and Sligo (1926).*

Carroll, Mark (football)

▶ *Native of Laois; played football for Laois, 1967-68.*
Career/honours: four senior club championship medals with Portlaoise 1967, 1968, 1970 and 1971. Inter-county management experience with Kildare U21 team.

Carroll, Mike (hurling)

▶ *Native of Kerry; hurled for Kerry, 1976-83.*
Career/honours: **two All-Ireland senior 'B' medals; one All-Ireland minor 'B' medal;** *seven senior county club championship medals with Ballyduff.*

Carroll, Ted (football)

▶ *Native of Clare; played football for Clare in the 1950s. Later resigned from the Force and emigrated to the United States.*

Carter, Martha (ladies' football)

▶ *Native of Mayo; played for Mayo, 2003 to present.*
Career/honours: **All-Ireland senior medal, 2003; All Star Award 2009 (centre back);** *two National League medals (Division 1), 2004, 2007;* **five All-Ireland club championship medals with Carnacon, 2002, 2007, 2008, 2011 and 2013.**

Carty, T. (football)

▶ *Native of Dublin; played football for Dublin in 1927.*

Carty, Tom (football)

▶ *Native of Tipperary; played football for Tipperary, 1924-26.*
Career/honours: **All-Ireland junior football medal, 1923**.

Casey, Denis (hurling)

▶ *Native of Tipperary; hurled for Westmeath, 1968.*
Career/honours: senior club championship medal in 1968 with St Brigid's; 1968: U21 medal for weaker counties.

Casey, Michelle (camogie)

▶ *Native of Limerick; played camogie for Limerick.*
Career/honours: **All-Ireland senior 'B' championship** *and senior 'B' league medals; five senior county championship medals with Killeedy.* **All-Ireland junior league medal, 1996;** *All Star nomination, 2006; All-Ireland Pan Celtic medal. Limerick Senior Player of the Year, 2001. Club: Killeedy.*

Casey, Noel (hurling)

▶ *Native of Clare; hurled for Clare, 1968-80.*
Career/honours: **All Star award 1978 (centre forward);** *Railway Cup medals, 1976 and 1978; National League medal,1977-78. Played U21 hurling for Clare.*

Casey, Pat (football)

▶ *Native of Mayo; played senior with Mayo in 2006.*
Career/honours: Mayo junior 'A' championship medal with The Neale, 2012; All-Ireland Colleges 'B' medal, 1999 with Ballinrobe.

Casey, Sean (football)

▸ *Native of Offaly; played senior for Offaly, 2006–07. Club: St Brigid's.*

Cashen, Martin (hurling)

▸ *Native of Offaly native, hurled for Offaly, 1976–85.*
Career/honours: **two All-Ireland senior medals, 1981 and 1985**; *played minor, U21 and junior hurling for Offaly; three Leinster SHC medals, 1980, 1981 and 1985; one Leinster U21 medal, 1978. Four senior club championship medals; three junior, one intermediate, one U21 club and eight championship medals with club Carrig/Riverstown.*

Cawley, Cathal (football)

▸ *Native of Sligo; played senior for Sligo, 1960–73, and also junior football.*
Career/honours: Railway Cup with Connacht, 1964–69; county club championship medal with Claremorris, 1971; county club championship medal with Crossmolina.

Chatten, Jack (football)

▸ *Native of Sligo; played senior football for Sligo, 1952–58.*
Career/honours: minor football 1952–53 (captain); senior and minor championship medals with Craobh Rua, Sligo, 1952; Longford county senior championship medal.

Clarke, Annette (ladies' football)

▸ *Native of Galway; played for Galway, 2003–16.*
Career/honours: **captained Galway to senior All-Ireland victory, 2004; two All Stars, 2004 and 2013; junior All-Ireland medal, 2002.** *Played with the Munster inter-provincial team.*

Clarke, David (football)

▸ *Native of Mayo; played for Mayo, 2001 to present.*
Career/honours: **two All Star awards, goalkeeper, 2016, 2017**; *four All-Ireland senior runners-up medals, 2006, 2012, 2016 and 2017; county senior medal, 2007. 7 Connaught championship medals, 1 National League medal Played inter-provincial football for Connacht.* **One All Ireland Club championship medal (2004/05)** *and two senior Connacht club medals, 2004 and 2007, county minor medals, 1999, 2000 and 2001; county U21 medal, 2000 with Ballina Stephenites.*
Only the sixth goalkeeper in GAA history to win back to back All Star Awards.

Cleary, Eoin (football)

▸ *Native of Clare; played football for Clare, 2014 to present.*
Career/honours: played minor football for Clare, 2011 and 2012; played U21 football for Clare, 2013, 2014, 2015; junior football for Clare, 2015; Division 3 National League medal, 2016. Senior club championship medal with St Joseph's Miltown Malbay, 2015; intermediate club medal, 2013.

Cleary, John (hurling)

▸ *Native of Tipperary; hurled for Waterford in 1974.*
Also played soccer for Thurles Town and Waterford.

Cleary, Pat (hurling)

▶ *Native of Offaly; hurled for Offaly, 1982-92*
Career/honours: **All-Ireland senior medal, 1985; All Star Award, 1995 (right corner forward);** *five Leinster championship medals; one National League medal; two Offaly U21 and intermediate medals. Clubs: Ballyskenagh and Kilmacud Crokes.*
Named man of the match in the 1985 All-Ireland SHC final, scoring two goals from play.

Cleary, Tommy (football)

▶ *Native of Westmeath; played senior football for Westmeath, 1997-98, 2001, 2005.*
Career/honours: **All-Ireland minor football medal, 1995;** *two senior club championship medals with The Downs, 2003 and 2005.*

Cleere, Mick

▶ *Native of Kilkenny; hurled for Kilkenny at senior grade, 1986-92.*
Career/honours: **All-Ireland junior medals, 1984 and 1986;** *played minor, U21 and junior hurling for Kilkenny; All-Ireland minor finalist, 1978; National League medal, 1989/90; Railway Cup medal, 1988. Minor, U21 and intermediate club championship medals with O'Loughlin Gaels.*

Clifford, Con

▶ *Native of Kerry; played junior for Kerry, 1961, 1964. Club: Dr Crokes.*

Clifford, Jerry (football/hurling)

▶ *Native of Cork; played football and hurling for Louth (1964-67).*
Career/honours: five senior club championship medals with Newtown Blues, Drogheda (football); one junior club championship medal with Ballynacargy (Westmeath, football).

Clifford, Jim (football)

▶ *Native of Galway; played football for Galway (1942) and Kerry (1943-44).*
Career/honours: Munster senior medal, 1944; senior club championship medal with Fermoy, 1945; All-Ireland senior finalist in 1942 and 1944. Won a Connacht SFC medal, 1942. Other clubs: St Mary's and the Geraldines.

Cloonan, Diarmaid (hurling)

▶ *Native of Galway; played for Galway (2001-07).*
Career/honours: minor and U21 hurling for Galway; All-Ireland senior finalist, 2001; National League medal, 2004; two All-Ireland U21 finalist medals, 1999, 2000; one All-Ireland minor finalist medal, 1997. Club: Athenry.

Clooney, James (hurling)

▶ *Native of Wexford native;*
hurled for Donegal, and won an Ulster SHC medal in 1923.

Cluskey, Noel (football)

▶ *Native of Louth; played senior football for Louth (1979-89).*
Career/honours: played minor U21 and junior for Louth; Leinster U21 medal, 1981; Dublin senior league medal with Garda, 1991.

Coen, Brian (football)

▸ *Native of Tipperary; played senior football for Tipperary (2006-11) and Wicklow (2013).*
Career/honours: played U21 and junior football for Tipperary; senior club championship medal with Fethard, 2001; U21 club championship medals, 2000, 2001 and 2002.

Coen, Jimmy (hurling)

▸ *Native of Galway; hurled for Cavan (1988).*
Career/honours: played minor hurling for Galway; two senior Club championship medals with Cavan Gaels and Woodford.

Coen, Johnny

▸ *Galway and Cavan.*

Coen, Mick (football)

▸ *Native of Galway; played senior for Galway, 1964-65.*
Career/honours: **All-Ireland senior medal, 1964;** *played minor, U21 and junior football for Galway; senior club championship medal (1964) with Tuam Stars.*

Coghlan, Hugh (football)

▸ *Native of Tipperary; played for Tipperary, 2004-14.*
Career/honours: Division 4 league runner-up, 2007; Division 3 league medal, 2008; GPA Player of the Month, May 2008; Division 4 league medal, 2014. Intermediate championship medal with Moyne/Templetuohy, 2004; Dublin senior football championship runner-up with St Vincent's, 2006; Dublin, Leinster and All-Ireland senior football championship medals, 2007-08; three Laois senior football championship medals with Portlaoise, 2010, 2011 and 2012; Tipperary intermediate hurling championship medal with Moyne/Templetuohy, 2014. World Police & Fire Games Gold Medal, 2013

Coleman, C.J. (hurling)

▸ *Native of Kilkenny; played for Kilkenny (1925-26).*

Coleman, Colin (football)

▸ *Native of Roscommon; played football for Roscommon (1995-96).*
Career/honours: minor and U21 football with Roscommon; intermediate championship medal with Éire Óg, 1991; junior championship medal with Johnstownbridge, Kildare, 2000.

Coleman, Enda (football)

▸ *Native of Laois; played senior for Laois, 1999. Club: Portlaoise.*

Coleman, Mattie (football)

▸ *Native of Galway; played for Galway during the 1980s.*
Career/honours: **All-Ireland minor medal, 1976;** *National League medal, 1981; All-Ireland senior finalist, 1983; inter-provincial football for Connacht. Club championship hurling medal with Abbeyknockmoy, 1988 and football medal with Monivea- Abbeyknockmoy.*

Coleman, Thomas (football)

▸ *Native of Mayo; played football for Mayo (1955), Clare (1956-57) and Limerick (1958).*
Career/honours: Connacht junior championship medal, 1953; club championship medal with Garda, Limerick, 1958.

Colleran, Luke (football)

▸ *Native of Sligo; played for Sligo, 1928.*

Colleran, Noel (football)

▸ *Native of Galway; played for Galway, 1968-72. Brother of Enda Colleran.*

Colleran, Paddy (football)

▸ *Native of Sligo; played football for Sligo, Cavan, Galway, Mayo, Tipperary and Waterford (1923-33).*
Career/honours: Connacht senior medal, 1928; five senior club championship medals in Sligo, Cavan and Waterford; senior league medal and President's Cup with Garda, Dublin, 1926; played for Connacht (only Sligo player), and also played with Munster and Ulster. Played in Garda vs Army matches. Played club hurling for Dungourney, Cork. Played for Ireland vs USA in the Tailteann Games of 1928.

In 1922, he and three of his brothers were prominent in a Sligo team that beat Tipperary in the 1922 All-Ireland senior semi-final .... but the Western county did not contest the final! Instead, following an objection, Sligo and Galway met in Connacht; Galway won that clash and then lost the All-Ireland final.

Collins, Ger (hurling)

▸ *Native of Tipperary; played hurling for Louth (1996-2007).*

Collins, Martin (football/hurling)

▸ *Native of Galway; played inter-county for Tipperary, Leitrim and Galway during the 1950s.*
Career/honours: **All-Ireland minor medal with Galway, 1952**; *seven senior club championship medals – Galway (1), Tipperary (2), Leitrim (3) and Cork (1).*

Collum, Sean (football/hurling)

▸ *Native of Tipperary; played football for Tipperary (1991-2005) and hurling in 1995. Also hurled at minor and U21 level for Tipperary.*

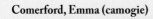

Comerford, Emma (camogie)

▸ *Played senior camogie for Kilkenny.*

Comerford, George (football)

▸ *Native of Clare; played senior football for Clare, Louth, Dublin and Kildare in the 1920s and 1930s.*
Career/honours: three senior club championship medals with Garda club in 1933, 1934 and 1935; one Kildare senior club championship medal with Athy (1937, captain). Won a senior club championship medal with Dundalk Gaels, and played Railway Cup football for Leinster and Munster.
Only non-Kerryman on the Munster Railway Cup team of 1921; represented Ireland in the 1932 Tailteann Games;

Compton, Colin (football)

▸ *Native of Roscommon; played football for Roscommon (2012 to present). Career/honours: NFL Division 2 medal, 2018; Trench Cup medal with Garda College, 2015; selected on the Higher Education GAA Independent Rising Stars football team, 2015.*

Comyns, Mick (football)

▸ *Native of Clare; played football for Clare, 1986-90. Career/honours: two Clare senior club championship medals with St Senan's, Kilkee, 1984 and 1989;* **three All-Ireland interfirm medals with Cork Garda, 1986, 1987 and 1996**. *Also played with St Finbar's.*

Conlon, Declan (hurling)

▸ *Native of Dublin; played for Dublin during the 1990s.*

Conlon, Liam (football)

▸ *Native of Leitrim; played football for Leitrim, 1988-98. Career/honours: Connacht championship medal, 1994;* **U21 All-Ireland 'B', 1992**. *Four senior club championship medals with Sean O'Heslin's.*

Conneely, Kevin (hurling)

▸ *Native of Roscommon; hurled for Roscommon (2009-12) and Longford (2012-present). Career/honours: Division 3B National League medal with Roscommon in 2010; Division 3B National League medal with Longford, 2013; Lory Meagher Cup medal, 2014.*

Connell, Eoghan (hurling)

▸ *Hurled for Monaghan in the 1990s. Career/honours:* **All-Ireland junior medal, 1997.**

Connell, Fiona (camogie)

▸ *Native of Roscommon; played camogie for Roscommon. Career/honours: two Connacht medals with Roscommon; two Connacht club medals.*

Connell, J. (football)

▸ *Native of Mayo; played for Garda Club, Dublin during the 1950s.*

Connell, Senan (football)

▸ *Native of Clare; played football for Clare, 1952-59. Career/honours: one minor, one intermediate, one senior and five league club championship medals.*

Connelly, Pat (hurling)

▸ *Native of Galway; hurled at senior level for Galway, 1982-83. Career/honours: Connacht medal, 1982. Club: Glenamaddy.*

Connellan, Donal (football)

▸ *Native of Roscommon; played football for Roscommon, 1992-2002.*

Connolly, Brendan (football)

▸ *Native of Monaghan; played football for Monaghan, 1969–73.*
Career/honours: Hackett Cup (1969) and Ward Cup (1974) medals with Drumhowan. Played for Monaghan in an exhibition match in New York in 1970. Scott medalist (1986).

Connolly, Denis (football)

▸ *Native of Sligo; played football for Sligo, 1969–75.*
Career/honours: Connacht senior championship medal, 1975.

Connolly, Gerard (football)

▸ *Native of Monaghan; played senior football for Monaghan, 1984. Club: Currin.*

Connolly, Johanna (ladies' football)

▸ *Native of Galway; played football for Galway, 2000–present.*
Career/honours: **All-Ireland senior medal, 2004**; *All-Ireland junior medal, 2002; nine senior Connacht titles; Lynch Cup medal with Garda College, 2005; O'Connor Cup medal with Sligo IT; All-Ireland intermediate club medal, 1999 (Kilkerrin/Clonterne); intermediate All-Ireland Club 7s winner 2013, 2014 (Glenamaddy, Williamstown).*

Connolly, John

▸ *Native of Galway. Club: Milltown.*

Connolly, Martin (football)

▸ *Native of Monaghan, played senior football for Monaghan, 1979. Club: Currin.*

Connolly, Padraig (hurling)

▸ *Native of Wicklow; played senior football for Wicklow, 1998–99.*

Connolly, Sean (football)

▸ *Native of Monaghan; played football for Leitrim, 1967–68.*
Career/honours: played minor football for Monaghan; played U21 football for Leitrim. Senior championship medal with Manorhamilton, 1975; also played for Dromohare and Melvin Gaels.

Connolly, Tom (football)

▸ *Native of Cork, played senior football for Cork (1954–56) and Kildare (1957–60).*
Career/honours: Munster minor medal, 1952; **All-Ireland junior medal with Cork, 1955**. *Senior club championship medals in Cork, 1952, and Kildare, 1959.* Received a gold Scott medal for bravery in 1976. Author of Detective: a life upholding the law.

Connor, Matt (football)

▶ *Native of Offaly; played football for Offaly (1974-82).*
Career/honours: **one All-Ireland senior medal, 1982; three All Star Awards: right corner forward, 1980, left half forward, 1982 and centre forward, 1983**. *Played minor and U21 football for Offaly; three Leinster senior medals, 1980, 1981 and 1982; Leinster U21 medals, 1977 and 1979; Railway Cup with Leinster. Six County senior championship medals with Walsh Island, 1978-83; two Leinster senior club championship medals, 1978, 1979. Played 161 games for Offaly amassing a total of 82 goals and 606 points. Played for Ireland v Australia Compromise Rules, 1984*
His goal against Kerry in 1980 was voted goal of the year. Ranked at No. 8 in the *Irish Independent 125 Greatest Stars of the GAA*. Full forward on Offaly team of the Millennium. Centre forward on football All Stars Super Stars Team. Millennium GAA Football Award, 2000. Garda Hall Of Fame Award 1995. Top Scorer in Gaelic football in Ireland, 1980, 1981, 1982, 1983 and 1984. Inducted into the GAA Hall of Fame in 2017. Also in 2017, chosen as the Greatest Offaly Sportsperson ever in the *Offaly Express*. His tally of 2-9 against Kerry in the 1980 All-Ireland semi-finals ranks as one of Gaelic football's most outstanding performances

Conroy, Ian (hurling)

▶ *Native of Dublin; hurled for Dublin (2005-06) and Wicklow (2000).*
Career/honours: minor, U21 and intermediate hurling for Dublin; two Division 2 senior league medals; **U21 'B' championship medal**. *Club: Cuala.*

Conroy, Jimmy (hurling)

▶ *Native of Galway; hurled for Galway (1958-67).*
Career/honours: played minor hurling for Galway; three Connacht minor championship medals; **All-Ireland minor medal***; All-Ireland senior finalist, 1958; senior club championship medals in Clare. Club: Toomevara.*

Conway, James (hurling)

▶ *Native of Dublin; hurled for Dublin, 1923-25.*

Conway, Tom (hurling)

▶ *Native of Galway native, hurled for Galway, 1958-63.*

Coogan, Ned (football/hurling)

▶ *Native of Kilkenny; hurled for Kilkenny (senior) in 1963; played football for Kilkenny, 1968-69.*
Career/honours: senior club championship medal in football with Muckalee, 1968; club championship medals with Coon – junior 1967, intermediate 1973; club championship intermediate medal with St Brigid's, Blanchardstown, 1975.

Cooke, Shane (football/hurling)

▶ *Native of Dublin; played senior hurling and football for Dublin (1994-96) and senior football for Laois (2001-02, 2004-06).*
Career/honours: played minor (1992, 1993) and U21 (1994-96) in football and hurling for Dublin; O'Byrne Cup medal, 2004; senior hurling championship medal with Rathcoole in 2004; represented Ireland in shinty, 1995. Club: football with St Mary's, Saggart; Senior Division 1 League, 2004; St Vincent De Paul and Floodlight Cup medals, 2004.

Coone, Pat (hurling)

▸ *Native of Meath; played for Meath, 1995-2006.*
Career/honours: minor and U21 hurling for Meath; **All-Ireland junior medal, 1998***; All-Ireland junior finalist, 1997; two All-Ireland intermediate medals in 2000 and 2001; Division 2 National League medal, 2000; two Kehoe Cup medals, 2000 and 2005; four Dublin interfirms medals, 1998, 1999, 2000 and 2001; two Leinster interfirms, 2000 and 2001;* **All-Ireland interfirms medal, 2000**.

Cooney, Brian (hurling)

▸ *Native of Dublin; played for Dublin in the 1960s.*
Career/honours: **All-Ireland minor medal, 1959;** *senior championship medal, 1963.*

Cooney, James (football)

▸ *Native of Waterford; played football for Waterford, 2000-01.*

Cooper, John (football/hurling)

▸ *Native of Wexford; played football (1992-2007) and hurling (1993) for Wexford. Career/honours: O'Byrne Cup medal, 1995; junior club (1995) and intermediate (1996) medals with club Adamstown. Trench Cup (1993, 1994) and Ryan Cup (1995) medals with Garda College.*

Corcoran, Bill (football)

▸ *Native of Offaly; played football for Offaly, 1983-86.*
Career/honours: played minor football, 1980; U21 football, 1981-83.

Corcoran, Brendan (hurling)

▸ *Native of Galway , hurled for Kildare (2008-10) and played minor hurling for Galway.*

Corey, Frank

▸ *Native of Clare.*

Cornish, Paul (football)

▸ *Native of Kildare; played football for Kildare.*
Career/honours: played minor 1998, 1999 and U21, 2000, 2001 for Kildare. Clubs: Monasterevin and Round Towers.

Corrigan, Tara (camogie)

▸ *Native of Dublin; played camogie for Dublin, 2009-12.*

Cosgrove, Jack (football)

▸ *Native of Galway; played for Galway, 1968-76.*
Career/honours: **All Star award in 1971 at full back***; three All-Ireland finalists medals vs Offaly in 1971, vs Cork in 1973 and vs Dublin in 1974; five Connacht senior medals; played minor, U21 and junior for Galway.*

Costello, Anthony (football)

▸ *Native of Galway; played for Galway, 2002-05.*

271

Costello, Paul (football)

▸ *Native of Tipperary; played for Tipperary, 1991-97 football.*

Costigan, Gary (hurling)

▸ *Native of Laois; hurled for Monaghan, 1998-2001.*

Cotter, Brian (football)

▸ *Native of Donegal; played for Donegal (1954-59) and Leitrim (1960-66). Career/honours: McKenna Cup medal; senior county league medal with Carrick-on-Shannon.*

Cotter, Frank (football)

▸ *Native of Clare; played football for Clare in the 1960s.*

Coughlan, Brendan (football)

▸ *Native of Wexford; played senior football for Waterford (1961-62) and Cork.*

Coughlan, Enda (football)

▸ *Native of Clare; played for Clare, 2004-07, 2009-10, 2012 to present. Career/honours: one National League Division 3 medal, 2016; Tommy Murphy Cup medal; McGrath Cup medal; All-Ireland Club finalist medal; six senior club championship medals with Kilmurry Ibrickane. 5 U21 and 2 minor Club championship medals. Club: Kilmurry Ibrickane.*

Coughlan, Fergus (hurling)

▸ *Native of Westmeath; played hurling for Wexford (1928-30, 1933-35) and Westmeath (1931-32). Clubs: Castlebridge and Taughmon.*

Courtney, John (football)

▸ *Native of Kerry; played football for Kerry in the 1950s.*
Career/honours: **All-Ireland minor medal, 1946;** *Club: Castlegregory.*
Was Superintendent of the 'Murder Squad' Author of *It Was Murder.*

Cox, Dominic (hurling)

▸ *Native of Roscommon; hurled for Roscommon (1974-83) Career/honours: played minor and U21 football for Roscommon;* **All-Ireland junior medal, 1974.**

Cox, Neil (football)

▸ *Native of Fermanagh; played for Fermanagh, 1994-2003 Career/honours: Ulster U21 football championship medal, 1994; seven Fermanagh senior football championship medals, 1992, 1999, 2000, 2001, 2002, 2003, 2006.*

Coyle, Jim (football)

▸ *Native of Louth; played for Louth, 1936. Career/honours: Railway Cup medals with Leinster, 1935 and 1939.*

Coyle, Martin (football)

▸ *Native of Clare; played football for Mayo, 1952-59.*

Coyle, Patsy (football)

▸ *Native of Galway; played football for Galway, 1958-59.*
Career/honours: **Junior All-Ireland medal, 1958.**

Coyle, Tom (football)

▸ *Native of Longford; played for Longford, 1991.*
Career/honours: five intermediate championship medals with Abbeylara.

Coyne, Colm (football)

▸ *Native of Westmeath; played football for Westmeath, 1999.*
Career/honours: senior club championship medal with Coralstown/Kinnegad in 1996; U21 medal in 1996. Played for Garda Club.

Creagh, Dick (football)

▸ *Native of Mayo; played senior football for Mayo, 1926-27.*
Career/honours: captained Mayo and played for Connacht; founder member of the Garda Club.

Creagh, R.

▸ *Native of*
played inter-county for Dublin, 1931.

Cremin, Ger (football)

▸ *Native of Kerry; played football for Kerry in the 1990s.*
Career/honours: **minor All-Ireland medal for Kerry, 1994**; *played junior football for Kerry, 1996. Club: Gneeveguilla.*

Cremin, Kieran (football)

▸ *Native of Kerry native;*
layed football for Kerry, 2004-08.
Career/honours: **three All-Ireland senior medals, 2004, 2006 and 2007**; *two National League medals, 2004 and 2006; three Munster championship medals, 2004, 2005 and 2007; two senior club championship medals; one senior club Munster championship medal; four senior Division 1 county club medals; eight senior East Kerry club championship medals. Club: Dr Crokes.*

Cribbin, Sarah (camogie)

▸ *Native of*
Played senior camogie for Kildare.

Cribbin, John (football)

▸ *Native of Kildare; played senior for Kildare, 1985-86.*
Career/honours: played played minor football for Kildare; six senior club championship medals with Clane, 1980, 1984, 1991, 1992, 1995 and 1996.

Croke, Aidan

▸ *Native of*
played inter-county for Galway during the 1950s.

Cronin, Matty (football)

▸ *played senior football for Waterford in the early 1970s;*

Crotty, Donal (football)

▸ *played senior football for Waterford in the 1960s and 1970s.*

Crotty, Jason (football)

▸ *Native of Waterford; played for Waterford, 1998-99.*
Career/honours: played junior football for Waterford; three senior club championship medals with Rathgormack, 1995, 1996 and 1999.

Crowley, Colin (football)

▸ *Native of Cork; played senior for Cork, 2002. Club: Castlehaven.*

Crowley, Con (football)

▸ *Native of Cork; played senior football for Waterford, 1949-57.*
Career/honours: played junior football for Waterford 1948; Munster junior championship medal, 1948; four county senior championship medals with Mount Sion; minor hurling medal with Bandon, 1942. Starred in Waterford's defeat of Kerry in the first round of the Munster championship in 1957 (as captain).
Inter-county referee; father of RTÉ television personalities, Carrie and Sinead Crowley.

Crowley, D. J. (football)

▸ *Native of Kerry; played for Kerry, 1967-72.*
Career/honours: **two All-Ireland senior medals, 1969 and 1970**; *three National League medals; three Munster senior medals; three county club championship medals. Clubs: Rathmore and East Kerry. Midfield partner of Mick O'Connell, 1967-1971.*
In 1969, D. J.'s outstanding second half display in the final inspired Kerry to a great victory over Offaly. In the 1970 final, he scored a goal shortly before the end of the match to secure victory. D. J. was only in his mid-twenties when he had to retire because of injury.

Crowley, Johnny (football)

▸ *Native of Kerry; played senior football for Kerry, 1994-2004.*
Career/honours: **three All-Ireland medals – 1997 vs Mayo, 2000 vs Galway, 2004 vs Mayo; All Star award, 2001 (left corner forward); All-Ireland junior medal in 1994**; *Railway Cup for Munster; Ireland International Rules team, 2001; played minor,* **U21 (one All-Ireland)** *and junior football for Kerry. Clubs: Glenflesk and East Kerry (won three county titles with the latter).*

Culbert, Brian (hurling)

▸ *Native of Clare; hurled for Clare, 2001-05.*
Career/honours: played minor hurling for Clare, 2000 (captain); played U21 hurling for Clare, 2003 (captain). Club: Sixmilebridge.

Culhane, Mick

▸ *played inter-county for Roscommon during the 1950s.*

Culhane, Richie (football)

▸ *Native of Longford; played senior football for Louth (1980-90) and Longford (1978-80 and 1990-94).*
Career/honours: played minor and U21 football for Longford; three O'Byrne Cup medals with Louth; **Over 40's All-Ireland Masters medal with Longford, 2000***; three senior club championship medals with Newtown Blues (Louth), 1981, 1986 and 1987.*
Played League of Ireland soccer with Drogheda United; Fine Gael councillor and former Mayor of Drogheda.

Culkin, John (football)

▸ *Native of Mayo; played inter-county football in the 1970s.*

Cullen, Aoife (camogie)

▸ *Native of Dublin; played camogie for Dublin in the 2000s.*
Career/honours: Leinster medal, 2005; **All-Ireland junior medal;** *played with Leinster senior camogie team. Leinster and club championship medals with St Vincent's; Purcell Cup medal with Garda College, 2005; selected on All Star Purcell team, 2005.*

Cullen, Claire (ladies' football).

▸ *Wexford and Dublin.*

Cullen, Pat (hurling)

▸ *Native of Longford; played for Longford, 1997-2015.*
Career/honours: **minor 'C' All-Ireland, 1997***; National Hurling League Division 3, 2002; Leinster Hurling Shield, 2005, 2006; Lory Meagher Cup medalist – 2010 and 2014; GPA/GAA Lory Meagher Champion 15 All Star, 2009 and 2014.*

Culligan, Paddy (football)

▸ *Native of Kerry; played inter-county football for Cork and Kerry, 1958-60.*
Career/honours: played junior football with Kerry, 1955-56; Munster junior medal with Kerry, 1955; Munster Colleges medal with St Brendan's, Killarney, 1953. Clubs: Killarney Legion and Dr Croke's. Three senior championship medals with the Legion: 1953, 1954 and 1955.
Rose to the rank of Garda Commissioner; played international basketball for Ireland, 1955-57.

Cullinane, John (hurling)

▸ *Native of Monaghan; hurled for Monaghan, 1997-99.*

Cullinan, Johnny (hurling)

▸ *Native of Clare; hurled for Clare in the 1960s.*

Cumiskey, Noel (football)

▸ *Native of Longford; played for Longford, 1968-73.*
Career/honours: Leinster senior championship medal, 1968; club championship medal Clane, Co. Kildare, 1975; intermediate, junior, U21, championship medals with Kenagh, Longford; All-Ireland Colleges medal St Mel's, Longford, 1963.

Cummins, Angela (ladies' football)

▸ *Native of Sligo; played for Sligo, 1993-2002.*
Career/honours: National League Division 3 medal (1995); Connacht junior championship medals (1995 and 1996); Louth junior Club championship medal with St Fechin's GAA (1997); Dublin senior club championship runners-up medal with the Garda Ladies' GAA (2004, 2005 and 2006).

Cummins, Frank (hurling)

▸ *Native of Kilkenny; hurled for Kilkenny, 1966-86.*
Career/honours: **eight All-Ireland senior medals, 1967, 1969, 1972, 1974, 1975, 1979, 1982 and 1983; four All Star Awards 1971, 1972, 1982 and 1983 (all midfield); three All-Ireland senior club championship medals with Blackrock (Cork) 1972, 1974 and 1979;** *two All-Ireland finalist medals, 1973 and 1978; eleven Leinster senior medals, 1967, 1969, 1971, 1972, 1973, 1974, 1975, 1978, 1979, 1982, 1983; U21 minor and U21 hurling for Kilkenny; Leinster and All-Ireland finalist medals, 1968; minor club championship medal with Ballyhale Shamrocks (1965); six county championship (all at midfield) medals with Blackrock (Cork).*
Ranked at No. 26 on the *Irish Independent 125 Greatest stars of the GAA. Selected at midfield on the Supreme All Star Hurling Team. Selected at centreback on the Club Hurling Silver Jubilee Team, 1971-96. Texaco Hurler of the Year, 1983.*

Cunniffe, Clement (hurling)

▸ *Native of Leitrim; hurled for Leitrim 2001 to present.*
Career/honours: U21 football for Leitrim, **Lory Meagher Champion 15 Award, 2013 and 2015.Club; St Mary's, Carrick on Shannon, 14 senior club championship medals,in hurling and 3 championship medals in football**

Cunniffe, Frank (football)

▸ *Native of Galway; played football for Galway, 1930s and 1940s.*
Career/honours: **one All-Ireland senior medal, 1938;** *two All-Ireland finalist medals, 1940 and 1941.*

Cunniffe, Martin (hurling)

▸ *Native of Galway; hurled for Leitrim in the 1970s and 1980s.*
Career/honours: Leitrim Hurler of the Year with St Mary's.

Cunningham, Shane (football)

▸ *Native of Dublin; played senior football for Dublin, 2017.*
Career/honours: O'Byrne Cup medal, 2017; played minor football for Dublin, 2012 (won All-Ireland); U21, 2014 (won All-Ireland) and 2015. Has played senior football with club Kilmacud Crokes since 2013. Won Division 1 colleges' senior football titles with St Benildus College.

Curtin, Gerry (hurling)

▸ *Native of Galway; hurled for Galway, 1980-81.*
Career/honours: **All-Ireland senior medal, 1980;** *Railway Cup hurling for Connacht, 1980. Club: Kinvara.*

Cush, Steven (football)

▸ *Native of Wicklow; played senior for Wicklow, 2000-08.*
Career/honours: Leinster minor finalist, 1997 (beaten by Laois); U21 for Wicklow, 1998-2000. Club: Coolkenno GFC. Club achievements: junior 'B' championship, 1997; Division 4 league, 1997; intermediate championship, 2002; senior championship, 2011 (group team, St Mary's); intermediate champions, 2013; Division 2 league, 2013, Division 1A league, 2014. With Garda, Dublin: Dublin Interfirms winners, 2006; Leinster Interfirms winners, 2006; All-Ireland Interfirms runners-up, 2006. Management career to date: trained Coolkenno to a Wicklow IFC and Division 2 league in 2013; trained Castletown/Liam Mellows to a Wicklow Division 1 title, 2016. Wicklow U21 football manager, 2013-14. Currently a selector with the Wicklow senior football team.

Cushen, Siobhan (ladies' football)

▸ *Native of Kerry; played for Kerry senior ladies, 1994-2005.*
Career/honours: **All-Ireland minor medal, 1995;** *Kerry minor, 1992, 1993, 1994, 1995; county minor championship, 1993 and 1994; county junior championship, 1995; county league (senior), 1997. Cork championship medal with Donoughmore; Munster championship medal with Donoughmore (2002) and with Chorca Dhuine, St Pat's, Blennerville (Kerry); Kerry county championship medal in 2003; Munster minor championship, 1995.*

Cussen, Michael (football/hurling)

▸ *Native of Cork; played football (2007-15) and hurling (2010-15) for Cork.*
Career/honours: Munster championship football medals, 2008 and 2009; National Football League medal, 2009. Clubs: Sarsfields and Glanmire; two senior club championship medals, 2008 and 2010; U21 championship medal, 2005; Munster U21 medal, 2006.

D

Dalton, Dermot (football)

▸ *Native of Meath; played senior football for Meath (1971-72) and Cavan (1975-79).*
Career/honours: three senior championship medals with Navan O'Mahony's, Meath; three senior and one league championship medals with Cavan Gaels, Cavan; one intermediate championship medal with Garda. Player for the Year, Cavan, 1978.

Dalton, Jim (hurling)

▸ *Native of Kilkenny; hurled with Monaghan during the 1990s.*

Daly, Cathal (football)

▸ *Native of Offaly; played football for Offaly, 1996-99.*
Career/honours: **All Star Award 1997;** *National League medal, 1998; Leinster senior medal, 1997; International Rules player, 2003; played inter-provincial football for Leinster; U21 Leinster medal, 1995; two O'Byrne Cup medals, 1997, 1998; Railway Cup player; senior club championship medals, 2000, 2002 and 2007.*

Daly, Enda (football)

▶ *Native of Roscommon; played senior football for Roscommon, 2000-15.*
Career/honours: played minor and U21 football for Roscommon; senior Connacht medal in 2001; U21 Connacht medal in 1999; two club championship senior medals for Roscommon Gaels.

Daly, Killian (football)

▶ *Native of Westmeath; plays senior football for Westmeath (2014 to present).*
Career/honours: played played minor football for Westmeath, 2011-12; Division 4 League medal, 2017; senior club championship medal with Mullingar Shamrocks, 2012; U21 championship medal, 2012.

Daly, Liam (football)

▶ *Native of Westmeath; played senior football for Westmeath, 1976-77.*
Career/honours: Intermediate medal with Leixlip 1978; also played for Mullingar Shamrocks.

Daly, Gerry (football)

▶ *Native of Galway; played football for Galway, 1954-59.*
Career/honours: **All-Ireland medal, 1956**; *four Connacht senior medals, 1956-59; Galway minor football, 1948; Galway junior football, 1952. Played for Garda Club, Dublin.*

Daly, Mark (football)

▶ *Native of Monaghan; played senior for Monaghan (2007-08).*
Career/honours: Ulster finalist medal, 2007; Monaghan intermediate medal, 2012; Intermediate Player of the Year in Monaghan, 2012.

Daly, Mark (football)

▶ *Native of Offaly; played senior football for Offaly, 1992-2006.*
Career/honours: Leinster senior medal. Club: Clara.

Daly, Mick (hurling)

▶ *Native of Laois; played senior hurling for Wicklow, 1963-69.*
Career/honours: Leinster and **All-Ireland junior medals with Wicklow 1967**; *hurled for Wicklow vs London in Wembley Stadium, 1967.*

Daly, Paddy (football)

▶ *Native of Mayo; played for Kildare, 1952-56.*
Career/honours: Kildare senior club championship medals in 1955, 1957 and 1958.

Daly, Peadar (hurling)

▶ *Native of Limerick; hurled for Limerick, 1967.*
Career/honours: played minor hurling, 1960; county championship medal with Young Irelands, 1965 (Dublin); top scorer in Clare in 1989.
In 1966, scored five goals for the Gardaí versus the Army; played his last game at the age of 57 with his two sons for his club, Bodyke.

Daly, Peter (football)

▶ *Native of Offaly; played senior for Offaly, 2007-08.*
Career/honours: played played minor football for Offaly, 2003-04.

Daly, Sean (hurling)

▶ *Native of Offaly; hurled for Cavan, 1983-87.*
Career/honours: Ulster junior championship medal, 1984; two senior hurling championship and league medals with Cavan Gaels; one junior championship medal with Daingean, 1988.

Davis, Don (football)

▶ *Native of Cork; played senior football for Cork, 1993-2000.*
Career/honours: **U21 All-Ireland medal, 1989***; minor All-Ireland finalist medal, 1987; minor Munster medal, 1987; four Munster senior medals, 1993, 1994, 1995, 1999; two All-Ireland finalist medals, 1993, 1999; National League medal, 1999. Senior club county, Munster and* **All-Ireland medal with O'Donovan Rossa (1993)***; three senior interfirm Munsters and All-Irelands with Cork Gardaí.*

Davis, Pat (football)

▶ *Native of Cork; played senior for Cork in 1993.*
Career/honours: **All-Ireland senior club championship medal with O'Donovan Rossa, 1993***; minor football 1986; U21 football, 1988; Munster minor and All-Ireland finalist minor medal, 1986.*

Davis, Tony (football)

▶ *Native of Cork; played senior football for Cork, 1985-94.*
Career/honours: **two All-Ireland senior medals, 1989, 1990; two All-Ireland U21 medals, 1983, 1984 (captain); All-Ireland minor medal, 1981; All Star award, 1989 (left half back); All-Ireland senior county championship medal with O'Donovan Rossa, 1993; All-Ireland junior medal, 1984;** *seven Munster senior medals; played minor and U21 football for Cork.* **Two All-Ireland Interfirms titles in 1986 and 1987 with Cork Gardaí.**

Tony is the only player to have won All-Ireland medals at minor, U21, junior, senior and senior club. Former analyst on the Sunday Game (RTÉ). Three brothers, three members, who all played senior football for Cork.

Deasy, Dermot (football)

▶ *Native of Dublin; played for Dublin, 1993-96*
Career/honours: **two All-Ireland senior medals, 1993 and 1995; All Star Award, 1993, at full back;** *three Leinster championship medals, 1993, 1994 and 1995; National League medal, 1993; minor football with Dublin; two senior club championship medals with Ballymun Kickhams, 1982 and 1985.*

Deegan, Bernie (football)

▶ *Native of Laois; played for Laois during the 1990s and 2000s.*
Career/honours: two All Star awards, 1992 and 1993 (goalkeeper). Club: Timahoe

Deehan, Garrett (hurling)

▶ *Native of Wicklow; hurled for Wicklow, 2001-02.*
Career/honours: Kehoe Cup medal, 2002.

Delaney, Aidan (football)

▶ *Native of Laois; played for Louth, 1993-96.*
Career/honours: played minor, U21 and junior for Louth; three intermediate club championships and on Leinster medal with Dundalk Gaels.

Delaney, Chris (football)

▸ *Native of Laois; played senior football for Laois and Carlow, 1930–46.*
Career/honours: Leinster senior medals, 1936, 1937 and 1938; Railway Cup
with Leinster, 1939, 1940, 1944 and 1945; club championship medals with
Stradbally, Garda (Dublin) and Tullamore.

Delaney, Ian (hurling)

▸ *Native of Tipperary; hurled for Roscommon 2008–16*
Career/honours; Minor and under 21 hurling for Tipperary, Munster minor and
U21 championship medals with Tipperary, Nicky Rackard medal 2015, National
league medals 2015

Delaney, Joe (hurling)

▸ *Native of Louth; hurled for Louth, 1967–78.*
Career/honours: three National League Division 3 medals; two Leinster junior
championship medals, 1969, 1973; **two junior All-Ireland medals, 1976,**
1977.

Delaney, Liam (hurling)

▸ *Native of Laois; hurled for Laois, 1976–77. Played U21 hurling for Laois.*

Delaney, Paddy

▸ *Native of Carlow; played senior football for Carlow in 1954, and club football for*
Tinryland.

Denvir, Sarah (ladies' football)

▸ *Native of Dublin; played for Dublin, 2002–10.*
Career/honours: All-Ireland senior finalist medal, 2002; **All-Ireland 'B' medal,**
2010.

Dermody, Ken (hurling).

▸ *Native of Tipperary; hurled for Kerry (1961–65). Club: Lixnaw.*

Devane, John (football)

▸ *Native of Galway; played inter-county senior football for Galway (2002–06).*
Career/honours: **U21 All-Ireland medal, 2002**.

Devaney, David (football)

▸ *Native of Galway; played senior football for Louth, 2004–07.*
Career/honours: played junior football for Louth, and played minor football for
Galway; one Leinster junior medal, 2009; one All-Ireland minor finalist medal,
1994; two Connacht minor medals, 1994 and 1995; one Connacht U21 title; one
Hogan Cup medal with St Jarlath's, Tuam, 1994. Clubs: Tuam Stars and Glyde
Rangers.

Devenney, Enda (football)

▸ *Native of Mayo; played senior for Mayo, 2007.*
Career/honours: played minor and U21 football for Mayo.

Devitt, Dan (hurling)

▶ *Native of Tipperary; hurled for Dublin, 1940–45.*
Career/honours: three Leinster medals, 1941, 1942, 1944; All-Ireland senior finalist medal, 1942; eight senior championship medals and eight senior league medals with Faugh's; Railway Cup with Leinster.
Marked Christy Ring and Mick Mackey in matches and held both scoreless. Author of *A Garda remembers and reflects.*

Dilleen, Kevin (football/hurling)

▶ *Native of Clare; played senior football (2004–06, 2009) and hurling (2007) for Clare.*
Career/honours: All-Ireland intermediate hurling medal with Clare, 2011; Munster interprovincial panel, 2006. Club: St Joseph's Doora Barefield.

Dillon, Graham (football/hurling)

▶ *Native of Westmeath; played senior football for Westmeath (2005–07); hurled for Fingal (2011, 2013). Clubs: St Paul's and Brownstown (Westmeath), Trinity Gaels (Dublin).*

Dineen, Dabhach (football)

▶ *Native of Dublin; played senior football for Dublin, 2005–06.*
Career/honours: played minor and U21 football for Dublin; two U21 Leinster medals, 2003, 2005. Club: St Brigid's; senior county and Leinster championship medals, 2003.

Doherty, Joe (football)

▶ *Native of Mayo; played inter-county football for Mayo.*

Doherty, Kevin (hurling)

▶ *Native of Leitrim; hurled for Leitrim, 1984–88.*

Doherty, Liam (football)

▶ *Native of Leitrim; played senior football for Leitrim, 1982–82. Club: St Mary's, Carrick-on-Shannon.*

Doherty, Pearse (hurling)

▶ *Native of Donegal; hurled for Donegal (2000) and Louth (2004).*

Dolan, Christy (football)

▶ *Native of Mayo; played inter-county for Mayo and Roscommon during the 1960s.*
Career/honours: played played minor football for Mayo; won minor Connacht title, 1962 (Mayo); three senior club championship medals for Garrymore.

Dolan, Colin (hurling)

▶ *Native of Galway; hurled for Monaghan (2011).*
Career/honours: played minor hurling for Roscommon.

Dolan, Daragh (football)

▶ *Native of Donegal; played senior football for Donegal, 1993.*
Career/honours: played minor football for Donegal; Ulster minor football medal, 1991.

Dolan, Michael (hurling)

▸ *Native of Galway; hurled for Monaghan during the 1990s.*

Dolan, Paddy 'Big Paddy' (football)

▸ *Native of Mayo; played senior football for Mayo and Leitrim.*

Dolan, Patrick

▸ *Played inter-county for Galway during the 1950s.*

Donegan, Denis (hurling)

▸ *Native of Kerry; played senior hurling for Kerry, 1975.*
Career/honours: Senior club championship medal with Ballyboden St Enda's, 1972; also played with Causeway.

Donlon, Leonard (football)

▸ *Native of Kildare; played senior football for Kildare, 1997 and 2001.*
Career/honours: Leinster minor medal for Kildare, 1991 (captain); U21 and minor club captain; minor championship medal, 1991 and intermediate championship medal, 2003 with St Brigid's; three senior club championship medals with Round Towers, 1996, 1998 and 2003.

Donnellan, Jim (football)

▸ *Played inter-county senior football for Donegal during the 1960s.*

Donnellan, Paddy (football)

▸ *Native of Galway; played football for Limerick (1961) and Galway (1955-59).*
Career/honours: Railway Cup football with Munster; senior championship medal with Garda Limerick, 1958. Played tournament games with Galway.

Donnelly, Clara (ladies' football)

▸ *plays senior ladies' football for Wexford.*

Donnelly, Hugh (football)

▸ *Native of Tyrone; played senior football for Tyrone (1954-57).*
Career/honours: played minor football, 1952-53 (captain); two Ulster medals; five club Tyrone senior championship medals for Omagh, St Enda's, 1952, 1953, 1954, 1957 and 1963.

Donnelly, Kevin (football)

▸ *Native of Kerry; played senior football for Kerry (1968).*
Career/honours: **All-Ireland minor medal, 1963; All-Ireland U21 medal, 1964**; *played minor and U21 football for Kerry. Club: Waterville.*

Donoghue, Martin (hurling)

▸ *Native of Galway ; hurled at senior level for Galway during the 1980s.*
Career/honours: **All-Ireland U21 medal, 1983**; *played minor (1980), U21 (1983) and junior (1982-86) hurling for Galway.*
Member of first Galway team to win eight consecutive All-Ireland Inter-county Vocational Schools titles in 1980.

Donoghue, Pierce (hurling)

▸ *Native of Wexford; hurled at senior level for Wexford during the 2000s.*
Career/honours: played minor and U21 Hurling; one Leinster senior medal,
2004; two U21 Leinster hurling medals, 2001 and 2002.

Donoghue, Tony (hurling)

▸ *Native of Galway; played senior hurling for Westmeath, 1966-68.*
Career/honours: Senior championship medal with Raharney. Served as chairman
of Raharney Hurling Club.
Was a founder member of and heavily involved in the underage structure
of St Oliver Plunkett's Hurling Club in Mullingar. A 'Tony Donoghue
Memorial Day' was held in his honour at St Oliver Plunkett's Hurling Club,
Robinstown, Mullingar on 28 September 2015.

Donohue, Claire (ladies' football)

▸ *Native of Laois; played for Laois, 1997-2000.*
Career/honours: played junior football for Laois, 2012.

Donohue, Kevin (football)

▸ *Native of Roscommon; played senior football for Roscommon, 1968-69.*

Donohue, Pat (football)

▸ *Native of Leitrim; played inter-county senior football for Leitrim, 1988-99.*
Career/honours: **All-Ireland 'B' football medal, 1990**; *Connacht senior*
championship medal, 1994; Trench Cup medal for Garda College; All Star
nomination in 1994 at midfield; intermediate club championship medal, 1998;
eleven senior club championship finalist medals; All-Ireland international finalist
medal; club championship junior medal (Dublin).

Donohue, Martin (hurling)

▸ *Native of Galway; hurled for Galway in 1978.*

Dooley, Conor (hurling)

▸ *Native of Dublin; played for senior hurling for Dublin (2015-17).*
Career/honours: Walsh Cup medal. Club: Ballyboden St Enda's; Dublin
minor hurling championship, U21 hurling championship and senior hurling
championship medals; also won Dublin senior football medal, a Leinster club SFC
medal, and an All-Ireland club SFC medal.

Doran, Jim (hurling)

▸ *Hurled for Dublin in 1969.*

Doran, Martin (football)

▸ *Native of Dublin; played senior football for Dublin, 1990, 1992-97.*
Career/honours: National League, 1993; Leinster medal, 1993; Division 2
League with Clontarf; intermediate championship medal with St Finian's,
Swords.

Doris, Frank (football)

▸ *Native of Longford; played senior football for Longford, 1943-51.*
Career/honours: senior club championship medal for Garda, 1948; Senior Colleges
Leinster medal for St Mel's, Longford.

Doyle, Brian (football)

▸ *Native of Leitrim; played senior football for Leitrim, 1985-88 and 1992-95. Career/honours: played U21 football for Leitrim; intermediate championship medal with Carraigallen, 1991.*

Doyle, James (hurling)

▸ *Played senior hurling for Louth (1953) and Monaghan (1954-55).*

Doyle, Jim (hurling)

▸ *Native of Kilkenny; hurled for Wexford, 1994-95.*

Doyle, Robin (football)

▸ *Native of Galway; played senior football for Galway, 1997-2000. Career/honours:* **All-Ireland senior medal, 1998**; *Galway minor footballer, 1992-93; captain of the 1993 minor team and winners of Connacht championship, 1993; Galway U21 team, 1994-96; winners of Connacht championship, 1996; 1995 Galway junior team member; winners of Connacht championship, 1995.*

Doyle, Oliver "Willie" (hurling)

▸ *Native of Wexford; hurled for Wexford at senior level, 1964. Clubs: Rathgarogue/Cushinstown (Wexford), St Finbarr's, Cork.*

Doyle, Tim (football/hurling)

▸ *Native of Kerry; played senior football for Kerry, 1967-70, and senior hurling, 1961. Career/honours: Munster U21 medal; club championship medal with Mid Kerry, 1967. Club football: Laune Rangers.* Author of *Get Up Them Steps* and *Peaks and Valleys.*

Doyle, Tim Jnr (football)

▸ *Native of Dublin; played senior football for Dublin, 2002-03. Career/honours: senior club championship medal with St Vincent's, 2003.*

Doyle, Willie (football/hurling)

▸ *Native of Wexford; played football (1958-65) and hurling (1963-64) for Wexford. Career/honours: played minor hurling and football for Wexford, 1958; county senior championship medal with St Finbarr's, Cork, 1965.*

Drumm, Mick

▸ *Native of Longford; county championship medals with Dublin Garda and Cork Garda.*

Duff, Jack (football)

▸ *Native of Kerry; played inter-county football during the 1950s. Club: Garda, Dublin.*

Duff, Vincent

▸ *Native of Tipperary; played inter-county for Tipperary, 1965-72. Clubs: Borrisokane, Tipperary, New Ireland and Faugh's, Dublin.*

Duffy, Leo (football)

▸ *Native of Roscommon; played senior football for Limerick.*
Career/honours: senior club championship medal for Garda, Limerick, 1958.

Duffy, Michael (football)

▸ *Native of Westmeath; played senior football for Westmeath, 1957-68.*
Career/honours: O'Byrne Cup medal; three senior championship and league medals for Athlone.

Duggan, Con (football)

▸ *Native of Wexford; played senior football for Wexford in the 1950s.*

Duggan, Derek

▸ *Native of Roscommon; played senior football for Roscommon, 1990-2000.*
Career/honours: played minor and U21 football for Roscommon; Connacht minor medal, 1989; Connacht senior medal, 1991; All Star nomination, 1991; three senior club championship medals with Castlerea; two FBD Senior League medals; three Trench Cup medals, Sligo RTC 1992, Garda College, 1993, 1994; played inter-provincial football for Connacht; also played with the Garda Club, Dublin
Scored "a monster equalising point" for Roscommon vs Mayo, 1991.

Duggan, Ken (football)

▸ *Native of Roscommon; played senior football for Roscommon, 1994-98.*
Career/honours: U21, 1993 and 1994; minor, 1990 and 1991.

Duggan, Triona (ladies' football)

▸ *Plays senior ladies' football for Kildare 2014.*

Duignan, Brian (football)

▸ *Native of Wicklow; played senior football for Wicklow, 1977-78. Club: Ashford.*

Dunne, Patrick (football)

▸ *Native of Kildare; played senior football for Kildare, 1995-97.*
Career/honours: U16 (1990), minor (1992), U21 (1994 and 1995), junior (1995, 1996) and was **Kildare All Star full back in 1995**– *U21s, juniors and seniors. Won junior club and intermediate championships with Caragh, Prosperous.*

Dunne, Richie (hurling)

▸ *Native of Kilkenny; senior hurler for Kilkenny (1973) and Laois (1983-84).*
Career/honours: played minor hurling for Kilkenny, 1970.

Dunphy, Bill 'Watty' (hurling)

Native of Kilkenny; hurled for Dublin, 1926-31.
Career/honours: senior league medal with Garda, Dublin, 1925.

Dunphy, John (hurling)

▸ *Native of Laois; played senior hurling for Laois, 1962. Club: Cullohill.*

Durkan, Seamus (football)

▸ *Native of Sligo; played inter-county senior football for Sligo (1961–70). Career/honours: two senior club championship medals for St Eunan's, 1969 and 1972; two junior club championship medals for Bunninadden; played for Sligo v Cavan in Wembley, 1967.*

Durkin, David (football)

▸ *Native of Sligo; played senior football for Sligo, 1995–2005. Career/honours: eight senior club championship medals with Tourlestrane (Sligo).*

Dwyer, Josie (camogie/ladies' football)

▸ *Native of Wexford; played senior camogie for Wexford, 2003–14, and ladies' football for Wexford. Career/honours:* **Camogie – three All-Ireland senior championship medals, 2010, 2011 and 2012;** *National League Division 1 medals, 2009, 2010 and 2011; five Leinster senior championship medals, 2004, 2009, 2010, 2011 and 2014; Leinster junior championship medal, 2003 and 2004; All Star nominations, 2010, 2011, 2012 and 2014.* **Ladies' football** *– All-Ireland intermediate football finalist medal, 2007; Leinster junior championship, 2005, 2006 (captain) and 2007; Purcell Cup medal with Garda College, 2005; Ashbourne Shield medal with Garda College, 2007. Clubs: St Aidan's (camogie) and Clonee (ladies' football).*

E

Earley, David (football)

▸ *Native of Kildare; played senior football for Kildare, 1994, 1995, 1997–99. Career/honours: minor (1992–93) and U21 (1993–95) football for Kildare; three club championship medals with Sarsfields 1993, 1994 and 1999.*

Earls, Eddie (football)

▸ *Native of Wicklow (Greystones); played senior football for Kildare, 1954–55. Career/honours: won a Kildare SFC title with Kilcoole in 1954. Now resident in New South Wales, Australia.*

Egan, Conor (hurling)

▸ *Native of Offaly ; hurled at senior level for Longford, 2008–14. Career/honours: two Lory Meagher Cup medals, 2010 and 2014; Division 3B National League medal, 2013;* **Lory Meagher All Star Award, 2014;** *played minor and U21 hurling for Offaly.*

Egan, Denis (hurling)

▸ *Native of Laois; senior hurler for Laois, 1996–97.*

Egan, Joe (football)

▸ *Native of Galway; played senior football for Galway, 1964. Career/honours: played minor and junior football with Galway.* Rose to the rank of Assistant Commissioner. Won Scott medal, 1984.

286

Egan, John (football)

▶ *Native of Kerry; played senior football for Kerry, 1975-84. Club: Sneem and South Kerry (won two county championships with the latter).*
Career/honours: **six All-Ireland senior medals, 1975, 1978, 1979, 1980, 1981 and 1984; five All Star awards – 1975 (right corner forward), 1977 (left corner forward), 1978 (left corner forward), 1980 (left corner forward) and 1982 (left corner forward); All-Ireland U21 medal, 1973**; *nine Munster senior medals, 1975, 1976, 1977, 1978, 1979, 1980, 1981, 1982 and 1984; two All-Ireland senior finalist medals, 1976 and 1982; four National Football League medals.*
Ranked at no. 28 in the *Irish Independent 125 Greatest Stars of the GAA*. Garda Hall of Fame award, 1998. Was captain of the 1982 All-Ireland defeated Kerry team attempting to win five in a row. "One of the greatest corner forwards ever in Gaelic football, one who never craved the spotlight. He was a gentle giant and warrior." – Pat Spillane

Egan, Liam (football)

▶ *Native of Mayo; played senior football for Limerick (1957, 1959).*
Career/honours: senior club championship medal with Garda 1958.

Egan, Noel (hurling)

▶ *Native of Roscommon; played senior hurling for Roscommon, 1981-87.*
Career/honours: **All-Ireland 'B' medal, 1977**; *senior club championship medal with Longford Slashers, 1977; Dublin junior championship medal with New Irelands, 1983 and St Jude's, 1989. Also played with Roscommon Gaels and Ballygar.*
Founder member of Newtowncashel Hurling Club, Longford.

Egan, Nuala (ladies' football)

▶ *played for Roscommon in the 1970s and 1980s.*
Career/honours: **All-Ireland senior medal, 1978; All Star Award 1980 (full back), first Ladies All Star awards.** Club: St Barry's.

Egan, Tom (football)

▶ *Played senior football for Meath in the 1950s. Club: Western Gaels.*

English, Leo (football)

▶ *Native of Roscommon; played senior football for Roscommon (1955-56) and Tipperary (1957-59).*
Career/honours: junior football for Tipperary, 1957; minor football and hurling for Roscommon, 1949-50; three senior club championship medals for St Patrick's, Knockcroghery (Roscommon), 1949; won medals for Clonmel Commercials, 1956 and Fethard, 1957 (both Tipperary); junior hurling championship medal for Tremane (Roscommon), 1949-50.

English, Paddy (football)

▶ *Native of Roscommon; played senior football for Roscommon and Donegal during the 1950s.*
Career/honours: senior club championship medals with Knockcroghery, 1951 and 1952 Railway Cup with Connacht.

English, Sean (hurling)

▸ *Native of Wexford; played inter-county senior hurling for Wexford (1960-61) and Tipperary (1963).*
Career/honours: **All-Ireland senior medal, Wexford, 1960**; *Leinster senior championship medal, 1960.*

Evans, John (football)

▸ *played senior football for Kerry, 1976.*
Career/honours: played minor (1973) and U21 (1975) football with Kerry Four senior club championship medals and one minor championship medal with Laune Rangers. **Managed Laune Rangers to All-Ireland Club victory, 1996**, *and two Munster championship titles, 1995 and 1996. Also managed Kerins O'Rahillys. Inter-county manager of both Tipperary and Roscommon; brought both teams through the leagues on promotion.*

Evers, Frank (football)

▸ *Native of Galway; played senior football for Galway (1952-63) and Westmeath (1952).*
Career/honours: **one senior All-Ireland medal (Galway), 1956;** *All-Ireland senior finalist, 1959; six Connacht senior medals; one National Football League medal; two Railway Cup medals; one Leinster minor medal (Westmeath); one senior club championship medal for Tuam Stars, 1962; one Leinster Senior Colleges medal; played for Garda Club, Dublin.Later joined the United Nations Police Force; now resident in Canada.*
Although while winning an All-Ireland medal in 1959, Frank is also remembered for an outstanding display in the 1959 final.

F

Fahy, Brian (football)

▸ *Native of Kildare; played senior football for Kildare, 1991-98.*
Career/honours: played minor and U21 football for Kildare; Leinster U21 medal, 1992; two Leinster senior finalists medals.
An accomplished athlete, Brian received an offer to play soccer in England at the age of eighteen, but turned it down.

Fahy, Gerry (hurling)

▸ *Native of Galway; played senior hurling for Monaghan, 1983.*
Career/honours: played minor football for Roscommon; played U21 football for Galway.
Gerry is a grandnephew of the legendary Mick Gill. He is a former inter-county manager of Galway, 1997, and Offaly, 2003-04. Also managed Galway minor and U21 teams (leading the latter to an All-Ireland final in 2017), and NUIG's winning Sigerson Cup team in 2003.Managed Galway's U20 footballers, under the new grading format.

Fahy, Ned (hurling)

▸ *Native of Clare; hurled for Dublin in the 1920s.*
Career/honours: **one All-Ireland senior medal, 1927**; *junior football for Clare; represented Leinster in the Railway Cup.*

Fallon, Peter (hurling)

▶ *Native of Roscommon; played senior hurling for Roscommon, 1968.*
Career/honours: **U21 'B' All-Ireland medal, 1967**; *two club championship medals in 1975 and 1978 with Athleague.*

Fallon, Peter (football)

▶ *Native of Galway; played senior football for Galway, 1919-22.*
Founder member of St Maur's GAA Club, Rush, Co Dublin.

Farragher, Padraig (football)

▶ *Native of Galway; played for inter-county senior football for Donegal, 1984-86.*
Career/honours: played minor and U21 football for Galway 1974-77.

Farran, Paddy (football)

▶ *Native of Donegal; played senior football for Kerry, 1925-26. Club: Faha Ballybunion.*

Farrell, Joe (football)

▶ *Native of Mayo; played senior football for Monaghan, 1927.*
Career/honours: Railway Cup football for Ulster, 1927.

Farrell, Kieran (hurling)

▶ *Native of Roscommon; played senior hurling for Roscommon, 1975-86.*
Career/honours: Division 3 National League medal, 1984; Connacht senior medal with Tremane in 1977. Member of the Roscommon senior hurling management team that won the All-Ireland 'B' championship in 1995.

Farrell, Seamus (hurling)

▶ *Native of Roscommon; played senior hurling for Roscommon, 1978-1993.*
Career/honours: Division 3 National League medal, 1984; special minor 'B' All-Ireland medal, 1975; Connacht senior medal with Tremone, 1977; three senior club championship medals with Tremone The three Farrell brothers, Sean, Seamus and Kieran – all members of the Force – all played for Roscommon in the same era

Farrell, Sean (hurling)

▶ *Native of Roscommon; played senior hurling for Roscommon (1970-87), Donegal (1987-90) and Cavan (1991-98)*
Career/honours: **thirty senior club medals in three different counties**; **All-Ireland junior medal with Roscommon, 1974; All-Ireland minor 'B' hurling medal, Roscommon, 1969**; *Railway Cup with Connacht, 1973 and 1977; Division 3 National League medal, Roscommon, 1984; six senior championship medals with Tremane; two senior county championship medals with Burt, Donegal, and twenty-two senior county championship medals with Mullahoran, Cavan. Founder member of Mullahoran St Joseph's Hurling Club, Cavan in 1990 and* **won twenty-one consecutive county championships 1990 to 2010 – a national record.** *Played for the All-Ireland Garda hurling team. Inter-county manager (Cavan) and member of the Roscommon senior hurling management team which won the Nicky Rackard Cup in 2007.*

Farrell, Tommy (football)

▶ *Native of Longford; played senior football for Longford, 1985-93.*
Career/honours: two Division 4 medals; Leinster player, 1990; Longford player of the year, 1990.

Farrelly, Frank (football)

▸ *Native of Meath (Kells); played senior football for Waterford.*
Career/honours: played for Waterford in the 1946 Munster football final versus Kerry; sub for Waterford vs Clare in the first round of the Munster SFC in May 1952; played junior football for Dungarvan in 1953. Played minor and junior football for Meath.

Farrelly, Frank (football)

▸ *Played senior football for Donegal, 1954. Club: St Eunan's.*

Farrelly, Frank

▸ *Meath and Cavan.*

Farrelly, P. J. (football)

▸ *Played senior football for Cavan, 1947.*
Career/honours: played junior football for Cavan. Club: Annagh

Faulkner, Bartle (football)

▸ *Native of Louth; played inter-county football for Louth.*

Fawl, John (hurling)

▸ *Native of Galway; played senior hurling for Galway, 1969-75.*
Career/honours: played U21 hurling, 1966-67; National League medal, 1975.

Fayne, Brendan (football)

▸ *Native of Longford; played senior football for Longford, 1973-77.*
Career/honours: senior club championship medal with Rathcline, 1976; also played with Edenderry.

Feely, Sean (football)

▸ *Native of Roscommon; played senior football for Roscommon (1962-67, 1970-71) and Longford (1968).*
Career/honours: played minor football for Roscommon, captain, 1962; played U21 football for Roscommon, 1966; Connacht junior medal, 1964; Leinster senior championship medal for Longford, 1968; senior club championship medal with Shannon Gaels, Roscommon, 1964.

Feely, Willie (football)

▸ *Native of Roscommon; played senior football for Roscommon during the 1970s.*
Career/honours: minor and U21 football for Roscommon; intermediate and junior championship medals with Tourmakeady; former inter-county manager of Mayo minor team.

Feeney, Pat (football/hurling)

▸ *Native of Dublin; played senior football (1956-57) and hurling (1957-59, 1962) for Dublin.*
*Career/honours: **All-Ireland minor football and hurling medals, 1954;** Leinster minor football and hurling medals, 1954. Club: Na Fianna.*
Pat played at Wembley with Dublin in 1962.

Fennell, Shane (hurling)

▶ *Native of Westmeath; senior hurler for Louth, 2005-13.*
Career/honours: **Nicky Rackard All Star award, 2012; Ireland Shinty team, 2012.** *Four Nicky Rackard Cup finalist medals.*

Fennelly, Pat 'Papa' (hurling)

▶ *Native of Laois; hurled at senior level for Laois, 1970-74.*
Career/honours: U21 hurling for Laois, minor hurling (1966), Laois Masters (over 40's).

Ferguson, Seamus (football)

▶ *Native of Galway; played senior football for Galway in the 1950s. Club: Garda, Dublin.*

Ferriter, Sean (football)

▶ *Native of Donegal; played senior football for Donegal, 1956-75.*
Career/honours: Railway Cup for Ulster, four in a row; **named on greatest ever Donegal XV at midfield;** *senior championship medal with St Eunan's, 1967, 1969, 1972; three McKenna Cup medals; three Lagan Cup medals.*
Garda Hall of Fame award, 2005; played in the Cardinal Cushing Games in USA, a tournament for the game's eight or nine "elite" hurlers or footballers, would travel to Boston to play the local teams in the 1960s.

Filan, Kevin (football)

▶ *Native of Mayo.*

Finan, Gerry (football)

▶ *Played senior football for Sligo in the 1980s.*
Career/honours: Connacht senior club medal with St Mary's, Sligo, 1983.

Finn, Mick (hurling)

Galway; senior hurler for Dublin, 1920s and 1930s.

Finn, Rebecca (camogie)

▶ *Native of*
Career/honours: Played camogie for Cork from primary game through to intermediate level. Club: Milford, with whom she won **three All-Ireland senior club,** *four Munster club and four county titles in a four-year span.*

Finnegan, John 'Fingers' (hurling)

▶ *Native of Dublin; played senior hurling for Dublin, 1991-2002.*
Career/honours: National League Division 2 medal; played minor hurling for Dublin; **Ireland shinty team, 1992;** *Senior 'B', intermediate and U21 medals Division 3 medal with Commercials.*

Finnerty, Pat (football)

▶ *Native of Mayo; played senior football for Donegal (1959).*
Career/honours: played junior football for Donegal, 1960 and 1961; two senior club championship medals (Donegal), 1959, 1962; one junior club championship medal, May 1955.

Finnerty, Peter (hurling)

▸ *Native of Galway; played senior hurling for Galway, 1984-94.*
Career/honours: **two All-Ireland senior medals, 1987 and 1988; four All Star awards, 1985, 1986, 1987, 1988 and 1990 (all at right half back); one All-Ireland U21 medal, 1983**; *three All-Ireland senior finalist medals, 1985, 1990 and 1993; one All-Ireland minor finalist medal, 1982; played minor hurling, 1980–82 and U21 hurling for Galway; three Railway Cup medals; three Oireachtas medals.* **Selected on Galway Hurling Team of the Millennium 2000. Ranked at no. 39 on the** *Irish Independent* **125 Greatest Stars of the GAA.** *Inter-county management: Sligo. Club: Mullagh. Former analyst on RTÉ's The Sunday Game.*

Fitzgerald, Aidan (hurling)

▸ *Native of Limerick; played senior hurling for Limerick.*

Fitzgerald, David (football)

▸ *Native of Tipperary; played for Tipperary during the 1970s.*
Career/honours: Division 2 League medal, 1970/1971.

Fitzgerald, Denise (ladies' football)

▸ *Native of Tipperary; played for Tipperary, 1998-2007.*
Career/honours: Ladies' NFL Division 3 medal, 2002; Munster junior medal, 2003 (captain); Ladies' NFL Division 3 medal, 2005; Munster intermediate medal, 2007; junior club and intermediate medals with Brian Boru Ladies' GFC. **All-Ireland intermediate club medal, 2009.**

Fitzgerald, Joe (football)

▸ *Native of Kerry; played senior football for Dublin, 1942.*
Career/honours: **All-Ireland senior medal in 1942 (captain**). *Club: Geraldines.*

Fitzgerald, Kieran (football)

▸ *Native of Galway; played senior football for Galway, 2000-11.*
Career/honours: **All-Ireland senior medal, 2001; one All Star award (2001), right corner back; All-Ireland U21 medal, 2002**; *five Connacht senior medals, 2000, 2002, 2003, 2005, 2008; two Connacht U21 medals, 2000, 2002;* **captain of Galway, 2007**. *Ten senior club championship medals; two county club Connacht championship medals;* **two All-Ireland senior club championship medals with Corofin, 2015, 2018; one All-Ireland Senior 7s medal, 2004**; *played inter-provincial football for Connacht; three Connacht senior club medals, 2008, 2009, 2014, 2017; nine Galway county senior medals, 1999-2014; four Galway county U21 medals, 1998-2002; four Galway county minor medals, 1996-1999; one All-Ireland Féile club medal, 1995. Capped in International Rules, 2006.*

Fitzgerald, Mike (hurling)

▸ *Native of Limerick; hurled for Limerick, 2006-09.*
Career/honours: played minor, U21 and senior hurling for Limerick; All-Ireland Club finalist medal, 2007. Club: Doon.

Fitzgerald, Niall

▸ *Played inter-county for Limerick.*

Fitzgerald, Niall (football)

▸ *Native of Tipperary; played senior football for Tipperary. Club: Moyle Rovers.*

Fitzhenry, Noel (football)

▸ *Native of Wexford; played senior football for Wexford, 1988-1993. Club: Duffry Rovers.*

Fitzmaurice, Shane (football)

▸ *Native of Mayo; played senior football for Mayo, 1996-97, 2002, 2005. Career/honours: county U21 junior and intermediate titles; county senior league title (Castlebar Mitchels); Connacht Minor League and Connacht U21 championship with Mayo. Trench Cup (Galway RTC);* **three All-Ireland senior interfirms medals with Garda (Galway Division).**

Fitzpatrick, Brian (football)

▸ *Native of Wicklow; played senior football for Wicklow, 1988. Career/honours:* **one All-Ireland club championship medal, 1990 (captain***); twelve senior club championship medals, all with Baltinglass; on senior Baltinglass team from 1979 to 1997.*

Fitzpatrick, Colin (football)

▸ *Native of Louth; played senior football for Louth, 1999. Career/honours: played U21 football for Louth (captain). Club: Oliver Plunketts, Drogheda*

Fitzpatrick, Martin (football)

▸ *Native of Mayo; played senior football for Mayo, 1960-64 and 1969. Career/honours: played minor football for Mayo, 1958-59; Connacht senior medal, 1969; Connacht junior medal, 1963; one senior club championship medal for Claughaun (Limerick); two minor, one junior and one intermediate championship medals for Garrymore (Mayo).*

Fitzpatrick, Mick (football)

▸ *Native of Cavan; played minor, U21 and senior football for Cavan.*

Flaherty, Ollie (hurling)

▸ *Native of Donegal; played senior hurling for Donegal (1998-2001). Career/honours: Donegal senior hurler of the year, 2000.*

Flanagan, Aidan (hurling)

▸ *Native of Tipperary; hurled for Tipperary, 1997-98.*

Flanagan, Ger (hurling)

▸ *Native of Tipperary; hurled for Tipperary, 1997-98.*

Flanagan, Gerry (football/hurling)

▸ *Native of Roscommon; played senior hurling (1964-74) and football (1962-71) for Roscommon.*
Career/honours: **two All-Ireland junior medals, 1965 and 1974**; *six senior club championship medals with Roscommon Gaels, 1964, 1965, 1966, 1968, 1969 and 1970; Senior League club medal with Garda Club, Dublin, 1972; Junior medals in football and hurling with Maynooth; junior and intermediate medals with Dunshaughlin.*

Flanagan, Vincent

▸ *Played inter-county for Monaghan.*

Flannery, Conor (football)

▸ *Native of Wicklow; played senior football for Wicklow, 2001-02, 2004, 2006-07. Career/honours: played minor and U21 football for Wicklow; club minor championship medal with Bray Emmetts, 1999.*

Fleming, Jim (football)

▸ *Native of Mayo; played inter-county senior football for Mayo (1958-61, 1964-65, 1967-68) and Donegal (1963-64).*
Career/honours: Connacht senior, junior and minor medals; two senior Mayo club medals, two junior and one intermediate championship medals; one senior, one junior club Donegal championship medals.

Fleming, Seamus (football)

▸ *Native of Laois; played senior football for Laois, 1967-69.*
Career/honours: played junior football for Laois; **All-Ireland junior medal, 1973**; *played minor football for Laois, 1965-67; Leinster minor medals, 1966 and 1967; All-Ireland minor finalist medal, 1967; All-Ireland junior medal, 1970 (London); senior club championship medal for St Joseph's, Laois.*

Flood, Gavin (football)

▸ *Played inter-county football for Roscommon.*

Flood, Paul (football)

▸ *Native of Kildare; played senior football for Kildare, 1997-2011.*
Career/honours: two Leinster titles with Kildare, one junior and one senior, 1998; one county junior title with Maynooth; three county intermediate titles with Maynooth; one Leinster intermediate title with Maynooth, 2009; second and third in the Cic Fada in Bray, 2011 and 2012 respectively.
Played League of Ireland soccer with Kildare Town.

Flynn, Brendan (football)

▸ *Native of Leitrim; played senior football for Leitrim, 1971-72.*
Career/honours: played minor football for Leitrim; junior club championship medal with Fenagh, 1967, and senior league medal with Aughnasheelin, 1969.

Flynn, Dominic (football)

▸ *Native of Roscommon; played senior football for Roscommon, 1974.*

Flynn, Martin

▸ *Played inter-county for Meath.*

Flynn, Michael (hurling)

▶ *Native of Kilkenny; played senior hurling for Kildare, 1962-66.*
Career/honours: **All-Ireland junior medal, 1962.** *Played football with Kilcullen.*
Approached by Kilkenny selectors to travel for trial, but could not, because he had no car.

Flynn, Michael

▶ *Played inter-county for Leitrim during the 1980s.*

Flynn, Mick (hurling)

▶ *Native of Cork; hurled at senior for Dublin, 1938-40*
Career/honours: **All-Ireland senior medal, 1938**; *National League medal, 1939; Railway Cup hurling for Leinster.*
Gold Scott medal, 1948. The only member of the Force to win an All-Ireland senior medal and a gold Scott medal.

Flynn, Pat (football)

▶ *Native of Leitrim; played senior football for Leitrim, 1980-85.*
Career/honours: U21 championship medal, 1974; three senior championship medals.

Flynn, Patrick

▶ *Native of Sligo; played inter-county for Sligo (1925, 1926) and Dublin (1927). Club: Garda, Dublin.*

Flynn, Patrick (football)
▶ *Played senior and U21 football for Waterford. Brother of Tom Flynn (below).*

Flynn, Pat (football)

▶ *Native of Wexford; played senior football for Wexford.*

Flynn, Paul (hurling)

▶ *Native of Galway; played senior hurling for Galway, 2008.*
Career/honours: **All-Ireland U21 medal, 2005**; *intermediate hurling for Galway. Club: Tommy Larkins. Tragically killed in a car accident in Galway, October 2008.*

Flynn, Tom (football)

▶ *Native of Waterford; played senior football for Waterford (1964-66) and Wexford. Club: Geraldine O'Hanrahans (New Ross), Kilrossanty (Waterford). Won a Waterford SFC title with Kilrossanty in 1964.*

Fogarty, Vincent (football)

▶ *Native of Mayo; played inter-county senior football for Wicklow (1958) and Mayo (1959).*
Career/honours: **All-Ireland minor medal, 1953 (Mayo).**

Foley, Donal (football)

▸ *Native of Tipperary; played senior football for Tipperary (1981–89).*
Career/honours: played minor (1979) and U21 (1981-82) football; also played
junior football (1989-93). Four senior club championship medals for Moyle
Rovers.

Foley, Peter (football)

▸ *Native of Wicklow; played senior football for Wicklow.*
In 1979 Wicklow arrived in Nowlan park to play Kilkenny with only 10
players as one of the team buses broke down in torrential rain. 17 years
old supporter Peter Foley lined out for Wicklow to make up the full
fifteen.

Forde, Gerry (hurling)

▸ *Played senior hurling for Galway and Sligo, 1970-74.*

Forde, John (football)

▸ *Native of Mayo; played for Mayo, 1917-33.*
Career/honours: Railway Cup football with Connacht; six Connacht
championship medals with Mayo, 1918, 1920, 1921, 1924, 1929, 1930 and
possibly 1931 and 1932 (unconfirmed); Mayo senior club championship medal
with Lacken Sarsfields in 1917, and a Roscommon senior championship medal
with Strokestown in 1926. John played at midfield for the Gardaí versus the Army
in Croke Park on 26 June 1921, and won a prestigious Croke Cup tournament
medal, when Mayo defeated Dublin in Croke Park on 27 November 1921.

Forde, Kevin (football)

▸ *Native of Offaly; played senior football for Offaly, 1987*
Career/honours: played U21 football for Offaly, 1983; senior club and U21
championship medals with Clara; Munster Colleges football medal with North
Monastery, 1980.

Forde, Sean (football/hurling)

▸ *Native of Mayo; played senior football for Waterford (1957), Mayo (1960) and*
Leitrim (1961), and senior hurling for Leitrim (1959-62).
Career/honours: played junior football for Waterford and Leitrim; senior
club championship medals for Moyle Rovers (football); played in the famous
championship victory over Kerry in 1957.

Foy, Louise (ladies' football)

▸ *Native of Leitrim; played football for Leitrim, 1987-96.*

Fox, Leon (football)

▸ *Native of Offaly; played senior football for Offaly, 2016 to present. Club: Ferbane.*

Fox, Paddy (hurling)

▸ *Native of Dublin; played senior hurling for Dublin, 1966-68.*
Career/honours: senior club championship medal with Kilmacud Crokes, 1966.

Freaney, Enda (football)

▶ *Native of Kildare; career ran from 1992 to 2012.*
Career/honours: senior football for Kildare, 1995-97; played minor (1993), U21 (1994-96) and junior (1998) football, and minor hurling; six senior club championship medals (1993, 1994, 1999, 2001, 2005, 2012) with Sarsfields; minor (1993), U21 (1992-93).
Scored a goal in the Kildare minor, U21 and senior club championship finals of 1993.

Freaney, Pierce (hurling)

▶ *Native of Kilkenny; played senior hurling for Carlow (1963-64), Kilkenny (1968) and Kildare (1973-74).*
Career/honours: **two All-Ireland minor medals, 1960, 1961;** *minor (1960-61) and junior (1962) hurling for Kilkenny; one Munster senior club championship medal with St Finbarr's, Cork, 1968; two All-Ireland Colleges medals with St Kieran's, Kilkenny, 1959, 1961. Inter-county referee.*

Frehill, Gary (hurling)

▶ *Native of Galway; played senior hurling for Kerry (1997-98). Club: Ballyheigue.*

Furlong, Colin (football)

▶ *Native of Wexford; played senior football for Wexford, 1996-97.*
Career/honours: U21 hurling and football for Wexford; junior football for Wexford. Senior championship medal with St Patrick's, Wicklow; junior championship hurling medal with St Patrick's, Ballyoughter, Wexford; two senior hurling championship medals and a Leinster medal with O'Loughlin Gaels, Kilkenny, 2001 and 2003.

Furlong, Eamonn

▶ *Played inter-county for Wexford and Wicklow.*

Furlong, J. (football)

▶ *Native of Wexford; played senior football for Waterford, 1926.*

G

Galavan, Liam (hurling)

▶ *Native of Kilkenny; played senior hurling for the Cats, 1974.*
Career/honours: Leinster U21 medal. Club: The Rower, Inistioge.

Gallagher, Bosco (football)

▶ *Native of Donegal; played senior football for Donegal, 1979-81.*
Career/honours: played minor and junior football for Donegal.

Gallagher, Darren (football)

▶ *Native of Longford; played senior football for Longford, 2015 to present.*
Career/honours: played minor football for Longford; Leinster minor medal, 2010; played U21 football for Longford, 2011-13; Hastings Cup medal.

Gallagher, James (hurling)

▶ *Native of Monaghan; played senior hurling for Monaghan, 2002-05.*

Gallagher, Jim (football)

▶ *Native of Donegal; played senior football for Leitrim (1975-80) and minor for Donegal (1968).*
Career/honours: **Masters for Sligo, 1991 and 1992**; *Leitrim Senior League with Glencar/Manorhamilton in 1976 (captain) and first senior championship with Glencar Manorhamilton in 1977; two minor championships with Dungloe, 1967 and 1968. Won a senior championship with St Mary's in Sligo in 1981, and a junior championship in Sligo with St John's in 1989.*

Gallagher, Michael (football)

▶ *Native of Donegal; played senior football for Donegal, 1978-84.*
Career/honours: McKenna Cup medal, senior club championship medal for Naomh Columba, Glencolmcille, 1978.

Gallagher, Tom (football)

▶ *Native of Leitrim; played senior football for Leitrim during the 1970s. Club: Aughnasheelin.*

Gallen, Andy (football)

▶ *Played inter-county football for Donegal.*

Gallery, Elaine (camogie)

▶ *Native of Clare; played camogie for Dublin and Clare, 2011-15.*
Career/honours: **All-Ireland championship medal with Dublin, 2013;** *All-Ireland National League medal with Dublin, 2012; played junior camogie for Dublin, 2012-14; played junior camogie for Clare, 2004-06; All-Ireland junior finalist medal with Clare, 2005; played minor camogie for Clare.*

Galligan, Tom (football)

▶ *Native of Cavan; played senior football for Cavan. Club: Virginia Blues; Ballybay, Pearse Brothers (Monaghan; won a senior football championship medal with them during then 1960s). Career: 1952-1973.*

Galvin, John Noel (football)

▶ *Native of Westmeath; played senior football for Westmeath, 1966-73.*
Career/honours: three senior club championship medals for Moate.

Galvin, Michael (football/hurling)

▶ *Native of Sligo; played senior football (1991-92) and hurling (1989) for Sligo.*
Career/honours: two senior club football championship medals for St Mary's, 1987-1996; Trench Cup medal, 1990/91, Sligo RTC; Trench Cup medal, 1994, Garda College; Division 4 National League medal, 1990; three senior club championship hurling medals with Craobh Rua and St Mary's. Player/manager with Sligo, 1998/99. Led Sligo hurlers to the Nicky Rackard Cup in 2008 and won promotion twice in the National League.

Galvin, Noel (football)

▶ *Native of Roscommon; played senior football for Roscommon, 2001-02.*
Career/honours: Connacht championship medal, 2001; **All-Ireland junior club**
medal.

Galwey, Charles (hurling)

▶ *Played senior hurling for Donegal and Sligo, 1977-78.*

Gannon, Seamus (football)

▶ *Native of Cavan; played senior football for Cavan, 1989-94.*
Career/honours: senior club championship medal (Cavan), 1998.

Gaul, Sean (football)

▶ *Native of Wexford; as played senior football for Wexford since 2009 (injured*
2014-16).
Career/honours: played full back for Wexford minors in 2008; beaten in Leinster
semi-final by Offaly; played wing forward and full forward for U21s, 2009-
11; won a Leinster U21 title in 2011 (beating Longford in the final; lost out
to Cavan in the All-Ireland semi-final); won a Leinster JFC in 2015, playing
at wing forward in the final against Meath; has won premier minor football,
premier U21 hurling and two senior football (2012, 2014) titles in Wexford.
Club: St Anne's.

Gaule, Charlie (football)

▶ *Played senior football for Wicklow and Kilkenny. Club: Castlebridge/Arklow.*

Garde, Maurice (football)

▶ *Native of Cork; played senior football for Tipperary, 1966-67.*
Career/honours: intermediate club medal with Castlemartyr, Cork; also played
intermediate hurling with the club.

Gately, Deirdre (ladies' football)

▶ *Native of Kildare; played football for Kildare during the 2000s.*

Gavin, Damien (football)

▶ *Native of Westmeath; played senior football for Westmeath, 1997-2004.*
Career/honours: **All-Ireland minor medal, 1995 (captain);** *Leinster senior*
medal, 2004. Club: St Mary's, Rochfortbridge. As of 2018, a selector with the
Westmeath senior football management setup.
"His finest moment in a senior jersey was undoubtedly his fisted winning
point in extra time in 2001 in the qualifier against Mayo in a heaving Hyde
Park."

Gaynor, Ciara (camogie)

▶ *played senior camogie for Tippeary, 1997-2005.*
Career/honours: **five senior All-Ireland medals, 1999, 2000, 2001, 2003**
and 2004; All Star award, 2004; intermediate All-Ireland title; *National*
League title, 2004; one senior club championship medal with Burgess Duharra,
2010; junior and intermediate club championship medals (one each) for Kilruane
McDonagh's.
Player of the Year, 2001; Lynchpin, 2003.

Gerrard, Simon (football)

▸ *Native of Louth; played senior football for Louth, 1999-2006.*
Career/honours: Division 2 National League medal, 2000; Railway Cup medal with Leinster, 2005; two senior championship club medals with Newtown Blues, 2000, 2001.

Gethins, Sean (football)

▸ *Native of Sligo; played senior football for Sligo, 1961-67.*
Career/honours: minor football, 1960-61; senior club championship medal, 1959.

Gibbons, J. J. (football)

▸ *Played senior football for Mayo during the 1960s. Club: Kilmaine.*

Gibbons, Russell (football)

▸ *Native of Mayo; played senior football for Clare.*
Career/honours: minor and U21 football for Mayo. Club: Éire Óg, Clare.

Giblin, Gerry (hurling)

▸ *played senior hurling for Louth, 1987-1990.*

Gielty, Michael (football)

▸ *Native of Mayo; played senior football for Mayo, 1978-79.*
Career/honours: All-Ireland Hogan Cup medal with St Jarlath's, Tuam, 1974; Dublin senior club medal with Civil Service, 1979.

Giles, Eamonn (hurling)

▸ *Native of Meath; played senior hurling with Meath, 1969-74.*
Career/honours: National Hurling League medal, 1972-73. Father of well-known Meath footballer, Trevor Giles.

Gill, Mick (hurling)

▸ *Native of Galway; hurled at senior level for Galway (1922-23, 1931-38) and Dublin (1924-30).*
Career/honours: **three All-Ireland senior medals (Galway, 1923, Dublin, 1924, 1927).** *Played hurling in the Tailteann Games, 1928. Four Leinster medals with Dublin: 1924, 1925, 1927 and 1930. Railway Cup with Leinster. Two National League medals. Six club championship medals for Garda, Dublin: 1925, 1926,1927, 1928, 1929 and 1931.*
The 1923 final was played on 14 September 1923, when Mick played for Galway. He then played for Dublin in the 1924 final, which was played on the 19 December 1924.

Gilmartin, Liam (football)

▸ *Native of Roscommon; played senior football for Roscommon, 1938-44.*
Career/honours: **two All-Ireland senior championship medals, 1943 and 1944; All-Ireland minor medal, 1939 (captain);** *All-Ireland senior finalist medal, 1946.*
Liam was regarded as the greatest midfielder of his era.

Gilmore, Brendan (football)

▸ *Native of Monaghan; played senior football for Longford, 1963-69.*
Football: National League football medal, 1966; O'Byrne Cup medal, 1965;
Leinster championship medal, 1968; senior club championship medal (Louth).

Gilton, Frank (football)

▸ *Native of Dublin; played senior football for Dublin in the 1960s.*
Career/honours: All-Ireland senior finalist medal, 1964. Club: O'Toole's.

Gilton, Paul (hurling)

▸ *Native of Dublin; played senior hurling for Dublin, 1985-86.*
Career/honours: U21 hurling for Dublin; Boland Cup medals, 1989, 1991 and
1994; Leinster Colleges medal with St Joseph's, Fairview. Club: Craobh Chiaráin.

Gilvarry, Hubert (football)

▸ *Native of Mayo; played senior football for Sligo, 1982-84 and 1987.*
Career/honours: four senior club championship medals, 1983, 1984, 1987 and
1996 and one Connacht championship medal, 1983, with St Mary's; junior
football for Sligo; Trench Cup medal with Sligo RTC, 1981; Overs 40s Masters
football with Sligo and Mayo.

Glancy, Frank (football)

▸ *Native of Roscommon; played senior football for Roscommon (1960-63) and*
Cavan (1967).
Career/honours: played minor (1959) and junior (1960) football for Roscommon;
senior club championship medal for Shannon Gaels (Roscommon); senior
Connacht championship medal, 1961; senior league medal for Cavan Gaels.

Gleeson, Conor (hurling)

▸ *Native of Tipperary; hurled at senior for Tipperary, 1995-2004.*
Career/honours: **one All-Ireland senior medal 2001.** *2 national league medals*
and one senior club championship medal with Boherlahan-Dualla 1996

Gleeson, Jack (hurling)

▸ *Native of Clare; played senior hurling for Dublin and Clare, 1927-35.*
Career/honours: **one All-Ireland senior medal with Dublin, 1927**; *All-*
Ireland senior finalist medal with Clare, 1932. Club: Toomevara.

Glennon, Denis (football)

▸ *Native of Westmeath; played senior football for Westmeath, 2004-17.*
Career/honours: played minor and U21 football for Westmeath; Leinster SFC
medal, 2004; Division 2 National League medal, 2008; Division 4 National
League medal, 2017; two senior championship medals, 2006 and 2007 and two
Feis Cups, 2012 and 2014, with Tyrrellspass; World Police and Fire Games gold
medal, 2013. Hurled with the St Brigid's club in Westmeath; continues to play
club football for Tyrrellspass.
Described on his inter-county retirement as "one of the best forwards
that ever put on the Westmeath jersey" by 2004 teammate, Alan Mangan.

Glennon, Liz (camogie)

▸ *Native of Roscommon; played camogie for Roscommon, 1999-2005.*
Career/honours: three Connacht county medals; Purcell Cup medal with Garda
College, 2005; **selected on All Star Purcell Cup team, 2005**; *Ashbourne Shield*
medal with Garda College, 2007.

Glynn, Sean (football)

▸ *Native of Galway; played senior football for Galway, 1985-93.*
Career/honours: two Connacht championship medals; one Division 3 National
League medal.

Godkin, Christy (football)

▸ *Native of Cork; played senior football for Cork, 1954-55.*
Career/honours: played for Garda Club, Dublin; founder member of St Raphael's
Garda Credit Union.

Gordon, Jacinta (camogie)

▸ *Played inter-county camogie for Wexford during the 2000s. Club: Blackwater.*

Gorman, Maeve (camogie)

▸ *Native of Kildare; played inter-county camogie for Kildare.*

Grace, Jim (hurling)

▸ *Native of Kilkenny; played senior hurling for Kilkenny, 1932-33*
Career/honours: **two All-Ireland senior medals, 1932 and 1933.**

Grace, Paul (hurling)

▸ *Native of*
played senior hurling for Kilkenny during the 1970s.

Grant, Jennifer (ladies' football)

▸ *Native of Tipperary; played football for Tipperary in the 2000s.*
Career/honours: All-Ireland intermediate finalist medal, 2013.

Gray, Patrick

Laois; played inter-county for Laois, 1919-23
Career/honours: played for Leinster in the Tailteann Games in 1924.

Greaney, Michael (hurling)

▸ *Native of Galway; played senior hurling for Monaghan, 2008.*
Career/honours: National League medal (Division 4) with Monaghan; played
minor, U21 and intermediate hurling for Galway; All-Ireland intermediate
finalist medal, 2001; Harty Cup and All-Ireland Colleges medals with St
Flannan's, 1998.

Greenan, Ray (football)

▸ *Native of Leitrim; played senior football for Leitrim, 1994-2000.*
Career/honours: two Division 1 National League medals, 1999 and 2001.

Greene, David (football)

▸ *Native of Donegal; played senior football for Donegal.*

Grehan, Jim (football)

▸ *Native of Westmeath; played senior football for Westmeath, 1959-64.*
Career/honours: junior championship medal with Kilbeggan Shamrocks, 1959.

Griffen, Tom (football)

▸ *Played inter-county senior football for Limerick.*

Griffin, Don (football)

▸ *Native of Wicklow; played senior football for Wicklow, 1988-90.*
Career/honours: All-Ireland Freshers medal with WRTC, 1986.

Griffin, Pat (football)

▸ *Native of Kerry; played senior football for Kerry (1963-74) and Kildare (1962).*
Career/honours: **two senior All-Ireland medals, 1969, 1970; one U21 All-Ireland medal, 1964 (first U21 championship)**; *Railway Cup football with Munster; seven Munster senior championship medals Railway Cup for Munster; played minor football for Kildare 1961-62; Kerry captain, 1968; three League medals, 1969, 1971 and 1972; two club championship senior medals with Mid Kerry, 1967 and 1971. Also played club football for Glenbeigh.*
Pat wore the no. 11 jersey for Kerry in five All-Ireland finals. According to author Raymond Smith: "Pat was far ahead of his time in thought and movement".

Griffin, Ralph (football)

▸ *Native of Galway; played senior football for Galway during the 1930s.*
Career/honours: **two All-Ireland senior medals, 1934 and 1938**; *Railway Cup with Connacht, 1936.*
Garda Hall of Fame award recipient.

Grogan, Enda (football)

▸ *Native of Meath; played inter-county football for Meath, 1954.*

Grogan, Rickard (football)

▸ *Native of Meath; played senior football for Meath during the 1940s and 1950s.*
Career/honours: played for Garda/Army vs the rest of Ireland in 1954.

Grogan (Jnr), Chris (football)

▸ *Native of Roscommon; played senior football for Roscommon during the 1980s and 1990s.*
Career/honours: one Connacht senior championship medal, 1991; one Connacht minor championship medal, 1984; one New York senior championship medal, 1989; four senior club championship medals with Roscommon Gaels; 1994, 1998, 1999 and 2004; played for the All-Ireland Garda and Combined Colleges teams.

Grogan (Snr), Christy (football)

▸ *Native of Roscommon; played senior football for Roscommon (1961-62) and Westmeath (1965).*
Career/honours: All-Ireland finalist medal, 1962; two Connacht senior medals, 1961 and 1962; senior club championship medal with Athlone, 1965.

Guinan, Niall (football)

▸ *Native of Wexford; played senior football for Wexford, 1992-97.*
Career/honours: **All-Ireland junior medal, 1993.** *Club: Bunclody.*

Guinan, Rory (football)

▸ *Native of Offaly; played senior football for Offaly, 2003-04, 2006 and 2009 Career/honours: U21 football, 2003-05; minor football, 2002. Club: Ballycumber.* Ulster Bank Rising Star award, 2008.

Guthrie, Mick (football)

▸ *Native of Clare; played senior football for Clare during the 1950s.*

H

Halligan, Brian (football)

▸ *Native of Offaly; played senior football for Offaly, 2001. Club: Ballycumber.*

Halligan, Michael

▸ *Played inter-county for Wicklow and Roscommon.*

Hallinan, P. J. (football)

▸ *Native of Sligo; played senior football for Sligo, 1965-71.*

Hallinan, Pat (football)

▸ *Native of Dublin; played senior football for Dublin.*
Career/honours: **minor All-Ireland medal, 1956***; minor football, 1967-1970;* **junior All-Ireland medal, 1960***; four senior club championship medals, 1966, 1967, 1970 and 1972 for St Vincent's; Leinster club championship medal, 1972; junior (1960) and intermediate (1960) championship medals.*

Hallissey, Andrew 'Andy' (football)

▸ *Native of Kerry; played senior football for Waterford in the early 1960s.*
Career/honours: played football for Brickey Rangers in Waterford and won a county title in 1963. A native of Templenoe, Co. Kerry.

Hanley, Edel (ladies' football)

▸ *Native of Tipperary; played football for Tipperary, 1999-2013.*
Career/honours: **All Star award, 2008; Intermediate All-Ireland medal, 2008***; senior county championship medals with Aherlow, Tipperary; senior county championship medal with Shanahoe, Laois; Munster senior club championship medal, 2011.*

Hanley, Ollie (football/hurling)

▸ *Native of Roscommon; played senior football (1974) and senior hurling (1963-80) for Roscommon.*
Career/honours: **All-Ireland junior hurling medal, 1974***; Senior League Club medal with Garda Club, 1971 and 1972; two junior club football (1968 and 1972) medals (Dublin) and one intermediate (1973) championship medal with St Pat's, Roscommon; Railway Cup with Connacht, 1969-71;* **Special All-Ireland Hurling U21 medal, 1967.**

Hannon, Ursula (camogie)

▸ *Club: St Vincent's.*

Hanrahan, David (hurling)

▸ *Played senior hurling for Monaghan, 1995-99*
Career/honours: **Junior All-Ireland medal with Monaghan, 1997.**

Haran, Mick (football)

▸ *Native of Sligo; played senior football for Sligo. Club: Curry and Kilrush Shamrocks.*

Hardiman, Albert (football)

▸ *Native of Clare; played senior football for Clare.*
Career/honours: senior club championship medal, 2000. Club: Éire Óg.

Harkins, Sid

▸ *Played inter-county for Laois, c. 1948.*

Harmon, Keri (ladies' football)

▸ *Native of Longford; played with Longford ladies from U14 through to adult level.*
Career/honours: **All-Ireland 'B' winners with Longford, 2011**; *colleges All-Ireland medal with Scoil Mhuire, Longford, 2011; Leinster medals, 2012, 2013. Clubs: Longford Slashers, Garda Westmanstown.*

Harnett, Pat (hurling)

▸ *Native of Louth; played senior hurling for Louth.*

Harrington, John (hurling)

▸ *Native of Monaghan; hurled for Monaghan (1972-78) and Kildare (1978-79).*
Career/honours: Ulster finalist medal, 1972-73; All-Ireland Masters finalist medal, 2001;
top scorer for Monaghan for three years.

Harrington, Mark (football/hurling)

▸ *Native of Cork; played football (2008-09) and hurling for Cork.*
Career/honours: Munster intermediate championship hurling medal; Munster senior club championship medal for Douglas, 2008; premier intermediate hurling medal, 2009.

Harrington, Paddy (football)

▸ *Native of Cork; played senior football for Cork in the 1950s.*
▸ *Native of Career/honours: played minor and junior football for Cork; two All-Ireland finalist medals, 1956 and 1957; two Munster senior championship medals, 1956 and 1957; two Munster championship medals, 1956 and 1957; Played for Ireland vs Combined Universities, 1957; nine inter-provincial seasons for Munster. Played for Garda Club, Dublin.*
Father of golfer Padraig Harrington. Driving force behind the foundation and building of Stackstown Golf Club in Dublin.

Harrington, Tadhg

▶ *Played inter-county for Cork.*

Hayden, D. (football)

▶ *Native of Clare; played senior football for Clare, 1924-25.*

Hayes, Andrew (hurling)

▶ *Native of Meath; played senior hurling for Meath.*
Career/honours: National League Division 2 medal; U21 special medal. Played U21 football for Meath.

Hayes, Billy (hurling)

▶ *Played senior hurling for Westmeath.*

Hayes, Dominic (hurling)

▶ *Native of Tipperary; played senior hurling for Tipperary, 1985*
Career/honours: **U21 All-Ireland medal, 1981***; minor 1978-79, U21 1981-82; played junior hurling for Tipperary; senior club championship medal with Faugh's, Dublin, 1987.*

Hayes, Joe (football)

▶ *Native of Clare; played senior football for Clare, 2002 - 17*
Career/honours: one National League Division 3 medal, 2016; two McGrath Cup medals, 2002, 2008; Munster finalist medal, 2012; one senior club championship and one league medal with Lissycassey, 2007; U17 Compromise Rules, 1999; Railway Cup medal, 2008; All-Ireland junior Interfirms with Limerick, 2009.

Hayes, Joe (hurling)

▶ *Native of Tipperary; hurled with Tipperary and Monaghan, 1987-94*
Career/honours: **two All-Ireland senior medals, 1989, 1991; minor All-Ireland medal;** *five Munster senior medals; two National League medals; two All-Ireland U21 finalist medals, 1983, 1984;* **junior All-Ireland medal***; Oireachtas Cup medal; club championship medal with Clonoulty-Rossmore, 1989.*
Managed Monaghan to All-Ireland junior success in 2007.

Hayes, Mick (hurling)

▶ *Native of Limerick; played senior hurling with Limerick, 1959-66*
Career/honours: two senior club hurling medals with Cappamore, 1959 and 1964 (Limerick); one junior club hurling medal with Dalkey Mitchells (1967, Dublin). Featured on All-Ireland Garda hurling team v Army, 1964, 1966 and 1967.

Hayes, Tom (football)

▶ *Native of Waterford; played senior football for Waterford, 1975-84.*
Career/honours: two intermediate and one junior championship club medals in Waterford; two All-Ireland Interfirms medals, 1986 and 1987, with Cork Garda.

Healy, Joe

▶ *Played inter-county for Wicklow, 1964-66*

Healy, John

▸ *Played inter-county for Sligo; resigned from the Force and became a District Court clerk.*

Hearne, John (hurling)

▸ *Native of Waterford; played senior hurling for Waterford, 1957-73.*
Career/honours: three senior club championship medals for Ballygunner, 1966, 1967 and 1968; three senior club championship medals for Faugh's (Dublin), 1970, 1972 and 1973; one intermediate club medal for Na Fianna, 1957.

Hearns, Dick (football)

▸ *Played senior football for Roscommon, Longford, Donegal, Cork, Dublin and Mayo; career ran from the 1930s to the 1950s.*
Career/honours: All-Ireland finalist medal for Mayo, 1932; trained Roscommon. Trained Mayo to All-Ireland success in 1936; Managed Shelbourne FC (soccer) for fourteen seasons. Boxed for Ireland, and won 173 of his 198 major amateur fights.

Heeran, Paddy (football)

▸ *Native of Leitrim; played senior football for Monaghan in the 1970s.*

Hegarty, Chris (football)

▸ *Played senior football for Mayo and Donegal.*
Career/honours: **senior All-Ireland medal with Mayo, 1950**. *Club: Charlestown.*

Hegarty, Pat (football)

▸ *Native of Cork; played senior football for Cork, 1992-98.*
Career/honours: **All-Ireland minor medal, 1991; All-Ireland U21 medal, 1994**; *All-Ireland Senior 'A' Colleges football medal with St Fachtna's, Skibbereen in 1991; Munster Senior Football Championship medal, 1993; two Trench cup medals with Garda College, 1993 and 1994; Cork County senior football championship (2014) with Carbery; five West Cork junior 'A' football championships between 1995 and 2006;* **three All-Ireland Interfirms medals with Cork Gardaí in 1994, 1999 and 2003.**

Hehir, Joe (football)

▸ *Native of Clare; played senior football for Clare during the 1970s.*

Heneghan, Brendan (football)

▸ *Native of Mayo; played senior football for Mayo during the 1990s. Club: Louisburgh.*

Hennessy, Sean (hurling)

▸ *Native of Wexford; played senior hurling for Wexford, 1950-52.*

Henry, Eamonn (football)

▸ *Native of Roscommon; played senior football for Roscommon (1987-90) and Kildare (1984-87)*
Career/honours: played minor (1980) and U21 (1982 and 1983) football for Kildare; senior club championship medal with Athy, 1987; Leinster U21 medal, 1983.

Henry, Gerry (football)

▸ *Native of Sligo; played senior football for Sligo. Clubs: Tubbercurry and Castlebar Mitchels.*

Herron, Colm (football)

▸ *Native of Donegal; played senior football for Sligo, 1984.*
Career/honours: senior championship medal with Aodh Rua, 1986.

Heslin, Shane (football/hurling)

▸ *Native of Leitrim; played senior hurling (1981-96) and football (spells between 1981 and 1996) for Leitrim.*
Career/honours: **All-Ireland 'B' medal, 1990;** *three senior club championship medals with Gortletteragh.*

Hession, Páraic (hurling)

▸ *Native of Galway; played senior hurling for Dublin, 1993-94*
Career/honours: minor and U21 hurling for Galway; Dublin senior hurling league medal; Boland Cup medal; two junior hurling championship medals in Galway.

Hickey, David (football)

▸ *Native of Waterford; played senior football for Waterford (2000-06).*
Career/honours: minor football and hurling, Western and county titles, 2003; U21 football and hurling, Western and county titles, 2006; Junior 'B' hurling, Western and county titles, 2000; Junior 'A' hurling, Western and county titles, 2005; intermediate football, Western titles, 2004 and 2006; intermediate football county title (2006) with Bricky Rangers. With Bishopstown, Cork: Tadhg Crowley senior football club competition, 2015; Munster U21 football title, 2003; Munster minor football round robin tournament champion, 2000.

Hickey, Mick (football)

▸ *Native of Tipperary; played senior football for Tipperary. Club: Bansha.*

Hickey, Shane (football)

▸ *Native of Clare; played senior football for Clare, 2005 to present.*
Career/honours: five senior county titles with Kilmurry Ibrickane; two senior Munster club titles; All-Ireland club final appearance in 2010.

Higgins, Mick (football)

▶ *Native of Native of New York, USA and (from childhood) Cavan; played senior football for Cavan, 1942-53.*
Career/honours: **three senior All-Ireland medals, 1947 (New York), 1948 and 1952 (captain);** *seven Ulster senior championship medals; two National League medals; Railway Cup football with Ulster; played on Ireland teams. Two county championship medals with Mountnugent, 1946, 1952; two McKenna Cup medals. All-time All Star award, 1987; Texaco Hall of Fame, 1989. Inter-county manager (Cavan, Longford, Donegal); inter-county referee.*
Ranked at no. 36 in the *Irish Independent 125 Greatest Stars of the GAA;* Garda Hall of Fame Award, 2001. Born in The Bronx, New York, USA, Mick is one of the few All-Ireland winning captains, hurling or football, born outside of Ireland. He was born on 22 August 1922, the same day Michael Collins was shot. Moved to Kilnaleck, Co. Cavan at the age of five. In his own words: "I never hit anyone; I played a clean game and I was never put off." Mick died on 28 January 2010. He was described by Eugene McGee as "a man who became a GAA superstar of his generation, despite limited coverage of games he played".

Hilliard, Denis (football)

▶ *Native of Wicklow; played senior football for Wicklow1974-1975 Football minor hurling and football for Wicklow, 1970 Senior football club championship medal in Wicklow.*

Histon, Kieran (football)

▶ *Native of Cork; played senior football with Cork, 2016.*
Career/honours: played minor hurling and football with Cork, 2013; U21 football with Cork, 2014-16; won two Munster U21 medals and was named on U21 team of the year in 2016; played U21 hurling with Cork, 2015; won a Cork senior hurling championship medal with Imokilly and a junior 'B' football medal with Cobh, both in 2017.

Hobbs, Dermot (football)

▶ *Native of Dublin; played senior football for Dublin, 1973*
Career/honours: played minor and U21 football with Dublin; Leinster minor and U21 medals; played with Garda Club, Dublin. Former chairman of St Raphael's Garda Credit Union.

Hoey, Aaron (football)

▶ *Native of Louth; played senior football for Louth, 1996-2012.*
Career/honours: **All-Ireland 'B' medal, 1997;** *National League Division 2 medals, 2000 and 2006; National League Division 3 medal, 2011; three Railway Cup medals with Leinster; three county hurling championship medals; played inter-provincial football for Ulster. Club: St Bride's, Knockbridge.*

Hoey, Eamonn (football)

▶ *Native of Monaghan; played senior football for Monaghan, 1997-98 and 2001-02.*
Career/honours: played minor and U21 football with Monaghan.

Hogan, Eamonn (football)

▸ *Native of Tipperary; played senior football for Tipperary, 1962-67.*
Career/honours: U21 and junior club championship medals with Grangemockler.
Nephew of Michael Hogan, the Tipperary player who was shot dead by British Crown forces in Croke Park on 'Bloody Sunday', 21 November 1920.

Hogan, John (hurling)

▸ *Native of Tipperary; played senior hurling for Cork, 1964. Also played junior hurling.*

Hogan, Ken (hurling)

▸ *Native of Tipperary; senior hurler with Tipperary, 1987-93.*
Career/honours: **two All-Ireland senior hurling championship medals, 1989 and 1991; one All Star award – goalkeeper, 1987; one All-Ireland minor hurling championship medal, 1980;** *played minor and U21 hurling for Tipp; five Munster senior hurling championship medals, 1987, 1988, 1989, 1991 and 1993; two National Hurling League medals, 1987 and 1988; two Munster U21 hurling championship medals, 1983 and 1984; one Munster minor hurling championship, 1980; Railway Cup medal, 1992; Oireachtas medal, 1990. Two North Senior Championsip medals with Lorrha. Inter-county manager of Tipperary, 2003. Coach with All-Ireland winners, 2001.*
All-Ireland U21 winning manager, 2010. Managed Irish shinty team, 1997.

Hogan, Liam (hurling)

▸ *Native of Offaly; senior hurler with Offaly, 1980-81.*
Career/honours: **All-Ireland senior medal, 1981;** *four senior club championship medals. Club: Coolderry.*

Hogan, Martin (football/hurling)

▸ *Native of Carlow; played senior football (1957-63) and hurling (1957-65) for Carlow.*
Career/honours: one Leinster junior championship medal, 1960; one Leinster intermediate hurling championship medal, 1962; **one All-Ireland intermediate hurling championship medal, 1962;** *one Railway Cup medal for Leinster, 1963.*

Hogan, Sean (football)

▸ *Native of Westmeath; played senior football for Westmeath. Club: Moate All Whites.*

Hogan, Stephen (hurling)

▸ *Native of Tipperary; played senior hurling for Tipperary, 1997.*
Career/honours: played intermediate hurling for Tipperary; county intermediate medal in 2007 with Lorrha-Dorrha; county senior championship medal with O'Loughlin Gaels in Kilkenny, 2001.

Hogan, Willie (football/hurling)

▸ *Native of Carlow; played senior football (1956-63) and hurling (1956-65) for Carlow.*
Career/honours: **All-Ireland intermediate hurling medal, 1962;** *two Division 2 National League medals, 1958, 1959; one Leinster junior championship medal, 1960; one Leinster intermediate hurling championship medal, 1962; Railway Cup medal with Leinster. Carlow Hall of Fame award, 1992. All-Ireland selection, 1962.*

Hogarty, Gerry (hurling)

▶ *Native of Dublin; played senior hurling for Dublin, 1983–85 and 1987. Career/honours: one senior club championship medal with Kilmacud Crokes, 1985.*

Holland, Teddy (football)

▶ *Native of Cork; played senior football for Cork, 1968-70.*
Career/honours: **All-Ireland junior medal, 1972; All-Ireland senior club championship medal with St Finbarr's, 1981;** *minor and U21 football for Cork; Munster minor medal, 1966; Munster U21 medal, 1969; senior club championship medals, 1969, 1971, 1980 and 1981 with Carbery and St Finbarr's;* **two All-Ireland Interfirms medals with Cork Garda, 1978 and 1986.** *Inter-county manager of Cork, 2007-08; also served as minor and U21 manager, and selector with the senior Cork team.*

Holohan, Jo Ann (ladies' football)

▶ *Native of Leitrim; played football for Leitrim, 1995-2000.*

Horgan, Keith (hurling)

▶ *Native of Dublin; senior hurler for Dublin, 1998-2004.*
Career/honours: four senior club championship medals for O'Toole's.

Houlihan, Johnny (football)

▶ *Native of Clare; played senior football for Clare in the 1970s. Club: Kilrush Shamrocks.*

Houlihan, P. J. (hurling)

▶ *Native of Kerry; senior hurler for Kerry (1976–84).*
Career/honours: Division 2 National League medal, 1978-79; six county senior championship medals with Ballyduff, Kerry.

Howard, Garrett (hurling)

▶ *Native of Limerick; played senior hurling for Limerick (1921-23 and 1933-36), Dublin (1924-29) and Tipperary (1929-32).*
Career/honours: **five All-Ireland senior medals – three for Limerick (1921,1934, 1936), two for Dublin (1924 and 1927)**; *two All-Ireland finalist medals; Railway Cup with Munster, 1931, and Leinster, 1927; five Munster senior medals, 1921, 1933, 1934, 1935 and 1936; three Leinster senior medals with Dublin, 1924, 1927 and 1928; five National League medals – one with Dublin, 1929 and four with Limerick, 1933, 1934, 1935 and 1936. Senior club championship medal with Croom, 1921; five senior club championship medals with Garda, Dublin, 1925, 1926, 1927, 1928 and 1929; senior club championship medals with Toomevara, 1930 and 1931; Thomond Feis medal with Tipperary, 1931; senior club league medals with Garda, 1924 and 1925; member of the All-Ireland hurling team in the Tailteann Games, 1924 and 1928. Inter-county manager of Clare, 1954-55.*
Listed at half back in the Team of the Millenium. Ranked no. 104 on the *Irish Independent* 125 Greatest Stars of the GAA. Played shinty for Ireland vs Scotland, 1924 and 1928. Bank of Ireland All-Time All Star, 1982; president of Burgess GAA Club.

311

Howard, Sheena (camogie)

▸ *Native of Tipperary; played camogie for Tipperary.*
Career/honours: **All-Ireland senior medal, 2001**; *Purcell Cup medal with Garda College, 2005;* **selected on the All Star Purcell Cup team, 2005;** *Ashbourne Shield medal with Garda College, 2007. Granddaughter of Garrett Howard. Club: Burgess Duharra.*

Hoyne, Nicky

▸ *Played inter-county for Kilkenny and Louth.*

Hughes, Enda (football)

▸ *Native of Mayo; played senior football for Louth, 2003. Clubs: Dowdallshill and The Neale.*

Hughes, Greg (football)

▸ *Native of Offaly; played senior football for Offaly, 1958-71*
Career/honours: **one All-Ireland football medal, 1971**; *two All-Ireland finalist medals; played minor football and hurling for Offaly. Two senior club championship medals with Colmcille, Meath, 1966 and 1968; three Railway Cup medals with Leinster (selected eight times; captain of Leinster, 1962). Played for Ireland vs Combined Universities in 1960.*
Described as the "prince of full backs".

Hughes, Jason (football/hurling)

▸ *Native of Carlow; played senior football (1992-2001) and hurling (1994-96) for Carlow.*
Career/honours: **senior All-Ireland 'B' medal, 1994;** *club championship medals in senior hurling, 1996, intermediate hurling 1992, junior football, 2013, intermediate football, 1992 and 2003 and minor hurling, 1989 with Ballinabranna, Carlow.*

Hughes, Jim (football)

▸ *Native of Laois; played senior football for Laois, 1960-72.*
Career/honours: played minor football and hurling for Laois; six club championship medals with Portlaoise, 1964, 1967, 1968, 1970 and 1971 (captain in 1964 and 1966); minor club championship medals with Portlaoise in football (1954) and hurling (1955 and 1956); Leinster senior championship medal, 1971-72. Former inter-county manager with Clare.

Hughes, Joe (football)

▸ *Native of Offaly; played senior football for Offaly, 1992, 1996-97.*
O'Byrne Cup medal, 1977; Leinster senior medal, 1997; two county senior championship medals, 2000 and 2002 for Tullamore.

Hughes, Seamus (football)

▸ *Native of Mayo; played senior football for Mayo during the 1970s.*
Career/honours: **All-Ireland minor medal, 1966.**

Hughes, Willie (football)

▸ *Native of Dublin; played senior football for Dublin, 1982-83.*
Career/honours: **All-Ireland football medal, 1983**; *Leinster senior medal, 1983; Leinster U21 medal, 1980; four senior club football championship medals with Garda Club; three senior club championship hurling medals with Faugh's, 1986, 1987 and 1992; All-Ireland U21 (1980) finalist medal.*

Hurley, Vincent (football/hurling)

▸ *Native of Cork; played senior hurling and football for Cork, 2005-07.*
Career/honours: **three All-Ireland junior football medals; two All-Ireland intermediate medals;** *three Munster junior football medals; three Munster intermediate hurling medals; McGrath Cup medal, 2007.*

Hurney, Pat (hurling)

▸ *Native of Galway; senior hurler for Galway during the 1980s.*
Career/honours: minor (1977) and U21 (1980) hurling for Galway; senior championship medal with Turloughmore, 1985. The Pat Hurney Memorial Tournament: between Gardaí and Turloughmore.

Hynes, Tony (football)

▸ *Played senior football for Mayo.*

I

Irwin, Gabriel (football)

▸ *Native of Tipperary; played senior football for Tipperary, 1980, 1984 and 1985.*
Career/honours: played minor and U21 football with Tipperary; junior hurling with Dublin, 1989. Captained Garda to Dublin senior football league Division 1, 1991. Played with Cashel King Cormacs, Garda and Faugh's.

Irwin, Paddy (football)

▸ *Native of Mayo; played senior football for Mayo in the 1940s and 1950s.*
Career/honours: **one All-Ireland senior medal, 1951;** *National League medal, 1954. In 1991, Paddy organised 400 people to come from the USA for the Mayo vs Roscommon Connacht senior football final.*

Ivess, Pat (football)

▸ *Native of Limerick; played senior football for Limerick, 1979-93*
Career/honours: three McGrath Cup medals; Railway Cup with Munster, 1988-89; three county senior leagues with Askeaton; one All-Ireland Interfirms, three Munster Interfirms.

J

Jevans, Cormac (football)

▸ *Native of Wexford; played senior football for Wexford, 1986-92. Club: Glynn-Barntown.*

Johnson, Basil (hurling)

▸ *Native of Offaly; played senior hurling for Offaly, 1962-80.*
Career/honours: minor and U21 hurling, 1963; minor football, 1963; National League Division 2 medal, 1966 (captain); **ten senior club championship medals with St Rynagh's;** *two Leinster club championship medals in 1970, 1971, 1972, 1973 with St Rynagh's; two All-Ireland club finalist medals; one senior club championship medal with Tremane (Roscommon), 1980.*

Jones, Ciaran (football)

▸ *Native of Wicklow; played senior football for Wicklow, 2007-08.*
Career/honours: Captained the Kilbride junior team to championship success in 2007. Wicklow junior player of the year 2007. Tragically drowned on 24 October 2011 in the River Liffey, while attempting to rescue people.

Jones, Maurice (football)

▸ *Native of Kerry; played senior football for Limerick during the 1950s.*
Career/honours: Senior club championship medal with Garda, Limerick, 1958.

Jones, Padraic (football)

▸ *Native of Longford; played senior football for Longford, 2000-01.*
Career/honours: one O'Byrne Cup medal with Longford, 2000; three senior championship medals; one intermediate championship medals with Dromard; three senior league medals; two Leader Cup medals.

K

Kavanagh, James (football)

▸ *Native of Kildare; played senior football for Kildare (2005-12) and Galway (2013).*
Career/honours: Kildare intermediate county championship medal, 2010; Leinster intermediate championship medal, 2010. All Star nominee. Clubd: Ballymore Eustace, Kildare; Milltown, Galway.

Kavanagh, Julie (ladies' football)

▸ *Native of Dublin; played for Dublin, 1988-2002.*
Career/honours: **All Star award, 1991 (midfield); Junior All-Ireland medal, 1989 (player of the match in replay)**; *All-Ireland finalist medal, 1990; Junior National League medal, 1988, 1989; Senior National League Division 3 medal, 1997; O'Connor Cup medal with Garda College; Leinster junior medal, 1988-89; minor Leinster champions, 1990; Leinster senior medal, 2002; replacement All Star, 1990. Club: St. Monica's*

Kavanagh, Tom (hurling)

▶ *Native of Galway; played senior hurling for Galway, 1999.*
Career/honours: played minor hurling, 1991 and U21 hurling for Galway, 1994;
Railway Cup with Connacht, 1999.

Keane, Alan (football)

▶ *Native of Galway; played senior football for Galway, 2001-08.*
Career/honours: **one All-Ireland senior medal, 2001**; *three Connacht senior*
medals. Club: Killererin.

Keane, Gerry (hurling)

▶ *Native of Limerick; Minor hurling for Limerick in 1950 at 16 years old. Senior*
hurling for Dublin 1955- 1957; Senior hurling for Limerick in 1958
Career/honours: Senior championship club medal with Kilmacud Crokes in 1966
scoring the winning point in the final.

Keane, Gerry (hurling)

▶ *Played senior hurling for Roscommon, 1965-69.*

Keane, John (football)

▶ *Native of Tipperary; played senior football for Tipperary, 1974-80.*
Career/honours: captain of Tipperary in 1979; senior club championship medal
with Fethard, 1978;Tipperary Player of the Year, 1978. Also played with
Tullamore.

Keane, Julie May (camogie)

▶ *Career/honours: third level Irish colleges team, 2004.*

Keane, Martin Joe (football/hurling)

▶ *Native of Roscommon; played senior football and hurling from 1965-72 for*
Roscommon and Galway.
Career/honours: **U21 All-Ireland football medal with Roscommon, 1966;**
junior All-Ireland hurling medal with Roscommon, 1965; *Railway Cup*
with Connacht, 1969; seven Roscommon senior hurling medals; one Galway
senior football medal.

Keane, Mick (football/hurling)

▶ *Native of Kerry; played senior football and hurling, 1965-69; represented Kerry*
and Leitrim in both codes.
Career/honours: played minor and junior for Kerry; captained club Gortletteragh
to senior final, 1970; leading scorer for Leitrim in 1967. Played for Ballylongford,
Shannon Rangers, Mohill, Carrick-on-Shannon and Gortletteragh. Founder of
Bord na nÓg in Leitrim; inter-county referee.

Kearns, Karl (football)

▶ *Native of Sligo; played senior football for Sligo (1991-96).*
Career/honours: minor football 1988-90, U21 1991-93; two Trench Cup medals
with Garda College, 1993 and 1994; two county championships with St Pat's,
Sligo 1989 and 1990.

Kearns, James (football)

▸ *Native of Sligo; played senior football for Sligo (1974-87).*
Career/honours: one Connacht senior championship medal, 1975; four county senior championship medals; six league medals.

Kearns, Liam (football)

▸ *Native of Kerry; played senior football for Kerry, 1984-90.*
Career/honours: **All-Ireland minor football medal, 1980***; played U21 football for Kerry; senior club championship medal with Austin Stacks, 1986. Inter-county Manager of Limerick (1999-2005), Laois (2006-08) and Tipperary (2015 to present).*

Keating, Connie (hurling)

▸ *Native of Limerick; played senior hurling for Limerick, 1976, 1980 and 1982.*
Career/honours: played minor and U21 hurling; Colleges All-Ireland with Moylish, Limerick (LIT), 1978; Munster section, 1980-81. Club: Mungret.

Keating, Dick (football and hurling)

▸ *Native of Tipperary; played senior football for Tipperary (1956-66) and senior football and hurling for Roscommon.*
Career/honours: played minor football with Tipperary (was on the All-Ireland losing team for Tipperary vs Dublin, 1955); four Tipperary senior championship medals with Ardfinnan.

Keating, John (football/hurling)

▸ *Native of Tipperary; played senior hurling (1957-60) and football (1957-77) for Tipperary.*
Career/honours: four county championship medals; Railway Cup with Munster, 1960-65.
In 1960, John had the distinction of joining eleven Kerrymen and three Corkmen on the Munster team.

Keating, Michael (football)

▸ *Native of Wicklow; played senior football for Wicklow, Mayo and Dublin, 1933-35.*
Career/honours: All-Ireland finalist medal with Dublin, 1934 (captain); three Dublin senior championship and league medals with Garda, Dublin; **All-Ireland junior medal with Wicklow in 1936 (scored the winning goal in the final);** *Munster junior medal with Limerick, 1929; eight county senior championship medals in four different counties; three provincial medals; Railway Cup football with Munster and Connacht.*
Known as "the Crown Prince of Wicklow football", and was described in his time as "certainly the most honoured Wicklow man to hit the GAA scene". Described in a newspaper article as "the finest midfielder and centre forward of his day" and "the greatest player who never won a senior All-Ireland medal".

Keegan, Oliver (football)

▸ *Native of Westmeath; played senior football for Westmeath.*

Keegan, Pat (football)

▸ *Native of Offaly; played senior football for Offaly, 1990-91.*

Keevans, Michael (football)

▶ *Native of Wexford; played minor football for Wexford, 1984-85. Also played for Naas.*
Career/honours: minor in 1982, U21 in 1985 (for Wexford).
In 1982, Michael, then seventeen, and his father Seamus, then forty-nine (the next player profile) played together for club Gusserane O'Rahilly's in the county senior final.

Keevans, Seamus (football)

▶ *Native of Wexford; played senior football for Sligo, Wexford, Cavan, Waterford and Cork in a career running from 1953-69.*
Career/honours: played in all four provincial senior inter-county championships; Railway Cup (1963) with Leinster. Refereed seven senior football finals. Started camogie in Olyegate, Co. Wexford. played for eighteen different clubs.
Won seven senior championship medals – Taughmon (two), 1955 and 1957, and Gusserane (one), 1975 in Wexford, Kill (three), 1966, 1967 and 1968 in Waterford and Cavan Gaels (one), 1965 in Cavan.

Keher, Seamus (football/hurling)

▶ *Native of Roscommon; played senior football and hurling for Roscommon in the 1960s.*
Career/honours: six senior club championship medals with Roscommon Gaels; first cousin of Kilkenny great, Eddie Keher, whose father was a member of the force was a native of Roscommon and was transferred to Kilkenny. Seamus was the first games master and PE instructor in Templemore Training Centre when it opened in 1964.

Kehilly, Mick (football)

▶ *Native of Cork; played senior football for Cork.*

Kehir, Stephen (football)

▶ *Native of Kilkenny; played senior football for Kilkenny.*

Kehoe, Brendan (football)

▶ *Native of Kildare; played senior football for Kildare (1957-61)*
Career/honours: played minor football for Kildare, 1952.

Kelleher, David (football)

▶ *Native of Cork; played senior football for Waterford, 2001.*
Career/honours: minor Cork championship medal, 1992; junior Wexford football championship medal, 2012; intermediate Wexford championship medal, 2013 for St Fintan's.
Played League of Ireland soccer for Waterford United.

Kellett, P. (football)

▶ *Played senior football for Monaghan, 1928.*

Kelliher, Kieran (football)

▶ *Native of Clare; played senior football for Clare, 1982-92*
Career/honours: Munster championship medal, 1992; league medal with Garda, 1991. Club: Ennistymon.

317

Kelliher, M.

▸ *Native of Clare; played senior hurling for Donegal, 1923.*
Career/honours: Ulster championship medal, 1923

Kelly, Alan (hurling)

▸ *Native of Tipperary; played senior hurling for Wicklow, 2013.*
Career/honours: played intermediate hurling for Tipperary (last four Munster finals); junior football for Tipperary, 2002.

Kelly, Danny (football)

▸ *Native of Donegal; played senior inter-county for Donegal (1974-75) and Westmeath (1976-77)*
Career/honours: two senior championships with Athlone, 1977 and 1979.

Kelly, Glenn (football)

▸ *Native of Dublin; played senior football for Waterford, 2008-11.*
Career/honours: played junior football for Dublin, 2003.
"Glen is the only player named by Michael Ó Muircheartagh on the *Late Late Show* in 2009 when asked by Pat Kenny if he had ever seen a player who was good enough, but for some reason had never been chosen to play for his county" - referring to the first series of TG4's underdogs show.

Kelly, Hud (hurling)

▸ *Native of Waterford; played senior hurling for Waterford (1995-97) and Carlow (1997-2000).*
Career/honours: played minor, U21 and junior hurling for Waterford; three senior championship medals in Waterford and one intermediate medal in Carlow; Division 2 Colleges (Ryan Cup) medal with Garda College.

Kelly, Jimmy (hurling)

▸ *Native of Cavan; played senior hurling for Cavan.*
Career/honours: Division 4 National League medal; two Ulster junior hurling medals.

Kelly, Jimmy (football)

▸ *Played senior football for Kerry, 1940-50.*

Kelly, Joachim (hurling)

▸ *Native of Offaly; played senior hurling for Offaly, 1974-93.*
▸ *Career/honours:* **two All-Ireland senior medals, 1981 and 1985; two All Star awards, 1980 and 1984 (both at midfield);** *minor and U21 hurling for Offaly; one All-Ireland senior finalist medal, 1984; one National League medal, 1990; seven Leinster senior medals, 1980, 1981, 1984, 1985, 1988, 1989 and 1990; Railway Cup medal, 1979. One senior county championship medal with Lusmagh, 1989. Former inter-county manager with Westmeath, Wexford and Roscommon; managed several clubs.*

Kelly, Joe (hurling)

▸ *Native of New York; played senior hurling for Galway in the 1920s.*

318

Kelly, Joe (hurling)

▸ *Played senior hurling for Dublin in 1931.*

Kelly, John (hurling)

▸ *Played senior hurling for Sligo.*

Kelly, Kenneth (hurling)

▸ *Native of Kildare; played senior hurling for Kildare.*

Kelly, Liam (football)

▸ *Native of Donegal; played senior football for Donegal, 1968.*
Career/honours: two Donegal senior championship and league medals.

Kelly, Luke (football/hurling)

▸ *Native of Carlow; played senior football and hurling for Carlow, 1980–89.*
Career/honours: Carlow intermediate, junior and minor club medals (one each).

Kelly, Martin (football)

▸ *Native of Galway; played senior football for Galway during the 1930s*
Career/honours: **two senior All-Ireland medals, 1934, 1938.**

Kelly, Michael (football)

▸ *Played senior football for Leitrim.*

Kelly, Michelle (ladies' football)

▸ *Native of Leitrim; played senior ladies' football for Leitrim.*

Kelly, Paddy (football/hurling)

▸ *Native of Meath; played senior hurling (1980-99) and football (1986) for Meath.*
Career/honours: two Meath senior hurling championship medals with Kiltale in 1982 and 1983 (as captain); **one All-Ireland 'B' hurling championship medal, 1993; one All-Ireland junior hurling championship medal, 1999;** *Railway Cup medal with Leinster, 1993; three Division 3 National hurling league medals; member of Leinster Railway Cup panel from 1989 until 1993. Football: one intermediate championship medal with Moynalvey, 1983; one junior championship medal with Moynalvey, 1981; one Leinster minor medal, 1980.*

Kelly, Pat (football)

▸ *Native of Mayo; played senior football for Mayo, 2003-06, 2008.*
Career/honours: **All-Ireland Club championship medal with St Vincent's (Dublin), 2006;** *Leinster club championship medal.*

Kelly, Patsy (football)

▸ *Native of Mayo; played senior football for Mayo, 1971.*
Career/honours: played minor and U21 football for Mayo.

Kelly, Peter (football)

▸ *Native of Wicklow; played senior football for Monaghan in the 1970s and 1980s.*
Career/honours: Monaghan intermediate championship medal, 1976.

Kelly, Phil (football)

▶ *Native of Donegal; played senior football for Cavan (1973-75) and Donegal (1975-77)*
Career/honours: Dr McKenna Cup medal; played minor and U21 football.

Kelly, Seamus (football)

▶ *Native of Cavan; played senior football for Wicklow, 1971.*
Career/honours: played minor football for Cavan, 1961; played U21 football for Cavan, 1964. Club: Baltinglass.

Kelly, Shane (football)

▶ *Native of Limerick; played senior football for Limerick, 2000-02.*
▶ *Native of Career/honours: McGrath Cup medal, 2001; senior club championship medal, 2015 with NE; county junior 'A' hurling championship medal, 2001; west senior football championship medals, 1998/2014; county intermediate championship medal, 2006; Ryan Cup medal with Athlone RTC, 1996.*

Kelly, Stephen (football)

▶ *Native of Limerick; played senior football for Limerick, 2002-10 and 2015.*
Career/honours: McGrath Cup medal, 2003; senior hurling (2001), intermediate hurling (2006, 2015) and west football championship medals (2015). 2003: **International Rules team.**
Played rugby with Munster 'A' and the Irish Wolfhounds and won an AIL with Shannon.

Kelly, Terry (hurling)

▶ *Native of Cork; played senior hurling for Cork (1951-65).*
Career/honours: **All-Ireland senior medal, 1954; minor All-Ireland medal, 1951;** *All-Ireland finalist medal, 1956; two Munster senior medals; Railway Cup with Munster; played junior hurling for Dublin. Clubs: Tracton (Cork), Éire Óg (Dublin). Played exhibition matches with Cork in New York and Boston, 1957.*

Kelly, Tommy (hurling)

▶ *Native of Galway; played senior hurling for Galway (1953-59) and Laois (1950-52).*
Career/honours: three All-Ireland finalist senior medals, 1953, 1955 and 1958; Railway Cup for Connacht, 1953 to 1959; junior (1950) and intermediate (1951) football championship medals with St Fintan's, Laois. Intermediate championship medal with Eyrecourt 1959.

Kenneally, Rose (camogie)

▶ *Native of Tipperary; played senior camogie for Tipperary, 2006-12.*
Career/honours: All-Ireland senior finalist medal, 2006; Munster senior medal. Club: Drom and Inch.

Kennedy, Damien (hurling)

▶ *Native of Clare; played senior hurling for Clare, 2002-03.*
Career/honours: one senior club championship medal with St Joseph's Doora Barefield, 2001; two senior club league medals, 2003, 2007; two Dr Harty Cup medals; one All-Ireland Colleges medal with St Flannan's, 1999/2000.

Kennedy, David (football/hurling)

▶ *Native of Tipperary; played hurling (1999-2005) and football (1998); represented Tipperary and Kildare.*
Career/honours: **Senior All-Ireland medal, 2001 with Tipperary; U21 All-Ireland medal, 1997;** *minor Munster hurling medal, 1995; National League, 2000-01; Christy Ring finalist medal, 2007; two National League medals with Kildare, Division 3, in 2009-2011; two senior hurling medals with Loughmore/Castleiney in 2007 and 2013; two senior football medals from 2005 and 2013.*

Kennedy, Frank (football)

▶ *Native of Clare; played senior football for Clare, 1952-67.*
Career/honours: Munster team, 1960-61; senior club championship medal with East Kerry and Portmagee Kerry, and also played with Coolmeen.

Kennedy, John (football/hurling)

▶ *Native of Cork; played senior hurling (1960, 1962 and 1965) and senior football (1959-66) for Wexford.*
Career/honours: **All-Ireland senior hurling medal, 1960;** *Leinster junior hurling medal with Wexford, 1959; three senior county championship hurling (1960, 1962 and 1965) and two football (1959 and 1960) medals with Faythe Harriers, Wexford. Also played for Sarsfields.*

Kennedy, John

▶ *Native of Wexford; played inter-county for Wicklow.*

Kennedy, Kevin (hurling)

▶ *Native of Clare; played senior hurling for Clare, 1977 and 1982.*
Career/honours: **manager of All-Ireland Clare intermediate winning team, 2011.**

Kennedy, Michael (hurling)

▶ *Native of Kerry; played senior hurling for Kerry in 1964. Club: Austin Stacks.*

Kennedy, Paddy (football)

▶ *Native of Kerry; played senior football for Kerry, 1936–47.*
Career/honours: **five All-Ireland senior football championship medals, 1937, 1939, 1940, 1941, 1946; All-Ireland senior football championship winning captain, 1946; one All-Ireland minor football championship medal, 1933;** *senior All-Ireland finalist medal, 1938; ten Munster senior football championship medals, 1936, 1937, 1938, 1939, 1940, 1941, 1942, 1944, 1946, 1947; one Munster minor football championship, 1933; two Railway Cup medals with Munster, 1941, 1946; won a Kerry county championship with Kerins O'Rahillys, 1939; four Dublin county championships, three with Geraldines and one with Garda Club. He joined in the late 1930s.*
Ranked at no. 46 in the *Irish Independent* 125 Greatest Stars of the GAA. Paddy Kennedy Memorial Park: Annascaul GAA Club's home ground, opened in 1984, is named Paddy Kennedy Memorial Park after him. Paddy is regarded by many as one of the all-time greats of Kerry football.

Kennedy, P. J. (football)

▶ *Native of Clare; played senior football for Clare, 1959-74. 1959-1974 Football*
Career/honours: Clare Footballer of the Year, 1970; winner of Cic Fada in 1969; played for Munster 1962-63; five senior championship county medals with Kilrush Shamrocks, 1975-79.

Kennelly, Ned (football)

▸ *Played senior football for Dublin and Kerry during the 1950s.*
Career/honours: **All-Ireland junior medal with Dublin, 1948.**

Kenny, Enda (football)

▸ *Native of Roscommon; played senior football for Roscommon, 2006–07.*
Club: St Faithleach's. Played soccer for Longford Town.

Kenny, Kieran (football)

▸ *Native of Sligo; played senior football for Sligo during the 1920s.*
Career/honours: Connacht championship medal, 1928; also played junior football
for Sligo. Club: Garda, Dublin.

Kenny, Pádraig (hurling)

▸ *Native of Roscommon; played senior hurling for Roscommon (1996–2003).*
Career/honours: **All-Ireland intermediate medal, 1999,** *2 senior club*
championship hurling medals with Oran 1992 and 1998 and 1 intermediate
football medal in 1997, 2 senior club championship medals with Sarsfields, 1998
and 2001.

Kenny, Tom (hurling)

▸ *Native of Kerry; played senior hurling for Kerry, 1964–70. Club: Crotta.*
Career/honours: **All-Ireland junior medal, 1972;** *National League Division 2*
medal. Won one senior championship medal with Crotta.

Kenoy, Tommy (football)

▸ *Native of Roscommon; played senior football for Roscommon, 1971–72 and*
1975–76.
Career/honours: played minor football for Roscommon, 1970; played U21 football
for Roscommon 1971–73; senior championship medal, 1983; played intermediate
(1981) and junior (1975) football for Roscommon.

Keogh, Brendan

▸ *Native of Kildare; played inter-county for Kildare.*

Keogh, Senan

▸ *Played inter-county for Louth.*

Keogh, Tom (football)

▸ *Native of Kildare; played football for Kildare and Laois in the 1920s.*
Career/honours: **two All-Ireland senior medals with Kildare, 1927 and**
1928; *All-Ireland finalist medal, 1935. Club: Portlaoise.*

Kerin, John (football)

▸ *Native of Clare; played senior football for Clare. Club: Michael Cusacks.*

Kerins, John (football)

▶ *Native of Cork; played senior football for Cork, 1983-96.*
Career/honours: **two All-Ireland senior medals, 1989-90; one All-Ireland U21 medal;** *three All-Ireland senior finalists medals, 1987, 1988 and 1993;* **two All Star awards, 1987 and 1990 (goalkeeper);** *six Munster medals, 1987, 1988, 1989, 1990, 1993 and 1994; one county senior championship medal, 1985 with St Finbarr's.*

Keyes, Tony

▶ *Played inter-county for Cavan.*

Kiernan, Dessie (hurling)

▶ *Native of Westmeath; played senior hurling for Westmeath, 1963-65.*
Career/honours: played minor hurling for Westmeath (captain); two senior club championship medals with Rickardstown, 1959 and 1963.

Kiernan, John (hurling)

▶ *Native of Westmeath; played senior hurling for Westmeath, 1963-65.*
Career/honours: two senior club championship medals with Rickardstown, 1959 and 1963. Also excelled in athletics, hockey and badminton. Brother of Dessie.

Kiernan, Mel (football)

▶ *Native of Leitrim; played senior football for Leitrim in the 1970s and 1980s.*
Career/honours: **scored three goals vs Kerry in the 1977 All-Ireland U21 semi-final, and had a goal disallowed.**

Kiernan, Philip (football)

▶ *Native of Longford; played senior football for Longford, 1977-88.*
Career/honours: Division 2 and 3 national football league medals; two senior club championship medals with Ardagh, 1978 and 1987; club championship medals with Longford and Kilbeggan Shamrocks. Played hurling for Castletown-Geoghegan in Westmeath. Served as a selector in the Westmeath senior football setup in recent years.

Kilbane, P. J. (football)

▶ *Played senior football for Mayo.*

Kilcoyne, Jim (hurling)

▶ *Native of Westmeath; played senior hurling for Westmeath during the 1980s.*
Career/honours: Division 2 National League medal, 1986; senior club championship medals with Ringtown, 1980 and 1987. Brother of Westmeath's only hurling All Star, David Kilcoyne.

Kilcoyne, Ursula (ladies' football)

▶ *Native of Roscommon; played football for Roscommon.*

Kilkelly, Brian (football)

▶ *Native of Mayo; played senior football for Mayo, 1983, 1989 and 1992.*
Career/honours: **All-Ireland U21 medal, 1983;** *played minor and U21 football; captain of Mayo U21 team in 1985; three Connacht U21 championship medals, 1983, 1984 and 1985; two Connacht senior championship medals, 1989 and 1992; county championship medals at minor and U21 level; county senior championship medals, 1986, 1988 and 1993 with Castlebar Mitchels; All-Ireland Vocational Schools medal.*

Killeen, Timmy (football)

▶ *Native of Clare; played senior football for Clare, 1981-86.*
Career/honours: McGrath Cup medal, 1984; four county senior club championship medals with Doonbeg, 1982, 1983, 1988 and 1991.

Killion, Tom (hurling)

▶ *Native of Roscommon; played senior hurling for Roscommon, 1983-96.*
Career/honours: played minor and U21 football, 1982; **All-Ireland senior 'B' hurling medal, 1995;** *Roscommon senior club championship medals, 1994-99.*

Killoran, Jimmy (football)

▶ *Native of Sligo; played senior football for Sligo in the 1960s.*
Career/honours: All-Ireland senior finalist medal, 1965.

Kilroy, Jack (hurling)

▶ *Native of Roscommon; played senior hurling for Roscommon, 1974-86.*
Career/honours: **All-Ireland junior hurling medal, 1974;** *National League Division 3 medal, 1983/84; six county senior club championship and seven county club league medals with Tremane; Connacht senior club championship medal, 1977 (captain) with Tremane.* **Manager of the Roscommon junior All-Ireland winning team, 2001.**

Kilroy, Matt (hurling)

▶ *Native of Roscommon; played senior hurling with Roscommon, 1973.*
Career/honours: Connacht senior club medal with Tremane, 1976.

Kilroy, Paddy (football/hurling)

▶ *Native of Galway; played senior football and hurling, 1923-30; represented Galway, Monaghan and Wexford.*
Career/honours: two Ulster medals, 1929 and 1930 (Monaghan); one Connacht medal, 1923 (Galway); All-Ireland finalist medal, 1930 (Monaghan); played senior football for Wexford; Leinster medal, 1925 (Wexford). Served as chairman of North Mayo county board.

King, Pat (football)

▶ *Native of Carlow; played senior football for Carlow during the 1960s.*

Kinneavy, Stephen (football)

▶ *Native of Galway; played senior football for Galway, 1974-76.*
Career/honours: **All Star award, 1983 (full back);** *All-Ireland senior finalist medal, 1983; interprovincial for Connacht; two Division 2 National League medals; one National League medal, 1982; four Connacht championship medals.*

Kinsella, Joe (hurling)

▶ *Native of Kildare; played senior hurling for Kildare during the 1980s. Career/honours: All-Ireland 'B' final in 1988; club championship with Leixlip, 1986.*

Kinsella, John (hurling)

▶ *Native of Kilkenny; played senior hurling for Wicklow. Career/honours: Leinster JHC medal, 1965.*

Kirby, Ned (football)

▶ *Native of Cork; played senior football for Cork, 1969-75.* Career/honours: **All-Ireland senior medal, 1973; All-Ireland U21 medal, 1970; All-Ireland minor medal, 1967;** *Munster minor football and hurling medals, 1967; Munster senior medals, 1971, 1973 and 1974; Munster junior medal, 1970.*

Kirby, Tom (hurling)

▶ *Native of Kerry; hurled at senior level for Kerry, 1961-72. Career/honours:* **junior All-Ireland medal, 1961**; *three National League Division 3 medals; three county senior championship medals with Ballyduff (Kerry), 1959, 1960 and 1961; two county senior championship medals with St Finbarr's (Cork), 1965 and 1968. Kerry Hurling Sports Star award, 1972.* Described as "one of the finest hurlers to ever come out of Kerry".

Kirwan, Darren

▶ *Native of Louth; played senior football for Louth, 1999-2001. Career/honours: Division 2 National League medal; two senior club championship medals with St Patrick's, 2003 and 2004 (captain); two senior club league medals with St Patrick's, 1999 and 2003, one ACC medal, 2001.*

Kirwan, John (hurling)

▶ *Native of Galway; played senior hurling for Galway (1924) and Dublin (1927). Career/honours: senior championship medal, 1927; senior league medal, 1926 with Garda, Dublin.*

Kirwan, James (football)

▶ *Native of Wexford; played senior football for Wexford (1926) and Dublin (1929). Career/honours: played for Garda vs Army in President's Cup, 1926-27.*

Kirwan, Paddy (football)

▶ *Native of Cavan; played senior football for Dublin, Cavan and Wexford.* Career/honours: **three All-Ireland senior medals, 1921, 1922 and 1923 for Dublin.** *One of the founders of the St Vincent's club. Played for Garda, Dublin.*

L

Lacey, Andrew (football)

▶ *Native of Tipperary; played senior football for Tipperary, 1999-2000. Career/honours: minor captain, 1997 and played U21 football for Tipperary; county minor and intermediate championship medals with Arradale Rovers; five West Tipperary senior medals.*

Lacey, Mairead (ladies' football)

▶ *Played senior ladies' football for Laois.*

Lafferty, Joe (hurling)

▶ *Played senior hurling for Cavan, 2007-11.*

Laffey, Peter (football)

▶ *Native of Mayo; played senior football for Mayo, 1936-39. Career/honours:* **one All-Ireland senior medal, 1936;** *six National League medals, 1934-39; Railway Cup football with Connacht, 1937, 1938.*

Laing, Hugh (football)

Roscommon; played senior football for Roscommon during the 1960s.

Lally, Mick (football)

▶ *Native of Louth; played senior football for Louth, 1967-68. Career/honours: played minor and U21 football for Louth, and minor hurling; two county senior championship medals with Wolfe Tones, 1964-65.*

Lamb, Harry (football)

▶ *Played senior football for Dublin, 1967-68. Club: Parnells. Career/honours: Accomplished soccer and tennis player. Inter-county referee.*

Lambe, James 'Chops' (football)

▶ *Native of Kildare; played senior football for Kildare, 2011-12. Career/honours: played junior football for Kildare; Leinster junior medal, 2012; All-Ireland junior finalist medal, 2012; U21 club championship medal.*

Lambe, Mick (football)

▶ *Native of Laois; played senior football for Laois. Club: The Heath.*

Lambe, P. (football)

▶ *Played senior football for Dublin, 1933.*

Lambe, Pat (football)

▶ *Native of Monaghan; played senior football for Louth, 1965. Career/honours: played junior football with Monaghan, 1970.*

Lambe, Peter (football)

▶ *Native of Monaghan; played senior football for Monaghan, and featured for the Farney County in their 1930 All-Ireland SFC final defeat against Kerry.*

Lane, Noel (hurling)

▶ *Native of Tipperary; played senior hurling for Tipperary, 1969-72.*
Career/honours: **All-Ireland senior medal, 1971; All-Ireland U21 medal, 1964;** *Munster minor medal, 1961; played Railway Cup hurling with Munster.*

Lang, Tom (football)

▶ *Native of Meath; played senior football for Sligo, Roscommon and Meath.*
Career/honours: senior football for Sligo 1956-67; played minor and junior football for Sligo; played senior football for Roscommon, and junior football for Roscommon and Meath. Clubs: Craobh Rua (Sligo), St Ronan's (Ballyfarnon/Keadue), Roscommon. Founder member of Naomh Mhuire, now St Mary's, Sligo.

Langan, Tom (football)

▶ *Native of Mayo; played senior football for Mayo, 1943-56.*
Career/honours: **two All-Ireland senior medals, 1950 and 1951;** *five Connacht championship medals; two National League medals; Railway Cup football for Connacht. Played for Garda Club, Dublin. Senior club championship medals with Ballycastle, Mayo, Sean McDermotts, Dublin and Garda, Dublin, 1948. Dublin junior handball champion; Leinster junior basketball medal.*
Named on the GAA Football Team of the Century (full forward) and Football Team of the Millennium. GAA Hall of Fame award recipient. Ranked at no. 16 in the *Irish Independent 125 Greatest Stars of the GAA*. Played for Ireland in 1951, 1952, 1953 and 1954. Tom Langan Park, Ballycastle is named after him.

Larkin, Frank (hurling)

▶ *Native of Galway; played senior hurling for Galway, 1976-79 and 1982.*
Career/honours: All-Ireland minor finalist medal, 1973; played U21 hurling for Galway; Oireachtas medal, 1976; three senior club championships, two U21 medals, two minor medals; Connacht junior football medal, 1983.

Larkin, Kenny (football)

▶ *Native of Westmeath; played senior football for Westmeath, 2003-04.*
Career/honours: played minor and U21 football for Westmeath. Leinster minor medal, 2000; National League Division 2 medal, 2003. Club: Castledaly Received a broken jaw in a challenge match versus Down in 2003, with Down's James McCartan prosecuted in an ensuing court case.

Lawlor, Jason (football/hurling)

▶ *Native of Wexford; played senior football for Wexford, 1995-2005, and senior hurling for Wexford, 2000.*
Career/honours: O'Byrne Cup medal, 1995; played minor football and U21 football and hurling for Wexford; Leinster minor finalist medal, 1994; two Leinster U21 medals, 1996, 1997. Club: Adamstown.

Leahy, Michael (hurling)

▶ *Native of Kilkenny; played senior hurling for Kildare in the 1960s.*
Career/honours: **All-Ireland junior medal, 1962.**

Leamy, John (hurling)

▸ *Native of Tipperary; played senior hurling for Tipperary, 1988-90.*
Career/honours: **All-Ireland senior medal, 1989; All-Ireland minor medal, 1982; U21 All-Ireland medal, 1985; All-Ireland junior medal, 1991;** *played minor, U21 and junior hurling for Tipperary; one intermediate club football championship medal for Golden/Kilfeacle, 1982*

Ledwith, Enda (football)

▸ *Native of Longford; played senior football for Longford, 1995-2007.*
Career/honours: two senior club championship medals for Abbeylara, 2000 and 2006; one intermediate championship medal, 1994.

Lee, Peter (football)

▸ *Native of Galway; played senior football for Galway, 1977-86.*
Career/honours: two National League medals, 1981 and 1983; four Connacht medals in 1982, 1983, 1984 and 1986. Nominated for All Stars, 1981 and 1983. County intermediate championship with Caherlistrane, 1977. Manager of Killanin senior team from 1994 to 2001.

Leeson, Joe (hurling)

▸ *played senior hurling for Dublin, 1931.*

Lenihan, Dan (hurling)

▸ *Native of Limerick; played senior hurling for Donegal, 1923.*
Career/honours: Ulster senior championship medal, 1923; senior club championship medal with Aodh Rua, 1924 (captain).

Lennon, Darren (football)

▸ *Native of Roscommon; played senior football for Roscommon, 2004-08.*
Career/honours: played minor and U21 football for Roscommon; senior successes – junior 'B', 'A', senior league (twice)

Leonard, Eric (football)

▸ *Native of Roscommon; played senior football for Roscommon, 1958-59.*
Career/honours: Connacht junior medal in 1959. Played with Rahara, Roscommon.

Leonard, Eugene (football)

▸ *Native of Limerick; played senior football for Limerick, 1978-93.*
Career/honours: played minor and U21 football and hurling, 1977 and 1980; three McGrath Cup medals; three county club championship medals with Castleisland (Kerry); one Limerick county club championship medal.

Leonard, Ronan (football)

▸ *Native of Galway; played senior football for Galway, 2002.*
Career/honours: Connacht senior medal, 2002; played minor football and hurling, 1997-98; U21 Connacht medal, 2000; senior club championship medal, 2001.

Lillis, Mick (football)

▶ *Native of Limerick; played senior football for Laois and Clare.*
Career/honours: **one All-Ireland club championship medal with Portlaoise, 1983;** *played minor and U21 football for Clare; five senior Laois championship medals, 1981, 1982, 1984, 1990 and 1991; one senior Clare championship medal, 1996. Inter-county manager of Laois.*

Linehan, Timmy (hurling)

▶ *Played senior hurling for Limerick and Wexford. Club: Dromcollogher.*

Loftus, Ronan (football)

▶ *Native of Mayo; played senior football for Mayo, 2001.*
Career/honours: one National Football League title, 2001; one Connacht U21 football championship, 2001 (losing All-Ireland finalist); one Hastings Cup U21, 2001; one Mayo senior league Division 2 medal; two Dublin club U21 'A' county football championships (UCD), 2000-01; one Mayo U21 'B' county title (Burrishoole).

Logue, Jennifer (camogie)

▶ *Played senior camogie for Tipperary, 2017.*
Career/honours: captained Tipperary U16s to Munster and All-Ireland titles, and made the minor Munster final with Tipperary minors; Ashbourne Cup medal, 2015; played senior camogie with Garda College, 2017-18.

Lohan, Gus (hurling)

▶ *Native of Galway; played senior hurling for Galway (1962-67) and Clare (1968-77)*
Career/honours: National League medal, Clare, 1977; senior hurling and football for Monaghan, 1962; **eleven senior hurling championship medals and two Munster club medals (1968 and 1969) with Newmarket-on-Fergus, Clare.** *Father of Brian and Frank Lohan of Clare hurling fame.*

Lohan, Helena (ladies' football)

▶ *Native of Mayo; played senior ladies's football for Mayo.*
Career/honours: **four senior All-Ireland medals, 1999, 2000, 2002, 2003 (captain); four All Star awards, 2000, 2002, 2003, 2004;** *three Division 1 National League medals, 2000, 2004; county intermediate medals, 2000 and 2008, and Connacht medal, 2008, with The Neale.*

Long, Eamonn (hurling)

▶ *Native of Clare; played senior hurling for Clare, 1959-64.*
Career/honours: three senior club championship and six league medals with Faugh's (Dublin).

Long, Kevin (hurling)

▶ *Native of Cork; played senior hurling for Cork, 1996. Also played minor hurling for the Rebels.*

Long, Martin

▶ *layed inter-county for Carlow and Wexford.*

Long, Peter (football)

▸ *Native of Louth; played senior football for Louth, 1976.*
Career/honours: three senior football championship medals with St Joseph's; one Ulster club championship medal.

Loughman, Elizabeth (ladies' football)

▸ *Native of Laois played football for Laois.*

Loughnane, Colman (hurling)

▸ *Native of Offaly; played senior hurling for Offaly, 1975-76.*
Career/honours: two senior club championship medals with Coolderry, 1977, 1980.

Loughnane, Donal (hurling)

▸ *Native of Offaly; played senior hurling for Waterford, 1990.*
Career/honours: played minor and U21 hurling for Offaly; junior hurling for Waterford; two senior championship medals with Coolderry, 1977 and 1980; three senior championship medals with Mount Sion, 1986, 1988 and 1994.

Lowney, Joe (football)

▸ *Native of Cork; played senior football for Galway during the 1950s.*
Career/honours: **All-Ireland senior medal, 1956.**

Lowry, Mick (football/hurling)

▸ *Native of Westmeath; played senior football and hurling for Westmeath, 1978-91.*
Career/honours: O'Byrne Cup medal, 1988; Divisions 3 and 4 National League medals; county club football championship medal with St Malachy's, 1981; four senior club hurling championship medals with Castletown-Geoghegan, 1972, 1982, 1986 and 1990; intermediate football medal with Tullamore, 1999. Inter-county manager of Offaly U21 footballers.

Lynagh, Jim (hurling)

▸ *Native of Westmeath; played senior hurling for Westmeath (1959-60), Leitrim (1962) and Kildare (1964).*
Career/honours: played minor, junior and senior hurling for Westmeath in the one year; junior hurling and football club championship medals in 1959; Leinster Colleges medal with Tullamore, 1959. Club: Castletown-Geoghegan (Westmeath).

Lynagh, Mick (football)

▸ *Native of Tipperary; played senior football for Tipperary, 2005-09.*

Lynam, John (football)

▸ *Native of Kildare; played inter-county for Kildare, 1927.*

Lynch, Barry (football)

▸ *Native of Meath; played senior football for Meath, 2006-07.*
Career/honours: O'Byrne cup medal, 2006; National League Division 2 medal, 2007; played U21 football for Meath, 2000-01; junior football for Meath, 2000-05; **All-Ireland junior football medal, 2003.**

Lynch, Brendan (football)

▸ *Native of Roscommon; played senior football for Roscommon, 1937-52.*
Career/honours: **All-Ireland senior medals, 1943 and 1944; All-Ireland minor medal, 1941;** *All-Ireland senior finalist medal, 1946; club championship medal with Garda, Dublin, 1948; Railway Cup for Connacht, 1944-52. Garda Hall of Fame award, 2004. Club: Garda, Dublin (captain). Played for Ireland vs Combined Universities in 1954.*
Quote from the man himself: "Sport is like life itself. If you have no ambition then you may as well not partake." Named in John Scally's book as one of "the GAA greats of Connacht". Named at wing half back in the Sunday Independent's 2017 'Football's Toughest Team' selection.

Lynch, John Joe (football)

▸ *Native of Cavan; played senior football for Cavan, 1962-72.*
Career/honours: three Ulster senior championship medals, 1964, 1967 and 1969; played junior football for Cavan; All-Ireland junior runner-up medal, 1962; played for the All-Ireland Garda team; seven senior club championship and league medals with Crosserlough.
Played for Cavan in Wembley against Sligo in 1966 and Galway in 1967.

Lynch, Louise (ladies' football)

▸ *Played senior ladies' football for Dublin.*

Lynch, Peadar (football)

▸ *Native of Clare; played senior football for Clare, 1955-62.*
Career/honours: two senior club championship medals; Railway Cup with Munster.

Lynch, Tom (football)

▸ *Native of Cavan; played senior football for Cavan, 1959-72.*
Career/honours: four Ulster senior medals, 1962, 1964, 1967 and 1969; one Railway Cup medal, 1966; one Ulster junior medal; two county championship medals with Mountnugent.

Lyng, Jim (hurling)

▸ *Native of Kilkenny; played senior hurling for Dublin, 1986-91.*
Career/honours: two Dublin senior club championship medals and four senior league medals with Faugh's. Replacement All Star, 1989.

Lyons, Aidan (football)

▸ *Native of Westmeath; played senior football for Westmeath, 1996, 1998, 1999, 2000 and 2001 Club: Mullingar Shamrocks.*

Lyons, John (football)

▸ *Native of Sligo; played senior football for Sligo, 1964-66.*

Lyons, John (football)

▸ *Native of Mayo; played senior football for Wicklow and Mayo, 1976-84.*
Career/honours: played minor football with Mayo, 1973; Connacht minor medal, 1973; Division 4 National League medal, 1980-81; Division 3 National League medal, 1981-82. **Player of the Year in Wicklow, 1978.**

Lyons, Patrick

▸ *played inter-county for Cavan during the 1950s.*

M

Mac Carthaigh, Aodhán (football)

▸ *Native of Clare; played senior football for Clare. Club: Éire Óg.*

Madden, Brendan (football)

▸ *Native of Westmeath; played senior football for Westmeath, 1982. Career/honours: played minor and U21 football for Westmeath; intermediate medal with St Paul's, Dunboyne. Also played with Moate All Whites.*

Magan, George (football)

▸ *Native of Kildare; played senior football for Kildare, 1918-25. Career/honours:* **one All-Ireland senior medal, 1919.** *Club: Celbridge. Was also a noted athlete, and a member of the Irish cross country international team in 1924.*

Magee, John (football)

▸ *Played senior football for Longford.*

Magennis, Aidan (football)

▸ *Native of Louth; played senior football for Louth, 1957. Career/honours:* **All-Ireland senior medal, 1957.** *Club: Garda, Dublin. Minor championship medal in Louth, 1954; three Louth senior championship medals, 1955, 1956 and 1960.*

Maguire, Brendan (football)

▸ *Played senior football for Meath in the 1950s. Career/honours: All-Ireland finalist medal, 1952.*

Maguire, Cyril (football)

▸ *Native of Dublin; played senior football for Westmeath and Monaghan, 1954-60. Career/honours: won a junior football title with Meath in 1961 and a Garda junior handball title in 1963 with the late John Fleming, who later became an Assistant Commissioner. In 1982, with his son Jim – also a member – he won the All-Ireland Garda junior doubles title in handball. He was in his fiftieth year. Won All-Ireland intermediate and senior pole vault titles.*

Maguire, Des (football)

▸ *played senior football for Cavan during the 1950s. Career/honours:* **All-Ireland senior medal, 1952.**

Maguire, Fergal (football)

▸ *Native of Clare; played senior football for Clare during the 1990s. Club: Shamrocks.*

Maguire, Liam (football)

▸ *Native of Cavan; played senior football for Cavan during the 1950s.*
Career/honours: **All-Ireland senior medal, 1952;** *senior club championship medal with Ballybay, 1957.* **Inter-county referee; refereed the All-Ireland final in 1961 before a 91,000-strong crowd.** *Inter-county manager: Monaghan.*
Liam had a brother Des also playing for Cavan in the final, and another brother Brendan playing for Meath in 1952 – a unique happening in Gaelic games.

Maguire, Tom (football)

▸ *Native of Cavan; played senior football for Cavan, 1953-66.*
Career/honours: All-Ireland minor finalist medal, 1952 (captain); All-Ireland senior finalist medal, 1955; played minor football for Cavan; four Ulster senior championship medals, 1954, 1955, 1962 and 1964; three Dr McKenna Cup medals, 1955, 1956 and 1962; National League runners-up medal, 1960 (captain); five Railway Cup medals, 1956, 1960, 1963, 1964 and 1965.
Played for Garda Club, Dublin. Represented Ireland in the Cardinal Cushing Games in the USA (the forerunner of today's All Stars).

Maher, Brendan (hurling)

▸ *Native of Offaly; played senior hurling for Offaly, 1965-67. Club: Killavilla.*

Maher, Greg (football)

▸ *Native of Mayo; played senior football for Mayo.*
Career/honours: **All-Ireland minor medal, 1985;** *All-Ireland senior finalist medal, 1989. Club: Claremorris.*

Maher, Liam (hurling)

▸ *Native of Tipperary; played senior hurling for Tipperary, 1983-86.*
Career/honours: senior club championship medal in Tipperary, 1996. Club: Boherlahan-Dualla.

Maher, Pádraic (hurling)

▸ *Native of Tipperary; played senior hurling for Tipperary, 2009 to present.*
Career/honours: minor hurling for Tipperary, 2006, 2007; U21 hurling for Tipp, 2008-11; **All-Ireland senior hurling medals, 2010, 2016;** *five Munster SHC medals, 2009, 2011, 2012, 2015, 2016;* **All-Ireland U21 hurling medal, 2010;** *Munster U21 hurling medals, 2008, 2010 (captain);* **All-Ireland minor hurling medals, 2006, 2007;** *Munster MHC medal, 2007; Waterford Crystal Cup, 2012, 2014. Club (Thurles Sarsfields) – seven Tipperary SHC medals, 2009, 2010, 2012, 2014, 2015, 2016, 2017; Munster Club SHC medal, 2012. Interprovincial medal for Munster, 2016. Won a Ryan Cup medal with Garda College in 2017.* **Has won five All Stars (2009, 2011, 2014, 2016 and 2017).** *Captain of Tipperary senior hurlers, 2017-18.*

Maher, Tom

▸ *Native of Galway; played inter-county for Galway during the 1950s.*
Career/honours: senior club championship medal, 1956, with St Finbarr's.

Maher, Willie (hurling)

▸ *Played senior hurling for Dublin in 1931.*

Mahony, Martin (hurling)

▸ *Kilkenny; played senior hurling for Laois during the 1970s.*

Mahony, Jim (hurling)

▸ *played senior hurling for Laois.*

Malcolmson, Paula (camogie)

▸ *Native of Dublin; played senior camogie for Dublin (2007 to 2012). Played junior camogie with Dublin. Club: Thomas Davis.*

Mallon, Malachy (football)

▸ *Native of Tyrone; played senior football for Tyrone, 1925-31.*
Career/honours: Railway Cup football with Ulster, 1926. Club: Dungannon.
He is seen taking the first filmed penalty kick in Gaelic football in a newsreel from a Tyrone vs Antrim match in 1929.

Manicle, John (football)

▸ *played senior football for Longford, 1967.*

Mann, Oliver (hurling)

▸ *Native of Limerick; played senior hurling for Leitrim, 1973-75.*

Mannion, Jarlath (football)

▸ *Native of Mayo; played senior football for Mayo, 1964-66.*
Career/honours: four senior club championship medals with Claremorris; one junior club championship medal with Claremorris.

Mannion, Padraig (hurling)

▸ *Played senior hurling for Sligo during the 1980s.*

Marley, Seamus (football)

▸ *Played senior football for Donegal, 1977-83.*

Marron, Pat (football)

▸ *Native of Limerick; played senior football for Limerick (1978-79) and Wicklow (1981-85)*
Career/honours: also played minor hurling for Limerick, 1974.

Marshall, Dave (football)

▸ *Native of Dublin; played senior football for Dublin, 2003-04.*
Career/honours: **All-Ireland U21 medal, 2003;** *Leinster medal, 2003.*

Martin, Con (football)

▸ *Native of Roscommon; played senior football for Offaly, 1974-75.*

Martin, Eddie (hurling)

▸ *Native of Roscommon; played senior hurling for Longford, 1985-88.*
Career/honours: played minor football and hurling for Roscommon, 1969; **All-Ireland minor 'B' medal in hurling for Roscommon.** *Founder member of Foghney Hurling Club, Longford, 1980.*

Martin, James (football)

▸ *Native of Longford; played senior football for Longford, 1999, 2001-10. Career/honours: played junior football for Longford; won O'Byrne Cup in 2000; played in six senior county finals with Dromard since club debut in 1997; Sigerson Cup final with Garda College, 2008, defeated by UU Jordanstown after extra time; Played in the Leinster junior final vs Kildare in 2013.*

Martin, J. J. (football)

▸ *Native of Cavan; played senior football for Cavan, 1971-80. Career/honours: intermediate and junior club championship medals with Templeport; three Dublin senior club championship medals and two Leinster club medals with Thomas Davis. Captain of Cavan over 40s all Ireland winners.*

Martin, Paddy (football)

▸ *Native of Kildare played senior football for Kildare in the 1920s.* Career/honours: **two senior All-Ireland medals, 1927 and 1928 (1928 was the first year that the Sam Maguire Cup was awarded to the winners);** *three senior All-Ireland finalist medals, 1926, 1929 and 1931.* **Played in six All-Ireland finals.**

Masters, James (football)

▸ *Native of Cork; played senior football for Cork, 2005-10.* Career/honours: **All-Ireland minor medal, 2000 (captain); one All-Ireland club championship medal, 2002-03 with Nemo Rangers;** *minor football (2000) and U21 football with Cork; three Munster senior medals, 2006, 2008 and 2009; one National League medal, Division 2; two All-Ireland senior finalist medals, 2007; nine senior club championship medals; five Munster senior championship medals; World Police and Fire Games gold medal, 2013.*

Masterson, P.

▸ *Native of Leitrim; played senior inter-county football, 1927.*

Mayock, Paul (hurling)

▸ *Native of Kildare; played senior hurling for Kildare, 1993-2000. Career/honours: played league and championship hurling for Kildare. Played all age groups, underage through to senior in both codes, for St Mary's, Leixlip,*

McArdle, Ben (football)

▸ *Native of Armagh; played senior football for Armagh, 1953-55.*

McArdle, Frank (football)

▸ *played senior football for Louth in the 1950s.*

McArdle, Gerry (football)

▸ *Native of Meath; played senior football for Dublin, 1949.* Career/honours: *played junior football for Meath;* **All-Ireland junior championship medal with Meath, 1947;** *senior club championship medal with Garda, Dublin, 1948; county junior championship medal with Drumconrath, Meath, 1963.*

McCaffrey, Dan (football)

▸ *Native of Cavan; played senior football for Cavan, 1947–58.*
Career/honours: **All-Ireland senior medal, 1952***; played minor football for Cavan, 1947; nominated on first All Star selection; Dr McKenna Cup medal. Played for Garda Club, Dublin.*

McCaffrey, Ivan (football)

▸ *Native of Mayo; played senior football for Mayo, 1955–65.*
Career/honours: played minor football for Mayo; Connacht minor championship medal, 1955; **All-Ireland junior medal, 1957***; Mayo county junior championship 1959; Scott medal, 1988.*

McCallion, John (football)

▸ *Native of Mayo; played senior football for Mayo, 1993–96.*
Career/honours: **All-Ireland junior medal, 1997***; Connacht FBD League medal; National League Division 3 medal; Mayo county intermediate championship medals, 1994 and 1999,*

McCann, Brendan (football)

▸ *Native of Westmeath; played senior football for Westmeath, 1954–62.*
Career/honours: one county medal, and two junior championship medals with Ballynacargy.

McCarrick, Gerry (football)

▸ *Native of Sligo; played senior football for Sligo, 1971–84.*
Career/honours: county senior championship medal with Tubbercurry, 1976 (captain); junior league medal with Garda, 1984.

McCarron, Martin (football)

▸ *Native of Leitrim; played senior football for Leitrim, 2001–02.*
Career/honours: played minor, U21 and junior football for Leitrim; two senior club championship medals with Melvin Gaels.

McCarthy, Brian (football)

▸ *Native of Kerry; played senior football for Kerry, 1996.*
Career/honours: played minor and U21 football for Kerry; **won two All-Ireland U21 medals, 1995 and 1996.** *Club: Dr Crokes.*

McCarthy, John (football)

▸ *Native of Dublin; played senior football for Dublin, 1970–81.*
▸ *Native of Career/honours:* **three senior All-Ireland medals, 1974, 1976 and 1977.** *Clubs: Ballymun Kickhams, Na Fianna and Garda.* **Played in six successive All-Ireland finals. Garda Hall of Fame award, 2002.**
John was once described by former Donegal manager Brian McEniff as "the most lethal of the six Dublin forwards" at the time. John once scored 3-7 from play in a Leinster championship match vs Carlow in 1978. He also scored the first goal in the 1976 All-Ireland final, and was fouled for the penalty for the second goal.

McCarthy, Mike (football)

▸ *Native of Cork; played senior football for Cork. Club: O'Donovan Rossa.*

McCarthy, Paddy (football)

▶ *Native of Clare; played senior football for Clare, 1955-59.*
Career/honours: played for Garda Club, Dublin.

McCaughney, Mick (football)

▶ *Native of Tyrone; played senior football for Cavan and Monaghan in the 1950s*
and 1960s.
Career/honours: three senior club championship medals with Ballybay Pearse
Brothers, 1957, 1959 and 1962; Division 1 medal with Cavan Slashers, 1956;
intermediate medal with Arva, of whom he was a founder member and player
manager, 1978.
Worked in Croke Park, 1978-88. Author of The Trillick Story, 50 years
a-playing and The west Tyrone Board, 1931-1974.

McConnon, Peter (football)

▶ *Native of Kildare; played senior football for Kildare, 1988-96.*
Career/honours: O'Byrne Cup medal, 1980; two county championship medals
with Round Towers, 1997 and 1998.

McCormack, Damien (hurling)

▶ *Native of Dublin; played senior hurling for Dublin, 1996-2001.*

McCormack, Denis (hurling)

Kilkenny; played senior hurling for Kilkenny (1972-73, 1981-83) and Westmeath
(1984-86).
Career/honours: **All-Ireland senior medal, 1982; two All-Ireland club**
championship medals with James Stephens, 1976 and 1982; *two National*
League medals, 1982 and 1983; two Leinster senior medals, 1972 and 1982;
Leinster minor medal, 1969; three senior club championship medals with James
Stephens, 1976 and 1981; **All-Ireland 'B' medal with Westmeath 1984,**
National League Division 2 medal with Westmeath, 1985. Played club hurling
with Raharney and Cullion in Westmeath.

McCormack, John (hurling)

▶ *Native of Tipperary; played senior hurling for Tipperary. Club: Knockavilla*
Kickhams. Inter-county referee.

McCormack, Michael (football)

▶ *Played senior football for Longford. Former inter-county manager of Monaghan.*

McCormack, Michelle (ladies' football)

▶ *Plays senior ladies' football for Longford.*

McDaniel, Tommy (football)

▶ *Native of Westmeath; played senior football for Westmeath, 2017 to present.*
Career/honours: Formerly a Ballinagore clubman, now playing for Castleknock
(Dublin); scored three points for winners Westmeath in the Division 4 NFL final
in 2017. Played for Garda College in the 2018 Sigerson Cup, scoring 1-2 in a
win over Athlone IT.

McDermott, P. J. (football)

▸ *Native of Sligo; played senior football for Donegal (1958-62) and Sligo (1963). Career/honours: played minor football for Mayo, 1954-55; McKenna Cup medal with Donegal; two Connacht minor championship medals with Mayo.*

McDonagh, Patrick (football)

▸ *Native of Sligo; played senior football for Sligo during the 1950s. Career/honours: two county senior league medals with Easkey; county senior championship medal with Garda, Limerick 1958.*

McDonagh, Pauline (ladies' football)

▸ *Native of Leitrim; plays ladies' senior football for Leitrim. Club: Drumkeerin.*

McDonald, John (hurling)

▸ *Native of Wexford; played senior hurling for Wexford, 1981-90. Career/honours: played minor, U21 and junior for Wexford; two Leinster finalists medals.*

McDonnell, Andy (football)

▸ *Native of Louth; played senior football for Louth, 2010-14, 2016 to present. Career/honours: National League Division 3 medal, 2011; two senior club championship medals with Newtown Blues, 2013 and 2017 (captain).*

McDonnell, Derek (hurling)

▸ *Native of Mayo; played senior hurling for Mayo, 1997-2014. Career/honours:* **Christy Ring Cup Champion 15 award, 2013.**

McDonnell, Mick (football/hurling)

▸ *Native of Laois; played senior hurling for Laois (1953-57) and senior football for Laois and Cork during the 1950s. Career/honours: played midfield for Cork footballers, 1957; county senior championship medal with Sarsfields (Cork), 1957; minor and U21 hurling and football for Laois.*

McDwyer, Oliver (football)

▸ *Native of Sligo; played senior football for Sligo in the 1950s and 1960s.*

McElkenney, Michael (football)

▸ *Native of Tyrone; played senior football for Galway (1956, 1957, 1960) and Tyrone (1955) Career/honours: Ulster senior championship medal with Tyrone, 1957* Described by legendary commentator Micheál O'Hehir as "the man with the musical name".

McEvoy, Darragh (football)

▸ *Native of Laois; played senior football for Laois, 2002-04. Career/honours: two senior club championship medals for Stradbally (Laois), 1998 and 2005; one senior club championship medal for St Patrick's, Wicklow, 2012.*

McEvoy, Johnny (football)

▶ *Native of Kildare; played senior football for Kildare, 1936–48.*
Career/honours: Kildare county championship medal, 1937; Dublin county
championship medal with Garda, Dublin, 1948.

McFadden, Con (football)

▶ *Native of Donegal; played senior football for Kilkenny, 1956–59.*
Career/honours: four senior club championships with Railyard.

McFarland, Declan (football)

▶ *Native of Monaghan; played senior football for Monaghan, 1969.*

McGahern, John (football)

▶ *Played senior football for Cavan and Mayo.*
Career/honours: Ulster senior championship medals with Cavan, 1918, 1920;
Connacht senior football medal with Mayo, 1929; All-Ireland junior football
finalist medal with Mayo, 1925; played for Connacht, 1927. Played with the
Garda Club, Dublin.

McGann, Bob (hurling)

▶ *Native of Tipperary; played senior hurling for Dublin during the 1920s and*
1930s.
Career/honours: **All-Ireland senior championship medal, 1927.** *Club:*
Nenagh

McGann, Kieran (football)

▶ *Native of Clare; played senior football for Clare, 1972–76.*
Career/honours: junior county championship medal with Fermoy, 1974. Club in
Clare: Michael Cusacks. His son Kieran won an All-Ireland hurling medal with
Cork in 2005.

McGarry, Mick (hurling)

▶ *Played senior hurling for Louth.*

McGarry, Ross (hurling)

▶ *Native of Dublin; played senior hurling for Fingal, 2007 to present.*
Career/honours: Kehoe Shield medal; two National League Division 3A
medals; two junior club hurling championship medals; one Dublin intermediate
championship medal (football); minor and U21 championship club medals
(football).

McGauren, Andy

▶ *Native of Longford; played inter-county for Longford during the 1980s and*
1990s.

McGee, John (football)

▶ *Native of Longford; played senior football for Longford, 1968–69.*
Career/honours: played minor football for Longford; two intermediate club
championship medals and three league medals with Cashel; Leinster Colleges
senior football medal with Belcamp College, Dublin.

McGee, Pat (hurling)

▶ *Native of Wexford; played senior hurling for Louth.*
Career/honours: Scott medal, 1984.

McGee, Peter (football)

▶ *Native of Donegal; played senior football for Donegal, 2012-13.*
Career/honours: **All-Ireland senior medal, 2012;** *Trench Cup medal with Garda College, 2015.*

McGee, Willie (football)

▶ *Native of Mayo; played senior football for Mayo, 1967-76.*
Career/honours: **All-Ireland U21 medal, 1967;** *one Connacht senior championship medal, 1969; one National League medal, 1969-70; Railway Cup with Connacht; two Masters with Kildare 1991, 1992.*
Scored four goals in the U21 All-Ireland final, 1967. Scored seventeen goals from play in one competitive season. Known as four goal Willie Named in John Scally's book as one of the "GAA greats of Connacht". Also featured in Scally's book *All-Ireland Ambitions.*

McGill, Cormac (football)

▶ *Native of Meath; played senior football for Meath, 2007-12.*
Career/honours: one club IFC, 2007 (Donaghmore/Ashbourne, Meath); one club AFL Division 1, 2011 (Meath); one club AFL Division 2, 2008 (Meath); one club AFL Division 3, 2007 (Meath); one Higher Education League, 2008/2009 (Garda College); one Meath Green Star, 2008 (Meath); one Sigerson Ulster Bank Rising Star Award, 2008 (Garda College); one intermediate All-Ireland, 2005 (UCD).

McGinley, Eamonn (football)

▶ *Native of Donegal; played senior football for Donegal (2009) and Roscommon (2011)*
Career/honours: McKenna Cup medal with Donegal, 2009; All-Ireland Gaeltacht medal, 2008 and 2014; Donegal Gaeltacht medal, 2014; Donegal Division 1 League medal, 2014, with Kilcar.

McGinley, John

▶ *Played inter-county for Louth.*

McGoldrick, J. (football)

▶ *Played senior football for Sligo (1925) and Limerick (1926).*

McGovern, Greg (football)

▶ *Native of Dublin; played senior football for Fermanagh, 1993-99.*
Career/honours: Garda Junior Footballer of the Year, 1999.
Greg was the first player to play under the "parentage" rule; his father is from Fermanagh.

McGovern, Joe (football)

▶ *Native of Fermanagh; played senior football for Offaly (1952-53) and Fermanagh (1954-55).*
Career/honours: county senior championship and league medal with Rosemount (Westmeath) in 1951.

McGovern, Peter (football and hurling)

▸ *Native of Carlow; played senior football and senior hurling during the 1960s; represented Carlow and Waterford.*
Career/honours: two county intermediate championship medals with Erin's Own, Waterford; junior All-Ireland finalist medal in hurling for Carlow, 1960.

McGowan, Martin (football)

▸ *Native of Leitrim; played senior football for Leitrim, 1988-93.*
Career/honours: **All-Ireland 'B' medal, 1989-90**; *U21 football for Leitrim; Division 3 National League medal, 1989-90.*

McGowan, Paddy 'Paudge' (football)

▸ *Native of Leitrim; played senior football for Leitrim, 1960-66.*
Career/honours: senior club championship medals with Melvin Gaels-Kinlough.

McGrath, Ciaran (football/hurling)

▸ *Native of Galway; played senior football for Galway, 2010-12, and senior hurling for Mayo, 2008-10.*
Career/honours: two senior club All-Ireland medals with Corofin, 2015, 2018; seven senior county medals with Corofin; three senior Connacht medals.

McGrath, Con (football)

▸ *Native of Galway; played senior football for Galway (1946) and Cork (1947-53).*
Career/honours: one senior club championship medal with Cork Garda, 1950; one National League medal, 1952; two senior Munster championship medals, 1949 and 1952 (Cork); two Railway Cup medals, Munster, 1948 and 1949; three selections on the All-Ireland team vs Combined Universities, 1950, 1951, 1952.

McGrath, Des (football)

▸ *Native of Mayo; played senior football for Mayo.*
Career/honours: two junior and two intermediate championship medals with Kilmaine, Mayo.

McGrath, Frank (football)

▸ *Native of Dublin; played senior football for Dublin, 1982-86.*
Career/honours: **All-Ireland senior medal, 1983**; *played minor and U21 football for Dublin; Leinster senior medals, 1983, 1984 and 1985;* **All-Ireland minor medal, 1982**; *Leinster U21 medal, 1984; two county Dublin championship medals, 1983 and 1986.*

McGrath, John (football)

▸ *Native of Clare; played senior football for Clare, 1975-89.*
Career/honours: Railway Cup medal, Munster, 1978; two McGrath Cup medals, 1981 and 1983; two senior club championship medals with Shannon Gaels, 1975 and 1976; three senior league championships medals with Garda, 1988, 1989 and 1991; All-Ireland Interfirm medal with Garda, 1986.

McGrath, Michelle

▸ *Played senior camogie for Clare.*

McGrath, Patrick F. (football)

▸ *Played senior football for Wexford, 1925.*

McGrath, Paddy (football)

▸ *Native of Longford; played senior football for Longford, 1945-53.*
Career/honours: Leinster minor medal, 1938; senior Dublin League medal with
Ard Craobh, 1945; senior club championship medal with Garda, Dublin, 1948.

McGrath, Pakey (football)

▸ *Native of Clare; played senior football for Clare, 1971.*
Career/honours: played minor and U21 football.

McGrath, Shane (football)

▸ *Native of Dublin; played senior football for Dublin (2010) and Clare (2012 to*
present)
Career/honours: Munster finalist medal, 2012; Division 1 League medal, 2005;
World Police and Fire Games gold medal, 2013. Club: Thomas Davis.

McGrath, Jack (football)

▸ *Native of Tipperary; played senior football for Tipperary, 1971. Club: Garda*
Club, Cork.

McGraynor, Liam (football)

▸ *Native of Wicklow; played senior football for Wicklow, 1975-79.*
Career/honours: one senior championship and league medals.

McGrory, Paula (ladies' football)

▸ *Native of Donegal; plays ladies' senior football for Donegal, 2015 to present.*
Career/honours: Division 2 league winners, 2016; senior Ulster champions,
2017. Club: Buncrana GAA (junior 'A' championship winners, 2016; Division 2
league winners, 2016).

McGuinness, John (football)

▸ *Native of Mayo; played senior football for Mayo, 1964-67.*
Career/honours: Connacht championship medal, 1967; Gaelic weekly champions,
1966; club championship and league medals for Claremorris, 1965. Played in an
All-Ireland final with Over 40's with Dublin in the mid 1980s. Ran over forty
marathons from 1981 to 1995, including in Dublin, London, New York, Belfast
and Amsterdam. Also participated in the World Police and Fire Games between
1991 and 1997, winning two gold, one silver and one bronze medals.

McGurrin, Hugh (football)

▸ *Native of Leitrim; played senior football for Leitrim, 1988-89.*

McHale, Eddie (football)

▸ *Native of Mayo; played senior football for Mayo (1973, 1982-83), Leitrim*
(1976) and Sligo (1978-81)
Career/honours: six senior championship football medals with St Mary's and two
senior hurling championship medals with Craobh Rua. Clubs: Knockmore, Allen
Gaels and St Mary's. Also excelled in boxing and rugby.

McHale, Eugene (football)

▸ *Native of Mayo; played senior football for Mayo, 1975–86.*
Career/honours: two Connacht senior championship medals, 1981 and 1985; Connacht minor league medal; five senior club championship medals with Knockmore. Inter-county referee.

McHugh, Aidan (football)

▸ *Native of Roscommon; played senior football for Roscommon.*
Career/honours: **All-Ireland U21 medal, 1978**; *Masters football with Roscommon.*

McHugh, Danny (football)

▸ *Native of Sligo; played senior football for Sligo from 1964– 69*
Career/honours: three North divisional junior championship medals 1959, 1963 and 1969 with Cliffoney and Grange

McHugh, Tom (football)

▸ *Native of Leitrim; played senior inter-county football during the 1970s.*

McInerney, Julie (ladies' football)

▸ *Native of Dublin; played senior ladies' football for Dublin, 1996-2001.*

McInerney, Pat ('Pa') 'Fowler' (hurling)

▸ *Native of Clare; played senior hurling for Clare (1913-26) and Dublin (1927-31, 1932-33)*
Career/honours: **two All-Ireland senior medals with Clare (1914) and Dublin (1927)**; *All-Ireland finalist medal with Clare, 1932; two Munster senior medals, 1914, 1932; three Leinster senior medals, 1927, 1928, 1930; one National League medal, 1929; Railway Cup hurling with Leinster, 1927; six club championship medals with O'Callaghan Mills and Garda. Played for Garda Club, Dublin. Played in Tailteann Games.*
GAA All-Time All Star award, 1983. Ranked at no. 75 in the *Irish Independent 125 Greatest Stars of the GAA.*

McInerney, P. J. (hurling)

▸ *Native of Clare; played senior hurling for Clare during the 1960s.*

McInerney, Zoe (camogie)

▸ *Played senior camogie for Clare.*

McIntyre, P. J. (football/hurling)

▸ *Native of Offaly; played senior football (1968) and senior hurling (1967-74) for Kerry; senior hurling and senior football for Offaly (1960-65)*
Career/honours: played minor and U21 hurling for Offaly; **junior All-Ireland hurling medal, 1967-1968**; *senior championship medal with Kenmare, 1974. Clubs: Kenmare (Kerry), St Rynagh's (Offaly). Scott medalist.*

McKenna, Eugene (football)

▸ *Native of Louth; played senior football for Monaghan, 1970-72. Club: Scotstown.*

McKenna, Lonan (hurling)

▸ *Native of Cavan; played senior hurling for Cavan, 2008-10.*
Career/honours: senior club championship medals with Ballymachugh, 2011, and
Cootehill, 2014 and 2015.

McIntyre, Seamus (hurling)

▸ *Native of Kerry; played senior hurling for Kerry, 1988-95.*
Career/honours: played junior football for Kerry; Munster junior football
championship medal, 1995; Munster minor football medal, 1989; Munster U21
football medal, 1995. Played with Kenmare, Gort, and Ballincollig. Captained
the Garda College to a Fitzgibbon final in 1997 when they lost to UCC.
Died in service on 22 April 2001. A Seamus McIntyre Memorial
Tournament is held every year since 2001.

McLoughlin, Donie

▸ *played inter-county for Monaghan, and played for Galway under the name P.*
Rooney

McLoughlin, Eddie (football)

▸ *Native of Mayo; played senior football for Mayo.*
Career/honours: All-Ireland Senior Colleges medal with St Colman's, Claremorris,
1977.

McLoughlin, Frank (football)

▸ *Native of Offaly; played senior football for Offaly and Carlow, 1954-65.*
Career/honours: O'Byrne Cup medal with Offaly, 1954; played minor, junior and
senior for Offaly in one year.

McLoughlin, John (football)

▸ *Played senior football for Mayo.*

McLoughlin, Paddy (football)

▸ *Native of Donegal; played senior football for Cavan and Monaghan during the*
1940s.
Career/honours: Dr Ward Cup medal for Monaghan Harps, 1944-45. Rose to the
rank of Commissioner. Missed out on a trip with Cavan to the 1947 All-Ireland
final in New York, because of his transfer to Monaghan.

McLoughlin, T. P. (football)

▸ *Native of Leitrim; played senior football for Leitrim, 1988-91.*
Career/honours: played minor and U21 football with Leitrim; three senior league
medals with Fenagh. Beaten in four senior championship finals.

McLoughlin, Tony (football)

▸ *Native of Kildare; played senior football for Kildare, 1982-90.*
Career/honours: played minor and U21 football for Kildare; Leinster U21 medal;
National League Division 2 medal; O'Byrne Cup medal, 1983.

McMahon, Edward (football)

▸ *Native of Monaghan; played senior football for Monaghan.*

McMahon, John (football)

▶ *Native of Cavan; played senior football for Cavan, 1960-61.*
Career/honours: played minor football (1956-58) for Cavan; junior football, 1959; one junior club and one intermediate championship medal.

McMahon, Sean (football)

▶ *Native of Tipperary; played senior football for Tipperary during the 1990s.*
Career/honours: minor and U21 football for Tipperary.

McMahon, P. (hurling)

▶ *Native of Clare; played senior hurling for Donegal in 1923.*
Career/honours: Ulster championship medal with Donegal, 1923.

McMahon, Pat (hurling)

▶ *Native of Kerry; played senior hurling for Kerry, 1980-86.*
Career/honours: **All-Ireland 'B' medal, 1986;** *Division 2 National League medal; two senior club championship medals with Lixnaw, 1983 and 1985.*

McMahon, Phil (football)

▶ *Native of Leitrim; played senior football for Leitrim and Monaghan during the 1920s.*
Career/honours: Connacht senior medal, 1927.

McMahon, Terry (football)

▶ *Native of Sligo; played senior football for Sligo, 1991.*
Career/honours: Trench Cup medal with Sligo IT, 1991.

McMahon, William 'Bill'

▶ *Native of Clare; played inter-county for Tipperary. Clubs: Éire Óg and Clonmel Commercials.*

McManamon, Sean (football)

▶ *Native of Mayo; played senior football for Laois (1962-63) and Roscommon (1975-76).*
Career/honours: senior club championship medal for O'Dempseys (Laois); junior club championship medal for Claremorris (Mayo), 1960; three senior club championship medals for Castlerea (Roscommon), 1969, 1971 and 1973. Inter-county referee.

McManus, Eamonn 'Junior' (football)

▶ *Native of Roscommon; played senior football for Roscommon, 1983-95.*
Career/honours: five All-Ireland Club finalists medals; played minor and U21 football; two senior Connacht championship medals; one U21 and one minor Connacht championship medals; thirteen club championship medals for Clann na Gael; eight Connacht club championship medals.

McManus, Jerry (football)

▶ *Native of Sligo; played senior football for Sligo, 1959-67.*
Career/honours: senior club championship medal, 1958; junior club championship medals, 1963, 1967; Hogan Cup medal, 1957. Inter-county manager, Kerry (hurling).

McManus, Jim (football)

▸ *Native of Roscommon; played senior football for Roscommon, 1980.*
Career/honours: All-Ireland senior finalist medal, 1980.

McManus, Pat (football)

▸ *Native of Roscommon; played senior football for Roscommon (1965-71) and*
Meath (1973-75).
Career/honours: Connacht junior medal (Roscommon); two club championship
medals for Clann na Gael.

McManus, Thomas

▸ *Native of Roscommon; played inter-county for Roscommon (1965-66) and*
Wicklow (1971-72).
Career/honours: two senior club championship medals in Roscommon; one
intermediate club championship medal in Wicklow.

McMenamin, Colm (football)

▸ *Native of Tipperary; played senior football for Tipperary, 1997-99 and 2002.*
Career/honours: Munster finalist medal, 2002. Club: Scarriff

McMenamin, John Dan (football)

▸ *Native of Donegal; played senior football for Donegal, 1961-67.*
Career/honours: played minor and U21 football for Donegal; three Ulster U21
medals; Dr McKenna Cup medal; Railway Cup football for Ulster; three senior
club Donegal championship medals with Ballybofey, captain in 1963 and 1964.
Played with Dublin Garda Club, 1964-65.

McMenamon, Sean (football)

▸ *Native of Mayo; played senior football for Laois (1960s) and Roscommon (1975-*
76).
Career/honours: three senior club championship medals with Castlerea
(Roscommon), O'Dempseys (Laois) and Castlebar (Mayo). Also played with
Salthill (Galway).

McNamara, Conor (hurling)

▸ *Native of Clare; played senior hurling for Clare in the 2000s. Club: Scariff.*

McNeal, Pat

▸ *Played inter-county for Monaghan, c. 1970.*

McNeela, Michael (football)

▸ *Native of Mayo; played senior football for Roscommon (1968-72) and Mayo*
(1973).
Career/honours: four Roscommon senior club championship medals for Roscommon
Gaels, 1974, 1975, 1978, 1980; two Connacht senior championship medals.

McPolin, Gary (football)

▸ *Native of Cork; played senior football for Cork, 1989, 1990 and 1993-97.*
Career/honours: **two All-Ireland junior medals, 1990 and 1993**; *All-Ireland*
minor finalist, 1987; Munster minor winner, 1987; Munster U21 championship
medal, 1989; **All-Ireland U21 medal, 1989**; *Munster senior medal, 1994.*
Coached Muskerry to a county final in 2005. **Interfirm All-Ireland medals**
with Garda (Cork City Division), 1991, 1994, 1996, 2000.

McNulty, Anthony (football)

▸ *Native of Dublin; played senior football for Dublin, 2002. Clubs: O'Dwyer's, Balbriggan and Garda, Dublin.*

McQuillan, J. J. (football)

▸ *Native of Roscommon; played senior football for Roscommon, 1943–44. Career/honours:* **two All-Ireland medals, 1943 and 1944.**

Meally, Michael (football)

▸ *Native of Kilkenny; played senior football for Kilkenny, 1960–77. Career/honours: ten senior club championship medals with Railyard; two minor club championship medals with Railyard; Division 2 league medal with Garda, 1972.*

Mee, Tommy (football)

▸ *Native of Galway; played senior football for Clare in the 1960s. Career/honours: played junior football for Galway; Cusack Cup medal, 1963. Clubs: Milltown Malbay and Glenamaddy.*

Melia, Mick (football/hurling)

▸ *Native of Kilkenny; played senior football for Kilkenny (1961–79) and senior hurling for Wicklow (1965). Career/honours: Leinster junior medal, 1971; eleven county club championship medals with Railyard; Division 2 football medal with Garda, Dublin.*

Mellett, Colm (hurling)

▸ *Played senior hurling for Meath in the 2000s. Career/honours: U21 hurling for Meath.*

Mellett, Seamus

▸ *Played inter-county for Meath.*

Merrigan, Michael (football)

▸ *Native of Wexford; played senior football for Wexford in the 1970s. Club: Bray Emmetts.*

Miller, Tom (football)

▸ *Native of Laois; played senior football 1963–72; represented Laois and Wexford. Career/honours: played senior football for Wexford, 1965; one senior championship medal with Timahoe (Laois), 1969 (one of five brothers on the team);* **eight senior club championship medals with Duffry Rovers (Wexford), including seven-in-a-row (1986–92).**

Miller, Tom (football)

▸ *Native of Laois; played senior football for Laois, 1993.*

Mimnagh, Mark (football)

▸ *Native of Longford; played senior football for Longford, 1984–89. Career/honours: three senior club championship medals with Killoe, 1988, 1993 and 1995; one senior league medal, 1985; played minor football for Longford.* **Longford Player of the Year, 1993.**

Milner, Michael (hurling)

▸ *Native of Cork; played senior hurling for Kerry, 2016 to present.*
Career/honours: minor and U21 football for Cork; two U21 Munster football
medals with Cork; senior club championship medal with Carbery, 2004; senior
club championship medals with Dr Crokes, 2014, 2016, **and an All-Ireland**
Club SFC medal, 2017. *Sigerson League with Garda College, 2009. Clubs;*
Dohenys and Carbery, Cork, and Dr Crokes, Kerry.

Minnock, Carthage (football)

▸ *Native of Offaly; played senior football for Offaly, 1962. Club: Blackwood Rovers.*

Miskella, John (football)

▸ *Native of Cork; played senior football for Cork, 1999-2011.*
Career/honours: **All-Ireland senior medal, 2010; one All Star award, 2009**
(left half back*); one county senior club championship medal with Ballincollig,*
2014; four Munster championship medals; three National League medals, 1999,
2010, 2011. Played interprovincial football for Munster. **International Rules**
player, 2008*. World Police and Fire Games medal, 2013.*

Mitchell, John (hurling)

▸ *Native of Kilkenny; played senior hurling for Wexford (1953, 1960-62) and Kerry*
(1955-59).
Career/honours: **All-Ireland senior medal with Wexford, 1960***; two Leinster*
senior medals with Wexford, 1960, 1962; one Munster league medal with Kerry,
1957; three senior club championship medals with St Aidan's ,Wexford, 1952,
1953, 1959; one senior club championship medal with Kilgarvan, Kerry, 1956.

Mockler, Paul (football)

▸ *Native of Roscommon; played senior football for Roscommon, 1966–69.*
Career/honours: **U21 All-Ireland medal, 1966***; senior championship medal*
with Garryowen (London) in 1972. Won a county junior football championship
with St Croan's, Ballintubber in 1963, and an intermediate title in 1978. Also
played with Éire Óg, Ennis, where he ended his career in 1983. Mentored and
managed teams up to 2007.

Mollahan, Siobhan (ladies' football)

▸ *Native of Leitrim; played ladies' senior football for Leitrim (2000-07) and*
Donegal (2007-08).

Molloy, Barry John (football)

▸ *Native of Carlow; played senior football for Carlow (2010 to present).*
Career/honours: Trench Cup medal with Garda College, 2015.

Molloy, Laz (football)

▸ *Native of Offaly; played senior football for Offaly, 1983-91.*
Career/honours: Division 3 league medal in 1990; played minor, U21 and junior
for Offaly; Division 3 League medal, 1990.
In the 1984 Leinster SFC quarter-final vs Longford at Croke Park, Laz
was in the stand when he was asked to report to the Offaly dressing room
at half time. He came on as sub goalie, kept a clean sheet and they won
the match.

Molloy, Rob (hurling)

▸ *Native of Galway; played senior hurling for Galway, 2009-12.*

Molloy, Willie (football)

▸ *Native of Offaly; played senior football for Offaly, 2002-03. Club: Ferbane.*

Maloncy, Billy (hurling)

▸ *Native of Kerry; played senior hurling for Kerry, 1963-67.*
Career/honours: played club hurling with Killarney, winning a senior championship in 1969

Moloney, John (football)

▸ *Native of Kilkenny; played senior football for Kilkenny, 1978-79.*

Moloney, Niall (hurling)

▸ *Native of Kilkenny native;*
hurled at senior grade for Kilkenny, 1997-2000.
Career/honours: two All-Ireland finalist medals, 1998 and 1999; U21 hurling for Kilkenny, 1995 and 1996; U21 All-Ireland finalist medal, 1995.

Moloney, Pat (football)

▸ *Native of Limerick; played senior football for Limerick, 1959-62.*
Career/honours: **in 1959, Pat played minor, junior and senior football for Limerick.** *Captain of Abbeyfeale minors when they won the county championships in 1958. Captain of the county minor team in 1959. Kelliher Shield medal, 1964.*

Moloney, T. (hurling)

▸ *Native of Waterford; played senior hurling for Waterford in the 1920s. Club: Lismore.*

Molyneaux, Mattie (football)

▸ *Native of Kerry; played senior football for Clare, 1973-74.*
Career/honours: played minor football for Kerry.

Monaghan, Brian (football)

▸ *Native of Offaly; played senior football for Offaly, 1998-2001.*
Career/honours: National League and O'Byrne Cups, 1998, 1999, 2000, 2001; played minor hurling and football, 1991-92 with Offaly; U21 football, 1994-95; intermediate hurling 1997-98; intermediate football with Offaly (and Leinster title), 1999.

Monahan, Eugene (hurling)

▸ *Native of Galway; played senior hurling for Galway (1954-55).*
Career/honours: senior club championship medals with Glen Rovers, 1948 (with Christy Ring and Jack Lynch) and Sarsfields, 1951. Also hurled for Ballinakill (now Tommy Larkins). Railway Cup with Connacht.

Monaghan, M. (football)

▸ *Native of Cavan; played senior football for Waterford, 1926.*

349

Monahan, Fintan

▸ *Native of Galway; played inter-county for Sligo, 1952-54. Club: Ballinakill.*

Mongey, Tom (football)

▸ *Native of Meath; played senior football for Meath, 1962-63.*
Career/honours: played minor football, 1958; junior football 1959, 1960, 1962 and 1966. Club minor championship medal with Boyne Emmetts, 1958 (captain).

Mooney, Lisa (ladies' football)

▸ *Plays senior ladies' football for Longford.*

Mooney, Seamus (football)

▸ *Native of Sligo; played senior football for Sligo.*

Moore, Joanne (ladies' football)

▸ *Played ladies' senior football for Cavan.*
*Career/honours: **All-Ireland intermediate medal, 2013.***

Moran, Ciara (camogie)

▸ *Native of Roscommon; played senior camogie for Roscommon, 1999-2011.*
*Career/honours: **All-Ireland junior medal, 2011**; two senior club championship medals with Athleague; three Connacht junior club medals.*

Moran, Colm (football)

▸ *Native of Kildare; played senior football for Kildare, 1980-89.*
Career/honours: two O'Byrne Cup medals; one senior club championship medal with Athy, 1987.

Moran, Jack

▸ *Played senior inter-county for Waterford, 1924.*

Moran, Joe (football)

▸ *Native of Westmeath; played senior football for Westmeath in the 1960s.*
Career/honours: senior championship medal with Moorefield, Kildare (1963) in hurling.

Moran, Michael (football)

▸ *Native of Kerry; played senior football for Monaghan, 1975-76.*

Moran, Padraig (football)

▸ *Native of Offaly; played senior football for Offaly, 1988-99*
Career/honours: played U21 (1988) and won Leinster and All-Ireland; minor 'B', junior, intermediate, senior 'B' championships with Tubber (Offaly); junior 'C' hurling championship with Tubber; Leinster and All-Ireland Vocational Schools medal with Clara.

Moran, S. (football)

▸ *Played senior football for Mayo, 1931.*

Morgan, Martin (football)

▶ *Native of Leitrim; played senior football for Leitrim and Galway during the 1920s.*
Career/honours: Connacht senior medal, 1927. Leitrim handball champion.

Morgan, W. (football)

▶ *Played senior football for Kildare, 1935.*

Moriarty, Dermot (football)

▶ *Played senior football for Donegal and Cavan during the 1940s.*

Moriarty, Eddie 'Ned' (football)

▶ *Native of Roscommon; played senior football for Mayo, 1951–59.*
Career/honours: two Connacht senior medals, 1955; National League medal, 1954; played in the Polo Grounds, New York in 1954 for the St Brendan Cup; Railway Cup for Connacht.

Moriarty, Mick (football)

▶ *Native of Kerry; played senior football for Kerry, 1953. Clubs: Austin Stacks and Castlegregory.*

Morley, John (football)

▶ *Native of Mayo; played senior football for Mayo, 1961-74.*
Career/honours: two senior Connacht medals,1967 and 1969; two Railway Cup medals in 1967 and 1969; Railway Cup for Connacht, 1970, 1971, 1973 and 1974; one National League medal, 1970; county senior club medal with Roscommon Gaels, 1978; selected on the Gaelic Weekly All–Ireland team, 1969; county senior club medal with East Mayo, 1967.
Quote from the late, great Dermot Earley: "You would have to consider John as one of the great players". Was murdered while on duty on 7 July 1980. Chosen on the Western People's best Mayo team, 1960-90. Featured in John Scally's book All-Ireland Ambitions.

Moroney, Bryan (football/hurling)

▶ *Native of Kerry; played senior football for Wicklow and Louth and senior hurling for Louth during the 1950s.*
Career/honours: two county senior championship medals with St Patrick's; senior hurling for Louth; two Division 3 National League medals.

Moroney, John (football)

▶ *Native of Louth; played senior football for Louth, 1997-99.*
Career/honours: **All-Ireland 'B' medal, 1997.**

Morris, Gillian (ladies' football)

▶ *Native of Dublin; played ladies' senior football for Dublin, 2001-02.*
Career/honours: also played junior football for Dublin.

Morris, Paddy (hurling)

▶ *Native of Galway; played senior hurling for Kildare.*
Career/honours: **All-Ireland junior medal, 1962 (match played in London).**
Club: Athy.

Morris, Tony (football)

▸ *Native of Cavan; played senior football for Cavan, 1961-67.*
Career/honours: minor football, 1957-60; All-Ireland minor finalist medal, 1959; three Ulster senior championship medals, 1962, 1964 and 1967; Railway Cup medals, 1963, 1965 and 1966; Dr McKenna Cup medal, 1962.

Morrissey, Annie (ladies' football)

▸ *Native of Clare; played ladies' senior football for Clare.*

Morrissey, Mick (football/hurling)

▸ *Native of Kilkenny; played senior hurling for Kilkenny (1987-92) and Dublin (1996-99); senior football for Kilkenny (1975-89).*
Career/honours: **senior All-Ireland medal (hurling), 1992; minor All-Ireland medal, 1981; U21 All-Ireland medal, 1984; junior All-Ireland medal, 1986 (captain)**. *Senior football for Kilkenny, 1975-1989; National League medal, 1987. Three senior club championship medals with Cuala (Dublin), 1989, 1991 and 1994. Two All-Ireland Colleges medal with Good Counsel, New Ross. Intermediate titles with Graiguenamanagh (1983, 1985).*

Morrissey, Moses (football/hurling)

▸ *Native of Wexford; played senior football and senior hurling for Wexford during the 1960s and 1970s.*
Career/honours: played minor and junior football for Wexford. County senior club championship medal with Gusserane, 1975 (junior, 1965).

Moyles, Sean (hurling)

▸ *Native of Dublin; played senior hurling for Dublin (1989-2003) and Meath (1997-98).*
Career/honours: two intermediate hurling championship medals Dunboyne, 1986 and 1989; one Dublin senior hurling league Division 1 medal with Faugh's (Dublin), 1990; one Dublin senior hurling championship medal with Faugh's (Dublin), 1992; one Meath junior football championship medal with St Paul's, Clonee (1999); **one All-Ireland junior hurling championship medal with Meath, 1999***; one Meath All-County Football League Division 3 medal, 2000; one Meath senior hurling championship medal with Kiltale, 2007.*

Moynihan, Con (football)

▸ *Native of Mayo; played senior football for Mayo, 1974-77.*
Career/honours: **All-Ireland minor medal, 1971; All-Ireland U21 medal, 1974***; played minor football for Mayo; Connacht minor medal, 1971; Connacht U21 medal, 1974; senior club championship medal with Ballaghaderreen; two Sigerson Cup medals with UCD, 1974 and 1975.*

Moynihan, Mark (football)

▸ *Played senior football for Mayo.*

Moynihan, Owen (football)

▸ *Native of Cork; played senior football for Cork, 1963-64.*
Career/honours: played junior football for Cork, 1961-63; Munster junior championship medal, 1962. Club: Muskerry.

Mulcahy, Pat (hurling)

▸ *Native of Kilkenny; played senior hurling for Wexford, 1975.*
Career/honours: played minor hurling for Kilkenny. Club: Faythe Harriers.
Played football with SarsfieldsWas featured in the Wexford local papers, because he
was a Kilkenny man who played for Wexford against Kilkenny.

Muldowney, John (hurling)

▸ *Laois native; played senior hurling for Cavan, 1958-59. Clubs: Belturbet,*
Crosskeys, Stradone (Cavan), Kildalkey (Meath), Aughavas (Leitrim), Erin's
Isle (Dublin).

Mulhare, Harry (football)

▸ *Native of Laois; played senior football for Laois (1968-75) and Tipperary (1975-*
82).
Career/honours: Leinster U21 championship medal, 1969; Leinster club
championship medal with Portlaoise, 1972; Railway cup medal – Munster, 1980;
three county senior championship medals in Laois, 1968, 1970 and 1971; one
county intermediate championship medal in Tipperary, 1980.
Played against all thirty-two counties in league or championship.

Mulhall, M. (hurling)

▸ *Native of Kilkenny; played senior hurling for Donegal, 1923.*
Career/honours: Ulster championship medal, 1923.

Mulhern, Noel (football)

▸ *Native of Leitrim; played senior football for Leitrim in the 1950s and 1960s.*

Mullahy, Darren (football)

▸ *Native of Galway; played senior football for Galway, 2003-10. Club: Milltown.*

Mullane, Jim (hurling)

▸ *Native of Clare; played senior hurling for Clare and Dublin, 1932-42.*
Career/honours: Munster championship medal with Clare, 1932; All-Ireland
finalist medal with Clare, 1932; All-Ireland senior finalist medal with Dublin,
1942; two senior club championship medals with Young Irelands, Limerick, 1930,
1932. Also played with Faugh's.

Mullarkey, Padraig (football)

▸ *Native of Kildare; played senior football for Kildare, 2000-10.*
Career/honours: Kildare senior football championship medal with Round Towers
in 2003; Kildare intermediate football championship medal with Ellistown in
2000; Kildare junior 'A' football championship medal with Ellistown in 1999.

Mullen, James (football)

▸ *Native of Offaly; played senior football for Offaly, 1988-95.*
Career/honours: **All-Ireland U21 medal, 1988**; *Division 3 National League*
medal, 1991 Leinster minor finalist medal, 1985; played minor and U21 football
for Offaly; senior club championship medal with Edenderry.

Mulligan, Donal (football)

▸ *Native of Dublin; played senior football for Dublin, 1964-65.*
Career/honours: **All-Ireland minor medal, 1958**; *played minor football, 1957-*
58; played junior football, 1960; **All-Ireland junior medal, 1960**; *Leinster*
senior medal, 1965; minor county championship medal with O'Tooles, 1957, and
a senior league medal, 1960.

Mulligan, Emlyn 'Muggsie' (football)

▸ *Native of Leitrim; played senior football for Leitrim, 2006-14.*
Career/honours: Leitrim senior league championship medal, 2012; played interprovincial football for Connacht; two FBD Insurance League medals, 2013, 2014; World Police and Fire Games gold medal, 2013. Club: Melvin Gaels.
Played soccer for Sligo Rovers.

Mulligan, Shane (football)

▸ *Native of Longford; played senior football for Longford.*
Career/honours: intermediate championship medal, 2007. Senior Leader Cup, 2013.

Mullins, Gerard (hurling)

▸ *Native of Dublin; played senior hurling for Dublin.*
Career/honours: also played U21 hurling for Dublin. Clubs: Crumlin and Faugs

Mulroy, Mick (football)

▸ *Native of Westmeath; played senior football for Westmeath, 1986-89. Club: Milltownpass.*

Mulryan, Kevin (football)

▸ *Native of Tipperary; played senior football for Tipperary, 2001-09.*
Career/honours: Tommy Murphy Cup medal, 2005; McGrath Cup medal, 2003; Munster minor hurling medal, 1999. Club: JK Brackens. Played minor and U21 football and hurling with Tipperary.

Mulvaney, John (football)

▸ *Played senior football for Cavan, 1977.*

Mulvee, Tom (football)

▸ *Native of Roscommon; played senior football for Roscommon, 1961.*
Career/honours: Connacht senior medal, 1961; played minor football. Three Roscommon county minor titles, 1957, 1958 and 1959.

Mulvihill, Patrick (football)

▸ *Native of Westmeath; played senior football for Westmeath, 2005-06.*
Career/honours: six Westmeath SFC medals with Garrycastle; one Roscommon SFC medal; World Police and Fire Games gold medal, 2013; one Leinster club SFC medal, 2012; played in an All-Ireland club SFC final for Garrycastle, Croke Park, 2012 (the Athlone outfit lost to Armagh's Crossmaglen after a replay). Clubs: Garrycastle (Westmeath) and St Brigid's (Roscommon).
Played soccer for Longford Town and Athlone Town.

Murphy, Barnes (football)

▸ *Native of Sligo; played senior football for Sligo, 1967-81.*
Career/honours: **All Star award, 1974 (centre back);** *minor, 1965 and U21, 1966-68; selected for the Connacht Railway Cup team for six years (captain, 1976); three Connacht club championship medals with St Mary's; All-Ireland 7-a-side medal with St Mary's.*

Murphy, Brian (football/hurling)

▶ *Native of Cork; played senior football (1972-79) and senior hurling (1972-83) for Cork.*
Career/honours: **three All-Ireland senior hurling medals, 1976, 1977 and 1978; one All-Ireland senior football medal, 1973; two All-Ireland U21 hurling medals, 1971, 1973; All-Ireland U21 football medal, 1971; two All-Ireland minor medals in hurling, 1969 and 1970; one All-Ireland minor football medal, 1969; two All Star football awards (1973, left corner back, 1976, left Corner back); two All Star hurling awards (1979, right corner back, 1981, right corner back); four All-Ireland senior club championship medals with Nemo Rangers, 1973, 1979, 1982 and 1984;** *played minor football and hurling for Cork, and U21 football; seven Munster senior football championship medals; four Munster senior hurling championship medals; four Railway Cup medals in football, 1975, 1976, 1977 and 1978; one Railway Cup medal in hurling, 1981; seven Munster senior club championship medals in football; one All-Ireland club SFC finalist medal, 1975.*
Garda Hall of Fame award, 1996. Named in John Scally's book as one of the "GAA greats of Munster".

Murphy, Brendan (football)

▶ *Native of Carlow; played senior football for Carlow, 2010-13, 2015 to present.*
Career/honours: Club minor (2004), U21 (2005 and 2006) and senior (2009 and 2014, captain) championship medals with club Rathvilly. Railway Cup for Leinster, 2012 and 2013. Played for Australian rules football for Sydney Swans.
Four international caps for Ireland.

Murphy, Bryan (hurling)

▶ *Native of Kerry; member of Kerry senior hurling panel since 2010 to present. Club: Causeway.*
Career/honours: two Christy Ring Cup medals; two National League medals; **two U21 All-Ireland 'B' medals; one All-Ireland minor 'B' medal; two U21 shinty/hurling medals with Ireland;** *three senior medals with the Irish senior shinty/hurling team; one U16 Vocational Schools 'A' All-Ireland medal with Causeway Comprehensive School; one Christy Ring All Star award.*

Murphy, Christy (football)

▶ *Native of Sligo; played senior football for Sligo (1974-78 and 1981-85) and Donegal (1979-80).*
Career/honours: Played for Connacht, 1982; played minor and U21 football for Sligo; two Sligo senior club championship medals with St Mary's, 1985 and 1987; three senior championship, one senior league and one intermediate championship medals with St Joseph's, Donegal.

Murphy, Connie (football)

▶ *Native of Kerry; played senior football for Kerry, 1987-94.*
Career/honours: played minor and U21 for Kerry; Munster senior championship medal, 1991; club county championship medal, 1991, Dr Crokes; **All-Ireland club championship medal, 1992, Dr Crokes.**

Murphy, Eileen (camogie)

▶ *Native of Galway; played senior camogie for Westmeath, 2008-14.*
Career/honours: All-Ireland (Division 3) League medal with Westmeath, 2014; **Junior 'A' All-Ireland medal with Westmeath, 2012;** *All-Ireland (Division 4) League medal with Westmeath, 2011.*

Murphy, Fachtna (football)

▶ *Native of Cork; played senior football for Cork, 1971.*
Career/honours: Senior championship medal with Carbery, 1971; marked Dermot Earley in the Army vs Garda match in 1973. Rose to the rank of Commissioner.

Murphy, Jack (football)

▶ *Native of Kerry; played senior football for Kerry, 1924-26. Club: St Mary's, Caherciveen.*
Career/honours: **one All-Ireland senior medal, 1924.**
Played in the drawn 1926 All-Ireland final against Kildare and was named man of the match. Tragically, he developed pneumonia after the match and died before Kerry won the replay. More can be found under the chapter *Did you know?*

Murphy, James 'Jas' (football)

▶ *Native of Kerry; played senior football for Cork (1947–49) and Kerry (1949–54).*
Career/honours: **All-Ireland senior medal with Kerry, 1953 (captain***); three Munster senior championship medals with Kerry, 1950, 1951 and 1953; played minor football for Kerry, 1941; club county championship medal with St Nicholas, Cork and one with Garda Club, Cork; played with Munster and the Rest of Ireland. Played club football in Kerry for Kerins O'Rahillys.*

Murphy, John (football)

▶ *Native of Clare; played senior football for Clare during the 1960s.*

Murphy, Liam (football)

▶ *Native of Wexford; played senior football for Wexford, 2006–07.*
Career/honours: county senior championship medal with Clongeen (Wexford) in 2007.

Murphy, Michael (football)

▶ *Native of Westmeath; played senior football for Westmeath, 1961–71.*
Career/honours: O'Byrne Cup medal; minor, junior and intermediate club championship medals with Ballymore.

Murphy, Michael (football/hurling)

▶ *Native of Wexford; played senior football (1977–81) and senior hurling (1978) for Wexford.*
Career/honours: **All-Ireland junior medal, 1985***; Division 2 National League medal, 1979–80; senior club and Leinster championship medals, 1981; minor with Raheens; U21 and junior football with Wexford. Club: Clongeen.*

Murphy, Pat (football)

▶ *Native of Kerry; played senior football for Donegal, 1961–63.*
Career/honours: county championship and league medals (Galway); county league medals in Donegal.

Murphy, Patrick (football)

▶ *Native of Cork; played senior football for London, 1991–92.*
Career/honours: played club football with St Brendan's and O'Donovan Rossa.

Murphy, Richard (football)

▸ *Native of Cork; played senior hurling for Kildare, 1993-94.*
Career/honours: one Christy Ring finalist medal, 1994; junior championship
medal with Confey, 1993.

Murphy, Seamus (football)

▸ *Native of Laois; played senior football for Laois, 1989.*
Career/honours: three county senior championship medals with St Joseph's, Laois,
1989, 1994 and 1996.

Murray, Brian (football)

▸ *Native of Donegal; played senior football for Donegal, 1984-98.*
Career/honours: **All-Ireland senior medal, 1992***; two senior championship*
medals, 1986 and 1987; two U21 medals, 1981, 1982 with Aodh Ruadh; All-
Ireland Colleges 1980 (De La Salle); Ulster SFC, 1990 and 1992; Railway Cup,
1994 and 1995; Ulster minor league, 1982; nominated in 1992 and 1993 for an
All Star; Dublin Senior Division League, 1992 (Civil Service GFC).

Murray, Dom (football)

▸ *Native of Laois; played senior football for Laois (1947), Cork (1946 and 1949),*
Donegal and Mayo.
Career/honours: played junior football for Donegal and Cork, and junior hurling
for Mayo; Munster junior championship medal with Cork, 1946 and 1951;
Munster senior championship medal with Cork, 1949; senior club championship
medal with Garda, Cork, 1950; senior club hurling championship medal with
Avondhu, Cork, 1952; Ulster junior championship medal with Donegal, 1954;
two senior club championship medals with Dungloe, Donegal, 1957 and 1958.
Played inter-county football and hurling in all four provinces.

Murray, Gerry (football)

▸ *Native of Galway; played senior hurling for Galway, 1965-66.*
Career/honours: All-Ireland minor finalist medal, 1955; played minor and junior
hurling for Galway. Marked the legendary Jimmy Doyle in the 1955 minor
defeat. Played senior football for Cavan Gaels.

Murray, Gerry (hurling)

▸ *Native of Offaly; played senior hurling for Meath (1975-78) and Louth (1984-*
87).
Career/honours: played minor hurling for Offaly.

Murray, Jimmy (football)

▸ *Native of Westmeath; played senior football for Westmeath.*
Career/honours: All-Ireland minor finalist medal, 1963; two senior club
championship medals with Kells.

Murray, Joseph

▸ *Native of Monaghan; played inter-county for Donegal in the early 1920s.*
Career/honours: more renowned as much-travelled GAA administrator, he
organised hurling and football clubs and county boards in Monaghan, Dublin,
Galway, Donegal and Waterford between 1909 and the mid-1920s; served as
acting secretary of Ulster Council (1913).

Murray, Mick (football)

▸ *Played senior football for Mayo in 1924.*

Murray, Pat (football)

▸ *Native of Westmeath; played senior football for Westmeath, 1981-93.*
Career/honours: O'Byrne Cup medal; two county senior championship medals with Moate, 1983 and 1997; two All-Ireland senior colleges medals with Carmelite College, Moate. Also played with Tullamore.

Murrihy, John (football)

▸ *Played senior football for Clare during the 1960s. Father of famed opera singer Paula Murrihy.*

Murtagh, Padraig (football)

▸ *Native of Longford; played senior football for Longford (2006).*
Career/honours: played minor and U21 football for Longford; three U21 'A' championship medals, 2001, 2002 and 2003; senior championship medal, 2008.

Myles, Ailish (camogie)

▸ *Native of Tipperary; played senior camogie for Tipperary, 1989-98.*
Career/honours: **All-Ireland junior medal, 1992***; two interprovincial titles with Munster; county junior 'A' championship (1997), junior 'B' league (1998) and intermediate championship (1998) with Templemore Camogie Club; interprovincial senior champions, 1993; three Munster junior medals, 1990, 1991 and 1992; U18 Munster champions, 1990;; interprovincial junior champions, 1992.*

N

Nally, John (football)

▸ *Played senior football for Mayo.*

Nally, Shane (football)

▸ *Native of Mayo; played senior football for Mayo, 2010, 2016 to present.*
Career/honours: played minor football for Mayo, 2007 and 2008 (captain in 2008); played U21 football for Mayo, 2010 and 2011; All-Ireland runners-up and Connacht medals, 2008.Club: Garrymore.

Nash, Michael (hurling)

▸ *Native of Kilkenny; played senior hurling for Kilkenny, 1977-82.*
Career/honours: **All-Ireland minor medal, 1977***; played minor and U21 hurling for Kilkenny; Leinster U21 and All-Ireland finalist medals, 1988; Leinster minor medal, 1977.*

Nash, Mike (hurling)

▸ *Native of Limerick; played senior hurling for Limerick, 1993-97.*
Career/honours: minor (1982) and U21 (1985-86); two All-Ireland finalist medals; two Munster senior championship medals; one National League medal. Club: South Liberties.

Naughton, Gerry (hurling)

▶ *Native of Roscommon; played senior hurling for Roscommon, 1971-88. Career/honours: Division 3 National League medal, 1983; two senior club championship medals with Athleague; junior club football championship medal with Colmcille, Longford.*

Naughton, Patrick (football)

▶ *Native of Sligo; played senior football for Sligo, 2000-08. Career/honours: FBD League medal, 2001. Club: Castleconnor – Connacht championship medal, 2007; intermediate club championship medal, 1998.*

Newton, Gerry (football)

▶ *Native of Leitrim; played senior football for Leitrim, 1985. Career/honours: played U21 Football for Leitrim.*

Newton, John (football)

▶ *Native of Roscommon; played senior football for Roscommon, 1983-95. Career/honours: two Connacht medals, 1990, 1991 (captain); National League medal, Division 2 1990; senior club league medals with Garda team; senior club league medal, Kildare. Nominated for four All Star awards: 1989, 1990, 1991 and 1993. Railway Cup career with Connacht: 1988-95. Former Roscommon Player of the Year.*

Neylon, Anthony (hurling)

▶ *Native of Clare; hurled at senior level for Clare, 1930-40. Club: Newmarket-on-Fergus.*

Nicholson, Fran (football)

▶ *Native of Roscommon; played senior football for Roscommon, 1984-87. Career/honours: four All-Ireland club finalist medals, 1983, 1987, 1988, 1990; minor Connacht championship medal with Clann na Gael;* **thirteen senior club championship medals, including eight in a row from 1984-91; seven Connacht club titles, including six in a row from 1984-89.**

Nohilly, Gerry (football)

▶ *Native of Galway; played senior football for Galway (1976-77) and Westmeath (1974-76 and 1980-82). Career/honours: three senior club championship medals with Mullingar Shamrocks; junior championship medal with Headford, Galway.*

Nolan, Louis (football)

▶ *Native of Kerry; played senior football for Kerry, 1962. Club: Killarney Legion, East Kerry. Won one senior championship with East Kerry.*

Nolan, Peter (football)

▶ *Native of Wicklow; played senior football for Wicklow, 1979.*
Wicklow arrived in Nowlan Park, Kilkenny for a league match with only ten players because one of the team buses broke down. They fielded a team with three Wicklow officials and a seventeen-year-old supporter called Peter Nolan, and went on to win the match by 0-8 to 0-3!

Noonan, Chris (football)

▸ *Native of Limerick; played senior football for Limerick, 1981-88.*
Career/honours: played junior and U21 football; junior club championship medal,
1996

Norton, Geraldine (ladies' football)

▸ *Plays senior ladies' football for Wicklow.*

Nugent, Barry (hurling)

▸ *Native of Clare; played senior hurling for Clare, 2002, 2004, 2005-10.*
Career/honours: two senior 'B'medals (2010 and 2014) and one intermediate
championship medal (2013) with Éire Óg, Ennis.

Nugent, Pamela (camogie)

▸ *Native of Offaly; played senior camogie for Offaly, 2011-12.*
Career/honours: played junior camogie for Offaly, 1996-99; Leinster junior
medal, 1999; London senior team, 2004-08. Club: Drumcullen. Played for Team
Great Britain in the International Camogie Games, 2004.

O

O'Brien, Conor (hurling)

▸ *Native of Tipperary; played senior hurling for Tipperary, 2007-17.*
*Career/honours: **two senior All-Ireland medals, 2010 and 2016**; three All-*
Ireland finalist medals ,2009, 2011, and 2014; four Munster senior medals, 2008,
2009, 2012 and 2015; Munster minor medal, 2003; Munster U21 medals, 2004
and 2006; National League medal, 2008; nominated for an All Star in 2008.
County intermediate championship medal, 2006; two West Tipperary senior
hurling medals, 2013 and 2014; two Fitzgibbon Cup medals with Waterford
IT, 2009 and 2006; county intermediate championship medal with Éire Óg
Annacarty, 2006.

O'Brien, Dermot (football)

▸ *Native of Dublin; played senior football for Dublin, 1983, 1986 and 1990.*
Career/honours: played U21 football for Dublin; All-Ireland U21 finalist medal,
1980; two senior county championship medals with Scoil Uí Chonaill in 1983
and 1986.

O'Brien, Dermot (football)

▸ *Native of Clare; played senior football for Clare, 1998-2008.*
Career/honours: played minor and U21 football for Clare; four senior and four
U21 club championship medals with Kilmurry Ibrickane; two Munster club
championship medals; Tommy Murphy Cup medal, 2004. Son of John O'Brien
(see below).

O'Brien, Des (football)

▸ *Played senior football for Galway, Tipperary and Offaly.*
*Career/honours: **All-Ireland 'B' medal in 1995**; Tommy Murphy Cup in 2005;*
captained Tipperary to win McGrath Cup in 2003; Railway Cup for Munster in
2003; three senior club championship medals with Clonmel Commercials.

O'Brien, John (football)

▶ *Native of Dublin; played senior football for Dublin, 2008.*
  Career/honours: U17 Leinster, 2003; U17 International Rules, 2003; Dublin
  minor (Leinster winners, All-Ireland runner-up) 2003; Dublin minor, 2004;
  Dublin U21 (2005 Leinster winner), 2005-07; O'Byrne Cup medal. Ulster
  Bank Rising Star award, 2008; World Police and Fire Games gold medal, 2013.

O'Brien, John (hurling)

▶ *Native of Clare; played senior hurling for Leitrim, 1976-78.*
  Career/honours: County senior championship medals in football and hurling.
  In 1977, he scored 3-1 out of a team total of 3-6 in the county senior
  hurling final with Allen Gaels, Drumshanbo, and also won the county
  football title with Glencar/Manorhamilton in the same year.

O'Brien, Mick (hurling)

▶ *Native of Limerick; played senior hurling for Limerick (1965–66).*
  Career/honours: played minor, intermediate and senior hurling, 1965–66; three
  county senior club championship medals in Limerick. Club: Monaleen.

O'Brien, Paul (football)

▶ *Native of Waterford; played senior football for Waterford, 1975.*
  Career/honours: senior county championship medal with Dunhill, 1975.

O'Brien, Sean (football)

▶ *Played senior football for Mayo.*
  Career/honours: also played minor and junior football for Mayo; junior and minor
  county championship medals with Swinford, 1951 and 1952.

O'Callaghan, Fergal (football)

▶ *Native of Tipperary; played senior football for Tipperary, 1999-2005.*
  Career/honours: **All-Ireland 'B' medal in 1995;** *Tommy Murphy Cup in 2005;*
  captained Tipperary to win the McGrath Cup in 2003; Railway Cup for Munster
  in 2003; three senior club championship medals with Clonmel Commercials.

O'Carroll, Seamus (football)

▶ *Native of Limerick; played senior football for Limerick, 2010-14.*
  Career/honours: two National League Division 4 medals, 2010 and 2013;
  Munster senior finalist medal, 2010; played U21 hurling for Limerick; junior 'A'
  club championship medal with Cappagh.

O'Carroll, Stephen (hurling)

▶ *Native of Kerry; played senior hurling for Kerry, 1974-78.*
  Career/honours: Won four senior hurling championship club medals with
  Causeway.

O'Connell, Aishling (ladies' football)

▶ *Has played senior for Kerry ladies since 2015 (to present).*
  Career/honours: two Munster ladies' SFC medals.

O'Connell, David (football)

▸ *Native of Galway; played senior football for Galway, 2013-15.*
Career/honours: club minor County championship medal, 2006 Connacht Colleges medals, 2004, 2005 and 2006

O'Connell, Graham (football)

▸ *Native of Kerry; played senior football for Limerick.*
Career/honours: **All-Ireland U21 medal with Kerry, 2008**; *two Kerry senior league medals with Austin Stacks. Club: Monaleen.*

O'Connell, J (football)

▸ *Played senior football for Waterford.*
Career/honours: a sub in Waterford's Munster SFC first round game against Clare, May 1952.

O'Connell, Joe (football)

▸ *Native of Mayo; played senior football for Mayo, 1952-59.*
Career/honours: played minor and junior football for Mayo; junior and minor county championship medals with Swinford.

O'Connell, Ken (football)

▸ *Native of Cork; played senior football for Cork, 1995-97.*
Career/honours: played minor 1992-93, U21 1995-96, and junior 1995-97 for Cork; **All-Ireland minor medal, 1993; All-Ireland junior medal, 1996.** *Club: St Kevin's.*

O'Connell, Linda (ladies' football)

▸ *Native of Cork; played ladies' senior football for Cork, 1997-2000.*
Career/honours: **one All-Ireland senior club medal with Donoughmore;** *played junior football, 2004-07. Eight county medals, three Munster medals.*

O'Connell, M.

▸ *Played inter-county for Donegal, 1924.*

O'Connell, Mick

▸ *Native of Cork; played inter-county for Cavan, 2004-11.*

O' Connell, Noel (hurling)

▸ *Native of Kerry; played senior hurling for Leitrim, and club hurling for Austin Stacks (Kerry).*

O'Connell, Pat (hurling)

▸ *Native of Kerry; played senior hurling for Kerry, 1994-96.*
Career/honours: Lixnaw – two Kerry senior hurling championships, 1999 and 2005; County Kerry senior hurling league medals. Finuge GFC – one North Kerry senior football championship,1996. Monaghan Harps Hurling Club – one Monaghan senior hurling championship, 1998. J. K. Brackens Hurling and Football Club – one Tipperary county junior football championship, 2003. Railway Cup hurling with Munster.

O'Connell, Sarah (ladies' football)

▶ *Native of Cork; played ladies' senior football for Cork, 2005-06.*

O'Connell, Sean (football)

▶ *Played senior football for Offaly during the 1950s. Founder member of St Raphael's Garda Credit Union.*

O'Connell, Shane (football)

▶ *Native of Clare; played senior football for Clare, 2012. Club: Éire Óg.*

O'Connell, Stephen (hurling)

▶ *Native of Kerry; played senior hurling for Kerry, 1979.*
Career/honours: played minor hurling and football, and U21 hurling .

O'Connor, Arthur (football)

▶ *Native of Longford; played senior football for Longford, 2000-10. Club: Abbeylara.*

O'Connor, Brendan (football)

▶ *Native of Roscommon; played senior football for Roscommon during the 1960s.*

O'Connor, Carrie (ladies' football)

▶ *Native of Dublin; played ladies' senior football for Dublin, 2008-10.*
Career/honours: **All-Ireland senior medal, 2010**. *Club: Clontarf.*

O'Connor, David (football)

▶ *Native of Roscommon; played senior football for Roscommon (1989-97).*
Career/honours: two Connacht senior championship medals; captained the Roscommon team. Played minor and U21 football. Clubs: Garda, Dublin and St Dominic's.

O'Connor, Donal (hurling)

▶ *Native of Kerry; played senior hurling for Kerry, 1975-77. Club: Kilgarvan.*
Career/honours: **All-Ireland 'B' medal, 1976**; *Munster minor medal, 1970;* **All-Ireland Interfirms medal with Cork, 1978**; *U21 championship medal with Roughty Rovers; Munster minor football medal with Kerry, 1970; intermediate championship medal with Kenmare.*

O'Connor, Jerry (hurling)

▶ *Native of Cork; played senior hurling for Cork, 2000-09.*
Career/honours: **two All-Ireland senior medals, 2004 and 2005; three All Star awards, 2004, 2005 and 2006 (all at midfield); Hurler of the Year, 2005; one All-Ireland senior club medal with Newtownshandrum, 2003-04**; *four Munster senior hurling medals, 2000, 2003, 2005 and 2006. With Newtownshandrum: four Cork County senior hurling medals, 2000, 2003, 2005 and 2009; three Munster senior club hurling medals, 2003, 2005 and 2009.*

O'Connor, Marie (camogie)

▶ *Native of Kilkenny; played senior camogie for Kilkenny, 2000-12.*
Career/honours: **junior All-Ireland medal, 2002; three All-Ireland club medals with St Lachtains, Freshford, Kilkenny, 2004, 2005 and 2006; All-Ireland club player of the match, 2006**; *five Leinster Club medals;* **twelve senior club county medals**; *two National League medals, (captain in 2008); Purcell Cup medal with Garda College, 2005; Ashbourne Shield medal with Garda College, 2007.*

O'Connor, Mossie (football)

▶ *Native of Kerry; played senior football for Kerry, 1969.*
Career/honours: two county and league championship medals; Munster senior club championship medal. Club: Castlegregory.

O'Connor, Paddy (football)

▶ *Native of Kerry; played senior football for Kerry.*
Career/honours: played his club football with Waterville; won an All-Ireland Vocational Schools medal with the Kerry Techs in 1973; played minor football for Kerry, 1973.

O'Connor, Ronan (hurling)

▶ *Native of Kerry; played senior hurling for Kerry and London. Club: Ballyduff.*

O'Connor, Sean (football)

▶ *Native of Kerry; played senior football for Kerry during the 1940s and 1950s.*
Career/honours: played minor football; two Munster minor medals, 1947 and 1948; one Munster senior medal, 1951; senior county championship medal with Castleisland, 1950.

O'Dare, Jack (football)

▶ *Native of Meath; played senior football for Meath, 1961-63.*
Career/honours: played minor hurling for Meath; senior club championship medal with Trim, 1961.

O'Dea, Ned (hurling)

▶ *Native of Cork; played senior hurling for Cork (1952) and Dublin (1958-59).*
Career/honours: Senior club championship medals with Avondhu, Cork (1952) and in Dublin (1955-59)Other clubs: Garda, Dublin and New Irelands.

O'Donnell, Fergal (football)

▶ *Native of Roscommon; played senior football for Roscommon, 1995-2004.*
Career/honours: played minor football; Connacht minor medal, 1989; Connacht senior medal, 2001 (captain); five county senior championship medals with Roscommon Gaels, 1994, 1998, 1999, 2001, 2004; Trench Cup medal, Garda College, 1994. Inter-county manager with Roscommon, 2015 and Roscommon minor team, 2006 and 2013.

O'Donnell, James (football)

▶ *Native of Mayo; played senior football for Dublin, 2000.*

O'Donnell, Jim (hurling)

▸ *Native of Limerick; played senior hurling for Limerick, 1964–74.*
Career/honours: **All-Ireland senior medal, 1973;** *played minor and intermediate hurling; two Munster championship medals, 1973 and 1974; National League medal, 1971. Nominated for All Star award, 1971; county minor medal with Doon, 1959.*

O'Donnell, Jim (football)

▸ *Native of Kildare; played senior football for Kildare, 1956–64.*
Career/honours: two senior championship medals with Clane, 1963 and 1967.

O'Donnell, Michael (hurling)

▸ *Played senior hurling for Limerick, 2001–08. Club: Doon.*

O'Donnell, Niall (football)

▸ *Native of Louth; played senior football for Louth, 1987–99.*
Career/honours: four Louth senior championships; eight Louth senior leagues; four Louth ACC Cups; **one All-Ireland 'B' championship***; one Division 3 National League medal; one Division 2 National League medal.*

O'Donnell, Seamus (football)

▸ *Native of Mayo; played senior football for Mayo (1952–56) and Louth (1957–60)*
Career/honours: **All-Ireland senior medal, 1957 (Louth***); played minor football for Mayo, 1950–52; Connacht senior medal with Mayo, 1955; Leinster senior medal with Louth, 1957; National League medal with Mayo, 1954; Connacht minor medal with Mayo, 1950; senior county championship in Meath with Athboy.*

O'Donnell, Tim (football)

▸ *Played senior football for Dublin in 1935.*

O'Donnell, Tim (football)

▸ *Native of Kerry; played senior football for Kerry in the 1920s and 1930s. Clubs: Camp and Dr Crokes.*
Career/honours: **three All-Ireland senior medals***; six Munster SFC medals; three National League medals; Garda Hall of Fame award, 1997.*

O'Donnell, Tom (hurling)

▸ *Played senior hurling for Limerick.*

O'Donnell, Vincent (football)

▸ *Native of Tipperary; played senior football for Tipperary in the 1970s and 1980s.*
Career/honours: Railway Cup with Munster, 1978. Club: Galtee Rovers.

O'Donoghue, Jim (football)

▸ *Native of Cork; played senior football for Cork, 2002–03.*
Career/honours: Munster club championship medal, 2002; Premier intermediate club medal with St Finbarr's, 2008.

O'Donoghue, Noel (football/hurling)

▶ *Native of Limerick; played senior hurling (1979-91) and senior football (1976-77); represented both Limerick and Kildare.*
Career/honours: **made the Kildare "All Star" team of 1995**.

O'Donovan, Brian (football)

▶ *Native of Cork; played senior football for Cork (1993-95).*
Career/honours: **All-Ireland Club medal with O' Donovan Rossa, 1993**; *Munster senior club medal; county senior club medal with O'Donovan Rossa,* **1992; one All-Ireland Interfirms medal in 1996 with Cork Garda.**

O'Dowd, Fred (football)

▶ *Native of Sligo; played senior football for Sligo and Donegal during the 1960s.*
Career/honours: two senior championship medals, one with St Eunan's (1969), one with Bundoran (1979).

O'Dowd, Gerry Noel (football)

▶ *Native of Roscommon; played senior football for Roscommon, 1975-78.*
Career/honours: Connacht senior medal, 1977; intermediate county medal with Boyle, 1983.

O'Dowd, Harry (football)

▶ *Native of Leitrim; played senior football for Sligo in the 1950s.*
Career/honours: four senior club championship medals with Sean O'Heslins, 1967-69 (three in a row) and 1972.

O'Dowd, Mattie (football)

▶ *Native of Cavan; played senior football for Monaghan during the 1950s.*
Career/honours: played minor and junior football; three minor county championship medals with Monaghan, 1952, 1953 and 1954; **All-Ireland junior medal with Monaghan, 1956**. *Played with the Cork Garda team.*

O'Driscoll, Ger (football)

▶ *Native of Kerry; played senior football for Kerry, 1975-82.*
Career/honours: **two senior All-Ireland medals, 1975 and 1980; one U21 All-Ireland medal, 1975; one junior All-Ireland medal, 1983**; *one All-Ireland senior finalist medal, 1976; one National League medal; one Railway Cup medal, Munster; played interprovincial football for Munster; two senior county championship medals with Young Irelanders. Also played for Valentia and South Kerry.*

O'Driscoll, Paddy (football/hurling)

▶ *Native of Cork; played senior football for Cork (1948-59) and senior hurling for Kerry.*
Career/honours: **All-Ireland junior medal with Cork;** *played junior hurling for Cork, 1949-51; played senior hurling for Kerry; captain of Cork, 1958; All-Ireland senior football finalist medal for Cork 1959; four Munster senior championship medals with Cork; three National League medals with Cork. Clubs: Russell Rovers and Garda. Selector on Cork's All-Ireland winning team of 1973. Played for Ireland in 1953, 1954 and 1957.*

O'Dwyer, Brian (hurling)

▸ *Native of Tipperary; played senior hurling for Tipperary 1994.*
Career/honours: played minor and intermediate with Tipperary, and intermediate
hurling with Limerick. Minor B U21a U21B and Intermediate Championship
medals with Moneygall.
Shinty interantional cap 1993

O'Dwyer, Kevin (football)

▸ *Native of Cork native, played senior football for Cork, 1993-2005.*
Career/honours: **one All Star award – goalkeeper; minor All-Ireland medal,**
1991; U21 All-Ireland medal, 1994; All-Ireland senior club medal with
O'Donovan Rossa, 1993; *five Munster medals; one National League medal;*
Cork County senior championship medal, 1992; Munster Club medal, 1992.

O'Dwyer, Tom (hurling)

▸ *Native of Tipperary; played senior hurling for Tipperary, 1993-94.*
Career/honours: National League medal, 1993-94.

Ó Giollain, Colm (hurling)

▸ *Native of Dublin; played senior hurling for Dublin, 1989-93.*
Career/honours: two Dublin senior championship medals with Cuala, 1989,
1991.

O'Grady, Dan (football)

▸ *Native of Mayo; played senior football for Leitrim.*

O'Grady, Sean (football)

▸ *Native of Mayo; played senior football for Mayo, 1969-74.*
Career/honours: minor (1965-67) and U21 (1968-70) football; senior county
championship medal with Roscommon Gaels, 1979-81; National League medal,
1970; three minor Connacht medals; two U21 Connacht medals; one senior
Connacht medal.

O'Gorman, Canice (hurling)

▸ *Native of Kilkenny; played senior hurling for Louth, 1984-88.*
Career/honours: played minor hurling for Kilkenny, 1980.

O'Gorman, Paudge (hurling)

▸ *Played senior hurling for Wexford.*

Ó Griofa, Peadar Óg (football)

▸ *Native of Galway; played senior football for Galway, 2014-16.*
Career/honours: played minor and U21 football for Galway. Club: Micheál
Breathnach.

O'Hanlon, Seamus (football)

▸ *Native of Armagh; played senior football for Tipperary, 1958-59.*
Career/honours: played junior football for Tipperary, 1958; played minor football
for Armagh, 1952-53; Munster interprovincial team, 1959; minor Ulster
championship medal, 1953; McRory Cup and Rannafast medals with St Patrick's
College, 1953. Also played with Rockwell Rovers and New Inn.

O'Hara, Ronan (hurling)

▶ *Native of Clare; played senior hurling for Clare, 1995-2000.*
Career/honours: played minor football and hurling; U21 hurling; Munster finalist
medal, 1999. Club: Cratloe.

O'Keeffe, Brian (football)

▶ *Native of Wicklow; played senior football for Wicklow.*
Career/honours: **All-Ireland junior medal, 2002;** *played minor and U21*
football for Wicklow.

O'Keeffe, Declan (football)

▶ *Native of Kerry; played senior football for Kerry, 1996-2003.*
Career/honours: **two senior All-Ireland medals, 1997 and 2000; two All**
Star Awards – goalkeeper, 1997 and 2000; *three Munster U21 medals, 1991-*
93; **All-Ireland junior football medal, 1994;** *six senior Munster medals; one*
National Football League medal; one Munster medal, 1990; Railway Cup,
Munster; three county senior championship medals with East Kerry, 1978, 1979,
1980. **International Rules player, 1990.** *Club: Rathmore.*

O'Keeffe, Phil (football)

▶ *Native of Laois; played senior football for Cork. Also played minor football for*
Laois.

O'Keeffe, Valerie (camogie)

▶ *Played senior camogie for Cork in the 2000s.*
Career/honours: **All-Ireland junior camogie medal (2004, captain).** *Club:*
Timoleague.

O'Kelly, Derek (football)

▶ *Native of Mayo; played senior football for Mayo, 1967.*

O'Leary, Colm (hurling)

▶ *Native of Tipperary; played senior hurling for Wexford, 1989.*
Career/honours: two senior club and league championship medals with Cuala
(Dublin).

O'Leary, Denis (football)

▶ *Native of Cork; played senior football for Wicklow, 1956-60.*
Career/honours: O'Byrne Cup medal, 1957; father of All-Ireland winning
captain John O'Leary, 1995.

O'Leary, Tim 'Gunner' (football)

▶ *Native of Cork; played senior football for Cork, 1958-66.*
Career/honours: played minor football, 1955-56; played junior football for Cork;
one Munster senior medal, 1966; two senior and one minor county championship
medals with Macroom. Played with Cork Garda GAA Club.

O'Loughlin, Mick (football)

▶ *Native of Cork; played senior football for Cork, 1963-71.*
Career/honours: All-Ireland finalist medal, 1967; intermediate hurling, 1967-
71; **All-Ireland junior medal, 1964;** *senior county hurling championship medal*
with Blackrock and intermediate football championship medal with Bishopstown.

O'Mahony, Aidan (football)

▶ *Native of Kerry; played senior football for Kerry, 2004 to present. Club: Rathmore.* *Career/honours:* **five All-Ireland senior medals, 2004, 2006, 2007, 2009 and 2014; man of the match in 2006 final; two All Star Awards (left half back, 2006 and centre half back, 2007)**; *seven Munster championship medals; one junior championship senior medal, 1998; one Munster junior championship, 1998; one intermediate senior medal, 1999; one county senior championship medal with East Kerry, 1999; one U21 county championship medal with East Kerry, 1999; one senior club championship, 2011; two O'Donoghue Cup medals, 2005 and 2014.Played interprovincial football for Munster.* Club: Rathmore. He once played on in a club match having sustained a broken leg, scoring two points. Played in six successive All-Ireland finals.

O'Mahony, Cian (hurling)

▶ *Native of Dublin; played senior hurling for Fingal, 2008-11.* *Career/honours: Cian scored a hat trick of goals in four minutes in a Kehoe Cup match against Louth.*

O'Mahony, Liam (football)

▶ *Native of Offaly; played senior football for Offaly in the 1980s.* *Career/honours:* **All-Ireland senior medal, 1982**; *Leinster medal, 1982. Club: St Rynagh's.*

O'Mahony, Owen (football)

▶ *Native of Cork; played senior football for Cork, 1981-89.* *Career/honours:* **All-Ireland senior medal, 1989; All-Ireland minor medal, 1981**; *U21 and junior football for Cork. Interprovincial football for Munster.* **Won an All-Ireland Club championship medal with Nemo Rangers in 1989 scoring 1-8 (record only equalised twice). Three All-Ireland Interfirms medals in 1986, 1987 and 1996 with Cork Garda.**

O'Mahony, Pat (football)

▶ *Native of Kerry; played senior football for Kerry, 1977-78. Club: Skellig Rangers.* *Career/honours:* **All-Ireland senior medal, 1978; All-Ireland junior football medal, 1983**; *minor football Kerry 1972-73; four county championship medals with East Kerry and South Kerry.*

O'Malley, Padraic (hurling)

▶ *Native of Kildare; played senior hurling for Kildare, 1994-95.* *Career/honours: played minor and U21 hurling for Kildare; two All-Ireland 'B' Hurling finalist medals, 1994, 1995.*

O'Malley, Ronan (hurling)

▶ *Native of Kildare; played senior hurling for Kildare, 1995-99, 2005-08.* *Career/honours: senior club hurling championship medal for Ardclough, 2004 and 2006; Leinster intermediate club championship medal, 2006; captain of Kildare, 2007.*

O'Mara, Phil (football)

▶ *Native of Waterford; played senior football for Tipperary, 1963.* *Career/honours: won three senior club championship medals with Railyard, Kilkenny; won numerous county junior hurling and football medals with different clubs.*

O'Meara, Ronan (hurling)

▶ *Native of Tipperary; played senior hurling for Roscommon, 2013 to present. Career/honours: one Nicky Rackard finalist medal, 2013; Nicky Rackard winners medal, 2015; intermediate championship medal with Lorrha, 2007; Nicky Rackard Champion 15 award, 2013.*

O'Neill, Dan (football)

▶ *Native of Mayo; played senior football for Mayo (1952-55, 1962-63) and Louth (1956-62).*
Career/honours: **All-Ireland senior medal with Louth, 1957**; *Connacht senior medal, 1955; Leinster senior medal, 1957; National League medal with Mayo, 1954; five county championship medals with Castlebar Mitchels, 1951, 1953, 1954, 1957, 1963; Leinster Railway Cup team.*
Author of Divided Loyalties – the story of why he dramatically quit his native Mayo and went on to All-Ireland success with Louth.

O'Neill, Mick (football)

▶ *Native of Cork; played senior football with Cork in the 1960s. Career/honours: played minor football for Cork, 1957, scored 3-4 from play in one game. Clubs: Beara, Waterville and South Kerry. Inter-county referee. Scott medal, 1976.*

O'Neill, Pat (hurling)

▶ *Native of Tipperary; played senior hurling for Tipperary in the 1970s. Club: Cappawhite.*

O'Neill, Seamus (football)

▶ *Native of Limerick; played senior football for Limerick during the 1980s. Career/honours: junior football with Limerick; county, junior, intermediate and senior medals in Limerick.*

O'Neill, Shane (football)

▶ *Native of Wicklow; played senior football with Wicklow, 1999-2002. Career/honours: O'Byrne Cup medal, 1996; Division 4 National League medal, 1996.*

O'Regan, Jim (football/hurling)

▶ *Native of Cork native played senior hurling (1925) and senior football for Cork; senior football and hurling for Dublin (1926-35).*
Career/honours: **four All-Ireland senior medals, 1926, 1928, 1929 and 1931**; *All-Ireland finalist medal, 1927; four Munster senior hurling medals; two National League hurling medals; Munster senior football medal; Railway Cup football and hurling for Munster; played junior hurling for Offaly; senior club championship medal with Garda. Clubs: Kinsale, Garda, Courcey Rovers.*
Played for Ireland vs USA in the Tailteann Games of 1932. Selector, Cork, All-Ireland winners, 1966. Inter-county referee.
Centre back on the Cork hurling team of the century. Refereed the All-Ireland hurling final between Limerick and Kilkenny in 1936.

O'Reilly, Declan (football)

▶ *Native of Dublin; played senior football for Dublin, 1995.*

O'Reilly, James (football)

▸ *Native of Kildare; played senior football for Kildare in the 1920s and 1930s.*
Career/honours: Leinster senior medal; Railway Cup football for Leinster, 1930.

O'Reilly, John Joe (football)

▸ *Native of Cavan; played senior football for Cavan, 1962-72.*
Career/honours: three senior Ulster championship medals, 1964, 1967 and 1969;
seven club championships in a row and league medals with Crosserlough; played
junior football for Cavan; All-Ireland junior runner-up medal, 1962. Played for
All-Ireland Garda team. Played in Wembley against Sligo, 1966 and Galway,
1967.

O'Reilly, Kathleen (ladies' football)

▸ *Native of Laois; played ladies' senior football for Laois in the 1990s.*

O'Reilly, Seamus (football)

▸ *Native of Mayo; played senior football for Mayo (1971-76) and Donegal (1979-84).*
Career/honours: **All-Ireland minor medal, 1971, Mayo; All-Ireland U21 medal, 1974**, *Mayo; four Connacht senior and two minor championship medals, Mayo; one Ulster senior championship medal, Donegal, 1983; one All-Ireland U21 finalist medal, 1973. Nominated for an All Star award, 1974 (full back). Senior county championship medal with Bundoran, 1979. Inter-county management: Donegal U21s.*
The Seamus O' Reilly Memorial Tournament ran from 2002 to 2013. This involved the best players of each Garda Region playing each other. The tournament was dedicated to Seamus and his family kindly donated a trophy in his honour (see elsewhere in this book).

Organ, Eugene (hurling)

▸ *Played senior hurling for Donegal, 2003-14.*

O'Riordan, Michael (football/hurling)

▸ *Native of Tipperary; played senior hurling (1986-87) and senior football (1976-86) for Tipperary.*
Career/honours: played junior hurling; National League Division 2 medal; four senior county championship medals with Fethard; one junior championship medal with Simonstown (Meath).

Ormsby, George (football)

▸ *Native of Mayo; played senior football for Mayo during the 1930s.*
Career/honours: **All-Ireland senior medal, 1936**; *six National League medals, 1934-39 (record); Railway Cup football with Connacht.*
Involved in the 1938 case when he was suspended by Sligo GAA county board for attending a soccer match while on duty. He was reinstated by the Connacht Council when it was learned that he had been on duty at the match. The incident features in the book *The GAA v Douglas Hyde* by Cormac Moore.

O'Rourke, Kevin (football)

▸ *Native of Longford; played senior football for Cavan (1979-82) and Longford (1982-94).*
Career/honours: Division 3 National League medal; played U21 football for Cavan.

O'Rourke, Kevin (hurling)

▸ *Native of Meath; played senior hurling for Meath (2009).*
Career/honours: Nicky Rackard medal, 2009; five U21 county medals with Navan O'Mahony's.

O'Rourke, Tom (hurling)

▸ *Native of Clare; played senior hurling for Dublin and Clare during the 1920s.*
Career/honours: **All-Ireland senior medal with Dublin, 1927**; *All-Ireland senior finalist medal with Clare, 1932.*

O'Ryan, Martina (ladies' football)

▸ *Native of Waterford; played ladies' senior football for Waterford, 1989-2002.*
Career/honours: **five All-Ireland medals with Waterford, 1991, 1992, 1994, 1995 and 1998;**
nine club All-Ireland medals with Ballymacarbry, Waterford, 1989, 1990, 1991, 1992, 1993, 1994, 1995, 1997 and 1998;
four All Stars, 1991, 1992, 1994 at full back and 2000 at centre back;
fifteen county medals with Ballymacarbry, Waterford.

Ó Sé, Páidí (football)

▸ *Native of Kerry; played senior football for Kerry, 1974-88.*
Career/honours: **as player – eight All-Ireland senior football championship medals, 1975, 1978, 1979, 1980, 1981, 1984, 1985 (captain) and 1986; five All Star awards, 1981 (right half back), 1982 (right half back), 1983 (right full back), 1984 (right full back) and 1985 (right full back)**; *played minor and U21 football; eleven Munster senior football championship medals, 1975, 1976, 1977, 1978, 1979, 1980, 1981, 1982, 1984, 1985 (captain) and 1986; four National Football League medals, 1974, 1977, 1982 and 1984; four Railway Cup medals with Munster, 1976, 1978, 1981 and 1982; two county senior championship medals, 1984 and 1985; four Munster U21 football championship medals, 1973, 1974, 1975 and 1976;* **three All-Ireland U21 football championship medals, 1973, 1975 and 1976;As inter-county manager –** *Kerry: two All-Ireland senior football championships, 1997 and 2000; six Munster senior football championships 1996, 1997, 1998, 2000, 2001 and 2003. Kerry U21s: one All-Ireland U21 football championship, 1995; two Munster U21 football championships, 1993 and 1995; one National Football League, 1997. Westmeath: one Leinster senior football championship, 2004. West Kerry: three county senior championships 1984, 1985 (player/manager) and 1990. Was also inter-county manager of Clare.*
Uncle of Kerry football greats Darragh, Tomás and Marc Ó Sé. Club: An Ghaeltacht (with whom he won a West Kerry league medal, 1988). Played rugby for a year with Young Munster. Became a successful publican in his native Ventry; died suddenly on 15 December 2012.
Ranked at no. 26 in the *Irish Independent 125 Greatest GAA stars*. One of the few people who captained and managed a team to All-Ireland wins.

O'Shaughnessy, Brian (football)

Laois; played senior football for Laois. Club: Ballinakill.

O'Shea, Denis (football)

▸ *Native of Cork; played senior football for Cork (1958-59) and Galway (1962). Career/honours: played junior football for Galway; All-Ireland junior finalist medal with Galway, 1961; county senior championship medal with Macroom, 1958.*

O'Shea, James (football)

▸ *Native of Kerry; played senior football for Kerry (1996-99) and Cork (2002-04). Career/honours:* **minor All-Ireland medal (Kerry), 1994; All-Ireland U21 medal (Kerry), 1996;** *one Munster minor and three U21 medals (Kerry); one National League medal (Cork); one Munster senior championship medal (Cork), 2002. With St Michael's/Foilmore: one All-Ireland intermediate club title, 2009; two South Kerry championship medals, 2007 and 2008. With South Kerry (Divisional): Kerry county U21, minor championships medals. With Bishopstown: Munster senior league club title, 2001. With Cork Garda:* **five All-Ireland senior Interfirm titles between 1996 and 2010 (player/manager for the last one in 2010). One All-Ireland junior Interfirm title.** *Top scorer in the Sigerson Cup final in 1995-96 with 1-2.*

O'Shea, Joe (football)

▸ *Native of Clare; played senior football for Clare, 1971-75 and 1980-82. Club: St Senan's, Kilkee.*

O'Shea, John (football)

▸ *Native of Tipperary; played senior football for Tipperary, 1973-78. Career/honours: minor hurling, 1970; U21 hurling and football, 1973; two senior county hurling championship medals with Faugh's, 1986 and 1987; captain of Dublin junior hurling team, 1988; manager of Dublin intermediate team, 2003. Chairman of West Tipperary Board.*

O'Shea, Martin (hurling)

▸ *Native of Kilkenny; played senior hurling for Galway, 1984-85.*
  Career/honours: senior county championship medal with Castlegar, 1984.

O'Shea, Michael (football)

▸ *Native of Clare; played senior football for Clare, 1999 to present. Career/honours: two senior club championship medals for St Senan's, Kilkee, 2003 and 2005*

O'Sullivan, Ashley (football)

▸ *Native of Wicklow; played senior football for Wicklow, 1981-95. Career/honours:* **All-Ireland 'B' medal;** *Division 3 and 4 National League medals; O'Byrne Cup medal; senior county championship medal with Dunlavin, 1981; Division 1, 2, 3 and 4 League medals with Garda Club (Dublin).*

O'Sullivan, Charlie (football)

▸ *Native of Kerry; played senior football for Kerry, 1933-41. Career/honours:* **four All-Ireland senior medals, 1937, 1939, 1940 and 1941. Scored the winning point in the 1940 final.** *Seven Munster senior championship medals; Munster interprovincial player. Played with Garda, Dublin; Camp and Kerin O'Rahillys, Kerry.*

O'Sullivan, Dan (football)

▸ *Native of Kerry; played senior football for Kerry (1954) and Dublin (1952-54). Career/honours: founder member of the Garda basketball team; senior club championship medal with Garda, Dublin, 1948. The last non-Dubliner to play for Dublin. Clubs: Garda, Dublin, and Listry, Kerry.*

O'Sullivan, Eamon (hurling)

▸ *Native of Kerry; played senior hurling for Kerry, 1959-69. Career/honours:* **All-Ireland junior medal, 1961**; *three National League Division 3 medals; one Munster intermediate medal; one Munster junior football medal; eleven senior hurling county championship medals and eight senior league medals with Ballyduff (Kerry); one senior football county championship medal with Shannon Rangers.*

O'Sullivan, Frank (football)

▸ *Native of Limerick; played senior football for Limerick, 2000.*

O'Sullivan, Jeremiah F. (hurling)

▸ *Native of Kerry; played senior football for Kerry, 1948. Clubs: Templenoe and Killarney Legion.*

O'Sullivan, Jerry (hurling)

▸ *Native of Kerry; played senior hurling for Kerry, 1994-97. Club: St Mary's Firies.*

O'Sullivan, John F. (football)

▸ *Native of Kerry; played senior football for Kerry in the 1950s. Club: Garda, Dublin.*
"A master at judging the flight of the ball".

O'Sullivan, John Michael (hurling)

▸ *Native of Kerry; played senior hurling for Kerry, 1999. Career/honours: two junior hurling county championship medals; one North Kerry intermediate championship medal with Abbeydorney; one U16 'B' All-Ireland; one county and one Munster senior vocational schools championship with Causeway Comprehensive.*

O'Sullivan, Ollie Rua (football)

▸ *Native of Cork; played senior football for Cork in the 1990s. Career/honours: National League finalist medal, 1997.*

O'Sullivan, Teddy (football)

▸ *Native of Kerry; played senior football for Kerry, 1947-50. Career/honours:* **one All-Ireland senior medal, 1946**; *senior finalist medal, 1947, in New York; Railway Cup with Munster, 1948; senior championship medal with Garda, Dublin, 1948; senior league medals with the Legion, Killarney, 1943 and 1944. Played for Garda Club, Dublin.*
"A stylist supreme on the football pitch."

O'Sullivan, Teddy (football)

▶ *Native of Kerry; played senior football for Kerry, 1961.*
Career/honours: played club football for Templenoe and Shannon Rangers,
winning one senior county championship medal.

O'Sullivan, Tim (football)

▶ *Native of Kerry; played senior football for Kerry, 1979-80. Club: Finuge.*

O'Sullivan, Tom (football)

▶ *Native of Kerry; played senior football for Kerry, 1998-2011.*
**Career/honours: five All-Ireland senior championship medals, 2000, 2004,
2006, 2007 and 2009; two All Star Awards – 2004 (right full back) and 2009
(left full back); All-Ireland U21 championship medal, 1998; All-Ireland
senior final man of the match, 2009**; *eight Munster senior championship
medals, 2000, 2001, 2003, 2004, 2005, 2007, 2010 and 2011; two Munster
U21 championship medals, 1998 and 1999; three National Football League
medals, 2004, 2006 and 2009; two Kerry senior football championships with
East Kerry, 1998 and 1999; one Kerry club football championship, 2011; County
League Division 1 – 2002; Kerry intermediate football championship, 1999;
Kerry junior football championship, 2005; played interprovincial football for
Munster. Club: Rathmore.*
"Soundness personified at full back." Played in six successive All-Ireland
finals.

O'Toole, Joe (football)

▶ *Played senior football for Dublin, 1928-29.*

O'Toole, Michael (football)

▶ *Native of Mayo; played senior football for Mayo, 1977-82.*
*Career/honours: played minor and U21 football for Mayo; minor and U21
Connacht medals; replacement All Star, 1981; senior club league medal with
Belmullet, 1984.*

Owens, Anthony (hurling)

▶ *Native of Kilkenny; played senior hurling for Limerick 2010.* **Under 21 all
Ireland medal 2003-04.** *two Fitzgibbon Cup medals with WIT 2003-04 and
Munster intermediate club medal South Liberties 2010.*

P

Parnell, Oliver (hurling)

▶ *Native of Offaly; played senior hurling for Offaly in the 1970s.*
Career/honours: also played with Galway in the 1972 intermediate final.

Perry, T. (football)

▶ *Played senior football for Dublin, 1933.*

Pettit, Anthony (football)

▶ *Native of Wexford; played senior football for Wexford (1993-94).*
*Career/honours: played minor and U21 football for Wexford; Leinster junior
medal, 2000; two junior championship medals with St Fintan's.*

Phelan, Adrian (football)

▸ *Native of Laois; played senior football for Laois, 1991-2002.*
Career/honours: **All-Ireland 'B' football medal**; *two senior club championship medals; two O'Byrne Cup medals.* **Laois senior footballer of the year, 1995.**

Phelan, Bill (hurling)

▸ *Native of Kerry; played senior hurling for Kerry.*
Career/honours: played club hurling for Ballyduff, winning two senior county hurling championship medals.

Phelan, Willie (hurling)

▸ *Native of Laois; played senior hurling for Dublin.*
Career/honours: **All-Ireland senior medal, 1927.**

Phillips, Brendan (football)

▸ *Native of Sligo; played senior football for Sligo, 1999.*
Career/honours: played minor football for Sligo; senior club championship medal with Eastern Harps.

Power, Elizabeth (camogie)

▸ *Native of Cork; played senior camogie for Tipperary, 2012 to present.*
Career/honours: played intermediate camogie for Cork; one senior club championship medal with St Catherine's, Cork; Purcell Cup medal with Garda College, 2005; Ashbourne Shield medal with Garda College, 2007.

Power, Martin (football)

▸ *Native of Waterford; played senior football for Waterford, 1989-99.*
Career/honours: Railway Cup for Munster.

Power, Mattie (hurling)

▸ *Native of Kilkenny; played senior hurling for Kilkenny (1920-25 and 1931-37) and Dublin (1926-30).*
Career/honours: **five All Ireland senior medals with Kilkenny 1922, 1931, 1932, 1933 and 1935 and Dublin 1927**. *All-Ireland senior finalist medals with Kilkenny, 1926, 1936 and 1937 and Dublin, 1930; twelve Leinster senior medals with Kilkenny, 1922, 1923, 1931, 1932, 1933, 1935, 1936,1937, Dublin, 1927, 1928, 1930; two National League medals with Dublin, 1929.* **Played in eight All-Ireland finals**. *Six club championship medals with Garda; Railway Cup hurling with Leinster. Played for Ireland in the Tailteann Games of 1932. Clubs: Dicksboro and Garda, Dublin.*

Power, Nicky (hurling)

▸ *Native of Waterford; played senior hurling for Kilkenny (1960-63) and Waterford (1966-69).*
Career/honours: played minor (1956-58) and junior (1959-60) hurling for Waterford; Leinster senior medal with Kilkenny, 1963; National League medal with Kilkenny, 1962; eleven club championship medals in Kilkenny, Waterford, Dublin and Wicklow. Runner up in All-Ireland Poc Fada, 1967.

Power, Noel

▸ *Native of Cork; played inter-county for Kerry, 1968. Also played for the Garda team.*

Power, Noel (football and hurling)

▸ *Native of Waterford; played senior football for Kerry and Waterford and senior hurling for Kerry.*
Career/honours: junior football for Kerry; played minor football for Waterford, 1963; senior county football championship medal with Ardmore (Waterford), 1955; three senior county football championship medals with East Kerry, 1970, Austin Stacks, 1976, 1979; Munster **and All-Ireland Club championship medal, 1970-71 with East Kerry; Munster and All-Ireland Club championship medal, 1976-77 with Austin Stacks.**

Prendergast, Charles (football)

▸ *Native of Cavan; played senior football for Laois, 1981-82.*

Prendergast, Jim

▸ *Played inter-county for Kilkenny.*

Prendergast, Lisa (ladies' football)

▸ *Native of Waterford; played ladies' senior football for Waterford.*
Career/honours: Division 2 and 3 National League medals; Munster junior championship medal; club championship football medals (Old Parish, Thurles, Sarsfields); club championship hurling medals (An Rinn); U18 All-Ireland football medal; Intermediate 7s football medal. Sister of Waterford hurlers Seamus and Declan Prendergast.

Prendergast, Paddy (football)

▸ *Native of Mayo; played senior football for Mayo and Donegal, 1946-56.*
Career/honours: **two All-Ireland senior medals, 1950, 1951;** *National League medal; Railway Cup medal, 1951; five Connacht championship medals, 1948-55; West Mayo championship medal. Played for Ireland vs Combined Universities in 1952, 1956.*
"Definitely the most spectacular full back ever," according to Micheál Ó Muircheartaigh. Ranked no. 65 on the *Irish Independent 125 Greatest Stars of the GAA*. Selected on the Garda All Star team. Named in John Scally's book as one of the "GAA greats of Connacht".

Prendergast, Tom (football)

▸ *Native of Laois; played senior football for Laois, 1976-87.*
Career/honours: **one All-Ireland Club championship medal, 1983 (Portlaoise);** *four Leinster Club medals with Portlaoise; ten county championship medals, Portlaoise; National League medal, 1986; All Star replacement, 1978; Texaco Footballer Of The Year, 1980.*

Prendiville, Ray (football)

▸ *Native of Kerry; played senior football for Kerry (1975), Meath (1976) and Waterford (1985).*
Career/honours: Munster championship medal, 1975 (Kerry); O'Byrne Cup, 1977 (Meath). Club: Scartaglin. Ray was killed in 2013 following a shooting incident in Namibia, where he was involved in the security business.

Q

Quaid, Damien (football)

▶ *Native of Limerick; played senior football for Limerick, 2010–13.*
Career/honours: junior football county championship medal, 2011; intermediate football county championship medal, 2013; junior hurling county and Munster medals. Clubs: St Mary's/Sean Finns for Rathkeale in Limerick.

Quaid, Seamus (hurling)

▶ *Native of Limerick; played senior hurling for Limerick and Wexford, 1958–61.*
Career/honours: **one All-Ireland senior medal, 1960**; *one Leinster senior medal; three senior club championship medals with Faythe Harriers; played for Limerick vs Wexford in the National League final of 1958.*
Killed in the line of duty on 13 October 1980.

Quane, Bill

▶ *Native of Limerick; played inter-county for Limerick, 1958–63.*
Clubs: Anglesborough and Galtee Rovers, St Brigid's (Dublin).

Queally, Peter (football/hurling)

▶ *Native of Waterford; played senior football (1990–97) and senior hurling (1994–2003) for Waterford.*
Career/honours: Munster hurling championship medal, 2002; **All-Ireland junior football medal, 1999**; *two Railway Cup medals for Munster, 2000 and 2001; County junior championship medal for Ballydurn, 1990 and 2010; county intermediate championship medal for Newtown, 1993; Trench Cup medal, 1994. Also played for Sarsfields, Cork.* Inter-county manager of the Waterford senior football team.
Quote from *The Irish Sun Gaelic Games* monthly of August, 2002: "Queally was seen as a hurler who gave his all, who would cut through flying sticks as if they were confetti in the air, whose fearless attitude won him a string of admirers and who loved nothing better than getting a ball to try and hit it into the next parish."

Quigley, Liam (football)

▶ *Native of Carlow; played senior football for Carlow, 1954.*

Quille, Nicholas (hurling)

▶ *Native of Waterford; played senior hurling for Kerry, 1955–69.*
Career/honours: minor hurling for Waterford, 1954–55; **All-Ireland junior medal, 1961**, *Kerry; three National League Division 3 medals, 1962, 1967, 1968; two Kerry county championship medals, 1965, 1966. Played his club hurling with John Mitchels and Ballyduff.*

Quinlan, Tom (hurling)

▶ *Played senior hurling for Dublin, 1933.*

Quinn, Cormac (hurling)

▶ *Played senior hurling for Wexford during the 1980s.*
Career/honours: played minor and U21 hurling for Wexford.

Quinn, Jim (football)

▸ *Native of Galway; played senior football for Roscommon (1945–47) and Mayo (1952).*
Career/honours: **All-Ireland minor medal, 1941**; *Connacht senior medal, 1946. Jim resigned from An Garda Síochána and later re-joined the force.*

Quinn, Joe (football)

▸ *Native of Donegal; played senior football for Donegal (1958–59) and Cavan (1961–63).*
Career/honours: Ulster senior medal with Cavan, 1962; senior county club championship medal in Monaghan, 1961; Dr McKenna Cup medal; Donegal minor, 1955.

Quinn, Michael (football)

▸ *Native of Clare; played senior football for Clare, 1972–73, 1977–78.*
Career/honours: intermediate club championship medal with Cuala (Dublin).

Quirke, James (hurling)

▸ *Native of Waterford; played senior hurling for Wicklow, 2010 and 2013.*
Career/honours: played minor hurling for Waterford, 2002–04; Christy Ring Cup medal, 2011; National League Division 2B medal; three senior county and two Munster club medals with De La Salle; one senior All-Ireland Club finalist medal.

R

Raftery, Claire (ladies' football)

▸ *Native of Roscommon; played ladies' senior football for Roscommon, 2002–07, 2011–14.*
Career/honours: National League medal, 2004; seven senior club championship medals with Castlerea St Kevins.

Ramsbottom, Pat (football)

▸ *Native of Laois; played senior football for Laois. Club: Timahoe.*

Randles, Con (hurling)

▸ *Native of Kerry; played senior hurling for Kerry.*
Career/honours: played club hurling with Kilgarvan, winning three senior county championship medals.

Rankin, John

▸ *Native of Laois; played inter-county for Laois, 1965–66.*

Rankin, George (football/hurling)

▸ *Native of Laois; played senior football for Wexford (1960–67) and senior hurling for Laois (1965–67).*
Career/honours: played minor football (1955) and intermediate hurling for Laois. Wexford minor selector. Clubs: Bunclody and Park-Ratheniska, Laois.

Ravenhill, Paul (football)

▶ *Native of Offaly; played senior football for Offaly, 1985–86.*
Career/honours: county minor championship medal with Tullamore; Celbridge senior footballer of the year, 1992; Westmeath senior championship medal with Moate, 1997; minor, U21 and senior medals with Tullamore.

Reddy, Mick

▶ *Native of Laois; played inter-county with Cork, 1950.*
Career/honours: Played with Cork Garda team; Munster junior medal, 1961.

Redpath, Jimmy (football)

▶ *Native of Kerry; played senior football (1959) and hurling (1958), and senior football for Kildare (1961).*
Career/honours: junior football for Kildare, 1962; Munster senior medal, Kerry, 1959; Munster junior medal, Kerry, 1959. Clubs: Killarney Legion (football) and Killarney (hurling).

Regan, Mick (hurling)

▶ *Native of Cork; played senior hurling for Cork in the 1970s.*
Career/honours: All-Ireland senior finalist medal, 1956. Hurled with Christy Ring. Founder member of the Garda Male Choir in 1972.

Regan, Mick (hurling)

▶ *Native of Galway; played senior hurling for Galway, 1959–69.*
Career/honours: played minor and intermediate hurling for Galway.

Regan, Pat (hurling)

▶ *Native of Roscommon; hurled at senior level for Roscommon (1990–99)*
Career/honours: **All-Ireland intermediate medal, 1999**; *four county senior hurling championship medals with Oran; intermediate football medal with Oran.*

Reid, Robert (hurling)

▶ *Native of Dublin; played senior hurling for Dublin, 2005–08.*
Career/honours: Division 2 National Hurling League medal, 2006.

Reilly, Gerry (football)

▶ *Native of Roscommon; played senior football for Roscommon during the 1960s.*
Career/honours: All-Ireland finalist medal, 1962; two Connacht senior championship medals, 1961 and 1962; three county senior championship medals with Newtown Blues (Drogheda).

Reilly, Sean (football)

▶ *Native of Mayo; played senior football for Donegal (1958–59) and Mayo (1959–68).*
Career/honours: played minor and junior football for Mayo; Railway Cup for Ulster and Connacht.

Reynolds, Fergal (football)

▸ *Native of Leitrim; played senior football for Leitrim, 1993–2003.*
Career/honours: played minor football, 1990; U21, 1992-93; U21 Hastings Cup medal, 1992; Connacht senior championship medal, 1994; three senior club championship medals; two junior championship medals with St Mary's Kiltoghert (Leitrim) and a Feis Cup medal with St Loman's, Mullingar (Westmeath).

Reynolds, Frank (football)

▸ *Native of Leitrim; played senior football for Leitrim (1958–63), Westmeath (1964) and Mayo.*
Career/honours: O'Byrne Cup medal with Westmeath; two senior county championship medals in Leitrim, 1955 and 1956; two senior county championship medals with St Loman's, Mullingar (Westmeath). Played a few times with Mayo senior footballers.

Reynolds, Hubert (football)

▸ *Native of Leitrim; played senior football for Leitrim (1949, 1957-59) and Louth (1950-55).*
Career/honours: minor All-Ireland finalist medal with Leitrim, 1945; All-Ireland senior finalist medal Louth, 1950; two Leinster championship medals Louth, 1950 and 1953; Railway Cup with Connacht, 1948. Personal bodyguard of Pope John Paul II during his visit to Ireland in 1979.

Reynolds, Hugh (football)

▸ *Native of Cavan; played senior football for Cavan, 1970-75.*
Career/honours: played minor and U21 for Cavan; All-Ireland Colleges medal with St Pat's.

Reynolds, Jack (football)

▸ *Native of Leitrim; played senior football for Leitrim (1958-63) and Westmeath (1964).*
Career/honours: two senior championship medals with Aughavas, Leitrim, 1955 and 1956; two senior club championship medals St Loman's, Mullingar, 1961, 1963; O'Byrne Cup medal with Westmeath, 1964.

Reynolds, James (football)

▸ *Native of Leitrim; played senior football for Leitrim in the 1920s.*
Career/honours: Connacht senior medal, 1927.
"A tower of strength on the field."

Reynolds, John (football)

▸ *Native of Roscommon; played senior football for Roscommon (1921-22) and Tipperary (1923-24). Club: Thurles.*

Reynolds, Vincent (football)

▸ *Native of Meath; played senior football for Meath, 1999.*
Career/honours: intermediate medal with Oldcastle.

Rice, John (football)

▸ *Native of Tipperary; played senior football with Tipperary, 1930-40. Club: Nenagh.*

Rigney, John (hurling)

▸ *Native of Offaly; played senior hurling for Offaly, 1989-93.*
Career/honours: played minor (1983-85) and U21 (1988-89) hurling; two Leinster senior medals, 1989, 1990; National League medal, 1990; Walsh Cup medal, 1991.

Roberts, Peter (football)

▸ *Native of Carlow; played senior football for Carlow, 1959-73.*
Career/honours: three county senior championship medals with Kildavin, 1966, 1970 and 1973; two county junior hurling and one county junior football championship medals; Carlow footballer of the year, 1970.Inter-county referee.

Rochford, Tom (football/hurling)

▸ *Native of Mayo, played senior football and hurling for Mayo, 1958-63.*
Career/honours: minor, U21 and junior football and hurling; two minor Connacht championship medals (football); one junior Connacht championship medal (football); two county junior championship medals in Holp, 1958 and 1962. Played in eleven positions on the Mayo senior team.

Roche, Denis (football)

▸ *Native of Kerry; played senior football for Waterford, 1952-55.*
Career/honours: holder of an All-Ireland Garda medal, 1969.

Roddy, Michael (football)

▸ *Native of Laois; played senior football for Laois (1945) and Cork (1950).*

Rodgers, Jim (football)

▸ *Native of Wicklow; played senior football for Wicklow (1945-47) and Wexford (1948-50).*
Career/honours: four Railway Cup medals with Leinster, 1952-55; Leinster junior hurling medal with Wicklow, 1954. Clubs: Blackwater and Dulart.

Rogers, Gary (football)

▸ *Native of Longford; played senior football for Longford, 2017.*
Career/honours: played U21 for Longford, 2012. Club: Mullinalaghta; two Longford SFC medals, 2016, 2017; three Division 1 Leader cups, 2013, 2016, 2017; one Division 1 league, 2017; three U21 football championships; one minor football championship.

Rooney, Darren (football and hurling)

▸ *Native of Laois; played senior football and senior hurling for Laois, 1999-2011.*
Career/honours: **Senior 'B' All-Ireland medal (hurling);** *two Division 2 National League medals (hurling), 2002 and 2007*; **minor All-Ireland medal, 1997 (football***); Leinster minor championship medal, 1997 (football); Leinster senior championship medal, 2003 (football); Leinster U21 medal, 1998 (football); two Railway Cup medals; played minor and U21 hurling and football for Laois. Clubs: Clonaslee St Manman's (Laois) and Parnells (Dublin).*

Rooney, Eugene (football)

▸ *Native of Mayo; played senior football for Mayo, 1968-70.*
Career/honours: National League medal, 1970; Connacht Railway Cup team, 1970; All-Ireland Colleges medal, 1965.

Rouine, Brendan (football)

▸ *Native of Clare; played senior football for Clare, 1991-2002.*
Career/honours: captain, 1998-99 season; **All-Ireland senior 'B' medal***;*
Railway Cup for Munster, 1999; two Trench Cup medals, 1993 and 1994 with
Garda College; four McGrath Cup medals; Munster championship medal, 1992.
Club: Ennistymon.

Rourke, David (hurling)

▸ *Native of Clare; played senior hurling for Waterford, 1926.*

Rowesome, Declan (hurling)

▸ *Native of Wexford; played senior hurling for Wexford, 1974-82.*
Career/honours: two senior Leinster and All-Ireland finalist medals; All-Ireland
Colleges medal with St Peter's, 1974.

Ruane, Ronan (football)

▸ *Native of Mayo; played senior football for Mayo during the 1990s.*
Career/honours: Connacht club medal with Castlebar Mitchels; minor and U21
Connacht medals with Mayo; All-Ireland Club finalist medal, 1994; four senior
championship and two senior league medals with Muckalee (Kilkenny).

Ruane, Tony (football)

▸ *Played senior football for Mayo, 1993.*

Russell, Ciaran (football)

▸ *Native of Clare; has played senior football with Clare since 2014.*
Career/honours: won U21 hurling and football medals with the Éire Óg club.

Russell, Paddy

▸ *Native of Kerry; played inter-county for Kerry.*

Russell, Paul (football)

▸ *Native of Kerry; played senior football for Kerry (1923-33) and Waterford*
(1936-38). Club: Dr Crokes.
Career/honours: **six senior All-Ireland medals, 1924 (at age 17), 1926,**
1929, 1930, 1931 and 1932*; seven Munster championship medals; three*
National League medals; two Railway Cup medals with Munster, 1927 and
1928; one Railway Cup medal with Leinster, 1930. Captained the Waterford
senior footballers in 1936 when stationed in Dungarvan. Played Tailteann Cup
football. Inter-county manager of Kerry, Meath and Waterford.

Ryan, David (hurling)

▸ *Native of Monaghan; played senior hurling for Monaghan, 1979-93.*
Career/honours: four Ulster junior championship medals, 1985-88; two Division
4 National League medals, 1984, 1986. Inter-county manager (Monaghan).

Ryan, David (hurling)

▸ *Native of Waterford; played senior hurling for Waterford, 1994 and 1996.*
Career/honours: Division 2 National League medal, 1994-95; intermediate and
junior championship medals with Roanmore, 2010.

Ryan, Eric (football)

▸ *Native of Kerry; played senior hurling for Kerry (1954) and Cork (1955-63). Career/honours: played minor football for Kerry, 1951-52; National League medal with Cork, 1955-56; two Munster senior medals with Cork, 1956-57; two All-Ireland senior finalist medals, 1956, 1957. Selected twice on Ireland teams. County championship medal with Macroom. On Munster Railway Cup team for seven years.*

Ryan, Gordon (hurling)

▸ *Native of Kilkenny; played senior hurling for Kilkenny, 1983-84.*
Career/honours: **Senior All-Ireland medal, 1983;** *minor (1976-77) and U21 (1980-81) hurling for Kilkenny;* **junior All-Ireland medal, 1988;** *All-Ireland Senior Colleges medal with St Kieran's, 1975; Fitzgibbon Cup medal with UCD, 1979. Club: O'Loughlin Gaels.*

Ryan, John (hurling)

▸ *Played senior hurling for Dublin, 1925.*

Ryan, Jonathan (football)

▸ *Native of Galway; played senior football for Galway, 2009-11.*
Career/honours: **won a minor All-Ireland medal with Galway, 2007;** *U21, 2008-10; won FBD League with Galway seniors, 2009; won a county U21 championship with Kilkerrin/Clonberne in 2010. Captained his club Kilkerrin/ Clonberne at the age of twenty-two.*

Ryan, Liam (football)

▸ *Native of Limerick; played senior football for Limerick, 1996-97.*

Ryan, Liam (football)

▸ *Native of Waterford; played senior football for Waterford, 1977-78. Career/honours: minor football for Waterford, 1974; senior club championship medals with Ballyduff, 1974 and 1987; three senior club championship medals with Midleton, 1983, 1984 and 1986.*

Ryan, M. (hurling)

▸ *Native of Limerick; played senior hurling for Donegal, 1923. Career/honours: Ulster championship medal, 1923.*

Ryan, Michael (football)

▸ *Native of Mayo; played senior football 1950-62, representing Mayo and Cavan. Career/honours: Played for Cavan in the 1962 All-Ireland semi-final.*

Ryan, Michael (football)

▸ *Native of Roscommon; played senior football for Roscommon, 1997-2005. Career/honours: five senior county championship medals with Roscommon Gaels; played minor and U21 football for Roscommon; Railway Cup medal with Connacht, 1999.*

Ryan, Peadar

▸ *Native of Limerick; played inter-county for Limerick, 1968-70.*

Ryan, Ray (hurling)

▶ *Native of Cork; played senior hurling for Cork, 2009.*
Career/honours: named on Cork club team of the year, 2006; four senior club championship medals with Sarsfields, 2008, 2010, 2012 and 2014; Railway Cup hurling for Munster, 2009. **First Sarsfields captain of Cork for 51 years.**

Ryan, Tom 'The Trick' (hurling)

▶ *Native of Kilkenny; played senior hurling for Wexford during the 1950s.*
Career/honours: **two All-Ireland senior medals, 1955 and 1956;** *two National League medals; eight senior club championship medals with St Aidan's; one junior club championship football medal.*

Ryan, Tom (hurling)

▶ *Native of Limerick; hurled at senior grade with Monaghan in the 1990s.*

Ryland, Robert (hurling)

▶ *Native of Offaly; played senior hurling with Longford, 2009-11.*
Career/honours: one Lory Meagher Cup medal, 2010; one Division 4 National League runners-up medal, 2010.

S

Sands, Tom (football)

▶ *Native of Galway; played senior football for Galway, 1961-70.*
Career/honours: **three All-Ireland senior medals, 1964, 1965, 1966;** *National League medal, 1966;* **U21 medal, 1964;** *three county championship medals with Fr Griffin's, 1971, 1973 (captain), 1975.*

Scahill, Dave (football)

▶ *Native of Roscommon; played senior football for Roscommon, 2005.*
Career/honours: U21 Connacht medal, 1999; two senior club championship medals with Castlerea, 2003 and 2009.

Scally, Kevin (football)

▶ *Native of Offaly; played senior football with Offaly during the 1950s. Club: Garda, Dublin.*

Scally, Matt (football)

▶ *Native of Westmeath; played senior football for Westmeath, 1981-90.*
Career/honours: O'Byrne Cup medal, 1988; Railway Cup medal for Leinster, 1988; National League medal, Division 3, 1988; six club county senior championship medals for Athlone, 1977, 1979, 1982, 1984, 1988 and 1991. Played for Rest of Ireland vs Dublin in the Dublin Millennium match, 1988.

Scanlan, J. J. (football)

▶ *Native of Clare; played senior football for Clare and Dublin during the 1920s.*
Career/honours: played for Munster in the Tailteann Games, 1924.

Scanlan, Sean (football)

▶ *Native of Wexford; played senior football with Wexford in the 1920s and 1930s. Clubs: Enniscorthy Starlights and Sarsfields (Wexford).*

Scanlon, F. (football)

▶ *Native of Kerry; played senior football for Cork, 1949.*

Scannell, Andy (hurling)

▶ *Native of Kerry; played senior hurling for Kerry, 1965. Career/honours: played club hurling with Annascaul.*

Seward, Jason (football)

▶ *Native of Waterford; played senior football for Waterford, 2007-09. Club: Clashmore/Kinsalebeg.*

Sex, Liam (football)

▶ *Native of Kildare; played senior football for Kildare, 1992-93. Career/honours: played minor football and hurling for Kildare, 1990; U21 football, 1992; three senior county championship medals with Sarsfields, 1993, 1994 and 1999.*

Sexton, Pat (hurling)

▶ *Native of Cork; played senior hurling for Cork, 2000. Career/honours:* **All-Ireland U21 medal, 1998**; *U21 (1998-2000) and minor hurling (1996-97) for Cork; Vocational Schools All-Ireland hurling medals in 1996, 1997 and 1998 (captain); Vocational Schools Munster football medals, 1998 (captain); Cork County intermediate hurling championship, 1995; three intermediate hurling county leagues; New York senior hurling championship (2001) with Limerick club.*

Shanahan, Bill (football/hurling)

▶ *Native of Waterford; played senior hurling (1957) and senior football (1959); represented Waterford and Kerry. Club: Listowel (Kerry). Career/honours: played junior (1957) and minor football (1954); senior (1959), junior (1956) and minor (1953) championship medals (Waterford); played minor (1954) and junior (1955) hurling for Waterford; junior hurling with Kerry, 1961-62;* **All-Ireland junior hurling medal, 1961**; *All-Ireland/Munster Colleges medal.*

Shanahan, T. (hurling)

▶ *Played senior hurling for Donegal, 1925.*

Shanley, Oliver (football)

▶ *Native of Meath; played senior football for Meath. Career/honours:* **one All-Ireland senior medal, 1967**; *All-Ireland finalist medal, 1966.*

Shanley, Padraig (football)

▸ *Native of Longford; played senior football for Longford, 2008.*

Shannon, Bill (football)

▸ *Native of Mayo; played senior football for Mayo (1956-62) and Sligo (1962-66). Career/honours: senior county championship medal with Navan O'Mahony's, Meath, 1958; Connacht team, 1958, 1959, 1965 and 1966.*

Shannon, David (football)

▸ *Native of Cork; played senior football for Wexford, 2018. Career/honours: club minor 'A' championship, 2008, and U21 (2011_ medals with O'Donovan Rossa, Cork.*

Shannon, John (football)

▸ *Native of Clare; played senior football for Clare, 1975-78 and 1982-84. Career/honours: two Clare intermediate championship medals; one Louth senior league medal; one Dublin intermediate medal.*

Sheedy, Jack (football)

▸ *Native of Dublin; played senior football for Dublin, 1984-95. Career/honours:* **All Star award, 1994 (midfield),** *five Leinster senior football titles, 1984, 1992-95; two Leinster junior football titles, 1985 and 1987; two National League titles, 1990 and 1993; represented Leinster in Railway Cup on five occasions; captained Dublin to All-Ireland Masters title in 2004; Ireland Masters International Rules team vs Australia, 2004 and 2006; 1990 championship debut vs Meath in four game saga in 1991. Inter-county manager of Longford, 2015. Played for Garda Club, Dublin, and Lucan Sarsfields.*

Sheehan, Tim (football)

▸ *Native of Kerry; played senior football for Kerry, 1965-69. Club: Kilcummin. Career/honours: played minor, U21 and junior football; three Munster senior medals;* **one All-Ireland junior medal;** *involved in three losing All-Irelands, 1964, 1965 and 1966; three senior county championship medals in Kerry; two Munster county championship medals.*

Sheehy, Sean (hurling)

▸ *Native of Kerry; played senior hurling for Kerry, 1970-73. Career/honours: played his club hurling for Ballyduff, winning two senior county hurling championship medals.*

Sheelin, Eugene (football)

▸ *Native of Louth; played senior football for Louth, 1977.*

Sheil, Leo (football)

▸ *Native of Roscommon; played senior football for Roscommon, 1993-94.*

Sheridan, Cathal (football/hurling)

▸ *Played senior football for Meath (1992-97) and Kildare (1998-2000) and senior hurling for Meath (1993-95, 2002-06) and Kildare (2000-01).*
Career/honours: **All-Ireland senior football medal, 1996, Meath; All-Ireland minor football medal, 1990; All-Ireland U21 football medal, 1993; All-Ireland junior medal, 2003; All-Ireland 'B' hurling medal, 1993.**
Clubs: Moynalvey, Kiltale, Kilcock.

Sheridan, Dessie (football)

▸ *Native of Longford; played senior football for Longford.*
Career/honours: intermediate championship medal with Dromard.

Sheridan, Gerry (football)

▸ *Native of Cavan; played senior football for Cavan, 1980, 1984-93.*
Career/honours: Ulster junior championship medal; McKenna Cup medal; one senior club and two senior league championship medals.

Sheridan, Henry (football)

▸ *Native of Dublin; played senior football for Dublin, 1960. Club: Skerries.*

Sheridan, Jim (football)

▸ *Native of Donegal; played senior football for Donegal and Leitrim in the 1970s.*
Career/honours: intermediate medal with Leitrim; Donegal Sports Star Hall of Fame, 2016.
Played soccer for Finn Harps, Sligo Rovers, Longford Town, St Patrick's Athletic and Coleraine. Won fourteen amateur caps for the Republic of Ireland soccer team.

Sheridan, Niall (football)

▸ *Native of Longford; played senior football for Longford, 1995-2007. Club: Abbeylara.*

Sheridan, Robbie (hurling)

▸ *Native of Dublin; played senior hurling for Fingal, 2008 to 2015.*
Career/honours: Keogh Shield medals; two National League medals; Nicky Rackard finalist medal.

Sherlock, John (football)

▸ *Native of Dublin; played senior football for Dublin, 1923-29.*
Career/honours: **one senior All-Ireland medal, 1923.**

Sherlock, Sean (football)

▸ *Native of Sligo; played senior football for Sligo (1978) and Tipperary (1978-83).*
Career/honours: played U21 (1979) and minor (1976) football for Sligo; minor (1976), U21 (1977 and 1978), senior league (1975) and championship (1976) medals with Tubbercurry.

Shevlin, Nigel (football)

▸ *Native of Louth; played senior football for Louth, 2006.*
Career/honours: Division 2 National League medal, 2006; two intermediate club championship medals, 2001 and 2008.

Shields, Mal (football)

▸ *Native of Cavan; played senior football for Cavan, 1955-62.*
Career/honours: played minor football for Cavan; McKenna Cup medal.

Shine, Colm (football)

▸ *Native of Roscommon; played senior football for Roscommon, 1966-69.*
Career/honours: **All-Ireland U21 medal, 1966**; *county senior championship medal in Roscommon, 1966; Connacht junior championship medal, 1964.*

Shortall, John (hurling)

▸ *Native of Laois; played senior hurling for Laois, 1997-99.*
Career/honours: club championship intermediate medal, football, 1994; two junior club championship medals, football, 1989 and 2000; club U21 championship medal, hurling, 1990; county Division 1 league medal, hurling, 1997.

Shortt, Michelle (camogie)

▸ *Native of Tipperary; played senior camogie for Tipperary in the 2000s.*
Career/honours: **All-Ireland senior medal, 2003**; *Purcell Cup medal with Garda College, 2005; Ashbourne Shield medal with Garda College, 2007.* **Selected on the All Star Ashbourne Shield team, 2007.** *Club: Drom and Inch.*

Silke, Martin (football)

▸ *Native of Roscommon; played senior football for Roscommon during the 1970s.*
Career/honours:
as a sixty-seven-year-old, came on as a sub for Strokestown in a cup match in June 2014.

Silke, Pat (football)

▸ *Native of Galway; played senior football for Limerick (1955-63) and Galway (1950).*
Career/honours: senior club championship medal with Garda, Limerick, 1958.

Skelly, Willie (football)

▸ *Native of Longford; played senior football for Longford, 1997-2001, 2008-09.*
Career/honours: two intermediate championship medals with Killashee St Brigid's in 2003 and 2011.

Sloyan, Paddy (football)

▸ *Native of Mayo; played senior football for Mayo, 1956-58.*
Career/honours: played for Garda Club, Dublin.

Small, John (hurling)

▸ *Native of Dublin; played senior hurling for Dublin, 1995-96.*

Smiddy, Jimmy (hurling)

▸ *Native of Cork; played senior hurling for Cork, 1996.*
Career/honours: played minor and U21 hurling and football for Cork; **All-Ireland intermediate medal, 1997**; *two senior club championship medals (1997, 1998) with Imokilly; junior championship medal with Castlemartyr, 2014.*

Smith, Jim (football)

▸ *Native of Cavan; played senior football for Cavan, 1919-38.*
Career/honours: **two All-Ireland senior medals, 1933 (captain), and 1935***;*
thirteen senior Ulster championship medals, 1920, 1923-26, 1928, 1931-37;
played in five All-Ireland senior finals*; one senior county championship medal*
with Virginia Blues (Cavan), 1919; six Dublin county hurling championship
medals, 1924, 1926-29, 1931; six Dublin county hurling league medals; two
Dublin county football championship and league medals; Railway Cup football
for Ulster.Captain of Cavan, 1927. Played for Ireland vs England (1925) and
America (1932) in the International Tailteann Games.
Described as "undoubtedly the greatest footballer of the decade"
(1920s). Played in Croke Park for Erin's Isle in the curtain-raiser on
Bloody Sunday (November 1920) with Garda in Dublin.

Smith, Jim Jnr

▸ *Native of Cavan; played senior football for Cavan, 1952.*
Career/honours: played minor football, 1951.

Smith, Michael (football)

▸ *Played senior football for Roscommon in the 1920s.*

Smith, Noel (football)

▸ *Native of Cavan; played senior football for Cavan, 1964-65 and 1974.*
Career/honours: two Colleges medals with St Mel's, Longford, 1961-64.

Smith, Paul (football)

▸ *Native of Cavan; played senior football for Cavan, 2014-16.*
Career/honours: Trench Cup medal with Garda College, 2015.

Smith, Phil (football)

▸ *Native of Cavan; played senior football for Cavan.*
Career/honours: two intermediate championship medals, 1997 and 2004, and
two senior league medals, 1991 and 2005, with Lacken Celtic.

Smith, Sean (football)

▸ *Native of Mayo; played senior football for Mayo, 1994-98.*
Career/honours: played minor and U21 football for Mayo; Connacht junior
championship medal, 1998.

Smith, Val

▸ *Native of Offaly; played inter-county for Louth during the 1980s.*

Smyth, Donal (football)

▸ *Native of Mayo; played senior football for Meath, 1980-94.*
Career/honours: **two All-Ireland senior medals, 1987 and 1988***; Centenary*
Cup medal, 1984; Leinster senior football championship, 1986-88 and 1990-
1991; All-Ireland finalist medal, 1990; played in 1990 final (beaten by Cork);
National Football League titles, 1988, 1990 and 1994; seven county championship
medals and four senior League medals with Navan O'Mahony's, including a four
in a row sequence, 1987-90 inclusive.

Smyth, Michael (football)

▸ *Native of Roscommon; played senior football for Roscommon, 1918-26. Career/honours: interprovincial football with Connacht, 1926: Clubs; Kilbride, Roscommon and Garda, Dublin.*

Smyth, Noel (football)

▸ *Native of Galway; played senior football for Offaly, 1965-67. Also played U21 hurling for Offaly.*

Somers, Gerry (hurling)

▸ *Played senior hurling for Louth.*

Spillane, Dan (football)

▸ *Native of Kerry; played senior football for Wexford, 1948-53. Career/honours: played junior football, 1944-46.*

Spillane, Pat (football)

▸ *Native of Kerry; played senior football for Cork, 1950. Career/honours: county senior championship medal with Cork Garda, 1950.*

Spollen, Niamh (football)

▸ *Native of Offaly; played football for Offaly 1994-2000.*

Spollen, Pat (football)

▸ *Native of Offaly; played senior football for Offaly and Wicklow in the 1990s. Career/honours: senior championship medal with Duffry Rovers.*

Stack, Niall

▸ *Native of Offaly; played inter-county for Offaly, 1999-2000.*

Stafford, Michelle (ladies' football/camogie)

▸ *Native of Wexford; played ladies' senior football for Wexford (1991-2000) and senior camogie for Dublin (2000-04).*

Stanley, Larry (football)

▸ *Native of Kildare; played senior football for Kildare (1916-19, 1926-30) and Dublin (1920-25).*
Career/honours: **two All-Ireland medals with Kildare (1919, captain) and Dublin (1923); inaugural recipient of an All Time All Star award, 1980;** *two county championship medals with Caragh (Kildare); three Leinster senior championship medals*
Selected on the Kildare Millennium team; Garda Hall of Fame; GAA Hall Of Fame award, 1980. Played for Ireland vs Combined Universities, 1951, 1953 and 1954. "Reportedly could catch a ball in one hand." An accomplished athlete in the high jump (Irish champion), Larry was the first Irish competitor to represent Ireland in athletics in the 1924 Olympic Games in Paris.

Stapleton, David (hurling)

▸ *Native of Limerick; played senior hurling for Limerick, 1999-2002. Career/honours:* **All-Ireland U21 medal, 2002;** *Munster U21 medal, 2002; played intermediate hurling for Kilkenny; All-Ireland runner-up medal, 2008; Ryan Cup medal with Garda College, 2016.*

Starkin, Gabriel (football)

▶ *Native of Offaly; played senior football for Offaly in the 1960s and 1970s. Career/honours: junior (1969) and intermediate (1971) championship medals with Bunbrosna (Westmeath).*

Steede, Ronan (hurling)

▶ *Native of Galway; played senior hurling for Donegal, 2007. Career/honours: All-Ireland Colleges medal with GMIT Castlebar, 2000.*

Stenson, Jimmy (football)

▶ *Native of Leitrim; played senior football for Leitrim, 1992-93. Career/honours: played minor and U21 football.*

Stones, Marius (football)

▶ *Native of Offaly; played senior football for Offaly (2001-03). Career/honours: played minor football for Offaly.*

Studdard, Martin (football)

▶ *Played senior football for Clare in the 1950s.*

Sullivan, Con (football)

▶ *Native of Cork; played senior football for Cork and Dublin during the 1950s. Career/honours:* **All-Ireland junior medal with Dublin, 1948**. *Club: Garda, Dublin.*

Sullivan, Jeremiah Francis (football)

▶ *Native of Kerry; played senior football for Kerry, 1949. Career/honours: county championship medal, 1958 with Limerick Garda.*

Sullivan, J.J. (hurling)

▶ *Native of Played senior hurling for Monaghan. Career/honours:* **All-Ireland junior medal, 1997.**

Sullivan, Joe (football)

▶ *Native of Longford; played senior football for Monaghan, 1969-74.*

Sullivan, Teddy (football)

▶ *Native of Kerry; played senior football for Kerry, 1943-51.*
▶ *Native of Career/honours:* **All-Ireland senior medal, 1946.** *Played in the All-Ireland final 1947 in the Polo Grounds, New York, losing to Cavan.*

Swan, Jack (hurling)

▶ *Native of Kildare; played senior hurling for Cavan, 1999. Career/honours: Division 3 National League medal.*
"Jack's brother Neil was playing senior hurling for Kildare when Jack was playing for Cavan."

Sweeney, Declan (football)

▶ *Native of Mayo; played senior football for Mayo, 1996–2000, 2004–06.*
Career/honours: **two All-Ireland U21 medals, 1994 and 1995**; *four Connacht championship medals; three All-Ireland finalist medals; one All-Ireland club finalist medal, 1997; one Connacht club championship medal, 1996; three senior club championship medals, 1992, 1996 and 1997 with Knockmore; minor and U21 club championship medals with Knockmore.*

Sweeney, Dermot (football)

▶ *Played senior football with Kildare.*
Career/honours: **All-Ireland minor medals with Dublin, 1954 and 1955**.

Sweeney, Eamonn (football)

▶ *Native of Sligo; played senior football for Sligo, 1989–97.*
Career/honours: senior county league medals with Sligo, 1994 and 1998; Sligo senior club player of the year, 1998.

Sweeney, Michael (football)

▶ *Native of Donegal; played senior football for Donegal, 1972–76.*
Career/honours: Ulster senior championship medal, 1972; two county senior championship medal with St Eunan's.

Sweeney, Sean (football)

▶ *Native of Mayo; played senior football for Donegal.*

T

Taaffe, Frank

▶ *Played inter-county for Louth.*

Tanner, Declan (hurling)

▶ *Played senior hurling for Offaly (2002–06) and Longford (2008–10, 2013–14).*
Career/honours: **won two All-Ireland Lory Meagher Cup medals with Longford**.

Tansey, Ben (football/hurling)

▶ *Native of Galway; played senior football for Roscommon (1978–79) and Meath (1980–85), and senior hurling for Roscommon (1971–78) and Meath (1980–89).*
Career/honours: played minor and U21 football for Roscommon; Connacht senior football championship medal with Roscommon, 1978; **All-Ireland junior hurling medal with Roscommon, 1974**; *two Roscommon senior hurling medals with Four Roads; Connacht senior club medal, 1977; intermediate football medal with St Aidan's; club footballer of the year, 1975; seven senior football and two senior hurling championship medals with Navan O'Mahony's; club footballer and hurler of the year.*

Tarpey, Michael

▶ *Played inter-county for Roscommon 1999. Connaught junior medal 1999; Club: St. Dominics, Knockcroughery*

Taylor, Dan (hurling)

▶ *Native of Tipperary; played senior hurling for Donegal, 1923. Career/honours: Ulster championship medal, 1923.*

Thomas, Finbar

▶ *Played inter-county for Galway, 1991. Club: Killanin. Career/honours: holds Galway Masters medals.*

Thompson, Derek (football)

▶ *Native of Roscommon; played senior football for Roscommon, 1992-2003. Career/honours: FBD league medal, 1999; Connacht senior medal, 2001; AIB Cup medal with Garda GAA Club in Dublin; O'Rourke Cup (Division 1 League) with St Faithleach's, Roscommon; O'Gara Cup and League with St Faithleach's (intermediate championship and league); U21 Division 1 county title; Trench Cup and Division 2 league with Sligo RTC.*

Thornton, Frank (hurling)

▶ *Native of Kerry; played senior hurling for Kerry, 1970-75. Career/honours: played his club hurling for Lixnaw.*

Thornton, Jim (football)

▶ *Native of Mayo; played senior football for Mayo, 1950-51. Career/honours: Connacht championship medal, 1950*

Tiernan, David (football)

▶ *Native of Mayo; played senior football for Mayo, 2001-12. Career/honours: two county senior medals with Charlestown, 2001 and 2009; one Connacht senior medal, 2001 (as captain); two senior league medals; one county intermediate medal, 2012; one Connacht intermediate medal, 2012.*

Tierney, James (football)

▶ *Native of Tipperary; played senior football for Tipperary, 2009-10. Career/honours: Division 3 National League medal, 2009-10; various underage hurling and football medals; West Tipperary senior hurling medal; Tipperary U21 'A' county hurling medal; Dublin intermediate hurling medal with Trinity Gaels.*

Tierney, Padraic (hurling)

▶ *Native of Dublin; played senior hurling for Dublin, 1991-94. Career/honours: played minor, U21 football and hurling; minor, U21 (captained for three years) 1990, 1991 and 1992. U13 hurling development squad manager (2015).*

Tinkler, Sean (hurling)

▶ *Native of Offaly; played senior hurling for Offaly, 1984-87. Club: Gracefield.*

Tobin, P. (hurling)

▶ *Native of Clare; hurled at senior grade for Donegal in the 1920s. Career/honours: Ulster championship medal, 1923.*

Tobin, Ned (hurling)

▶ *Native of Laois; played senior hurling for Dublin, 1925-29.*
Career/honours: **one All-Ireland senior medal, 1927.** *Clubs: Faugh's, Dublin,*
and Garda, Dublin. Played with Munster in the Tailteann Games.

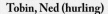

Tobin, Padraig (hurling)

▶ *Native of Limerick; played senior hurling for Limerick, 1993 and 1995-98.*
Career/honours: Munster senior medal, 1996; National League medal, 1997; two
senior club and Munster medals with Kilmallock, 1992 and 1994.

Tormey, Andrew (football)

▶ *Native of Meath; has played senior football for Meath since 2012.*
Career/honours: played minor for Meath, 2007-08, and won a Leinster MFC
title in 2008; U21, 2010-11. Club: Donaghmore-Ashbourne. Club achievements:
three Division 1 minor football championships, 2006-08; won a Meath IFC
medal in 2007, and an U21 championship medal in 2011.

Tormey, Joe (football)

▶ *Native of Galway; played senior football for Galway and Leitrim in the 1960s.*
Career/honours: Connacht junior medal, 1961; played junior football with
Leitrim. Awarded a Scott medal.

Treacy, Gerard

▶ *Played inter-county for Fermanagh, 1962-68.*

Tubman, Ray (football)

▶ *Native of Leitrim; played senior football for Leitrim, 1997.*

Tubridy, Joe (football)

▶ *Native of Clare; played senior football for Clare, 1960-69.*
Career/honours: two Munster junior football medals; four Clare county
championship medals; one **All-Ireland Interfirms medal with Cork Garda,**
1978.

Tuite, William

▶ *Native of Kildare; played senior football for Kildare (1924) and Sligo (1924-26).*

Tuohy, Brian (football)

▶ *Native of Donegal; played senior football for Donegal (1981-92) and Sligo*
(1993).
Career/honours: **All-Ireland U21 medal, 1982 (captain);** *played minor (1979-*
80) and U21 (1981-83) football for Donegal; Ulster senior championship medals,
1983 and 1990; four senior county championship medals with Aodh Ruadh,
Donegal.

Tuohy, Errol (hurling)

▶ *Native of Clare; played senior hurling for Kerry, 2002-05. Club: Dr Crokes. Also*
played minor hurling for Kildare.

Twomey, T. (hurling)

▶ *Native of Limerick; played senior hurling for Donegal in the 1920s.*
Career/honours: Ulster championship medal, 1923.

395

Twomey, Hugh (hurling)

▶ *Native of Kerry; played senior hurling for Kerry, 2001-03.*
Career/honours: National Hurling League Division 2 medal, 2001; four Kerry intermediate hurling championship medals with Kilgarvan in 2006, 2007, 2009 and 2010; three Kerry intermediate hurling league medals with Kilgarvan, 2001, 2006 and 2007; one Kerry football championship – Novice Shield final with Kilgarvan, 1999; **one All-Ireland senior Interfirms football championship with Cork Garda, 1999.**

Twomey, J. P. (hurling)

▶ *Native of Kerry; played senior hurling for Kerry in 1959.*
Career/honours: played minor, junior, intermediate and senior hurling for Kerry; club championship medal, 1968, with Crotta O'Neills; also played with Abbeydorney and Kilflynn.

Twomey, John (hurling)

▶ *Native of Dublin; played senior hurling for Dublin, 1982-96.*
Career/honours: two Leinster senior finalist medals, 1990 and 1992 (captain); Railway Cup hurling with Leinster; senior club championship medal with Erin's Isle in 1983 (hurling); senior club championship medal with Erin's Isle in 1993 (football).

Twomey, Moss (football)

▶ *Native of Cork; played senior football for Cork, 1961-62.*
Career/honours: played minor (1957-58) and junior (1960-61) football for Cork.

Tynan, Andy (football)

▶ *Native of Roscommon; played senior football for Longford, 1966-67.*
Career/honours: National League medal, 1966.

Tynan, Eddie (football)

▶ *Native of Westmeath; played senior football for Westmeath, 1980-83, 1987, 1988.*
Career/honours: junior championship with Shandonagh; captain in 1987.

V

Varley, Liam (hurling)

▶ *Native of Westmeath; played senior hurling for Westmeath, 2013 to present.*
Career/honours: played minor and U21 hurling for Westmeath; key player in Westmeath U21s' historic Leinster championship win over Kilkenny in 2016. Won an NHL Division 2A medal with Westmeath in 2016. Part of the Westmeath minor football team which reached a Leinster final in 2013 under the management of former Dublin player, Tom Carr. Played for Garda College in the 2018 Fitzgibbon Cup. Club: has represented and won medals with Castletown-Geoghegan at all underage grades, and won Westmeath SHC medals in 2013 and 2017 (captain).

W

Walker, Gerry (football)

▶ *Native of Westmeath; played senior football for Westmeath, 1985-89.*
Career/honours: O'Byrne Cup medal, 1988; captain of Westmeath, 1986. Club:
Tubberclair.

Walsh, Adrian (football)

▶ *Native of Dublin; played senior football for Dublin, 1980-82.*
Inter-county referee.

Walsh, Dan (hurling)

▶ *Played senior hurling for Galway.*

Walsh, Edward 'Ned' (hurling)

▶ *Native of Laois; played senior hurling for Wicklow, 1951-53.*
Career/honours: played minor hurling for Laois, 1941; Leinster minor
championship medal with Laois, 1941.

Walsh, Emma (camogie)

▶ *Played senior camogie for Wexford.*

Walsh, George (football)

▶ *Played senior football for Cork in the 1920s. Club: Macroom.*
Career/honours: a noted athlete, particularly with the shot putt.

Walsh, Kevin (football)

▶ *Native of Galway; played senior football for Galway, 1987-2003.*
Career/honours: **two All-Ireland senior medals, 1998 and 2001; one**
All-Ireland minor medal, 1986; All Star Awards 1998, 2001, 2003 (all
midfield); *five Connacht senior championship medals. Played interprovincial*
football for Connacht. Club: Killanin. Inter-county manager with Galway
(2015 to present) and Sligo (2008-13).
Named in John Scally's book as one of the "GAA greats of Connacht".

Walsh, Michael (hurling)

▶ *Native of Cork; played senior hurling for Waterford in the 1920s. Club: Lismore.*

Walsh, Michael (hurling)

▶ *Native of Dublin; played senior hurling for Dublin, 1988-89. Club; Whitehall*
Colmcille Also played football for Whitehall.

Walsh, Michael (hurling)

▶ *Played senior hurling for Donegal in the 1930s (team captain, 1932).*

Walsh, Michael (football)

▶ *Played senior football for Waterford, 1985-89.*
Career/honours: captained Waterford senior footballers, 1986. Club: Kilrossanty,
with whom he won Waterford SFC medals in 1985, 1986 and 1988.

Walsh, Mick (football)

▸ *Played senior football for Galway during the 1970s.*
Career/honours: played minor and U21 football for Galway; **All-Ireland minor medal, 1970 (captain).**

Walsh, Mossie (hurling)

▸ *Native of Waterford; played senior hurling for Waterford, 1974-85.*
Career/honours: **All Star award 1980 – midfield***; National League Division 2 medal; two senior county championship medals with Ballyduff, 1982 and 1987; former Waterford hurler of the year; one Railway Cup medal, Munster, 1982*

Walsh, Pat (football)

▸ *Native of Clare; played senior football for Clare, 1969-70.*
Career/honours: played minor (1966), U21 (1968-69) and junior (1969) football; five Clare county championship medals with Kilrush Shamrocks.

Walsh, Pat

▸ *Played inter-county for Galway during the 1950s.*

Walsh, Patrick (hurling)

▸ *Native of Waterford; played senior hurling for Westmeath (2013) and Longford (2016 to present)*
Career/honours: junior championship medal with Fourmilewater, 2012; intermediate and junior championship medals and Leinster League medal with Clonkill, 2014; senior and junior championship medals with Clonkill, 2015.

Walsh, Róisín (camogie)

▸ *Native of Kildare; played senior camogie for Kildare, 1995-2000 and 2002.*
Career/honours: two Leinster junior medals, 1995, 1996; thirteen senior championship medals, including twelve in a row; two Leinster medals, 1996 and 2004 with St Laurence's; All-Ireland rounders medal.

Walsh, Seamus (football)

▸ *Played senior football for Mayo.*

Walsh, Seamus (hurling)

▸ *Played senior hurling for Wexford during the 1950s and 1960s. Club: Faythe Harriers.*
Career/honours: Leinster junior medal, 1957.

Walsh, Tom (hurling)

▸ *Native of Cork; played senior hurling for Dublin and Antrim.*
Career/honours: junior championship medal with Tullylease, Cork, 1945; also played with young Irelands, Dublin, 1950-51.

Walsh, Willie (hurling)

▸ *Native of Carlow; played senior hurling for Carlow.*
Career/honours: **All-Ireland intermediate medal, 1962.**

Walshe, Jim (hurling)

▸ *Played senior hurling for Dublin, 1929.*

Ward, Francie (football)

▶ *Native of Monaghan; played senior football for Monaghan, 1966-68. Career/honours: played minor (1961-62) and U21 (1963) football for Monaghan; three county championship medals with St Joseph's, Laois, 1976, 1977 and 1979; one county championship medal with Tinryland, Carlow, 1975. Inter-county referee.*

Ward, Paddy

▶ *Native of Donegal; played senior football for Donegal and Leitrim in the 1960s and 1970s.*

Ward, Sean (football)

▶ *Native of Mayo; played senior football for Mayo, 1983-84. Career/honours:* **All-Ireland minor medal, 1978.**

Ward, Tom (football)

▶ *Native of Mayo; played senior football for Mayo, 1980-82. Career/honours: one Connacht senior championship medal, 1981; five county championship medals with Knockmore; two Connacht club championship medals.*

Ware, Garvan (football)

▶ *Native of Carlow; played senior football for Carlow, 1989-2002, and Kildare, 2001. Career/honours:* **All-Ireland 'B' championship in 1994;** *O'Byrne Cup medal, 2002; played with Clane, Kildare from 2000-06. With the Éire Óg club: U21 club championship medal, 1988; eight Carlow senior football championship medals; five Leinster club football championship medals, 1992, 1993, 1995, 1996 and 1998; losing All-Ireland finalist in the club football championship in 1993 and 1996.*
According to many, Garvan's finest hour was the All-Ireland Club final vs O'Donovan Rossa of Skibbereen on St Patrick's Day, 1992, when he gave an outstanding performance that many consider to be the finest display ever seen in the club championship.

Watters, Dessie (football)

▶ *Native of Sligo; played senior football for Sligo in the 1960s.*

Weldon, Willie (hurling)

▶ *Native of Westmeath; played senior hurling for Westmeath in the 1960s. Club: Lough Lene Gaels.*

Weymes, T. J. (football)

▶ *Played senior football for Monaghan, 1929-30. Club: Clones.*

Whelan, Eddie (football)

▶ *Native of Kildare; played senior football for Monaghan, 1980-81. Career/honours: U21 championship medal with Kildare, 1974; U21 Kildare footballer of the year in 1974. Clubs: Raheen and Caragh (Kildare), Monaghan Harps (football) and Éire Óg (Kildare). Hurling: three Hackett Cup medals.*

Whelan, John (football)

▶ *Native of Kildare; played senior football for Kildare, 1993-98.*
Career/honours: played minor football, 1992-93; U21 football, 1993-95; four senior county championship medals with Sarsfields, 1993, 1994, 1999 and 2001; U21 senior county championship medals, 1992 and 1993; minor championship medal; Kildare footballer of the year, 1993; club player of the year, 1999.

Whelan, Seamus (football)

▶ *Native of Wexford; played senior football for Wexford in the 1970s.*
Career/honours: played minor and junior football; two county senior championship medals with Tinryland (Carlow, 1984) and Starlight's (Wexford, 1993). Inter-county referee.

Whelehan, Paul (football)

▶ *Native of Galway; played senior football for Galway, 2014-15.*
Career/honours: **All-Ireland junior club championship medal with St Grellan's, Ballinasloe, 2013.**

White, Colin (football)

▶ *Native of Sligo; played senior football for Sligo, 1994-98.*
Career/honours: played U21 football for Sligo; clubman of the year, 1997; U21 and senior Connacht finalist medals.

White, E. (hurling)

▶ *Native of Kerry; played senior hurling for Donegal in the 1920s.*
Career/honours: Ulster championship medal, 1923.

White, Frank (football)

▶ *Native of Sligo; played senior football for Sligo (1943, 1947-57) and Donegal (1944-46, 1957, captain in 1946).*
Career/honours: played minor football for Sligo, 1941; one senior County championship medal with Dungloe, 1957; first member of Shamrock Gaels Hall of Fame award, 2012; Dungloe Hall of Fame, 2003; Railway Cup football for Connacht and Ulster (winners medal, 1951).Frank captained the Sligo team which played Mayo at the official opening of Countess Markievicz Park in 1955.

White, George (football)

▶ *Native of Kerry; played senior football for Waterford and Cork, 1957-61.*
Career/honours: played minor football for Kerry; All-Ireland minor finalist medal for Kerry, 1954. Played on the Waterford senior team that shocked his native Kerry in the 1957 Munster championship.

White, J.

▶ *Played inter-county for Cork, c. 1958.*

White, Joe (hurling)

▶ *Played senior hurling for Kerry, 1958. Club: Kenmare.*

White, Jeremiah (football)
▶ *Native of Tipperary; played senior football for Tipperary, 1978-79.*

Whyte, Mick (football)

▸ *Native of Roscommon; played senior football for Roscommon, 1973-77. Career/honours: played minor and U21 football for Roscommon; played minor hurling for Roscommon; Connacht senior medal, 1977; two senior hurling county championship medals with Tremane, 1973 and 1974; two intermediate club championship medals with Oran in 1974 and 1980.*

Williamson, Kevin (football)

▸ *Native of Offaly; played senior football for Offaly, 2011. Career/honours: Offaly senior championship medal (2013) with Tullamore.*

Wilson, Joe (football)

▸ *Native of Galway; played senior football for Roscommon.*

Wilson, Tara (camogie)

▸ *Played senior camogie for Carlow.*

Winston, Bernard (football)

▸ *Native of Roscommon; played senior football for Donegal in the 1940s. Career/honours: senior club championship medal with Dungloe, 1940.*

Woodlock, James (hurling)

▸ *Native of Tipperary; played senior hurling for Tipperary, 2006-15. Career/honours: one National League medal, 2008; Munster U21 championship medal, 2006; Munster minor championship medal, 2003; three Munster senior medals, 2008, 2009 and 2015; senior club championship medal for Drom and Inch, 2011; Railway Cup hurling for Munster.*

Wright, Tom (hurling)

▸ *Native of Limerick; played senior hurling for Wicklow. Career/honours: Leinster junior medal, 1964.*

Y

Yorke, John (football)

▸ *Native of Longford; played senior football for Longford, 1980-83.*

Young, James (hurling)

▸ *Native of Laois; played senior hurling for Laois, 2000-10. Career/honours: Nominated for an All Star in 2006 and 2007; two intermediate hurling, three intermediate football, senior 'B' and U21 championship medals with Clonaslee St Manman's.*

Young, Louise (camogie)

▸ *Native of Tipperary; played senior camogie for Tipperary. Career/honours:* **three All-Ireland senior medals; one All-Ireland junior medal, 2001;** *Purcell Cup medal with Garda College, 2005;* **selected on All Star Purcell Cup team, 2005;** *Ashbourne Shield medal with Garda College, 2007. Player of the All-Ireland Club 7s tournament (2011) with Toomevara.*

Player Profiles

*the Following list features members of An Garda Síochána who have played
senior inter-county football, hurling, ladies' football and camogie
but no further information could be unearthed*

Barry, Tom
Kerry, 1920s.

Beattie, Brendan
Roscommon.

Bonner, Pat (football)
Donegal.

Brady, Leo
Donegal.

Brennan, Gary (hurling)
Cavan.

Brennan, Mick
Meath/Cavan.

Brennan, Seamus
Sligo and Cavan.

Broderick, Tom

Brogan, James

Brown, Ollie
Dublin.

Brown, Willie (hurling)
Dublin.

Byrne, Declan (hurling)
Louth.

Byrne, Tom
Clare.

Cadden, Gerry (football)
Cavan.

Cahill, Dermot
Dublin.

Cahill, Michael
Wicklow.

Callaghan, Liam
Kildare.

Callan, Noel
Louth and Meath.

Campbell, Joe (football)
Mayo.

Carthy, Terry
*Wicklow (played in the
1950s).*

Casey, Bill
Longford.

Casey, Christy
Sligo.

Casey, Eamonn
Limerick.

Cawley, Nathy
Sligo.

Clarke, Jack (hurling)
Dublin, 1931.
Clarke, John (football)
Mayo.

Cleary, Johnny (football)
Tipperary.

Cleere, Damien
Kilkenny.

Clifford, Jim
Donegal and Mayo.

Cody, Edmond
Kilkenny.

Coll, Phil (football)
Limerick (1960s).

Connell, ?
*Played inter-county for
Waterford in 1950.*

Connolly, Tom
Limerick.

Connolly, Tom (football)
Mayo.

Connor, Jim
Donegal and Mayo.

Connor, John
Donegal and Mayo.

Conroy, Jack (hurling)
Dublin, 1920s.
Conroy, Tommy
Galway.

Conway, Dominic (football)
Mayo.

Cronin, Tom
Kerry.

Cunningham, Seamus
Wicklow.

Curley, Gerry
Monaghan.

Curran, Paudge
Kerry.

Curry, P.
Offaly.

Curtin, Andrew
Clare.

Darles, Eddie
Wicklow.

Delaney, Michael

Donnelly, Frank
Armagh and Sligo.

Donoghue, Nicky
Leitrim.

Dowd, ? (football)
Played inter-county football for Mayo, 1931.

Dowling, Tom
Dublin.

Dwyer, Bill
Laois.

Egan, T. J.,
Westmeath.

Fagan, Owen
Westmeath.

Fahey, Orla (ladies' football)
Tipperary.

Farrelly, Shane

Fitzgerald, Edel.

Gavin, Pat

Gibbons, Myles

Gordon, Eamonn
Played inter-county for Roscommon.

Griffin, Caroline
Meath.

Halton, Patrick
Cavan.

Hogan, Paul
Played inter-county for Carlow.

Hourihan, Pat
Played inter-county with Kilkenny.

Hyland, Christy
Galway native; played inter-county for Galway.

Kavanagh, Tom
Keane, Páidí (football)
Played senior football for Mayo.

Kellegher, John
Played inter-county for Clare.

Kelly, Pat
Galway native; played inter-county for Galway.

Kenny, Brian
Tipperary native, played inter-county for Tipperary.

Keoghan, Theresa

King, Martin
Offaly native; played inter-county for Wicklow.

Larkin, Sid
Played inter-county for Laois.

Lawlor, Gerry
Played inter-county for Kilkenny.

Lawlor, Pat
Played inter-county for Laois.

Leahy, Tony
Played inter-county for Kilkenny.

Lenihan, Liam
Played inter-county for Monaghan.
Lyttleton, Donal
Played inter-county for Carlow.

Macken, Benny
Played inter-county for Roscommon

McArdle, Pascal
Played inter-county for Monaghan during the 1950s.

McMahon, John Dan
Played inter-county for Donegal.

McManamon, John
Played inter-county for Donegal.

Meehan, Frank
Played inter-county for Monaghan.

Mitchell, Mick
Played inter-county for Meath.

Moore, David
Dublin native; played inter-county for Dublin.

Morrissey, Paddy
Played inter-county for Kildare.

Murphy, Tom

Murphy, Vincent
Played inter-county for Wexford.

Nolan, Con.

Nolan, John
Played inter-county for Kilkenny.

Noonan, Mick
Dublin.
Nugent, Jim
Played inter-county for Dublin.

O'Brien, Gerry
Played inter-county for Dublin.

O'Donoghue, Pat
Played inter-county for Leitrim.

O'Driscoll, Gerry
Clare native; played inter-county for Clare.

Piper, ? (hurling)
Played senior hurling for Louth.

403

Rowan, Peter J.
Played inter-county for Offaly.

Ryan, Christy
Played inter-county for Carlow.

Smith, Gerry
Played inter-county for Cavan.

Teehan, Johnny

Twomey, John
Kerry native; played inter-county for Kerry.

Walsh, Brendan
Played inter-county for Sligo.

Walsh, Martin
Kilkenny native; played inter-county for Kilkenny.

Walsh, P. J.
Played inter-county for Laois.

Wilson, Seamus

Winston, Dermot

Young, Joe
Kilkenny native; played inter-county for Kilkenny.

Photograph of a Dungloe G.A.A. team - 1948? - which included the entire Station Party of 4 Gardaí. The Sergeant obligingly did Station Orderly on many occasions to allow all of us to play. When unable to so a Garda from Burtonport would be sought.
Front: P. Clarke; M.Ward; Dom Bonner; N. Sweeney; Padraic Kennedy, now residing in Killarney; H. McCready; Sean Bonner.
Back: J.O'Donnell; Joe Wilson, now retired in Sligo; Paddy Prendergast, now in Tralee; Dan Bonner, father of current Donegal G.A.A. Team Manager; C. Campbell, Donegal custodian for many years; N. Gallagher; Frank White, Garda Pens. Assoc; J. McGlynn; Ref. - - Boyle. Eleven of the 15 are still alive.
The Garda involvement with the team must be something of a record. In later years Sean Ferriter, Pat Murphy, Tony Keys, Jim Connor (recently deceased) and the late Sean Concannon played with Dungloe G.A.A. team but may not have played together and did not represent the entire Garda strength. Photograph courtesy of Paddy Prendergast.

Leabharlanna Poiblí Chathair Baile Átha Cliath
Dublin City Public Libraries

Acknowledgements

Sponsorship:

The authors would like to thank the following for their sponsorship during the early stages of the project. Without their generous help, we would not have got to the publishing stage.
Eddie Doyle of D&N Group, Mullingar; Joe Gallagher of Lir Business Centre, Mullingar; Coiste Siamsa; St Raphael's Garda Credit Union Ltd; St Paul's Garda Credit Union; GRMSA, the Retired Members' Association.

Brian Willoughby acknowledgement:

In 1998, I remember getting a request from my then Chief Superintendent Willie Ryan asking me to trawl the Division – which was then Longford/Westmeath – for members of the Gardaí who had represented the Force at senior level. I was told that the work was for a retired member named Noel Hynes, who was compiling a book on the subject. I was delighted to do the research because although my limited talent on the GAA fields did not extend beyond underage with my home club, Lismore, I have always had a seriously keen interest in GAA matters – particularly Waterford GAA – and so, I subsequently forwarded two lists to Noel.

I effectively forgot about it until 2014 when I was attending the Garda vs Army Gaelic football and hurling matches in Mullingar. I met former Offaly great John Rigney, and I remembered Noel and his project. I asked John if Noel had ever finished the book. John didn't know, but said he would get Noel's number for me. He duly did, I rang Noel, and the rest is history.

I would like to thank Noel for his willingness to co-operate me in completing the project, and for his boundless enthusiasm and good humour during our research together. The completion of the task would not have been possible without the Trojan work which Noel had already done.

I would like to thank my wife Marie and son Matthew for their incredible patience and tolerance while I was working on the project. I would also like to thank my biggest fan, my mother-in-law Olive Oates, my brother-in-law All Ireland Garda Hurling Rep, Mick Morrissey for his input.

Noel Hynes acknowledgement:

It would not have been possible to complete this book without the help and support of many people during the course of my research dating back to 1998 – in particular to members of my family, my late wife, Eimer, my daughter Auveen McGrath, my son Fergal, all whom graciously accepted my absence while on my laptop and phone for long periods. I am indeed indebted to the curator of the Garda Museum in Dublin Castle, now retired Inspector Pat McGee, for his generous help and guidance while trawling through numerous editions of Iris An Garda dating back to the 1920s and 1930s. I am also deeply grateful to John Dunne of J. F. Dunne Insurance, Naas, for the use of his office during the early years of my research. Matters were put on the back burner in 2007 when my wife died, but receiving a phone call from one Brian Willoughby, currently a Detective Sergeant in Mullingar, in 2014, reignited my desire to finalise the project. I wish to state categorically that this book would never have seen the light of day without Brian's intervention. He very kindly accepted my request to come on board. He is imbued with great human qualities and impressed me with his GAA enthusiasm, his depth of knowledge regarding the playing careers of members of An Garda Síochána, and his expertise in modern technology, left no doubt in my mind that this project should be completed.

Both of us hope that the fruits of our labour will be enjoyed by all who peruse this book, particularly all those members of An Garda Síochána who performed at senior inter-county level with distinction on the playing fields of Ireland, and indeed by the wider GAA community. It has to be stated that both An Garda Síochána and the GAA are synonymous with life in this great little nation known as Ireland.

General Acknowledgements

This mammoth task would not have been possible without the assistance of a lot of people who provided fantastic help and encouragement. We acknowledge with deep gratitude to those who helped in our research and to those who generously volunteered the loan of photographs and newspaper cuttings. There were those who went above and beyond the call of duty in their assistance, and we list these people below. We sincerely regret any omissions.

Mary O'Sullivan, on behalf of her dad the late Daniel O'Sullivan: Dan had embarked on a project similar to ours and had amassed a wealth of knowledge about the Gardaí and the GAA, which his wife and daughter graciously handed over to ourselves to include in the book.

Dermot Keating, who submitted extraordinary lists of players, their clubs and counties.

Similarly, Aiden Donnelly, for his lists and efforts made by him to uncover as much information as possible, including a visit to Mullingar Garda Station to assist.

Eugene Comiskey, for the many lists he has submitted.

Eugene Dunne, Department of History, Maynooth University, for his help in researching articles in newspaper archives.

Eugene O'Sullivan, Garda GAA Club historian, for his assistance.

Keith Heffernan, an expert in Laois GAA.

Joe Ward, a Leitrim GAA enthusiast.

Sean Farrell, an expert in Roscommon GAA.

Ken Hogan, for his invaluable knowledge of players.

Former Dublin GAA chairman Gerry Harrington for his advice.

Tadhg Cowhig for his advice and generosity.

Mary Hennessy of the Garda Portal.

All who submitted photographs for publication, particularly Sportsfile and Inpho.

The following people contributed handsomely to the project and we are very appreciative for their help: Alan Aherne, Tom Ahearne, Eamonn Barry, Gabriel Bell, Tim Bowe, Des Brennan, Pascal Brennan, Liam Cahill, Paddy Casey, Gerard Connolly, Jim Connor, Matt Connor, Daithí Cronin, Danny Culloty, Gerry Curley, Peter Dennehy, Noeleen Dobson (who had to constantly listen to me in our office !), Tony Donoghue, Paul Downey, Tom Fagan, Tony Fagan, Frank Ferry, Weeshie Fogarty, Gerry Gacquin, Hugh Gallagher, Liz Glennon, John Gray, Chris Grogan Jnr, Damien Hand of Hand Imaging, Mullingar, Alf Harvey, Joe Hayes (Clare), Liam Hayes, Philip Higgins of Naas Printing Ltd., Gabriel Irwin, John Keating, Keith Heffernan, Paul Hughes, Charlie Jordan, Michael Kearns, Brian Kelly, David Kelly, Hud Kelly, Joachim Kelly, John Kelly, Philip Kinahan of Sportsfile, Andrew Lacey, Larry Langdon, John Leamy, James Lundon, Colm Lydon, Adrian Lyons, Alan Lynch, Declan Lynch, P. J. Maxwell, Sharon Mangan, Donal McAnallen, Gearóid McCarthy, Brona McCrystal, Martin McGowan, Pat McGee, Alan Milton, Brendan Minnock, Tom Mongey, Seamus Moriarity, Cathy Morley, Jim Murphy, Padraig Murtagh, Peter Nolan, Michael O'Connor, Sinead O'Connor, Pat O'Connell, Tim O'Connor, Phil O'Dea, Roisin O'Dea, Aidan Ó Murchú, Adrian O'Neill, Anne O'Neill, Michael O'Neill, Roger Nicholson, Liam Rabbitte, Adrian Russell, John Scally, Mark Stokes, Tim Slattery, Paddy Smith.